Washington delivering his first inaugural address.

To:
Dev. Butcher

THE PRESIDENTS

My Best Wishes

Bill White
12/12/77

The White House, home of our Presidents.

THE
PRESIDENTS

FROM THE INAUGURATION OF GEORGE WASHINGTON TO THE INAUGURATION OF JIMMY CARTER

Historic Places Commemorating the Chief Executives of the United States

ROBERT G. FERRIS
Series Editor

UNITED STATES DEPARTMENT OF THE INTERIOR
NATIONAL PARK SERVICE
Washington, D.C. Rev. Ed. 1977

ASSOCIATE DIRECTOR, PRESERVATION OF HISTORIC PROPERTIES
Ernest Allen Connally

CHIEF, OFFICE OF ARCHEOLOGY AND
HISTORIC PRESERVATION
Jerry L. Rogers

ACTING CHIEF, HISTORIC SITES SURVEY DIVISION
George F. Emery

The Biographical Sketches section of this volume was based on a study prepared under contract by Prof. Charles H. McCormick, Fairmont State College, W. Va. Survey and evaluation reports prepared by various National Park Service historians and contract personnel were utilized in preparing the Survey of Historic Sites and Buildings portion. These reports were reviewed by the Advisory Board on National Parks, Historic Sites, Buildings, and Monuments and the Consulting Committee for the National Survey of Historic Sites and Buildings. Current members of these groups are listed in the Acknowledgments. Editorial Assistants Richard E. Morris and Richard E. Dean, Jr., assisted with various phases of manuscript preparation.

ASSISTANT EDITOR: JAMES H. CHARLETON

Photographic Editor: Dorothy Chatfield Buffmire

Designer: Patrick A. Hurley

Library of Congress Cataloging in Publication Data
United States. National Park Service.
  The Presidents.
  (The National survey of historic sites and buildings, v. 20)
  Bibliography: p.
  1. Presidents—United States—Homes. 2. Presidents—United States—Biography.
3. Historic sites—United States. I. Title. II. Series.
E159.U55   1977   973'.0992 [B]   77–608061

For sale by the Superintendent of Documents, U.S. Government Printing Office
Washington, D.C. 20402

Stock No. 024–005–00683–4

Foreword

We Americans are intrigued and inspired by the lives of our Presidents, whom we elevate from our midst to the highest office in the land. In this awesome position, which involves grave responsibilities, the Chief Executives not only symbolize our national ideals and goals, but also help shape our global destiny.

In reading of their experiences, we rejoice in their triumphs, sympathize with their problems, warm to their personal joys, and grieve over their sorrows.

This book, which emphasizes the sites and buildings associated with the Presidents, provides a new and unique dimension in understanding them and should further stimulate public interest in their careers.

I heartily recommend this volume to all my fellow citizens.

CECIL D. ANDRUS
Secretary of the Interior

Preface

This book will increase public knowledge of the lives of our Presidents. It will also guide citizens to visit the various Park System areas and National Historic Landmarks that honor them. These sites reflect the persistent efforts of historic preservationists in all parts of the country.

Credit for the preparation of this book is shared widely by persons both in and out of the National Park Service. The Service appreciates the assistance of the many individuals and institutions who contributed. The National Survey of Historic Sites and Buildings, which is cosponsored by the National Trust for Historic Preservation, is authorized by the Historic Sites Act of 1935.

WILLIAM J. WHALEN
Director
National Park Service

Contents

Part Three

The Presidents:
Survey of Historic Sites and Buildings   325

Part One

The Presidents:
Historical Background

ONE of the principal instruments Americans have always relied on to guide their destiny in an often precarious and troubled world, the Presidency is a bulwark of the Republic. Through turmoil and tragedy—world wars, a major civil conflict, depressions and panics, riots and upheavals—to the many peaks of national triumph and achievement, the 38 men who have occupied the office have not only directed and stabilized the course of the Nation, but also have exerted a major influence on global affairs.

The Presidents have ranged from strong and distinguished individuals, sharply attuned to the times in which they served, to average men who coped as best they could with the problems of their eras. Some were rich, some were poor; some intellectuals, some poorly educated; healthy and infirm; bold and vacillating; outgoing and reserved; compromising and unyielding; revered and scorned. Some seemed ideally suited for the position, some miscast; some enjoyed personal happiness, some suffered tragedies. They have been men of diverse talents, backgrounds, strengths, and limitations.

Yet, facing solemn responsibilities, carrying heavy burdens, and taking advantage of the opportunities history has presented, all the Chief Executives have provided national leadership. As custodians of the country's trust, they have striven to represent the entire populace, regardless of party or sectional differences. And, by his own particular attitude toward the Presidency and the stamp of his own character and personality, each one has contributed to its stature and evolution.

SINCE the Founding Fathers created the office at the Constitutional Convention in 1787, it has evolved into one of the most awesome in the world. In 1789, when the Constitution went into effect, the Nation was a small, rural Republic of but 13 States nestled along the eastern seaboard. Its inhabitants totaled only 4 million, and it

3

George Washington, who launched the Nation on its course to greatness, takes his oath of office on the balcony of New York City's Federal Hall on April 30, 1789.

carried slight weight in international affairs. During the ensuing span of time, it has grown into an urbanized, industrial country of 50 States extending as far westward as Alaska and Hawaii. The population exceeds 215 million, and the Nation ranks as a leading global power.

Paralleling that growth, especially in the 20th century, has been a tremendous increase in the scope and influence of the Presidency. This has occurred for a variety of reasons. To accomplish desired national ends, some Chief Executives have vigorously exerted powers that are implied but not stated in the Constitution. The unique talents of certain Cabinet members and special assistants and advisers have also strengthened the Presidency. Demands for the Government to provide various public services have swelled the executive branch. Then, too, the complexities and expansion of the economy have brought about the creation of a number of major regulatory agencies.

Pertinent also is the increased role of the Nation in international affairs, particularly during the nuclear age, in which the President's functions as commander in chief of the Armed Forces and as chief diplomat give him exceptional power and visibility. Also enhancing the strength of the office are all the tools of modern technology.

Fellow Citizens of the Senate
and
of the House of Representatives.

Among the vicissitudes incident to life, no event could have filled me with greater anxieties than that of which the notification was transmitted by your order, and received on the fourteenth day of the present month:——On the one hand, I was summoned by my Country, whose voice I can never hear but with veneration and love, from a retreat which I had chosen with the fondest predilection, and, in my flattering hopes, with an immutable decision, as the asylum of my declining years: a retreat which was rendered every day more necessary as well as more dear to me, by the addition of habit to inclination, and of frequent interruptions in my health to the gradual waste committed on it by time.——On the other hand, the magnitude and difficulty of the trust to which the voice of my Country called me, being sufficient to awaken in the wisest and most experienced of her citizens, a distrustful

Washington's first inaugural address (page one), in his own hand.

Presidential duties include representing the Nation on social and ceremonial occasions. Queen Elizabeth and Prince Philip of Great Britain greet President and Mrs. Eisenhower on their arrival at the British Embassy.

UNTIL about the end of the 19th century, the Government was relatively small and easy to administer. The Presidents received little secretarial-clerical assistance, and many of them personally drafted and even penned state papers in longhand. If special help were required, a few clerks or specialists might be borrowed from the various agencies and departments of the executive branch. For advice, the incumbent relied mainly on his Cabinet and friends or colleagues.

A few men guarded the Chief Executive, who did not begin to receive any sort of Secret Service protection until after Abraham Lincoln's assassination in 1865, and he was quite accessible to the public. His principal direct communication with the people was through speechmaking tours of the country.

Political party mechanisms were simple. Campaigns required relatively small amounts of funds; and State organizations, supplemented by a few congressional managers, performed most of the work. Some nominees, such as William McKinley, conducted "front-porch" campaigns, during which the people came to the

Jet aircraft have greatly enhanced the mobility of our Chief Executives. President Johnson confers with Vice President Hubert H. Humphrey (second from left) and other advisers aboard Air Force One.

candidate instead of vice versa.

Also, before 1828, from George Washington through John Quincy Adams, Presidential campaigns in the modern sense were not even conducted, and the Chief Executives were largely freed from the need to be popular politicians as well as statesmen. Congressional caucuses and State legislatures chose Presidential candidates. For these reasons, early Chief Executives mainly sought the approval of Congress and the legislatures rather than that of the masses of the voters, who played only an indirect role.

By 1828, however, all the States but Delaware and South Carolina had instituted popular selection of electors. Thus, in 1829 Jackson became the first President to be elected popularly in the modern sense. He opened the White House to his backwoods supporters and shared with them the political spoils of victory. Further democratization occurred in 1832, when political parties held their first national conventions to nominate candidates for President.

Then, in 1840, the elections became even more popularly oriented.

The Whigs appealed to the common man by portraying their candidate, William Henry Harrison, as a national hero who had lived in a log cabin. The use of campaign slogans and songs, as well as torchlight parades, brought far more voters to the polls than in earlier elections. For this reason, political parties subsequently began to choose their nominees in part for their popular image.

SINCE the beginning of the 20th century, the President's political, military, diplomatic, and economic powers have expanded immensely. At the same time, the size of the executive branch has mushroomed. The complexities of the office—especially in the era

Public appearances, though they sometimes burden the Secret Service, provide the principal opportunity for Chief Executives to maintain their contact with the people. President and Mrs. Coolidge arrive to dedicate Wicker Memorial Park, Hammond, Indiana, on Flag Day, June 14, 1927.

of electronic communication—require an array of special advisers. Television and radio, as well as extensive coverage in newspapers and periodicals, almost instantaneously bring the President's latest acts and opinions to the attention of the world. Jet aircraft allow him to fly speedily to any part of the globe. Since 1901, when William McKinley was assassinated, the Secret Service has progressively tightened its vigilance in protecting the President. As a result, he is less accessible to the public than in earlier decades.

Campaigning is hectic and exhausting. Even before the blossoming of the jet age, Harry S Truman, traveling more than 31,000 miles on a "whistle-stop" campaign in 1948, delivered 356 speeches during a 35-day period. The funds required, especially because of television costs, have soared into the millions of dollars. The diversity and ever-changing nature of the electorate dictate huge and specialized campaign staffs.

Party machinery and organization are intricate. Scheduling demands the careful allocation of the candidate's time in relation to speech and other appearances, transportation arrangements, and press coverage. Coordination of national, regional, and local efforts requires special skill. The standard, set speech is no longer as acceptable; increased platform and media exposure requires fresh and varied approaches.

Until the turn of the 20th century, Presidential administration was relatively simple. President McKinley (1897-1901) dictates to his secretary, John A. Porter.

Presidential election campaigns are the lifeblood of our political processes. An 1848 Whig banner.

President Truman beginning his 1948 "whistle-stop" campaign at Washington's Union Station. With him are his Vice-Presidential running mate, Alben W. Barkley, and his daughter, Margaret.

TODAY, the President bears many responsibilities, some of which have gradually evolved over the years. In one elective office he combines a panoply of roles that in parliamentary countries are shared by a monarch or largely ceremonial head of state and a prime minister or premier.

As Chief Executive, the President supervises one of the largest administrative complexes in the world, the executive branch of the U.S. Government. This involves continual awareness of the activities of the legislative and judicial branches, with which he participates in the checks and balances system established by the Constitution. As commander in chief of the Armed Services, representing the supremacy of civil over military authority in the United States, he exercises awesome power, particularly in times of war or national emergency.

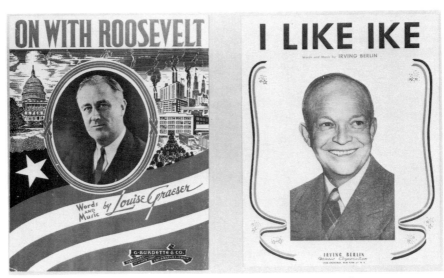

The spirited partisanship that prevails during Presidential campaigns even stimulates the writing of songs. Here are two, from 1936 (Franklin D. Roosevelt) and 1952 (Dwight D. Eisenhower).

During the 1960 campaign, Senator John F. Kennedy (left) and Vice President Richard Nixon (right) answer questions from a panel of newsmen during a series of televised "debates"—a historic first. These were more like press conferences than actual debates.

As chief diplomat, the President helps formulate and executes foreign policy, appoints and supervises a huge diplomatic corps, negotiates treaties with other nations, administers foreign aid, officially receives world rulers and dignitaries, attends international meetings and peace conferences, and as a good will ambassador of the United States visits various foreign countries. Especially since the beginning of the 20th century, as one international crisis after another has risen, he has become the prime defender of democracy at home and abroad.

The President also enjoys the somewhat contradictory distinction of being the leader of his party and at the same time bipartisan spokesman for the American people as a whole. In addition, he makes recommendations to Congress concerning legislation, seeks to maintain a stable and prosperous economy, assures domestic tranquillity, and provides relief during disasters. Finally, as chief of state, he participates in a wide range of ceremonial activities.

WHEN George Washington took his oath of office at New York's City Hall in 1789, he became the political equal of kings, emperors, and czars. Yet, though always an aristocrat, he chose to shun the exalted status and arbitrary power such monarchs enjoyed. If he had not accepted the position, had faltered in his leadership, or had soon died, our gamble in constitutional Government might have failed. Yet, devoted as he was to the principles of republican Government and fully aware of his precedent-making capabilities as the first President, during his two terms he sharply defined the office that the Constitution had only broadly delineated.

At the same time, Washington smoothly launched the new Republic—plagued by internal jealousies, economically unstable, and endangered by the rivalries of far more powerful nations—on its uncharted quest for a workable Government of the people. In the process, he helped formulate the national structure that the Constitution had created.

Providing what the Articles of Confederation lacked, a strong Executive independent of the Legislature but integrated into the constitutional structure, Washington asserted authority in fields where the Constitution did not specify whether the Congress or the President was to act. Yet he respected Congress and maintained amicable relations with it.

Washington's immediate successors John Adams, Thomas

Jefferson, James Madison, James Monroe, and John Quincy Adams further shaped the Presidency and the national political system. Just as important, they steered the Nation through its early, crisis-ridden years on the course Washington had set and perpetuated the Union—though they were unable to avoid the foreign entanglements he had feared. During Madison's administration, the War of 1812 with Britain broke out.

Although that conflict ended in more of a stalemate than a victory, the national effort involved and the reaffirmation of independence that resulted created an upsurge in nationalism. Democracy also flowered, except for those blacks who were victims of the slavery system and certain other groups. The population tripled. Millions of pioneers surmounted the Appalachian barrier and pushed the frontier to the Mississippi and beyond—doubling the national bounds. From an alliance of 13 virtually autonomous States during the War for Independence, the Nation melded into a strong Federal Union of 24 States.

The Presidents from Andrew Jackson through James Buchanan faced fundamentally different problems. As the country matured and mastered obstacle after obstacle—internal political strife, international crises, and war—it gained in strength and confidence. But sectionalistic debate persisted over the character of the Union and over whether sovereignty resided in the States or in the National Government. This debate was central to the slavery issue,

Early turnpikes, predecessors of modern expressways, linked the Nation. Scene in 1827 at the Fairview Inn, near Baltimore along the Frederick Pike, which ran from Baltimore to Cumberland.

Five major political protagonists, two of whom were to ascend to the Presidency, attend a reception. Secretary of State John Quincy Adams (right) held it for Senator and former General Andrew Jackson (middle) on January 8, 1824, the anniversary of the Battle of New Orleans. Also pictured are (left to right) John C. Calhoun, Daniel Webster, and Henry Clay (between Jackson and Adams). President Monroe did not attend.

over which the North and South clashed bitterly—the most persistent and critical problem posed to the Chief Executives of the era. Particularly explosive was the question of whether western areas should be admitted to the Union as free or slave States.

An interrelated phenomenon was the continuing westward surge of the Nation—at the expense of the Indians, who were shoved aside. Ten new States in the South and West joined the Union. Reflecting the new trend, Jackson was the first westerner to occupy the White House, and three others who served in the period were all elected from the same region: William Henry Harrison, James K. Polk, and Zachary Taylor.

Polk, who won office by advocating sweeping expansion, realized by war and diplomacy the American dream of pushing the national boundaries to the Pacific. Other Presidents grappled with western problems and their ramifications. The question of Texas plagued Martin Van Buren and John Tyler. Besetting Zachary Taylor and Millard Fillmore were the Territorial quarrels that erupted in the wake of the Mexican War. Franklin Pierce and James Buchanan were hard put to quell the turmoil in "bleeding Kansas."

Elsewhere, too, no permanent or peaceful solution to the slavery question could be found. Finally, after Lincoln's inauguration, the Nation fell into fratricide. Lincoln led the North through the Civil War and preserved the Union. Upon his assassination, Andrew Johnson felt the first brunt of the long acrimony that was to be engendered by Reconstruction—the difficult task of attempting to heal the rift between the North and South as well as to restore the Union on terms equable to the defeated South and the black people.

The Presidents from Grant to McKinley, supported by Supreme Court decisions, gradually restored relative amity between the North and the white South, but at the expense of equality for blacks. These Chief Executives presided over other profound changes in the Nation, which by the end of McKinley's term had grown to 45 States. An industrial revolution, stirring in the North before the Civil War, created a massive industrial complex and transformed living patterns. Also helping to reshape the country were inventors such as Alexander Graham Bell, Thomas A. Edison, and Henry Ford, as well as industrialists like Andrew Carnegie and John D. Rockefeller.

Seeking economic opportunities, millions of immigrants came to America; and millions left rural areas for the cities. The standard

The Civil War, which tragically pitted the North against the South, scarred the national consciousness. Portrayed here is the Battle of the Crater (1864), Petersburg, Virginia.

Lincoln and key military advisers discuss the prospects for peace in February 1865 at City Point, Virginia, aboard the *River Queen*, which had carried the President down the Potomac from Washington and up the James. Left to right: Gens. William T. Sherman and Ulysses S. Grant, Lincoln, and Adm. David D. Porter.

The economy of the South recovered slowly after the Civil War, though Atlanta, a railroad center, pictured here about 1887, boomed.

Mechanization of agriculture not only multiplied food output but also sped the growth of industrial technology. Steam thresher at work.

From the Nation's beginnings, immigrants have enriched our way of life. Arrival at Ellis Island, New York, about 1900.

of living rose, but such problems as child labor, inadequate industrial safety, absence of workmen's compensation laws, and substandard wages became rampant. In time, labor was to organize unions to correct these evils.

Settlers continued to pour into the West, driving back the Indians and destroying their way of life. The region boomed, however, and many prospectors, cattlemen, and wheat farmers enjoyed bonanzas. Many others, though, found disillusionment. Rail networks crept across the continent to the Pacific and further bound the Nation together.

In 1898 the United States triumphed in the Spanish-American War, asserted its will in Cuba, and annexed other erstwhile Spanish possessions in the Philippines, Guam, and Puerto Rico. This represented a foray into imperialism that continued well into the 20th century, when the country became an industrial colossus and major world power. In 1912 the last two of the contiguous 48

States came into the Union, and in 1959 they were to be joined by the two detached ones.

During the first two decades of the century, "progressive" Presidents Theodore Roosevelt, William Howard Taft, and Woodrow Wilson strove at home to reform the American way of life within the framework of the free enterprise system. Their aims included major improvements in political democracy, economic-social justice, restraint of corporations, and conservation of natural resources. The means were vigorous Government action and a scientific approach to social problems. Abroad, the progressives aimed for a more powerful role in world order. At the same time, as Wilson phrased it, they sought to make the world "safe for democracy"—a goal World War I did not attain.

Meantime, earlier in the century, the automobile and airplane had come into widespread use. These two new modes of transportation, along with an ascendant technology, were to revolutionize the entire American socioeconomic system. Mass production of automobiles would put the Nation on wheels. The growth of air transport would further integrate it and tie it closer to other peoples of the world.

Meanwhile, after the domestic prosperity of the 1920's, the Great Depression had struck. President Herbert Hoover, who advocated only enough Government intervention in the affairs of the citizenry to insure the free working of the economy, at first sought solutions in voluntary cooperation rather than compulsory Government actions. Although he eventually proposed legislation to counter the economic decline, most people favored more drastic measures and in 1932 they elected Franklin D. Roosevelt. Expanding the powers of the Federal Government, he took substantive steps to help pull the Nation out of the depression.

At the same time, however, the worldwide economic distress was helping bring into power Adolf Hitler and other aggressors, who fomented World War II. The Japanese attack on Pearl Harbor in December 1941 brought the United States into the global conflict. Before Germany was crushed in May 1945, it proved to be incredibly costly in terms of lives and resources. Some 3 months later, America used the devastating force of the atomic bomb to induce the surrender of Japan. To foster collective security and prevent the recurrence of world war, in 1945 the United Nations was founded.

Outgoing President William Howard Taft greets his successor, Woodrow Wilson, just before his inauguration on March 4, 1913.

One Chief Executive and a future one during World War II. President Roosevelt and General Eisenhower at Castelvetrano, Sicily, in December 1943. Gen. George S. Patton is at the far left.

U.S. industrial prowess is recognized worldwide. Molten steel flows from an open-hearth furnace.

Nevertheless, subsequent developments, including the "Cold War," the Korean and Viet-Nam conflicts, and the proliferation of nuclear weaponry, led to a long period of international tension. Principally for this reason, the Presidents who served in the middle decades of the 20th century—Harry S Truman through Jimmy Carter—have borne crushing responsibilities. Their principal tasks have been to maintain the peace in a turbulent world and to foster domestic stability and prosperity.

For the latter purpose, these leaders have utilized the resources of the Federal Government to prevent recessions from turning into depressions and to restrain the inflation that resulted from three decades of unprecedented prosperity—as the Nation advanced into an unparalleled era of industrial-scientific-technological activity spurred by the taming of the atom and initiation of the space program.

National growth has been synonymous with urban growth. New York City skyline from the roof of Rockefeller Center.

A rare photograph showing President Kennedy and two of the three ex-Presidents then living, Truman and Eisenhower. They were attending funeral ceremonies in 1961 at Bonham, Texas, for former House Speaker Samuel Rayburn. Hoover was not present.

Not all citizens shared in this prosperity, nor enjoyed all the benefits of our society. During a series of urban riots in the late 1960's and in other ways, black people vented their rage at the social and economic discrimination that have been inflicted on them. Indians, other minorities, and women expressed similar complaints. Recognizing their validity, the Government and private industry undertook comprehensive programs that were intended to alleviate injustices.

The Chief Executives from Truman through Carter have also marshaled the economic capabilities and armed power of the Nation to aid poor and threatened countries or to contribute to the progress of mankind and the pursuit of world peace. Harry S Truman fostered the Marshall Plan to rehabilitate the European economy, stricken by World War II. Dwight D. Eisenhower proposed his Atoms for Peace program to the United Nations. In 1961 John F. Kennedy established a national goal of landing a man on the moon within the decade, which was achieved in 1969. Both he and Lyndon B. Johnson furthered international cooperation.

During recent decades, the influence of black people in American political life has broadened significantly. Presidential aspirant Carter views his endorsement in the *Baltimore Afro-American* with Executive Editor Moses J. Newson.

Richard Nixon pursued détente with the Soviet Union and the People's Republic of China; and ended U.S. participation in the long Viet-Nam War, which had been opposed by a large segment of the American people. Coming to office in 1974 after Nixon resigned because of the "Watergate Affair," Gerald R. Ford took over the critical responsibility of maintaining global leadership and advancing the cause of peace, as well as restoring confidence in Government. Among Jimmy Carter's domestic goals were the furthering of social justice, restoration of economic vigor, and reorganization of the Government. Abroad, he planned new initiatives toward disarmament and international cooperation.

As the country entered the last quarter of the 20th century, it looked back on two centuries of progress and girded itself for the challenges of the future. As always, the Presidents will direct their solution and help fulfill the Nation's destiny.

Manned lunar exploration, which began with the first landing by Apollo 11 in 1969, marked a new epoch in world history. Here, James B. Irwin, on the fourth landing (Apollo 15) in 1971, salutes the flag. The lunar module is on the left, and the lunar rover on the right.

ALL the occupants of the White House, despite their accomplishments, have faced multitudinous problems. How well they have solved them and how successful their administrations were has depended to a considerable degree on their characters and talents, as well as their ability to gain public support for their goals and programs.

What sort of men were the Presidents, collectively and individually? What has motivated them? How have their background, education, qualifications, and experience differed from or been similar to those of other men? How did they rise to such an exalted position?

Part Two

The Presidents:
Biographical Sketches

DIVERSITY is the keynote to the 38 Presidents as a group. In physical appearance, temperament, place of birth, family background, role in national life, status of health, political affiliation, the nature and success of their administrations, popular reaction of their times and posterity toward them, and pursuits in later life, they demonstrate exceptional heterogeneity. Yet, in numerous respects, they exhibit similarities.

Among these is ethnic origin. All the Presidents have been of Northern European extraction and the preponderant number of British origins. English bloodlines predominate, followed by Scotch and Scotch-Irish. Both of Kennedy's parents were of Irish background. Although several Chief Executives carried traces of Continental European ancestry, the only ones directly descended from that area were Van Buren and the two Roosevelts, whose names reflect their Dutch forebears; and Hoover and Eisenhower, both of Swiss-German lineage. Most of the parents of the Presidents and their families have spent several generations in the United States; only a handful of Chief Executives, who by law are required to be American born, were the children of one or both immigrant parents.

A second area of resemblance is in occupation, where public service and the law rank high. Except for Taylor, Grant, and Eisenhower, who had been Army generals and whose earlier careers were essentially apolitical, practically all the Presidents played extensive roles in public life—Federal, State, and local, appointive and elective. The range is considerable, however. Buchanan, for example, enjoyed almost four decades of experience in State and Federal posts, including the diplomatic corps.

On the other hand, the only earlier elective office Arthur ever held was as Vice President. Lincoln's experience consisted only of four terms in the State legislature and a single term in the U.S. House of

Theodore (left) and Franklin D. (right) Roosevelt while they were serving as Assistant Secretaries of the Navy.

Representatives. Hoover, along with Taylor, Grant, and Eisenhower, never ran for any kind of public office prior to his Presidential nomination, though he had served as Secretary of Commerce, as World War I Food Administrator, and on various national and international relief commissions.

Thirteen Chief Executives (John Adams, Jefferson, Van Buren, Tyler, Fillmore, Andrew Johnson, Arthur, Theodore Roosevelt, Coolidge, Truman, Lyndon B. Johnson, Nixon, and Ford) had served as Vice Presidents. Nine were Cabinet members, Monroe holding two posts: six secretaries of State (Jefferson, Madison, Monroe, John Quincy Adams, Van Buren, and Buchanan); three Secretaries of War (Monroe, Grant, and Taft); and one Secretary of Commerce (Hoover). Other Presidents also held various sub-Cabinet posts and lesser U.S. Government positions.

Seven served as Ambassadors or Ministers: both Adamses, Jefferson, Monroe, Van Buren, Harrison, and Buchanan—all before the Civil War. Taft held the position of Governor General of the Philippines; and, after his Presidency, the Chief Justiceship of the United States, the only President who ever held a seat on the Supreme Court.

Except for 12, the rest enjoyed congressional experience, all before their incumbencies except for John Quincy Adams who held a seat in the House of Representatives afterward, as did also Andrew Johnson in the Senate. The first five Presidents had served in the Continental Congress. The last two of these, Madison and Monroe, also sat in Congress, the former in the House and the latter in the Senate.

Ten served in both Houses (John Quincy Adams, Jackson, William Henry Harrison, Tyler, Pierce, Buchanan, Andrew Johnson, Kennedy, Lyndon B. Johnson, and Nixon); five in the Senate only (Monroe, Van Buren, Benjamin Harrison, Harding, and Truman); and eight in the House (Madison, Polk, Fillmore, Lincoln, Hayes, Garfield, McKinley, and Ford).

Polk was the only Speaker of the House to become Chief Executive. Tyler held the office of President *pro tem* of the Senate for one session. Lyndon B. Johnson served as both Minority and Majority Leader of the Senate. Garfield and Ford were House Minority Leaders. Garfield was the only Chief Executive elected while serving as a Member of the House, though he was also a Senator-elect. Ford was appointed as Vice President while in the House, and then assumed the Presidency upon Nixon's resignation. Harding and Kennedy were elected while sitting in the Senate.

Sixteen individuals had earlier served as Governors of States or Territories: Jefferson, Monroe, Jackson, William Henry Harrison, Van Buren, Tyler, Polk, Andrew Johnson, Hayes, Cleveland, McKinley, Theodore Roosevelt, Wilson, Coolidge, Franklin D. Roosevelt, and Carter. Four were Governors when they became President (Hayes, Cleveland, Wilson, and Franklin D. Roosevelt), and McKinley had left office earlier in the year that he ran for the Presidency.

Many White House occupants also served in State legislatures or held such State posts as attorney general, Lieutenant Governor, and comptroller, as well as various county and city positions. Despite the prominence of large cities in U.S. history, only one mayor of a major city (Buffalo), Cleveland, ever occupied the highest office in the land.

More than two-thirds of the Presidents received training in the law, many in the days before formal school training when they "read the law." Most of the overall group were admitted to the bar. Some curtailed or abandoned law practice during long periods in public office and never returned to it actively. Wilson, for one, stopped practicing after a short time, to begin graduate studies in political science.

Several men, including Van Buren, Hayes, Cleveland, Benjamin Harrison, McKinley, Taft, and Coolidge, worked as county or city prosecuting attorneys or solicitors before they entered the mainstream of political life. Jackson held the position of attorney general of the Western District of North Carolina (present Tennessee), as well as justice of the Tennessee superior court. Taft also sat on a superior court, in Ohio, and was a Federal circuit judge.

A number of individuals were once elementary or secondary teachers: John Adams, Jackson, Fillmore, Pierce, Garfield, Arthur, Cleveland (at a school for the deaf), McKinley, Harding, and Lyndon B. Johnson. Arthur and Johnson also served as principals. Of the group, Garfield moved on to college teaching, the one-time principal occupation of John Quincy Adams, Taft, and Wilson. Garfield, Wilson, and Eisenhower, respectively, served as presidents of Western Reserve Eclectic Institute (later Hiram College) and Princeton and Columbia Universities. Taft was dean of the Cincinnati Law School.

Several Presidents were, by principal occupation, farm or

Coolidge as a young lawyer. He was one of the large number of Chief Executives who were trained in that profession.

Lyndon B. Johnson poses in 1928 with grade-school students at Cotulla, Texas, where he was both principal and teacher.

plantation owners or managers, and those who engaged in other professions sometimes pursued agriculture as an avocation. Theodore Roosevelt, for example, though from an urban background, operated ranches in North Dakota. Other Chief Executives purchased or inherited family farms or estates.

Other occupations include mining engineer (Hoover), tailor (Andrew Johnson), and newspaper editor (Harding). A considerable number of Chief Executives were professional or semiprofessional soldiers. None were doctors or ministers, though William Henry Harrison studied medicine for a while; and John Adams and Madison, theology.

During the course of their careers, numerous Presidents followed humble occupations and knew disappointment and failure. Fillmore worked as a wool carder. Grant, as a young officer unhappy with military service, resigned and worked as a clerk and real-estate agent, but he was unsuccessful in these fields as well as farming. Truman failed in the haberdashery business, as did Lincoln in storekeeping. A number of others at some point in their lives, particularly during their early years, were forced to work at menial jobs.

Another general similarity among the Presidents is that, despite the modest origins of many of them, a great number were either wealthy or well-to-do as they neared the ends of their lives. Hoover and Lyndon B. Johnson were self-made millionaires; Franklin D. Roosevelt and Kennedy, by inheritance. Others who enjoyed considerable wealth include Washington, Van Buren, Tyler, Polk, Taylor, Fillmore, Arthur, Benjamin Harrison, Theodore Roosevelt, Taft, Wilson, Harding, Coolidge, Truman, Eisenhower, and Nixon. On the other hand, Jefferson died in debt and Madison and Monroe ended their lives in genteel poverty, though all three had always lived in comfortable circumstances. A few others also enjoyed no more than modest wealth. At one point in his life, McKinley barely avoided bankruptcy.

Most Chief Executives have been well educated. The contrasts are marked, however. Lincoln enjoyed only a few months of low-level formal education, whereas Wilson earned his Doctor of Philosophy (Ph. D.) degree, the only Chief Executive to do so. Although historically speaking relatively few Americans have ever enjoyed the privilege of a college education, 27, or just over two-thirds, of the Presidents were graduates, and two others attended higher-level institutions but did not win a degree. Of the 27, at least half won honors or other academic distinction.

Five have been graduates of Harvard (the two Adamses, two Roosevelts, and Kennedy); two of the College of William and Mary (Jefferson and Tyler); two of Princeton (College of New Jersey) (Madison and Wilson); two of the U.S. Military Academy (Grant and Eisenhower); and 14 of other schools (Polk, University of North Carolina; Pierce, Bowdoin College; Buchanan, Dickinson College; Hayes, Kenyon College; Garfield, Williams College; Arthur, Union College; Benjamin Harrison, Miami [Ohio] University; Taft, Yale University; Harding, Ohio Central College; Coolidge, Amherst College; Hoover, Stanford University; Lyndon B. Johnson, Southwest Texas State Teachers College; Nixon, Whittier College; Ford, University of Michigan; and Carter, U.S. Naval Academy). A few of these individuals also studied at other colleges or universities on a preparatory or temporary basis.

Those attending college but not graduating were: Monroe (College of William and Mary), William Henry Harrison (Hampden-Sydney College), and McKinley (Allegheny College). The following nine men did not attend at all: Washington, Jackson, Van Buren, Taylor, Fillmore, Lincoln, Andrew Johnson, Cleveland, and Truman.

Wilson earned his Ph. D. in political science at Johns Hopkins. Except for John Adams, who received an M.A. from Harvard, no President ever was awarded one, though many of them won honorary degrees. Two undertook university-level study abroad, both briefly: John Quincy Adams at Holland's University of Leyden, and Kennedy at the London School of Economics. Madison accomplished a year of additional study at the College of New Jersey (now Princeton) following his graduation, as did also Franklin D. Roosevelt at Harvard.

Many Chief Executives undertook specialized professional training, particularly in the law. Graduates of law schools were Hayes (Harvard University), Taft (Cincinnati Law School), Wilson (University of Virginia), Nixon (Duke University), and Ford (Yale University). Those who attended schools but did not obtain degrees were McKinley (Albany Law School), both Roosevelts (Columbia University), Truman (Kansas City Law School), and Lyndon B. Johnson (Georgetown University).

The following read law in the days before formal training was available or commonplace: both Adamses, Jefferson, Madison, Monroe, Jackson, Van Buren, Tyler, Polk, Fillmore, Pierce, Buchanan, Lincoln, Garfield, Arthur, Cleveland, Benjamin Harrison, Harding, and Coolidge. In addition, at least three of those who matriculated at law schools—Hayes, McKinley, and Taft—also read law.

Another marked similarity is in the performance of military service. Twenty-four, or about two-thirds, of the Presidents have served in various branches of the Armed Forces or State militia units; one, Buchanan, in a private volunteer group during the War of 1812. Interestingly enough, all except him attained officer status, 11 as generals. A few worked their way up from the enlisted ranks. Three became commanders of the Army: Washington, Grant, and Eisenhower.

For at least 11, notable success as officers provided a stepping-stone on their way to the Presidency: Washington, Jackson, William Henry Harrison, Taylor, Pierce, Grant, Hayes, Garfield, Benjamin Harrison, Theodore Roosevelt, and Eisenhower—only three of whom (Taylor, Grant, and Eisenhower) were professional soldiers for the major part of their lives. The only erstwhile naval personnel among the Chief Executives have been the last five (Kennedy, Lyndon B. Johnson, Nixon, Ford, and Carter), all of whom served as officers below admiral rank.

Despite the trend toward urbanization in the United States from its earliest days, the Presidents have overwhelmingly hailed from small towns and rural areas. Only Theodore Roosevelt, Taft, Kennedy, and Ford were born in metropolitan areas or large cities. A number who came from rural areas, including Jackson, Polk, Fillmore, Buchanan, Lincoln, and Garfield, as well as possibly Taylor and Pierce, literally rose from "log cabins" to the White House. Most of the others were born in modest homes amid humble or middle-class surroundings. Van Buren was born in his father's tavern. A few individuals of agrarian origins belonged to well-to-do families; or they and members of their families subsequently advanced to positions of wealth and prominence.

In line with the predominance of rural origins, the fathers of more than half the Presidents were, at one time or another, farmers or plantation owners. Others were professional men or executives, including several lawyers, clergymen, teachers, and financiers.

About two-thirds of the Chief Executives have performed military service. Gen. Benjamin Harrison is pictured here during the Atlanta Campaign, in the Civil War.

Eisenhower was one of the three career soldiers who rose to the highest office in the land. Here, as a young second lieutenant, in 1916, he poses at Denver on his wedding day with his bride, "Mamie."

Additional diverse occupations include: ironmaker, livestock dealer, carpenter, blacksmith, tanner, tavernkeeper, surveyor, mechanic, storekeeper, merchant, and tavern porter.

The families of John Quincy Adams, the two Harrisons, Taft, Franklin D. Roosevelt, and Kennedy had already achieved national fame before they came to office. John Quincy Adams was the son of President and signer of the Declaration of Independence John Adams. Benjamin Harrison, whose father was a U.S. Congressman, was the grandson of Chief Executive William Henry Harrison and the great-grandson of Benjamin Harrison, another signer of the Declaration. Taft's father served as Secretary of War, Attorney General, and Minister to both Austria-Hungary and Russia. Kennedy's father was Ambassador to Great Britain. William Henry Harrison, Tyler, and Pierce were the sons of Governors. Several other fathers served in State legislatures.

Except for Buchanan, all the Presidents were married at some time during their lives. Five—Tyler, Fillmore, Benjamin Harrison, Theodore Roosevelt, and Wilson—were wed twice, all after their first wives died. No Chief Executive has been divorced, though Jackson, Harding, and Ford married divorced women. Six (Washington, Jefferson, Madison, Fillmore, Benjamin Harrison, and Wilson) wed widows.

Four individuals (Jefferson, Jackson, Van Buren, and Arthur) were widowers when they entered the White House. Cleveland, a bachelor at the time, married there, the only President to do so. Tyler and Wilson were remarried, though not in the Executive Mansion, during their terms of office.

THE First Ladies have been as diverse in appearance, personality, talents, and achievements as their spouses. Although a number have been reserved and avoided the limelight, especially before the 20th century, almost all of them in one way or the other have encouraged their husbands and contributed substantially to their careers. Two instances stand out. Eliza McCardle, who married Andrew Johnson when he was a struggling young tailor, taught him to write and improved his reading ability. Edith Bolling Galt Wilson helped manage her husband's affairs while he was incapacitated with a stroke near the end of his second term.

All in all, the wives have injected charm and graciousness into the White House and served the Nation in various other ways.

The First Ladies have contributed to the Nation in a variety of ways. Mrs. Calvin Coolidge served with the Red Cross.

While aiding their husbands and raising their children, they have managed the household, sometimes supervised refurnishing and remodelings of the mansion, and entertained world dignitaries.

The First Ladies have also taken part in civic-patriotic organizations and devoted themselves to worthwhile causes. Particularly in the 20th century, as the role of women in the country's life has intensified, the First Ladies have participated in such national programs as beautification of the environment, antipoverty activities, mental health, and women's rights.

A considerable number of the ladies have been well educated and widely traveled. A few have pursued professional careers of their own. Several were teachers. Eleanor Roosevelt's achievements are especially notable, particularly after Franklin succumbed. She advanced numerous humanitarian causes, wrote a nationally syndicated newspaper column, played a key role in Democratic Party affairs, sat in the U.S. delegation to the General Assembly of the United Nations (U.N.), and served as the U.S. member of the Human Rights Commission of the U.N. Economic and Social Council.

THIRTY-TWO of the 38 Chief Executives and their wives have had children and some of those who had none of their own (Washington, Madison, Jackson, Polk, Harding, and bachelor Buchanan) adopted or cared for those of their wives by earlier marriages or for those of close relatives or friends. In this category are Washington, Madison, and Jackson; and Buchanan acted as father to his niece, who served as his White House hostess. Tyler, by two wives, fathered the most children, 15.

The children of about two-thirds of the Presidents were fully grown or at least young adults while their fathers served in the White House. Only 11 raised young children (age 12 and under) there: Tyler, Lincoln, Grant, Hayes, Garfield, Arthur, Cleveland, Theodore Roosevelt, Taft, Kennedy, and Carter. The only child of a President ever to be born in the White House was a daughter of Cleveland.

The sons, as well as other descendants, of a large number of Chief Executives have led distinguished careers. John Quincy Adams, son of John, won the Presidency, as well as other distinction, as did also Benjamin, the grandson of William Henry Harrison. Charles Francis Adams, son of John Quincy, served as U.S. Representative and Minister to Great Britain. Other Adams progeny, John Quincy II, Charles Francis, Jr., Henry, and Brooks, excelled in politics, literature, and historiography. John Van Buren, John Scott Harrison (son of William Henry Harrison and father of Benjamin), David G. Tyler, Franklin D. Roosevelt, Jr., and James Roosevelt were all Members of the U.S. House of Representatives.

Robert Tyler was Register of the Confederate Treasury; Lyon G. Tyler, president of the College of William and Mary; Richard Taylor, Confederate general; Robert Todd Lincoln, Secretary of War and Minister to Great Britain; Frederick D. Grant, Minister to Austria-Hungary; Gen. Harry A. Garfield, president of Williams College and Fuel Administrator during World War I; James R. Garfield, U.S. Civil Service Commissioner and Secretary of the

Two eminent First Ladies. Dolley Madison (left) gained distinction for her social graces; Eleanor Roosevelt (right), for her humanitarianism.

Interior; Theodore Roosevelt, Jr., Assistant Secretary of the Navy, Governor of Puerto Rico, and Governor-General of the Philippines; and Robert A. Taft, U.S. Senator.

Just a few parents of Presidents survived to see their sons enter the White House, though most witnessed their early successes. The mothers of Washington, John Adams, Madison, Polk, Garfield, McKinley, Franklin D. Roosevelt, Truman, and Carter, the stepmothers of Lincoln, Harding, and Ford, and the fathers of John Quincy Adams, Fillmore, Harding, and Coolidge survived through their children's inaugurations. Coolidge's father even enjoyed the unique privilege of swearing in his son.

In addition to these, both parents of Grant and Kennedy lived to see their sons assume the highest office in the land. Kennedy's two parents also survived his assassination, as did Lincoln's stepmother and Garfield's mother. The mother of Polk was the only other one to outlive her son. George Harding and Joseph Kennedy were the only fathers to survive their sons. Abigail Adams had the distinction of being the wife of one President and the mother of another.

The untimely deaths of either or both parents sometimes brought difficult circumstances to future Presidents' families. Jackson and Hayes were posthumous sons. Other widowed mothers with young children include those of Washington, Jefferson, Monroe, Andrew Johnson, Garfield, Cleveland, and Hoover. The mothers of Jackson and Hoover also succumbed at early ages themselves and left their children as orphans. Lincoln and Coolidge lost their mothers when they were quite young, though stepmothers took over the task of raising them. Tyler's mother died when he was 7 years of age, and his father never remarried. Ford was adopted by his stepfather, his mother's second husband.

Practically all the Presidents except Kennedy, a Roman Catholic, were Protestants or demonstrated Protestant leanings. Official affiliations were as follows: Episcopalian, 10 (Washington, Madison, Monroe, William Henry Harrison, Tyler, Taylor, Pierce, Arthur, Franklin D. Roosevelt, and Ford); Presbyterian, six (Jackson, Buchanan, Cleveland, Benjamin Harrison, Wilson, and Eisenhower); Methodist, four (Polk, Andrew Johnson, Grant, and McKinley); Unitarian, four (the two Adamses, Fillmore, and Taft); Baptist, three (Harding, Truman, and Carter); Disciples of Christ (Christian Church), two (Garfield and Lyndon B. Johnson);

Reformed Church, two (Van Buren and Theodore Roosevelt); Quaker (Friends), two (Hoover and Nixon); and Congregationalist, one (Coolidge).

Lincoln and Hayes were never officially affiliated with any denomination, though the former occasionally attended Presbyterian services and the latter regularly those of the Methodist Church. Jefferson, originally an Episcopalian, later declared himself a Deist and expressed interest in Unitarianism. And not all the other Chief Executives were strongly identified with their churches. Some favored more than one denomination during their lifetime, and many at one time or another worshipped with various faiths.

No Presidents were ministers, though Garfield was a lay preacher, and John Adams and Madison studied theology and at one time considered the profession. Arthur, Cleveland, and Wilson were sons of clergymen, and Hoover's mother was a Quaker lay minister.

Another striking similarity among the Chief Executives is that most of them assumed the position at a mature age, and a large number were long lived. The average age upon entering office was a little less than 55 years. Theodore Roosevelt, who took over from McKinley, was the youngest to serve, at 42; and Kennedy, at 43, the youngest elected. The oldest at inauguration was William Henry Harrison, 68; Eisenhower, at 70, the oldest upon retirement from office.

The assassinations of four Presidents have shocked the country. Garfield was shot in 1881 at Washington's Baltimore and Potomac Railroad Station.

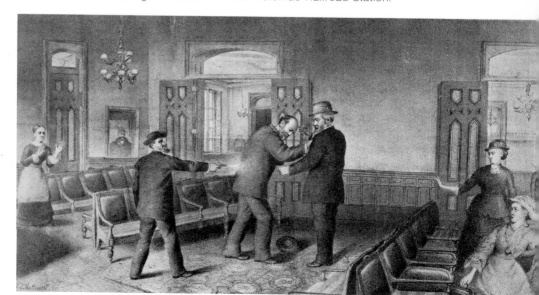

The average age at death was nearly 69, a remarkable figure considering the effect on the average of the four Presidents who were assassinated—Garfield and Kennedy in their forties, Lincoln at 56, and McKinley at 58. John Adams, who lived to be 90 years and 8 months old, was the longest lived; Hoover also reached 90. Of the 29 other deceased Chief Executives, four (Jefferson, Madison, John Quincy Adams, and Truman) died in their eighties; 10 passed away in their seventies; 12 in their sixties; and three others in their fifties.

Most of the Presidents were born in the Eastern States, 22 in the Thirteen Original States, and 32 of the 38 in the States east of the Mississippi. Reflecting the westward trend in our history, the 16th President, Lincoln, was the first born west of the Appalachians; Hoover, the 31st, the first born west of the Mississippi; and six of the last nine have been natives of States in the trans-Mississippi West. Nixon was the only one born in the Far West.

The bulk of the Chief Executives have been northerners by birth. Twenty-two were born in that region, versus 16 (including Lincoln and Truman, from the border states of Kentucky and Missouri, respectively) in the South. Nine of those who were southern-born (Washington, Jefferson, Madison, Monroe, Jackson, William Henry Harrison, Tyler, Polk, and Taylor) came to office before the Civil War, only three in the long interim until World War II (Lincoln, Andrew Johnson, and Wilson), and four (Truman, Eisenhower, Lyndon B. Johnson, and Carter) since that time.

By place of birth, the Presidents have represented 16 or 17 States, because both North and South Carolina claim Jackson. Virginia produced eight (Washington, Jefferson, Madison, Monroe, William Henry Harrison, Tyler, Taylor, and Wilson); Ohio, seven (Grant, Hayes, Garfield, Benjamin Harrison, McKinley, Taft, and Harding); New York, four (Van Buren, Fillmore, and both Roosevelts); Massachusetts, three (the two Adamses and Kennedy); North Carolina, two (Polk and Andrew Johnson) and claims, as does South Carolina, Andrew Jackson; Texas (Eisenhower and Lyndon B. Johnson) and Vermont (Arthur and Coolidge), each two; and nine other States, one each (New Hampshire, Pierce; Pennsylvania, Buchanan; Kentucky, Lincoln; New Jersey, Cleveland; Iowa, Hoover; Missouri, Truman; California, Nixon; Nebraska, Ford; and Georgia, Carter).

Some 16 of the 38 Chief Executives have come to office from other than the States of their birth. Leading the States in which the Presidents resided when they were originally elected or inaugurated is New York, which furnished eight: Van Buren, Fillmore, Arthur, Cleveland, Theodore Roosevelt, Franklin D. Roosevelt, Eisenhower, and Nixon; Ohio, six (William Henry Harrison, Hayes, Garfield, McKinley, Taft, and Harding); Virginia, five (Washington, Jefferson, Madison, Monroe, and Tyler); Massachusetts, four (both Adamses, Coolidge, and Kennedy); Tennessee, three (Jackson, Polk, and Andrew Johnson); Illinois, two (Lincoln and Grant); and ten other States, one each (Louisiana, Taylor; New Hampshire, Pierce; Pennsylvania, Buchanan; Indiana, Benjamin Harrison; New Jersey, Wilson; California, Hoover; Missouri, Truman; Texas, Lyndon B. Johnson; Michigan, Ford; and Georgia, Carter). Eisenhower and Nixon both changed their legal residences by the beginning of their second terms, from New York to Pennsylvania and California, respectively.

MOST Presidents remained associated with a certain political party from early in their careers until the ends of their lives, though a few changed their affiliations or did not make formal ones until shortly before their election. Some Chief Executives have championed the causes of their parties; others have often tried to subordinate partisan issues.

Washington disdained parties and dreaded their formation, though he seemed to favor the Federalists. Except for a few minor or short-term affiliations, the choices of his successors were as follows: Federalists, one (John Adams); Democratic-Republicans, four (Jefferson, Madison, Monroe, and John Quincy Adams); Whigs, four (William Henry Harrison, Tyler, Taylor, and Fillmore); Democrats, 12 (Jackson, Van Buren, Polk, Pierce, Buchanan, Cleveland, Wilson, Franklin D. Roosevelt, Truman, Kennedy, Lyndon B. Johnson, and Carter); and Republicans, 15 (Lincoln, Grant, Hayes, Garfield, Arthur, Benjamin Harrison, McKinley, Theodore Roosevelt, Taft, Harding, Coolidge, Hoover, Eisenhower, Nixon, and Ford).

Andrew Johnson, a former Democrat, ran on the National Union (Republican) ticket as Vice President and succeeded to the Presidency; his subsequent estrangement from the Republicans left him virtually without a party. Similarly, Tyler's ties to the Whigs frayed rapidly.

Jefferson and Madison founded the Democratic-Republican Party. The Whig Party grew out of it from John Quincy Adams' faction; the Democratic, from that of Jackson. The Republican Party, which drew most of its strength from Whigs and Free-Soil Democrats, was founded in 1854 primarily to oppose the extension of slavery.

JUST over half, or 20, of the 37 Presidents prior to Carter served single terms or less. The only one to hold the office more than the traditional two terms, slightly more than 12 years when he died near the beginning of his fourth term, was Franklin D. Roosevelt. Subsequently the 22d amendment (1951) to the Constitution

Vice President Truman, accompanied by his wife and surrounded by governmental leaders, takes the Presidential oath from Chief Justice Harlan F. Stone in the Cabinet Room of the White House upon the sudden death of Roosevelt in April 1945.

restricted future tenure to a maximum of two terms plus any unexpired term of less than 2 years to which an incumbent might have succeeded.

Nine Chief Executives served two full terms: Washington, Jefferson, Madison, Monroe, Jackson, Grant, Cleveland (nonconsecutive), Wilson, and Eisenhower. Lincoln and McKinley were elected to second terms, but were assassinated during them. Nixon resigned before completing his second term.

Theodore Roosevelt, Coolidge, Truman, and Lyndon B. Johnson, who all succeeded to office through the Vice-Presidency, were subsequently elected to full terms and lived to complete them. No Presidents who succeeded through the Vice-Presidency ever won second elective terms. Vice Presidents Tyler, Fillmore, Andrew Johnson, Arthur, and Ford succeeded to the Presidency, but never won election in their own right.

Judge Sarah T. Hughes, the first woman in history to swear in a Chief Executive, administers the oath to Vice President Johnson aboard Air Force One at Dallas in 1963. This occurred only a few hours after a sniper's bullet had struck down President Kennedy. The bereaved widow, Jacqueline, is at the right; Lady Bird Johnson, at the left.

The shortest term was that of William Henry Harrison, who was stricken soon after his inauguration and died after only a month in office. Only one Chief Executive, Andrew Johnson, was impeached by the House of Representatives, but he was not convicted by the Senate. Nixon, facing almost certain impeachment, resigned.

Incumbent Presidents who were defeated when they ran for reelection were the two Adamses, Van Buren, Cleveland, Benjamin Harrison, Taft, Hoover, and Ford. Five sitting Chief Executives sought but did not win their parties' renomination: Tyler, Fillmore, Pierce, Andrew Johnson, and Arthur. Jefferson, Jackson, William Henry Harrison, Cleveland, and Nixon lost Presidential elections but subsequently were successful.

Tyler and Franklin D. Roosevelt were the losing Vice-Presidential candidates of major parties before elevation to the Presidency. In those eight instances where a death in office has occurred, the succession—of Vice Presidents Tyler, Fillmore, Andrew Johnson, Arthur, Theodore Roosevelt, Coolidge, Truman, and Lyndon B. Johnson—has been automatic. Vice President Ford took office when Nixon resigned. John Adams, Jefferson, and Van Buren won nomination and election while serving as Vice President. Nixon is unique in that he lost his first bid for the Presidency at the end of his Vice-Presidential term, but was later able to capture the office.

ALTHOUGH the health of the Presidents during their tenure has varied considerably and the burdens of office have placed them under great stress, only Garfield (gunshot wounds), Wilson (stroke), and Eisenhower (heart attack) were incapacitated for extended periods. Franklin D. Roosevelt was handicapped throughout much of his adult life from the effects of infantile paralysis.

Of the eight Chief Executives who died in office, four were assassinated (Lincoln, Garfield, McKinley, and Kennedy). The others (William Henry Harrison, Taylor, Harding, and Franklin D. Roosevelt) died of natural causes. Jackson, Truman, and Ford weathered serious assassination attempts while they were President, as did also President-elect Franklin D. Roosevelt, as well as Theodore Roosevelt after his Presidency.

Tyler fortuitously escaped death in 1844 when a cannon exploded during a firing demonstration while he was aboard the *Princeton* on the Potomac River. Lincoln, while viewing a Confederate attack on Fort Stevens, D.C., was the only President to be under hostile fire while in office, though many were prior to their election while in military service. Before entering office, Jackson and Lincoln engaged in duels, and Jackson was seriously wounded during an altercation.

MOST Presidents have remained active in retirement, and blended participation in political and national affairs with pursuit of private concerns. For a number of them, the return to private life has brought vast relief. Buchanan and Hayes, for example, made unabashed statements of pleasure on departure from the White House. On the other hand, some individuals left office reluctantly and never fully adjusted to the change in status. Van Buren, Fillmore, Grant, Cleveland, and Theodore Roosevelt sought to regain the Presidency; only Cleveland succeeded.

Just a few of the men returned to major elective or appointive public office. Two went back to the U.S. Congress, Andrew Johnson briefly late in his life to the Senate and John Quincy Adams for an extended period in the House of Representatives. Taft was cochairman of the National War Labor Board during World War I, and in his twilight years Chief Justice of the United States.

Grant, who toured the world during his retirement, being received by the Emperor of Japan in 1879.

Various others also sat on Government boards, commissions, and committees; represented the incumbent Chief Executive on ceremonial occasions; advised him; or performed specific tasks at his request.

A few ex-Presidents, including Taft, Benjamin Harrison, Lyndon B. Johnson, and Ford, taught or lectured at universities. Numerous individuals served as officials or trustees, held honorary offices, or otherwise supported educational institutions, libraries, learned societies, and charitable and philanthropic organizations. Arthur, Cleveland, Benjamin Harrison, and Coolidge resumed their law practices, though they were usually less active in the profession than in earlier years.

Several men traveled extensively. Van Buren, Pierce, Fillmore, and Hoover visited Europe. Theodore Roosevelt traveled there as well as to Africa and Latin America. Grant journeyed leisurely around the world. Nixon flew to China.

Grant and Roosevelt subsequently described their travels and impressions in books. A large number of individuals wrote

Many ex-Presidents have continued to serve the Nation. One of the foremost of these was Herbert C. Hoover, shown meeting with President Truman in the White House.

memoirs, autobiographies, and books on other subjects, as well as magazine and newspaper articles, pamphlets, and tracts on national or political affairs, as well as miscellaneous subjects.

IN physical appearance the Presidents have ranged from handsome to homely. Some have worn beards, mustaches, and sideburns; some had long hair, some short; some were bald. Others have worn spectacles. Some were stylish dressers, and others favored informal attire. They ranged in height from Madison (5 feet 4 inches) to Lincoln (a full foot taller). Other short Presidents were the two Adamses, Van Buren, and Benjamin Harrison; tall, Washington, Jefferson, Arthur, Franklin D. Roosevelt, and Lyndon B. Johnson. Madison, the lightest, weighed a mere 100 pounds; Taft, 300 pounds, and Cleveland, 260 pounds.

FOR diversion, over the course of their careers the Chief Executives have enjoyed a variety of hobbies, some of which they pursued avidly and others casually. Their interest in sports, though often only in a spectator capacity, has been strong. Included are such individual pursuits as hunting, fishing, walking-hiking, horseback riding, swimming, golf, bowling, skiing, tennis, and exercising. Popular team sports have been baseball, softball, football, and basketball. Two of the most active sportsmen-Presidents, both of whom took part in and watched a wide range of athletic activities, were Theodore Roosevelt and Ford.

Other hobbies include: philately, bird watching, and collecting naval prints and models: Franklin D. Roosevelt; playing cards: Washington, John Quincy Adams, Van Buren, Buchanan, Harding, Truman, Eisenhower, and Nixon; painting and cooking: Eisenhower; the theater: Washington, Jefferson, John Quincy Adams, Lincoln, and Carter; movies: a number of the 20th-century Presidents.

Few individuals have exhibited any strong musical inclination, though some played instruments—with varying degrees of skill. Jefferson, Tyler, and Nixon played the violin; Truman and Nixon the piano; Coolidge the harmonica; and Harding the alto horn and cornet. Many of the Chief Executives have enjoyed listening to music and dancing. Nearly all have enjoyed reading—ranging from Shakespeare and other classical authors to mysteries and westerns as well as histories and biographies. In addition, many

Presidential hobbies have been as diversified as the men themselves. Eisenhower paints (upper left); Truman plays the piano (upper right); Harding golfs (lower left); and Carter plays tennis (lower right).

Many Chief Executives have enjoyed baseball. Coolidge throws out the first ball to open the 1925 American League season.

Presidents have enjoyed occasional cruises on the Presidential yacht. Most of them have sought whenever possible to rest away from the Capital, at official retreats or in their private residences or vacation homes.

George Washington

FIRST PRESIDENT   1789-1797

Peerless military leader of the War for Independence, able chairman of the Constitutional Convention, brilliant first President, and wise statesman, Washington more than any other man launched our Republic on its course to greatness. During his two precedent-setting terms, he shaped the role of the Presidency, pioneered its relations with Congress, unified the Nation, fostered political harmony, and maintained neutrality in foreign affairs. For all these reasons, he clearly deserves the epithet "Father of His Country."

Washington, the eldest of six children from his father's second marriage, was born into the landed gentry in 1732 at Wakefield plantation, Va. Until reaching 16 years of age, he lived there and at other plantations along the Potomac and Rappahannock Rivers, including the one that later became known as Mount Vernon.

Washington's education was rudimentary, probably provided by tutors but also possibly by private schools, and he learned surveying. After he lost his father when he was 11 years old, his half-brother Lawrence, who had served in the Royal Navy, acted as his mentor. As a result, the youth acquired an interest in pursuing a naval career, but his mother discouraged him from doing so.

At the age of 16, Washington joined a surveying party sent to the Shenandoah Valley by Lord Fairfax, a land baron. For the next few years, Washington conducted surveys in the frontier areas of Virginia and present West Virginia, and gained a lifetime interest in the West. In 1751-52 he accompanied Lawrence on a visit the latter made to Barbados, West Indies, for health reasons just prior to his death.

The next year, Washington began his military career when the Royal Governor appointed him to an adjutantship in the militia, as a major. That same year, as a gubernatorial emissary, accompanied by a guide, he traveled to Fort Le Boeuf, Pa., in the Ohio River Valley, and delivered to French authorities an ultimatum to cease fortification and settlement in British territory. During the trip, he tried to cement relations with various Indian tribes.

Winning the rank of lieutenant colonel and then colonel in the militia, in 1754 Washington led a force that sought to challenge French control of the Ohio River Valley, but met defeat at Fort Necessity, Pa.—an event that helped trigger the French and Indian War (1754-63). Late in 1754, irritated by the dilution of his rank because of the pending arrival of British regulars, he resigned his commission. That same year, he leased Mount Vernon, which he was to inherit in 1761.

In 1755 Washington reentered military service with the courtesy title of colonel as an aide to Gen. Edward Braddock, and barely escaped death when the French inflicted a defeat in the Battle of the Monongahela, Pa. As a reward for his bravery, Washington won his colonelcy and command of the Virginia militia forces, charged with defending the colony's frontier. Because of the shortage of men and equipment, he found the assignment challenging. Late in 1758 or early in 1759, disillusioned over governmental neglect of the militia and irked at not winning higher rank, he resigned and headed back to Mount Vernon.

The Continental Congress accepts General Washington's resignation on December 23, 1783, at the Maryland State House.

In this letter to John Langdon, President *pro tem* of the Senate in the First Congress, Washington accepts the Presidency.

In 1759 Washington wed Martha Dandridge Custis, a wealthy widow and mother of two children. The marriage produced no offspring, but Washington reared those of his wife as his own. During the period 1759-74, he managed his plantations and sat in the Virginia House of Burgesses. He supported the initial protests against British policies; took an active part in the nonimportation movement in Virginia; and, in time, particularly because of his military experience, became a Whig leader.

By the 1770's, relations of the colony with the mother country had become strained. Measured in his behavior but resentful of British restrictions and commercial exploitation, Washington represented Virginia at the First and Second Continental Congresses. In 1775, after the bloodshed at Lexington and Concord, Congress appointed him as commander in chief of the Continental Army. Overcoming severe obstacles, especially in supply, he eventually fashioned a well-trained and disciplined fighting force.

The strategy Washington evolved consisted of continual harassment of British forces while avoiding general actions. Although his troops yielded much ground and lost a number of battles, they persevered even during the dark winters at Valley Forge, Pa., and Morristown, N.J. Finally, with the aid of the French fleet and army, he won a climactic victory at the Battle of Yorktown, Va., in 1781.

During the next 2 years, while still commanding the unpaid and poorly supplied Continental Army, Washington denounced proposals that the military take over the Government, including one that planned to appoint him as king. But he supported army petitions to the Continental Congress for proper compensation.

Once the Treaty of Paris (1783) was signed, Washington resigned his commission and trekked back once again to Mount Vernon. His wartime financial sacrifices and long absence, as well as generous loans to friends, had severely impaired his extensive fortune, which consisted mainly of his plantations, slaves, and landholdings in the West. At this point, however, he was to have little time to repair his finances, for his retirement was brief.

Dissatisfied with national progress under the Articles of Confederation, Washington and other leaders advocated a stronger central Government. He hosted the Mount Vernon Conference (1785) at his estate after the initial meetings in Alexandria, Va., though he apparently did not directly participate in the discussions.

Despite Washington's sympathies with the goals of the Annapolis Convention (1786), he did not attend. But the following year, encouraged by many of his friends, he presided over the Constitutional Convention, whose success was immeasurably influenced by his presence. Following ratification of the new instrument of Government, the electoral college unanimously chose him as the first President.

On April 30, 1789, after a triumphal journey from Mount Vernon to New York City, Washington took the oath of office at Federal Hall. During his two terms, he governed with dignity as well as restraint. He provided the stability and authority the emergent Nation so sorely needed; gave substance to the Constitution, and reconciled competing factions and divergent policies within the Government and his administration.

Washington respected the role of Congress and did not infringe upon its prerogatives, but did challenge it on matters he felt to be of principle. He also tried to maintain harmony between Secretary of State Thomas Jefferson and Secretary of the Treasury Alexander Hamilton, whose differences typified evolving party divisions, from which the President attempted to keep aloof.

Yet, usually leaning upon Hamilton for advice, Washington supported his plan for the assumption of State debts, concurred in the constitutionality of the bill establishing the Bank of the United States, and favored enactment of tariffs by Congress to provide Federal revenue and protect domestic manufacturers.

Washington took other steps to strengthen governmental authority, including suppression of the Whisky Rebellion (1794)

President and Mrs. Washington with her grandchildren George Washington Parke Custis and Eleanor Parke ("Nelly") Custis.

and Indian resistance in the Northwest Territory. As a gesture of national unity, he toured the Northeast in 1789 and the South in 1791. During his tenure, the Government moved from New York to Philadelphia (1790), he superintended the planning for relocation to the District of Columbia, and he laid the cornerstone of the Capitol (1793).

In foreign affairs Washington exerted dominance. He fostered United States interests on the North American Continent by treaties with Britain and Spain, though Jay's Treaty with Britain was controversial. Yet, until the Nation was stronger, he insisted on the maintenance of neutrality. For example, when war broke out between France and England in the wake of the French Revolution, he ignored the remonstrances of pro-French Jefferson and pro-British Hamilton.

Although many people encouraged Washington to seek a third term, he was weary of politics and refused to do so. In his "Farewell Address" (1796), he urged his countrymen to forswear party spirit and sectional passions and to avoid entanglement in the wars and domestic policies of other nations.

Washington enjoyed only a few years of retirement at Mount Vernon. Even then, demonstrating his continued willingness to make sacrifices for his country, in 1798 when the country was on the verge of war with France, he agreed to command the Army, though his services were not ultimately required. He died at the age of 67 in 1799.

John Adams

SECOND PRESIDENT   1797–1801

**A giant among the Founding Fathers, Adams was
one of the leaders who generated the American
Revolution, for which his prolific writings provided
many of the politico-philosophical foundations. Not
only did he help draft the Declaration of Independence, but he also steered it through the Continental
Congress. He later served the Nation as one of its
premier diplomats, first Vice President, and second
President. He won office by only a narrow margin,
and headed a divided Federalist Party in an era of
sharp political strife and complicated international
relations. Yet he avoided a declared war against
France while defending U.S. sovereignty on the
high seas.**

Adams, descended from a long line of yeomen farmers and the
eldest of three sons, was born in 1735 at Braintree (later Quincy),
Mass., and was himself the progenitor of a distinguished family.
He graduated from Harvard College in 1755, and for a short time
taught school at Worcester, Mass. At that time, he considered
entering the ministry, but decided instead to follow the law and
began studying with a local lawyer.

Adams was admitted to the bar at Boston in 1758, the same year
he took an M.A. degree at Harvard, and began to practice in his
hometown. Six years later, he married Abigail Smith, who was to
give birth to three sons, one of whom was John Quincy, and two
daughters. She was thus the only woman in U.S. history to be the
wife of one President and the mother of another, and she was also
the first mistress of the White House.

Like many others, Adams was propelled into the Revolutionary
camp by the Stamp Act. In 1765 he wrote a protest for Braintree
that scores of other Massachusetts towns adopted. Three years
hence, he temporarily left his family behind and moved to Boston.
He advanced in the law, but devoted more and more of his time to
the patriot cause. In 1768 he achieved recognition throughout the
Colonies for his defense of John Hancock, whom British customs
officials had charged with smuggling.

John Adams (center, left), the "Atlas of American Independence," and the other members of the drafting committee present the Declaration of Independence to the Continental Congress.

Adams later yielded to a stern sense of legal duty but incurred some public hostility by representing the British soldiers charged with murder in the Boston Massacre (1770). Ill health forced him to return to Braintree following a term in the colonial legislature (1770-71), and for the next few years he divided his time between there and Boston.

A 3-year stint in the Continental Congress (1774-77), punctuated by short recuperative leaves and service in the colonial legislature in 1774-75, brought Adams national fame. Because he was sharply attuned to the temper of Congress and aware that many Members resented Massachusetts extremism, he at first acceded to conciliatory efforts with Britain and restrained himself publicly. When Congress opted for independence, he became its foremost advocate, eschewing conciliation and urging a colonial confederation.

Abigail Adams was not only a brilliant woman in her own right, but she also furthered the career of her husband, John. She was the only woman in history to be the wife of one President and the mother of another, John Quincy.

Adams was a master of workable compromise and meaningful debate, though he was sometimes impatient. He chaired 25 of the more than 90 congressional committees on which he sat, the most important of which dealt with military and naval affairs. He played an instrumental part in obtaining Washington's appointment as commander in chief of the Continental Army. Adams was a member of the five-man committee charged with drafting the Declaration of Independence in June 1776, though he probably made no major changes in Jefferson's draft. But, more directly involved, he defended it from its congressional detractors, advocated it to the wavering, and guided it to passage.

The declaration battle won, exhausted by the incessant toil and strain and worried about his finances and family, Adams in November 1777 retired from Congress. He headed back to Braintree intending to resume his law practice. But, before the month expired, Congress appointed him to a diplomatic post in Europe—a phase of his career that consumed more than a decade (1777-88).

Adams served in France during the period 1778-85, interrupted only by a visit to the United States in the summer of 1779, during which he attended the Massachusetts constitutional convention. Independent-minded and forthright, as well as somewhat jealous of the fame and accomplishments of others, he frequently found himself at odds with fellow diplomats Benjamin Franklin and Arthur Lee, as well as French officials, whose policies he mistrusted. He joined Franklin and John Jay, however, in negotiating the Treaty of Paris (1783), by which Britain recognized the independence of the United States.

Meanwhile, during the preceding 3 years, Adams had persuaded the Dutch to recognize the Colonies as an independent Nation, grant a series of loans, and negotiate a treaty of alliance. As the first American envoy to Great Britain (1785-88), he strove to resolve questions arising from the Treaty of Paris and to calm the harsh feelings between the two countries.

Back in the United States, Adams was soon elected as the first Vice President (1789-97), an office he considered insignificant but in which he emerged as the nominal leader of the Federalist Party. The real leader was Alexander Hamilton, whose political manipulations coupled with the peculiarities of the electoral system at the time, resulted in Adams being saddled as President with his political enemy Jefferson, the leader of the opposition Democratic-

I was born Octr. 19, 1735 in Quincy then the North Parish in Braintree, my Father was John Adams born in the Same Parish, My Grandfather was Joseph Adams Junior born in the Same Parish My Great Grandfather was Joseph Adams Senior, and my Great real Grandfather was Henry Adams who came from England. These all lived died and were buried in this Parish as their Gravestones in the Congregational Church yard distinctly show to this day My Mother was Suzanna Boylston a Daughter of Peter Boylston of Brokeline. I was educated partly at the public Grammar School and partly at a private Academy under Mr Joseph Marsh both in this Parish. In 1751 I entered Harvard Colledge in Cambridge. In 1755 took my degree of Batchelor of Arts, and immediately undertook the Care of the Publick Grammar School in Worcester where I lived in the Family and studied Law in the Office of James Putman, till 1758 when I took my Second Degree at Colledge and the Oath of an Attorney in Boston In 1761 I was admitted a Barrister at Law in Boston in the Superiour Court of Judicature of the Province of Massachusetts Bay. In 1764 I married a daughter of the Reverend William Smith. Abigail Smith, of Weymouth. In 1767 my Son John Quincy Adams was born in this Parish . . . .

In 1755 I took a decided part against France and Great Britain too; thoroughly disgusted with their Folly, the Ignorance, the Cowardice or Treachery of her Conduct of the War against Canada. This Indignation was much increased by her degrading Treatment of our Troops through the whole War.

In 1760 and 1761, upon the first Appearance of the Design of Great Britain to deprive Us of our Liberties by asserting the Souveraign Athority of Parliament over Us, I took a decided Part against her, and have persevered for Fifty five Years in opposing and resisting to the utmost of my power every Instance of her Injustice, and arbitrary Power, towards Us. I am Sir with much respect .

your humble Servant

John Adams

John Adams prepared this one-page biography for an unidentified correspondent. It was probably written around 1815, when he was 80 years of age.

Republican Party, as his Vice President—the only instance in U.S. history where such a situation occurred. Also, Adams' principal Cabinet members answered to Hamilton.

But the problems did not end there. Adams also faced a hostile Congress, and he inherited the deep political discord between the Hamiltonians and the Jeffersonians that had taken root during Washington's administration. The resulting party warfare, of which Adams bore the brunt, was generated by the strong personal and political differences between the two men and the partisanship that arose out of the philosophical, diplomatic, and economic ramifications of the wars of the French Revolution between Great Britain and France.

Britain was not particularly solicitous of the rights of American shipping, but the major obstacle to peace was the belligerency of France toward U.S. ships carrying British goods and seamen serving on British warships. Hamilton and most Federalists, drawing closer to the old enemy Britain, favored war with France as a way of uniting the country and building a strong Army and Navy. The Jeffersonians, controlling roughly half the votes in Congress and friendly toward War for Independence ally France, opposed war as far as they dared, but public opinion was bellicose.

If Adams had asked for a declaration of war, the antiwar party could not have stopped it. Rational discussion of political differences between the two parties degenerated into an ever more shrill exchange of insults. Bitter frustrations found release in the Federalist-backed Alien and Sedition Acts and in the Democratic-Republican response, the Kentucky Resolutions and the Virginia Resolutions.

The statesmanlike Adams maintained a neutral stance without abandoning his principles. He kept the United States out of a declared war with France and achieved an amicable peace. But, always more a political philosopher than a politician, he proved unable to unite his party, divided by the machinations of Hamilton, who spurred congressional opposition to Adams, and the implications of the French Revolution. The Jeffersonians pushed the Federalists out of office in the election of 1800, the same year that the Government and its 150 employees moved from Philadelphia to the incomplete Capital in the District of Columbia and the Adamses occupied the White House.

Adams spent his later years quietly at Quincy, where he resided in his home, "Peacefield," which he had purchased in 1787. The death of his wife in 1818 saddened him, but he never lost interest in public affairs and lived to see his son John Quincy become President. John, the longest lived Chief Executive, died at the age of 90 just a few hours after Jefferson, with whom he had become reconciled, on July 4, 1826—dramatically enough the 50th anniversary of the adoption of the Declaration of Independence.

Thomas Jefferson

THIRD PRESIDENT   1801-9

As author of the Declaration of Independence, political theorist, cofounder of the Democratic-Republican Party, Virginia legislator and Governor, distinguished diplomat, first U.S. Secretary of State, second Vice President, and third President, Jefferson has left an indelible impression on our governmental system and philosophy. Graced with a wide-ranging and probing mind that was interested in most fields of human endeavor, he ranked among the most outstanding men of his or any other time. During his Presidential administration, he more than doubled the size of the United States, laid the basis for its westward expansion, and maintained neutrality toward France and Britain during the Napoleonic Wars.

The eldest of two sons in a family of 10, Jefferson was born in 1743 at Shadwell, a frontier plantation in Goochland (present Albemarle) County, Va. But 2 years later his father, Peter, a self-made surveyor-magistrate-planter who had married into the distinguished Randolphs, moved his family eastward to Tuckahoe plantation, near Richmond. His reason for doing so was a promise he had made to his wife's newly deceased cousin, William Randolph, to act as guardian of his son. Young Jefferson passed most of his boyhood in the Randolph home, beginning his elementary education with private tutors.

In 1752, when Jefferson was about 9 years old, the family returned to Shadwell. His father died 5 years later and bequeathed him almost 3,000 acres; he became head of the family. In 1760, at the age of 17, he matriculated at the College of William and Mary, in Williamsburg. An incidental benefit was the chance to observe the operation of practical politics in the colonial capital. He graduated in 1762, studied law locally under the noted teacher George Wythe, and in 1767 was admitted to the bar.

At Shadwell, Jefferson assumed the civic responsibilities and prominence his father had enjoyed. In 1770, when fire consumed the structure, he moved to his nearby estate, Monticello, where he had already begun building a home. Two years later, he married Martha Wayles Skelton, a widow. During their decade of life together, she was to bear six children, one son and five daughters, but only two of the latter reached maturity.

Meanwhile, in 1769 at the age of 26, Jefferson had been elected to the House of Burgesses, in Williamsburg. He was a member continuously until 1775, and alined himself with the anti-British group. Unlike his smooth-tongued confreres Patrick Henry and Richard Henry Lee, Jefferson concentrated his efforts in committee work rather than in debate. A literary stylist, he drafted many of the Revolutionary documents adopted by the House of Burgesses.

Jefferson utilized the same methods in the Continental Congress (1775-76), where his decisiveness in committee contrasted markedly with his silence on the floor. His colleagues, however, rejected several of his drafts the first year because of their extreme anti-British tone. But, by the time he returned the following May, after spending the winter in Virginia, the temper of Congress had changed drastically. The very next month, though only 33 years old, he was assigned to the five-man committee chosen to write the Declaration of Independence, a task his associates assigned to him.

A notable career in the Virginia House of Delegates (1776-79), the lower house of the legislature, followed. Jefferson took over leadership of the "progressive" party from Patrick Henry, who relinquished it to become Governor. Highlights of this service included revision of the State laws (1776-79), in which Jefferson collaborated with George Wythe and Edmund Pendleton; and authorship of a bill for the establishment of religious freedom in Virginia, introduced in 1779 but not passed until 7 years later.

Although hampered as Governor (1779-81) by wartime conditions and constitutional limitations, Jefferson proved to be a weak executive, even in emergencies hesitating to wield his authority. When the British pressed their invasion of the State in 1781, he recommended the combining of civil and military agencies under Gen. Thomas Nelson, Jr., and virtually abdicated office. Although he was later formally vindicated, the action fostered a conservative takeover of the government and his reputation remained clouded for some time.

Jefferson stayed out of the limelight for 2 years, during which time his wife died. In 1783 he reentered Congress, where he

Thomas Jefferson (left) and political rival Alexander Hamilton (center) confer with President George Washington.

sponsored and drafted the Ordinance of 1784, forerunner of the Ordinance of 1787 (Northwest Ordinance). In 1784 he was sent to Paris to aid Benjamin Franklin and John Adams in their attempts to negotiate commercial treaties with European nations. During his 5-year stay, Jefferson succeeded Franklin as Minister to France (1785-89), gained various economic concessions from and strengthened relations with the French, visited England and Italy, absorbed European culture, and observed the beginnings of the French Revolution.

Jefferson returned to the United States in 1789. In the years that followed, interspersed with pleasant interludes and political exile at Monticello, he filled the highest offices in the land. Ever averse to political strife, he occupied these positions as much out of a sense of civic and party duty as personal ambition.

FOURTH of MARCH, 1801.

Wednesday last, agreeable to the constitution, the inauguration of Thomas Jefferson and Aaron Burr, as President and Vice President of the United States, took place. The happy event of a change in the administration of our government, and the placing the power thereof in the hands of the men whom " the people" delight to honor and confide in, was celebrated in an unusual and merited degree, by all the republicans in this city and county ;—The day was truly a day of jubilee and festivity.

A procession, under the direction of a committee of arrangement, was formed, which for splendor and extent, exceeded by far any thing of the kind ever exhibited in this city, excepting the pompous procession in 1787, on the ratification of the federal government. The military on this occasion made a handsome appearance. The Tammany Society, which attended the procession ; was numerous, and made a beautiful display of flags and other decorations. The True Republican Society also attracted deserved attention by their respectable appearance ; the ranks of the citizens were numerous and well filled, and the associated youth displayed an enthusiastic ardor of patriotism worthy the youthful heroes of '76.

We remarked that in that part of the procession composed of the civil officers of government, were the state officers only, not one of the civil officers of the federal government designing to shew an approbation of the choice of characters that have been chosen to preside over them—and in short no one except known democratic republicans made their appearance therein.

The musical part of the procession, as well in the church as the military bands in the procession, were very pleasing ; and among the pieces composed for the occasion, " Jefferson's March" merited and received distinguished applause.

The elegant schooner; " Thomas Jefferson" attracted a marked degree of attention from an admiring multitude—she was well officered, and manned by a crew of brave tars, accompanied by a number of that respectable and useful class of citizens, the ship-builders.

It is worthy of remark, that not only the cavalcade excited the admiration of our political opponents, but that they admit that good order was preserved by the democrats on this occasion.

The public dinners were numerous, and among the most conspicuous were that held at Francis's, in the house lately occupied by the president of the United States, and that held in the chamber lately occupied by the federal Senate.

Newspaper account of Jefferson's first inauguration.

Aggravating normal burdens and pressures were Jefferson's feuds with Alexander Hamilton on most aspects of national policy, as well as the vindictiveness of Federalist attacks. These clashes originated while Jefferson was Secretary of State (1790-93) in Washington's Cabinet. Unlike Hamilton, Jefferson sympathized with the French Revolution. He favored States rights and opposed a strong central Government. He also envisioned an agricultural America, peopled by well educated and politically astute yeomen farmers. Hamilton took the opposite position.

These political and philosophical conflicts resulted in time in the forming of the Federalist Party and Democratic-Republican Party, which Jefferson cofounded with James Madison. In 1793, because of his disagreements with Hamilton and Washington's growing reliance on Hamilton for advice in foreign affairs, Jefferson resigned as Secretary of State. For the next 3 years, he remained in semiretirement at Monticello.

In 1796 Jefferson lost the Presidential election to Federalist John Adams by only three electoral votes and, because the Constitution did not then provide separate tickets for the President and Vice President, became Vice President (1797-1801), though a member of the opposing party. In 1800 the same sort of deficiency, soon remedied by the 12th amendment, again became apparent when Democratic-Republican electors, in trying to select both a President and Vice President from their party, cast an equal vote for Jefferson and his running mate, Aaron Burr. Only after a tie-settling election in the Federalist-controlled House of Representatives that rended both parties did Jefferson capture the Presidency; Burr became Vice President.

Jefferson, who was the first Chief Executive to be inaugurated at the Capitol, called his victory a "revolution." Indeed, it did bring a new tone and philosophy to the White House, where an aura of democratic informality was to prevail. And, despite the interparty acrimony of the time, the transition of power was smooth and peaceful, and Jefferson continued many Federalist policies. Because the crisis with France had terminated, he slashed Army and Navy funds. He also substantially reduced the governmental budget. Although he believed in an agrarian America, he encouraged commerce.

In 1801-5 Jefferson deployed naval forces to the Mediterranean to subdue the Barbary pirates, who were harassing American

Fellow citizens of the Senate & House of Representatives.

Peace.

It is a circumstance of sincere gratification to me, that on meeting the great council of our nation, I am able to announce to them, on grounds of reasonable certainty, that the wars & troubles, which have for so many years afflicted our sister-nations, have at length come to an end; & that the communications of peace & commerce are once more opening among them. whilst we devoutly return thanks to the beneficent being who has been pleased to breathe into them the spirit of conciliation & forgiveness, we are bound, with peculiar gratitude, to be thankful to him that our own peace has been preserved through so perilous a season, & ourselves permitted quietly to cultivate the earth, & to practise and improve those arts which tend to increase our comforts. the assurances indeed of friend-ly disposition recieved from all the powers, with whom we have principal relations, had inspired a confidence that our peace with them would not have been disturbed. but a cessation of the irregularities which had afflicted the commerce of neutral nations, & of the irritations & injuries produced by them, cannot but add to this confidence; and strengthens, at the same time, the hope that wrongs committed on unoffending friends, under a pressure of circumstances, will now be reviewed with candor, & will be considered as founding just claims of retribution for the past, & new assurance for the future.

Indians.

Among our Indian neighbors also a spirit of peace and friendship generally pre--vails; & I am happy to inform you that the continued efforts to introduce among them the implements & the practice of husbandry, & of the houshold arts, have not been without suc--cess: that they are becoming more & more sensible of the superiority of this dependance, for clothing & subsistence, over the precarious resources of hunting & fishing: & already we are able to announce that, instead of that constant diminution of numbers produced by their wars & their wants, some of them begin to experience an increase of population.

Tripoli.

To this state of general peace with which we have been blessed, one only exception exists. Tripoli, the least considerable of the Barbary states, had come forward with demands unfounded either in right or in compact, & had permitted itself to denounce war, on our failure to comply before a given day. the style of the demand admitted but one answer. I sent a small squadron of frigates into the Mediterranean, with assurances to that pow--er of our sincere desire to remain in peace; but with orders to protect our commerce against

20381

First page of Jefferson's first annual message to Congress, December 8, 1801, in his own handwriting.

vessels. During his second term, to counter English and French interference with neutral American shipping during the Napoleonic Wars, he applied an embargo on foreign trade, for the purpose of avoiding involvement. But this measure proved to be unworkable and unpopular.

Jefferson's greatest achievements were in the realm of westward expansion, of which he was the architect. Foreseeing the continental destiny of the Nation, he sent the Lewis and Clark Expedition (1804-6) to the Pacific, though he knew it had to cross territory claimed by foreign powers. While that project was being organized, Jefferson's diplomats at Paris had consummated the Louisiana Purchase (1803), which doubled the size of the United States and extended its boundaries far beyond the Mississippi.

In 1809 Jefferson retired for the final time to Monticello. He continued to pursue his varied interests and corresponded with and entertained statesmen, politicians, scientists, explorers, scholars, and Indian chiefs. When the pace of life grew too hectic, he found haven at Poplar Forest, his retreat near Lynchburg. His pet project during most of his last decade was founding the University of Virginia (1819), in Charlottesville, but he also took pride in the realization that two of his disciples, Madison and Monroe, had followed him into the White House.

Painfully distressing to Jefferson, however, was the woeful state of his finances. His small salary in public office, the attendant neglect of his fortune and estate, general economic conditions, and debts he inherited from his wife had taken a heavy toll. When a friend defaulted on a note for a large sum, Jefferson fell hopelessly into debt and was forced to sell his library to the Government. It became the nucleus of the Library of Congress.

Jefferson died only a few hours before John Adams at the age of 83 on July 4, 1826, the fiftieth anniversary of the adoption of the Declaration of Independence.

James Madison

FOURTH PRESIDENT   1809-17

**Madison was a brilliant political philosopher and
pragmatic politician. He won recognition as the
"Father of the Constitution," served in the Continental
Congress as well as the House of Representatives,
and founded the Democratic-Republican Party with
his mentor, Jefferson. As President, Madison's efforts
to keep the peace through diplomacy failed, and he
led the Nation through the indecisive War of 1812
against Britain and the beginning of the ensuing
period of nationalistic fervor. Domestically, with the
support of Congress, he strengthened U.S. military
forces, created the Second Bank of the United States,
and enacted a protective tariff.**

A scion of the planter aristocracy, Madison was born in 1751 at
Port Conway, King George County, Va., while his mother was
visiting her parents. With her newborn son, the first of 10 children,
in a few weeks she journeyed back to Montpelier estate, in Orange
County, which became his lifelong home. He obtained his early
education from his parents, tutors, and a private school.

An excellent scholar though frail and sickly in his youth, in 1771
Madison graduated from the College of New Jersey (present
Princeton University), where he demonstrated special interest in
government and the law. But, considering the ministry for a career,
he stayed on for a year of postgraduate study in theology.

Back at Montpelier, still undecided on a profession, Madison
soon embraced the patriot cause, and State and local politics
absorbed much of his time. In 1775 he served on the Orange County committee of safety; the next year, at the Virginia Convention,
which advocated various revolutionary steps and framed the
Virginia constitution; in 1776-77 in the House of Delegates; and in
1778-80 in the Council of State. His ill health precluded military
service.

Madison was chosen in 1780 to represent Virginia in the
Continental Congress (1780-83 and 1786-88). Although originally
the youngest Delegate, he played a major role in its deliberations.

Meantime, in the years 1784-86, he had again sat in the Virginia House of Delegates.

Madison was a guiding force behind the Mount Vernon Conference (1785), attended the Annapolis Convention (1786), and was otherwise instrumental in the convening of the Constitutional Convention (1787). Preeminent at the Convention, he served on key committees and tirelessly advocated a strong Government. His Virginia Plan was in large part the basis of the Constitution. And his journal of the Convention, which was not published until after his death, remains the best single record of the event.

Madison also played a major part in guiding the Constitution through the Continental Congress. Leading the pro-ratification forces in Virginia, he successfully defended the instrument against powerful opponents. Earlier, in New York, where he was serving in the Congress, he collaborated with Alexander Hamilton and John Jay in a series of essays that in 1787-88 appeared in the newspapers and were later published in book form as *The Federalist* (1788), a classic in political theory.

As a U.S. Representative (1789-97), Madison helped frame and pass the Bill of Rights. He also assisted in organizing the executive department and creating a system of Federal taxation. As leaders of the opposition to Hamilton's policies, he and Jefferson founded the Democratic-Republican Party.

In 1794 Madison married a vivacious widow who was 16 years his junior, Dorothea ("Dolley") Payne Todd, who had a son; they were to raise no children of their own. Although spending the period 1797-1801 in semiretirement, Madison authored the Virginia Resolutions, which attacked the Alien and Sedition Acts. While he served as Secretary of State (1801-9), his wife often acted as President Jefferson's hostess. Her lavish parties at the White House dazzled the Capital City for years.

In 1809 Madison succeeded Jefferson. Like the first three Presidents, Madison was enmeshed in the ramifications of European wars. Diplomacy had failed to prevent the seizure of U.S. ships, goods, and men on the high seas; and a depression wracked the country. Madison continued to negotiate with the warring parties and applied economic sanctions, eventually effective to some degree.

But continued British interference with American shipping created strong congressional sentiment for war. The "War

Early in his career, Madison won the epithet "Father of the Constitution," the instrument he was later to uphold as President. In this painting, which portrays its adoption, he is seated directly to the left of the group of three standing men.

Hawks," a group of mostly young Democratic-Republican Congressmen from the South and West who were territorial expansionists as much as defenders of the national pride, urged naval action to punish the British, the conquest of Canada, and military measures to end British fomenting of the Indians in the West. Eventually agreeing that U.S. honor and economic independence were at stake, in 1812 Madison asked Congress to declare war against Britain.

The young Nation was ill prepared. Federalist alienation in New England sapped the war effort. Poor generalship, inadequate troop strength, and supply and transportation problems frustrated the Army's efforts to conquer lightly defended Canada. At sea, despite victories in individual encounters, the U.S. Navy found itself unable to cope with the Royal Navy, which blockaded the coast.

New England opposition hampered Madison's conduct of the War of 1812. This cartoon shows him "beheading," or repealing, his 1814 embargo (snapping turtle). He was forced to do so because of the objections of northeastern merchants, who profited by supplying British forces.

The British captured Washington, burned the White House, Capitol, and other buildings, and forced the Government to flee the city for a time. The war ended in stalemate in December 1814 when the inconclusive Treaty of Ghent, which nearly restored prewar conditions, was signed.

But thanks mainly to Andrew Jackson's spectacular victory at the Battle of New Orleans (Chalmette) in January of 1815, most Americans believed they had won. Twice tested, independence had survived and an ebullient nationalism marked Madison's last years in office, during which period the Democratic-Republicans held virtually uncontested sway.

During the last 3 years of his administration, Madison concentrated on his domestic program. Congress, concurring in three of his proposals, strengthened land and naval forces to avoid the repetition of raids on the Capital and to protect the country as a whole and its commerce; established the Second Bank of the United States; and enacted a protective tariff on foreign manufactures.

Imaginative British version of their attack on Washington in 1814, near the end of the War of 1812. The letters indicate key actions.

Although Madison favored internal improvements, he vetoed on constitutional grounds a congressional bill that sought to finance the building of roads and canals with Federal funds.

In retirement after his second term, Madison managed Montpelier, but continued to be active in public affairs. He served as cochairman of the Virginia constitutional convention of 1829-30 and as rector of the University of Virginia after 1826. Writing newspaper articles defending the administration of Monroe, he also acted as his foreign policy adviser.

Madison spoke out, too, against the emerging sectional controversy that threatened the existence of the Union. Although a slaveholder all his life, he was active during his later years in the American Colonization Society, whose mission was the resettlement of slaves in Africa. He passed away at the age of 85 in 1836.

James Monroe

FIFTH PRESIDENT   1817-25

Monroe, able political heir of Jefferson and Madison and last of the Virginia dynasty (1801-25), held office at a time when the Democratic-Republicans reigned supreme over the weak Federalists and was overwhelmingly elected to a second term. Yet the Panic of 1819 and the intersectional strife preceding the Missouri Compromise (1820) dashed the original hopes for an "Era of Good Feelings." The highlight of his administration was promulgation of the Monroe Doctrine. Earlier in his career, when he had helped negotiate the Louisiana Purchase and served as Madison's Secretary of State, he had also made a notable mark in diplomacy.

The son of a planter of modest means and the oldest of five children, Monroe was born in 1758 in Westmoreland County, Va. He received his elementary education at a private school. In 1776, some 2 years after his father died, he discontinued his studies at the College of William and Mary. He immediately entered active service in the Continental Army, which the year before had awarded him a lieutenant's commission. During 4 years of service, he was wounded twice and advanced to the rank of major. Upon his discharge in 1780, he read law for 3 years with Thomas Jefferson, who became his lifelong adviser and friend.

Becoming active in politics, in 1782 Monroe entered the Virginia House of Delegates. The following year, he took a seat in the Continental Congress (1783-86). In 1786, when he joined the bar and established a practice in Fredericksburg, he married Elizabeth Kortright. She was to bear two daughters and a son.

Meantime, Monroe had been reelected to the House of Delegates (1786-90) and attended the Annapolis Convention, one of the forerunners of the Constitutional Convention. Nevertheless, in 1788, indicative of his aversion to a strong central Government, he opposed the Constitution at the Virginia ratifying convention. That same year, James Madison soundly defeated him in a race for the U.S. House of Representatives.

In 1790, when Monroe moved to Charlottesville, the Virginia legislature appointed him to the U.S. Senate (1790-94), where he became an advocate of Jeffersonian policies. Service as Minister to France (1794-96) and Governor of Virginia (1799-1802) followed. Reentering the diplomatic arena in 1803, he helped Robert R. Livingston negotiate the Louisiana Purchase from France and then held the position of Minister to Great Britain (1803-7), during which time he headed a special mission to Spain (1804).

In 1808, the year after Monroe returned to the United States, he temporarily lost Madison's friendship by vainly challenging him for the Presidency. In 1810 Monroe once again won election to the Virginia House of Delegates, and the following year also to the governorship. But, after only 3 months, he became Madison's Secretary of State (1811-17). In 1814-15 he was concurrently Secretary of War.

Blessed by Madison and facing only slightly Federalist opposition, in 1816 Monroe was elected to the White House. The next year, only 2½ months after taking office, he toured the Middle Atlantic States and then New England, the old Federalist stronghold. A Boston newspaper suggested that the warm welcome he received augured a political "Era of Good Feelings" in the Nation. But, despite his appointment of a competent intersectional Cabinet, the "good feelings" soon evaporated.

A depression struck the country in 1819 and, in a sudden emergence of the slavery issue, sectional debates broke out in Congress when Missouri sought admission to the Union as a slave State. The struggle captured headlines for 2 years and threatened to sunder the country. Disaster was averted by the Missouri Compromise (1820), which admitted Missouri as a slave State and Maine as a free State and outlawed slavery in the Louisiana Purchase area north and west of the southern boundary of Missouri.

In diplomacy Monroe achieved successes. The Rush-Bagot Agreement (1817) with Britain brought arms limitations on the Great Lakes. In the Adams-Onís Treaty, the United States acquired Florida from Spain, and Spain recognized United States claims to the Northwest as far as the Pacific shores. In addition, agreement was reached with Britain to the joint occupancy of Oregon and to delineation of the northern boundary of the Louisiana Purchase.

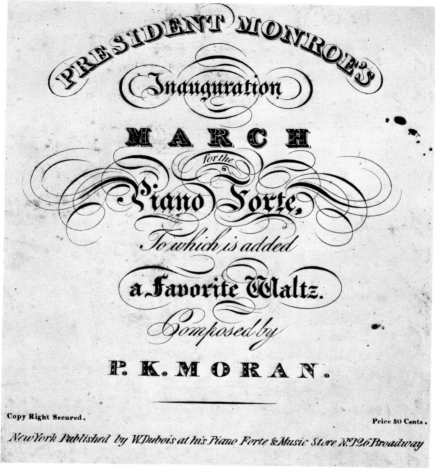

March composed in honor of Monroe's inauguration.

Monroe's greatest diplomatic accomplishment, however, was the Monroe Doctrine. Responding to the nationalistic revolutions that were freeing Latin America from Spanish and Portuguese control and fearing the intervention of various European powers, the British suggested a joint Anglo-American declaration that both nations would resist any intrusions in the area. Although Jefferson and Madison advised Monroe to accede to the British proposal, Secretary of State John Quincy Adams urged that the United States assert its independence by making its own declaration.

-ceeds from that, which exists in their respective Governments, and to the defence of our own, which has been atchieved by the loss of so much blood and treasure, and matured by the wisdom of their most enlightened Citizens, and under which we have enjoyed unexampled felicity, this whole nation is devoted. We owe it therefore to candor, and to the amicable relations existing between the United States and those powers, to declare that we should consider any attempt on their part to extend their system to any portion of this Hemisphere, as dangerous to our peace and safety. With the existing Colonies or dependencies of any European power, we have not interfered, and shall not interfere. But with the Governments who have declared their Independence, and maintained it, and whose Independence we have, on great consideration, and on just principles, acknowledged, we could not view any interposition for the purpose of oppressing them, or controling in any other manner, their destiny, by any European power, in any other light, than as the manifestation of an unfriendly disposition towards the United States. In the war between those new Governments and Spain, we declared our neutrality, at the time of their recognition, and to this we have adhered, and shall continue to adhere, provided no change shall occur, which in the judgment of the competent authorities of this Government shall make

Monroe's seventh annual message to Congress, dated December 2, 1823. Page 30, reproduced above, outlines the Monroe Doctrine. The message was transcribed by a clerk and signed by Monroe.

The President (at globe) formulates the Monroe Doctrine with his advisers. Secretary of State and the next Chief Executive John Quincy Adams (left) played a key role.

Monroe agreed and in his annual message to Congress in 1823, based on a draft prepared by Adams, he warned Europe against future colonization in the Western Hemisphere. This "Monroe Doctrine" was forgotten for many years, then revived by President James K. Polk at the time of the Mexican War (1846-48). By the late 19th century, the doctrine had become one of the cornerstones of U.S. foreign policy.

The years following Monroe's retirement to Oak Hill, Va., which he had completed in 1823, were filled with activity. He managed his estate, became a regent of the University of Virginia, served as cochairman of the State constitutional convention of 1829-30, acted as local magistrate, and even considered running again for Governor. But severe financial problems forced him to sell all his property, including his home, and in 1830 his wife died. He moved to New York City to live with one of his daughters. He died there, aged 73, on July 4 the following year.

John Quincy Adams

SIXTH PRESIDENT   1825-29

**John Quincy Adams was the only President who was
the son of another. Like his father, he demonstrated
determination and sometimes imperiousness;
preferred intellectual to social activities; rendered
outstanding service as a diplomat; evinced more
statesmanship than political pragmatism; suffered
strong political opposition; and failed to win
reelection. His visionary proposals for internal
improvements and national development were so far
ahead of his time that they failed to win public
sanction. Earlier, as Secretary of State, he had been a
prime mover behind the Monroe Doctrine. And, in his
post-Presidential years, he pursued a long and
remarkable career in the House of Representatives.**

The second child and eldest son of two remarkable parents, John
Quincy Adams was born in 1767 at Braintree (later Quincy), Mass.
Precocious, he attended private schools and absorbed Revolutionary ideas, as well as a lifelong anti-British attitude, from his father.
The youth spent the period 1778-85 in Europe, where his diplomat-
father was assigned. The experiences of John Quincy there were
broad and cosmopolitan, and he quickly achieved exceptional
maturity for his age. He was formally educated in Paris, Leyden,
and Amsterdam, but probably learned even more from his elders.

Mingling in diplomatic circles and holding discussions with
Franklin, Jay, and Jefferson, young Adams acquired an interest in
a wide range of subjects and became an accomplished linguist as
well as an avid diarist. In 1781 when he was a mere 14-year-old, he
became secretary to the first U.S. diplomatic agent to Russia. Back
in Paris, he witnessed the signing of the Treaty of 1783.

When his father was assigned to London in 1785, John Quincy
returned to the United States and matriculated at Harvard.
Graduating in 2 years, he read law at Newburyport, Mass., won
admittance to the bar in 1790, and set up practice in Boston. During
the next 4 years, he also wrote on political topics, mainly in defense
of Washington's administration, in which his father served as Vice
President.

John Quincy Adams, one of our most distinguished diplomats, sat for this portrait at the age of 29 while visiting London.

Washington then appointed Adams as Minister to Holland (1794-96). From 1797 to 1801, under his father, he served as Minister to Prussia. In the former year, he married Louisa C. Johnson, daughter of a U.S. consular official whom he had met earlier while in London on diplomatic business. They were to have three sons, including Charles Francis, and one daughter.

Returning to Boston in 1801, John Quincy resumed his law practice. The following year, failing to win election to the U.S. House of Representatives, he entered the State senate, soon followed by service in the U.S. Senate (1803-8). His independent actions, however, cost him the support of the Federalist Party and in 1808 he resigned from it and the Senate. Although he was later to become affiliated with the Democratic-Republican, National

Chief U.S. plenipotentiary John Quincy Adams shakes hands on Christmas Eve, 1814, with his British counterpart, Lord Gambier, after the signing of the Treaty of Ghent, which ended the War of 1812.

Republican, and Whig Parties, he was to exhibit individualistic political tendencies for the rest of his life.

Adams moved back to Cambridge, where 2 years earlier he had accepted a position as professor of rhetoric and oratory at Harvard (1806-9). While Minister to Russia (1809-14), under Madison, in 1811 he turned down a Presidential offer to sit on the U.S. Supreme Court. In 1814 he and four other commissioners negotiated the Treaty of Ghent, which ended the War of 1812. Subsequently he served as Minister to Britain (1815-17).

Back in the United States, in the period 1817-25 Adams made a notable mark as Monroe's Secretary of State. Among his other accomplishments, he was instrumental in the acquisition of Florida from Spain, arranged for joint Anglo-American occupancy of Oregon, gained Spanish recognition of U.S. claims to the Pacific Northwest, and helped formulate the Monroe Doctrine.

In 1824 Adams barely won election to the Presidency because of extreme factionalism in the one existing party, the Democratic-Republican. Three opposition candidates came to the fore from the South: William H. Crawford of Georgia, Andrew Jackson of Tennessee, and Henry Clay of Kentucky. Although Jackson won a plurality of the electoral votes, none of the four candidates obtained the required majority. In the subsequent maneuvering in the House of Representatives, Clay, who had drawn the least number and disliked Jackson, threw his support to Adams. When the latter appointed Clay as Secretary of State, Jackson's followers charged that the two had made a "corrupt bargain."

Despite his unsubstantial mandate, Adams advocated a bold program of domestic reform. To spur commerce, he urged the utilization of Federal funds to build a comprehensive system of roads and canals. As a means of stimulating manufacturing, he recommended a high protective tariff. He also stressed the need for Government encouragement of the arts and sciences, including establishment of a national university, erection of an observatory, and financing of scientific expeditions.

Because of the prevailing belief in a minimal governmental role in economic affairs, as well as opposition from constitutionalists and States righters, Adams' proposals failed to stir the public. Also his defense of Indian rights in Georgia, disdain of States rights, and distaste for slavery offended many groups. Even his nonpartisan appointments yielded him little credit.

By the time Adams sought reelection in 1828, his followers had coalesced with those of Clay to form the National Republicans. They encountered the superbly organized campaign apparatus of Jackson, whose party retained the Democratic-Republican name. In a mud-slinging contest, Adams met a disastrous defeat. Aged 61, he returned to his beloved "Peacefield," Mass. That same year, his 28-year-old son, the eldest, George Washington Adams, died under tragic circumstances.

Nevertheless, Adams inaugurated a distinguished 17-year career in the House of Representatives (1831-48)—the only ex-President to serve in that body. He won the epithet "Old Man Eloquent." Always an opponent of slavery, hopeful of eventual emancipation but not a rabid abolitionist, he fought against the extension of slavery into the western Territories and took other steps against the institution. He also protested the Mexican War (1846-48).

On the other hand, Adams pushed the advancement of science. He sponsored establishment of the Smithsonian Institution (1846), continued to advocate a Federal astronomical observatory, and favored the standardization of weights and measures. Somehow, during these years he also worked on his father's papers, wrote three volumes of poetry and two biographies, and sat on the Harvard board of overseers.

During a debate in February 1848, the 80-year-old Adams suffered a stroke in the House Chamber and died 2 days later.

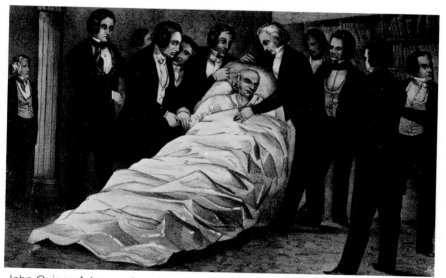

John Quincy Adams enjoyed a remarkable career in the U.S. House of Representatives after his Presidency. He died in the Capitol in 1848 not long after being stricken during a debate.

Andrew Jackson

SEVENTH PRESIDENT   1829-37

The first Chief Executive elected from west of the Alleghenies, the first from other than Virginia or Massachusetts, and the first nonaristocrat, frontier-born Jackson sought to represent the common man. Yet he had become a rich planter and had served in both Houses of Congress. But it was the charisma of "Old Hickory," his renown as a military hero and Indian fighter, and his astuteness in politics that assured his election as President. He not only expanded the powers of the office but also virtually redefined them.

Jackson was born of poor, newly immigrated parents in 1767. His first home was a log cabin in the Waxhaws region, on the North-South Carolina border. His boyhood was turbulent and insecure. He never knew his father, who died in an accident about 2 weeks before his birth. Andrew's two older brothers, Robert and Hugh, as well as an uncle with whom he stayed for awhile, furnished him with guidance, though he early demonstrated a strong temper and aggressive manner. He learned to read and write at a local school.

At the age of 13, during the War for Independence, Jackson enlisted in the militia and participated in some skirmishes. The next year, the British captured him and Robert, both of whom were wounded, but their mother won their release. En route home, Robert died of smallpox and exposure; Hugh had been killed earlier.

The following year, Mrs. Jackson died while on her way to Charleston to nurse two cousins who were incarcerated on a British prison ship. Young Andrew at first compensated for his loneliness with rowdiness and wild living. After a stay in Charleston, he returned to his relatives in the Waxhaws, where he taught school for a short time and then attended an academy in Charlotte, N.C.

In 1784, despite his meager education, Jackson journeyed to Salisbury, N.C., to read law and stayed there for about 2 years. He then lived briefly in Morganton and Martinsville, N.C., and was admitted to the bar in 1787. The next year, taking a position as a public prosecutor, he moved west to what was to become Tennessee, at first to Jonesboro and then Nashville; in 1790 he became attorney general of the Western District of North Carolina (present Tennessee).

Jackson married Rachel Donelson Robards in 1791; the ceremony had to be repeated several years later because of a legal technicality in her divorce from her first husband. This kept the tongues of Jackson's political enemies wagging throughout his career. Deeply devoted to each other, the couple forged a happy but childless marriage, though they adopted a son of Rachel's brother and renamed him Andrew Jackson, Jr.

Jackson thrived on the frontier. Yet, while active as public prosecutor, land-slave-horse speculator, judge advocate in the county militia, lawyer, landowner, storekeeper, and politician, he experienced many economic ups and downs. He also often brawled and fought several duels, in one of which he killed a man who had slurred Mrs. Jackson.

In 1796 Jackson attended the constitutional convention that organized the State of Tennessee. He served as its first U.S. Representative (1796-97), U.S. Senator (1797-98), and judge of the State superior court (1798-1804). During this time, in 1802, he was elected a major general in the Tennessee militia. Two years later, he purchased The Hermitage plantation and between then and 1812 spent most of his time managing it and his other holdings.

During the War of 1812 (1812-14), Jackson led his militia to victory over the Creek Indians at the Battle of Horseshoe Bend, Ala. (1814). This won him a major generalship in the Regular Army, as well as national fame. On January 8, 1815, after the treaty ending the war was signed, his hastily assembled and motley army defeated the British Regulars at the Battle of New Orleans (Chalmette). This further enhanced his prestige.

In 1817 Jackson commanded U.S. forces in the First Seminole War (1817-18), but, exceeding his instructions, he invaded Spanish West Florida. Following U.S. acquisition of Florida by treaty in 1821, he served a few months as its first Territorial Governor. In 1823 he was reelected to the U.S. Senate from Tennessee.

Spurred by his military fame and strong frontier support, in 1824 Jackson ran for President along with three other Democratic-Republican candidates; none of them gained a majority. Although Jackson won the greatest number of popular and electoral votes, he

Gen. Andrew Jackson.

This cartoon, which satirizes Jackson's vigorous assertion of Presidential authority, depicts him as a tyrannical veto-wielder who tramples on the Constitution, the judiciary, and Whig programs.

ON THE WAY TO ARABY!

In this 1836 cartoon, Jackson flees from banker Nicholas Biddle, who has frustrated his attempt to abolish the Bank of the United States. Jackson's mantle of office falls to Van Buren.

lost to John Quincy Adams when the House settled the election early in 1825. That same year, the aggrieved Jackson resigned from the Senate to devote his full time to pursuit of the Presidency.

During the mud-slinging campaign of 1828, John Quincy Adams' followers painted Jackson as an uncouth and dangerous savage whose election would bring the reign of the mob. On the other hand, Jackson's backers pictured him as a military hero, frontiersman, and champion of the average man; and Adams as a patrician easterner, who was a "corrupt bargainer." Jackson won, carrying the South and West and obtaining key votes in Pennsylvania and New York.

Jackson's victory was the first in the modern sense because by 1828 all States except Delaware and South Carolina chose their electors by popular vote. On inaugural day, his supporters— frontiersmen, farmers, planters, laborers, artisans, mechanics, tradespeople, and businessmen—took over the White House. But this event was tempered with sadness. His wife had died just after the election.

Jackson, who combined effectively the roles of chief of party, chief of state, and Chief Executive, substantially enhanced the power of the office. Asserting his authority and independence, he refused to yield to Congress or his department heads in policymaking, wielded strong party leadership, and vigorously applied the veto. To assure a politically loyal bureaucracy, he took one more step toward establishment of a "spoils system." He trusted his "kitchen cabinet," a group of unofficial advisers, more than his official Cabinet.

The National Republicans, or Whigs, led by Henry Clay and Daniel Webster, charged that Jackson was a dictator, "King Andrew I." But the majority of Americans disagreed and in 1832, by which time his party had adopted the Democratic name, decisively reelected him. Attesting to his success was his triumphant tour of the Middle Atlantic and New England States the following year.

One of Jackson's greatest coups, involving a bitter interparty fight, was the congressional upholding of his veto of the recharter of the Second Bank of the United States. It was a private corporation but for all practical purposes a Government-sponsored monopoly that regulated the money supply. He doubted its constitutionality and felt it was responsive only to the vested interests who controlled it.

Jackson won his second major victory during the nullification controversy. Although he held slaves himself and understood the anger of South Carolinians over the high tariff, which protected northern manufacturing, he refused to permit them to carry out Vice President John C. Calhoun's plan under which a State might nullify an unpopular Federal law.

Proclaiming "Union" to be the most fundamental of national values, in 1832 Jackson met the challenge to Federal authority, which included threats of secession, by mobilizing troops to enforce the tariff in South Carolina. Coupled with a congressional compromise that gradually reduced the tariff, Jackson's strong stand forced the nullifiers to back down.

In Indian affairs, reflecting his and other frontiersmen's dislike of natives, Jackson defied the Supreme Court and relocated the

Five Civilized Nations from the Southeast to present Oklahoma. To force the rebellious Seminoles to comply, he launched the Second Seminole War (1835-42).

Jackson was also active in foreign affairs. He sought to purchase Texas and California from Mexico, but met rebuff. When Texans revolted against the Mexican Government, Jackson kept the United States officially neutral, though he strongly sympathized with the Texan cause. As one of his last official acts, he appointed a Minister to the newly independent republic.

Jackson scored some diplomatic triumphs. He settled contested claims that the United States had long held against European states for property seized in the Napoleonic Wars; negotiated a reciprocal trade agreement with Great Britain to permit free trade with the British West Indies; and dispatched the first major American diplomatic mission to Asia, which resulted in treaties with Siam and Muscat.

Jackson helped his Vice President, Martin Van Buren, obtain the Presidential nomination and was the first President to campaign actively for his chosen successor. In 1837, almost 70 years of age, he retired to The Hermitage. He devoted considerable time to managing it and his other properties; experienced some financial woes, created principally by his spendthrift adopted son; advised Van Buren; continued to play a role in the Democratic Party; espoused the annexation of Texas; and helped expansionist James K. Polk, rather than Van Buren, who had opposed the annexation, win the Democratic nomination for the Presidency in 1844.

Almost deaf and also blind in one eye and suffering the effects from various illnesses and wounds that had plagued him over the years, Jackson died in 1845.

Martin Van Buren

EIGHTH PRESIDENT   1837-41

**A sagacious lawyer and master politician who earned
the epithet "Red Fox of Kinderhook," Van Buren was
the prime architect of the Democratic Party coalition
that helped elect Jackson, served as his Secretary of
State and Vice President, and was his handpicked
successor as President. Unfortunately, Van Buren's
term of office coincided with a severe economic
depression not of his own making, and his steps to
alleviate it were ineffective. His opposition to the
annexation of Texas further hurt his popularity, in the
West and South. His two attempts to regain the office
failed.**

The first President born after the Declaration of Independence
and the first under the U.S. flag, Van Buren began life at
Kinderhook, Columbia County, N.Y., in 1782. His father, who had
fought in the War for Independence, won his livelihood as a
tavernkeeper and farmer. Young Van Buren attended village
schools for several years. At the age of 14, he read law with a local
attorney but soon moved to New York City to pursue his legal
studies. He then returned to Kinderhook and was admitted to the
bar in 1803. Four years later, he wed Hannah Hoes, who was to give
birth to four sons before she died 12 years later; he never remarried.

Shortly after Van Buren's marriage, he moved to nearby
Hudson, N.Y. Between then and 1820, in a rapid political
ascendancy, he held the offices of surrogate of Columbia County,
State senator, and State attorney general; and organized the
Albany Regency, a powerful political organization whose chief tool
was patronage. In 1821, by which time he had become identified
with the Democratic-Republican Party, he was elected to the U.S.
Senate (1821-28), though he remained active in State politics. In the
national arena, he backed William H. Crawford for President in
1824, and opposed the John Quincy Adams administration.

By 1827 Van Buren had become the most influential northern
supporter of Andrew Jackson, and the following year engineered
the successful merger of Jackson, Calhoun, and Crawford forces

Van Buren as a young man.

that carried Jackson into the Presidency. To aid Jackson further and retain his power in the State, that same year Van Buren, who became known as the "Little Magician" for his small stature and political prowess, resigned from the Senate and won the governorship of New York. Within 3 months, however, he resigned to take the position of Secretary of State (1829-31), where he served with distinction and became Jackson's most trusted adviser. His loyalty during a Cabinet imbroglio brought him appointment as Minister to Great Britain, but the President's enemies in Congress blocked the confirmation.

In 1832 Van Buren replaced Calhoun as Vice President on the Jacksonian ticket. Four years later, in an invective-filled campaign, he won the Presidency over several sectionally nominated Whig candidates. Only 3 months later, the Panic of 1837, precipitated in part by Jackson's policies, particularly his stand on hard money, initiated a 5-year-long nationwide depression that lasted long enough to insure Van Buren's defeat in 1840.

Based on his belief that business recklessness and overextension of credit were the cause, Van Buren reduced Government spending, particularly aid for internal improvements, and employed other deflationary tactics. None succeeded. As part of his economic policy, like Jackson he opposed creation of a new bank of the United States on the pattern of the old one, but he disliked Jackson's practice of assigning Government funds to State banks. The remedy he proposed was an independent Government treasury system, which Congress refused to authorize until 1840.

Van Buren's inauguration, in the old House Chamber of the Capitol.

Van Buren sought the Presidency twice after he left office and was nominated once, by the antislavery Free Soil Party in 1848. Winning no electoral votes, he failed to bridge the chasm between the Democratic and Whig platforms, as this cartoon indicates. Salt River symbolizes political oblivion.

Van Buren had been elected on a platform that opposed the extension of slavery but allowed it to continue where it already existed. He tried to still southern secessionist rumblings and blocked the annexation of Texas because it would add to slave territory and carried a threat of war with Mexico. This cost him his popularity in the West and South, as well as Jackson's support.

Although disaster befell his domestic policies, Van Buren was successful in foreign affairs. When passions rose on both sides of the Canadian border over the aid of the American citizens to Canadian revolutionaries and over the exact location of the Maine-Canadian border, he acted with restraint to avoid bloodshed and initiated a diplomatic interchange that was later resolved in the Webster-Ashburton Treaty (1842).

Whig William Henry Harrison battered Van Buren in 1840. Many conservative Democrats defected, and Van Buren failed to win even his home State. Leaving office, he took up residence at Lindenwald, an estate in Kinderhook. He continued to figure prominently in National and State politics, though he rejected President John Tyler's offer of a seat on the Supreme Court.

In 1844 Van Buren failed in a bid for the Democratic Presidential nomination, mainly because of his continued opposition to the annexation of Texas. The next year, he spurned Polk's offer of the post of Minister to Great Britain. During the period 1846-48, he led the antislavery wing of the Democratic Party, which was alined against the expansionist policies of James K. Polk.

In 1848 Van Buren again ran for President as the Free Soil, or antislavery, candidate, but did not receive any electoral votes. Although he supported the Compromise of 1850, he became increasingly disenchanted with the pro-southern positions of Presidents Franklin Pierce and James Buchanan. Near the end of his life, Van Buren endorsed Lincoln's efforts to limit slavery and preserve the Union.

A highlight of Van Buren's twilight years was an extensive tour of western Europe in the years 1853-55. During this time, while staying at the Villa Falangola in Sorrento, Italy, he began work on his autobiography and a political history. But his stay was ended prematurely by the need to accompany home the body of one of his sons who had died in Paris. Van Buren died in 1862 at the age of 79.

William Henry Harrison

NINTH PRESIDENT 1841

"Tippecanoe" Harrison, the oldest President at inaugural and the last to be born a British subject, was the first Whig to hold the office and the first incumbent to die. His term, a mere month, was the shortest on record. Like Jackson, he was an erstwhile frontier general and war hero, but he was born in a Tidewater Virginia mansion instead of in a backwoods log cabin. His grandson, Benjamin, became the 23d President.

Harrison, the youngest of seven children, was the son of planter Benjamin Harrison, who signed the Declaration of Independence and served as Governor of Virginia. The youth was born in 1773 at Berkeley plantation. He received his elementary education at home and attended Hampden-Sydney College, probably some time during the years 1787-90, but apparently did not graduate. In the latter year, he matriculated at an academy in Southampton, Va., and later in the year began studying medicine in Richmond and then in Philadelphia, but he never qualified as a doctor.

In 1791, after his father's death, Harrison turned to a military career. Accepting a commission as an ensign in the Army, he was assigned to the Northwest Territory and based at Fort Washington, in the Cincinnati area. As an aide to Gen. "Mad Anthony" Wayne, in 1794 he fought against the Indians in the Battle of Fallen Timbers, Ohio. The next year, he married Anna Symmes, daughter of a prominent land speculator-colonizer, from whom the couple apparently purchased a log cabin and a large tract of land in North Bend, Ohio, near Cincinnati.

After 3 more years of military service, Harrison resigned from the Army and served briefly as Secretary of the Northwest Territory. As its first Delegate to Congress (1799-1800), he was instrumental in obtaining legislation splitting off Indiana Territory from the Northwest Territory. In the latter year, President John Adams appointed him as Governor of Indiana Territory (1801-12). During this time, he lived in Vincennes and resided mainly in Grouseland,

This portrait of William Henry Harrison, painted in Philadelphia, shows him at the age of 27 while he was serving as the Northwest Territory's Delegate to Congress.

which he built in 1803-4. Although theoretically he was charged with protecting the rights of the Indians, his actual primary assignment was to effect cession of their lands to expedite white settlement. His success generated strong Indian resistance.

In 1811, to suppress a confederation led by the Shawnee chief Tecumseh and his half-brother The Prophet, Harrison took advantage of the former's journey to the South in search of allies and attacked Prophet's Town, an Indian stronghold near Tippecanoe Creek. After a brief but bloody battle, Harrison's forces burned the town and scattered the inhabitants. Although the battle was celebrated as a great victory and was to make Harrison a national hero, it was actually indecisive and military losses were far heavier than those of the natives. The Indians were driven into the hands of the British, and resistance remained intense.

After the outbreak of the War of 1812, Harrison obtained another opportunity to quash the Indians. Quickly winning the rank of brigadier general in the Regular Army, he was chosen to command U.S. forces in the old Northwest. After training his inexperienced troops and participating in various engagements, he recaptured Detroit from the British and in October 1813, by which time he had become a major general, defeated them and their Indian allies in the Battle of the Thames, in Canada, during which Tecumseh was killed. Indian resistance in the Northwest disintegrated, and the British were afterward unable to mount offensive action there.

In 1814, after a disagreement with the Secretary of War, Harrison resigned his commission and moved back to North Bend. He mingled farming and some unsuccessful commercial ventures with political activity. His offices included U.S. Representative (1816-19), State senator (1819-21), U.S. Senator (1825-28), and Minister to Colombia (1828-29). For the next 7 years, to support his family, he held minor local governmental posts in North Bend and ran his farm, which grew into a thriving estate.

In 1836 Harrison was one of the regional Whig candidates who unsuccessfully challenged Van Buren for the Presidency. In the wake of the subsequent economic depression, the Whigs, sensing victory over Van Buren, decided to nominate a military hero for the 1840 race and rallied behind Harrison, hero of Tippecanoe, under the slogan "Tippecanoe and Tyler, too." In a circus-like and acrimonious campaign, the Whigs painted the aristocratic Harrison as a log-cabin-dwelling, hard-cider-drinking frontiersman who was a major military hero; Van Buren was labeled as a champagne-sipping dandy and plutocrat. Coonskin caps, miniature log cabins, and plenty of hard cider appeared at Whig rallies.

Harrison's solid victory brought joy to his party, especially to leaders Henry Clay and Daniel Webster, who anticipated they would dominate the administration. Webster accepted the office of Secretary of State, and Clay planned to supervise enactment of his long-advocated "American System" from the Senate. Harrison immediately summoned a special session of Congress to deal with the Nation's economic problems.

Sheet music published during Harrison's vigorous Presidential campaign in 1840. The Whigs claimed their aristocratic candidate was a log-cabin-dwelling frontiersman.

As Governor of Indiana Territory, Harrison shoved the Indians aside to expedite white settlement. This sketch depicts one of his acrimonious meetings with Tecumseh, who led the opposition.

But, within a month after taking office, Harrison was dead, at the age of 68, the victim of exhaustion and pneumonia, likely contracted during exertions associated with the inaugural. Mrs. Harrison, who had not yet arrived in Washington because of illness, survived him by more than 22 years. She had given birth to six sons and four daughters. Their father was buried in North Bend.

John Tyler

TENTH PRESIDENT   1841-45

Tyler, a Democrat turned Whig, was the first Vice President to succeed to the Presidency upon the death of an incumbent. Although his opponents labeled him "His Accidency," he rejected their belief that he should serve merely as an Acting President, and in a precedent-setting action pursued an independent course and claimed the full powers of the position. Because of his clash with his own party, he was threatened with impeachment. The major goal of his stormy administration was the annexation of Texas, which was in sight as his term ended.

Like his immediate predecessor, Harrison, Tyler was the scion of a distinguished Virginia planter family and came from the same county, Charles City. He was born at Greenway estate in 1790, the second son and sixth child of eight. His mother died when he was only 7 years of age. After attending a local private school, he studied at a grammar school associated with the College of William and Mary and then at the college itself, from which he graduated in 1807. He read law with his father, soon to be elected Governor, and then with Edmund J. Randolph in Richmond.

In 1809 Tyler was admitted to the bar and began practice in his home county. Two years later, he entered the Virginia House of Delegates (1811-16) and later the Council of State (1816). During the War of 1812, he served as a militia captain in the Williamsburg-Richmond area, but never saw action. In 1813 he married Letitia Christian; she was to bear eight children, three sons and five daughters, before her death at the White House in 1842. By a second wife, Julia Gardiner, whom he wed 2 years later, while still President, Tyler had five sons and two daughters.

In the U.S. House of Representatives (1816-21), a staunch Democratic-Republican, Tyler took proslavery, strict construction-ist, and States rights positions. Following another tour in the Virginia House of Delegates (1823-25) he served as Governor (1825-27), and then sat in the U.S. Senate (1827-36), during which time he took part in the Virginia constitutional convention of 1829-

117

30. As a Senator, he backed Jackson for President in 1828 as the lesser of two evils, though he personally disliked him and, like many other Tidewater planters, opposed many of his policies.

By 1836 Tyler's rupture with the Democrats was complete. He resigned his Senate seat and became a nominal Whig, though he disagreed with the ultranationalistic and antislavery positions of many party leaders. That year, as a southerner with a Democratic background to broaden the appeal of the ticket, he was selected as one of the Whig regional Vice-Presidential candidates. He was not elected but achieved the honor 4 years later, after a final period of service in the Virginia House of Delegates (1839-40).

Following the death of President Harrison, the Whigs had to reckon with "Tyler, too," the youngest President (51 years old) inaugurated until that time. When he insisted on the role of a duly-elected President rather than that of acting Chief Executive, the Whigs, most of whom represented a northern and western point of view and were led by Henry Clay, still hoped he would adopt their programs.

But many Whig ideas offended Tyler's principles. He opposed a national bank, a high tariff, and federally financed public improvements. The result was a controversial administration. After his second veto of a national bank bill, all his Cabinet members except Secretary of State Daniel Webster resigned. Tyler replaced them with conservatives and kept himself at odds with the congressional majority, repeatedly vetoing legislation it favored. The Whigs expelled him from the party, even considered impeaching him, the first time such an action was contemplated against a President, and pushed through a House resolution censuring him. Congress even refused to provide funds for the upkeep of the White House and, on the last day of his administration, for the first time in history, overrode a Presidential veto.

Despite these difficulties, Tyler accomplished much in foreign and domestic affairs. The Webster-Ashburton Treaty (1842) ended years of dispute over a section of the Canadian border and provided for joint United States-British naval patrols off Africa to suppress the slave trade. The Navy was reorganized, and the forerunners of the Naval Observatory and the Weather Bureau were established. The Second Seminole War came to an end. Far East trade increased because of a commercial treaty with China, the first the United States negotiated with that country. A congressional act, supported

Tyler, who fancied himself as something of a political "outlaw," renamed the estate he purchased in 1842 while President as "Sherwood Forest," after Robin Hood's hideout.

by Tyler, gave western settlers first claim to plots of land before they went on public sale and later the opportunity to buy them.

Tyler's last and perhaps most significant act as President paved the way for annexation of Texas. Most of the Whigs in Congress felt it would strengthen slavery. Aware of their sentiments but fearful that foreign intrigue might permanently alienate Texas and her rich cotton lands from the United States, Tyler opened negotiations with Texas. In 1844 officials signed a treaty agreeing to annexation if the U.S. Government would assume a substantial part of the Texas public debt. Northern antislavery forces in the Senate commanded enough votes to reject the treaty.

Tyler was undaunted. In 1844, virtually a man without a party, he accepted the Presidential nomination offered by a group of his followers, but threw his support to James K. Polk before the election. Taking Polk's victory as a mandate but realizing he could never obtain the necessary two-thirds majority for the annexation treaty in the Senate, Tyler used the remainder of his term to push it through Congress by means of a joint resolution of both Houses, which required only a simple majority vote. Just a few days before he left office, Congress approved the measure offering Texas the opportunity to join the Union.

Tyler retired to Sherwood Forest, an estate near his birthplace he had bought in 1842. Although a supporter of slavery, during the ensuing years of national tumult he long remained relatively inactive except for managing his plantation. In 1860, however,

THE MOUNTAIN IN LABOR.

The assertive Tyler, who assumed office upon the death of William Henry Harrison, met exceptional opposition both from his fellow Whigs, especially Henry Clay (left), and from the Democrats. He is shown here armed with his veto sword and beleaguered by political enemies (mice).

Tyler during his retirement.

alarmed at the growing national schism and hoping to avert a civil war, he appealed for moderation. He urged the secessionists to exercise caution, and chaired the ill-fated Washington Peace Convention (February 1861), which vainly sought a sectional compromise on the extension of slavery. He then served in the Virginia secession convention and won election to the Confederate Congress. In January 1862, while awaiting the convening of the latter body, in Richmond, Va., he was suddenly stricken ill and died there a few days later.

James K. Polk

Polk, who won office on an expansionistic platform, pushed the national boundaries to the Pacific, led the Nation through the Mexican War, and settled the Oregon question with Great Britain. A protégé of Jackson and sometimes called "Young Hickory," he was the first "dark-horse" Presidential candidate and an energetic and effective Chief Executive. By choice, he served only a single term, and died soon thereafter.

Polk, the eldest of 10 children, was born at a log farmhouse near the city of Charlotte, N.C., in 1795. When he was 11 years old, his family moved to the vicinity of Columbia, Tenn., where the father prospered in farming. Sickly during most of his childhood, the youth, though studious by nature, received little formal education.

In 1818 Polk graduated with honors from the University of North Carolina. He briefly returned to his home near Columbia and then read law in Nashville for a year; in 1820 he was admitted to the bar and began practicing in Columbia. Before long, he became prominent in the profession, and was elected to the lower house of the State legislature (1823-25). In 1824 he married Sarah Childress; they had no children. During this period, he initiated a lifetime political alliance and friendship with Gen. Andrew Jackson, a friend of his father.

During Polk's years in the U.S. House of Representatives (1825-39), including the speakership (1835-39), he came to lead Jackson's followers. During the years 1839-41, he served as Governor of Tennessee, but was afterward twice defeated for reelection. In 1840 he acquired Polk Place, in Nashville, his principal residence for the rest of his life.

In the Presidential election of 1844, Van Buren was the likely Democratic candidate, but his opposition to the annexation of Texas prevented him from mustering sufficient southern votes to win the nomination. A deadlock ensued and, Polk, a "dark horse" who had been mentioned as a Vice-Presidential possibility, was named.

This Democratic broadside, distributed during the 1844 campaign in Ohio, depicts Polk as a "coon dissector." The coon was a symbol of the Whig Party.

Polk campaigned against Whig Henry Clay on a platform favoring the annexation of Texas, the acquisition of California, and the "reoccupation" of Oregon ("54°40' or Fight"). Alluding to Polk's relative obscurity, the Whigs asked: "Who is James K. Polk?" But expansionist sentiment in the country was strong enough to bring him victory, though the election was extremely close and he did not even win his home State.

At 49 years of age, Polk was the youngest Chief Executive to serve until his time. Stating in advance that he would not seek reelection, he followed a strenuous schedule designed to carry out his program in a single term. One of his immediate problems was the possibility of war with Mexico. She severed diplomatic relations over the U.S. offer of annexation to Texas, which Polk nevertheless completed later in the year.

Hoping to settle matters peaceably but also determined to acquire California, Polk dispatched diplomat John Slidell to Mexico City with orders to obtain acceptance of the Rio Grande as the Texas boundary and to offer to purchase all or part of the present Southwest, including California. Mexican nationalists were outraged, and Slidell was not received. Meantime, Polk had deployed an army under Gen. Zachary Taylor to the disputed area between the Nueces and the Rio Grande in Texas. In April 1846 Mexican troops killed part of a patrol and captured the rest of it.

Polk, asserting that U.S. blood had been shed on U.S. soil, won a congressional declaration of war despite fervent opposition from antislavery northerners. In the months that followed, the Army won spectacular victories, which culminated in the capture of Mexico City in September 1847. The year before, California had fallen in the Bear Flag Revolt, accomplished by rebellious American settlers and abetted by naval and overland military forces. In the Treaty of Guadalupe Hidalgo (1848), Mexico surrendered the bulk of the present U.S. Southwest and recognized the Rio Grande as the boundary of Texas; the United States paid $15 million to Mexico and assumed the claims of American citizens against the Mexican Government.

In the Northwest, Polk did not resort to war, which neither the United States, involved in the Mexican War, nor Britain wanted. But he settled the problem of Oregon, which the two nations had jointly occupied since 1818. In 1846, well aware of the large British investment in northern Oregon, Polk agreed to a northern U.S.

By the President of the United States of America

A Proclamation.

Whereas, the Congress of the United States, by virtue of the constitutional authority vested in them, have declared by their act, bearing date this day, that, "by the act of the Republic of Mexico, a state of war exists between that Government and the United States."

Now, therefore, I, James K. Polk, President of the United States of America, do hereby proclaim the same to all whom it may concern: and I do specially enjoin on all persons holding offices, civil or military, under the authority of the United States, that they be vigilant and zealous, in discharging the duties respectively incident thereto: And I do moreover exhort all the good people of the United States, as they love their country; as they feel the wrongs which have forced on them the last resort of injured nations, and as they consult the best means, under the blessing of Divine Providence, of abridging its calamities; that they exert themselves in preserving order, in promoting concord in maintaining the authority and the efficacy of the laws, and in supporting and invigorating all the measures which may be adopted by the constituted authorities, for obtaining a speedy, a just, and an honorable peace.

In testimony whereof, I have hereunto set my hand, and caused the seal of the United States to be affixed to these presents. Done at the city of Washington, the thirteenth day of May, one thousand eight hundred and forty-six, and of the Independence of the United States the seventieth.

James K. Polk

By the President:
James Buchanan
Secretary of State.

XLIV

Proclamation of war against Mexico, signed by James K. Polk as well as Secretary of State and future President James Buchanan.

Polk's inauguration at the Capitol in 1845.

boundary line at the 49th parallel (except for the southern tip of Vancouver Island) instead of 54°40′. This dismayed northern expansionists, who resented his compromise on this issue in contrast to his apparent tenaciousness on behalf of southern slaveholders in the Southwest.

Thus, in a brief period, Polk completed the acquisition of the territory embracing the bulk of the present contiguous 48 States. But this spectacular success had its negative side. His actions helped divide the Democratic Party into anti- and pro-slavery wings; and the need to organize the new Territories precipitated quarrels in both parties over the extension of slavery. Furthermore, the military victories in the Mexican War strengthened the Whigs, for heroes Zachary Taylor and Winfield Scott were rapidly becoming their leading prospects as Presidential candidates.

Polk's domestic accomplishments were dwarfed by the magnitude of his territorial achievements. Tariffs were reduced, the Treasury was reorganized by the establishment of branches in big cities, and the U.S. Naval Academy and Smithsonian Institution were established.

As Polk had promised, he quit the Presidency in 1849 after a single term. Hard work had taken its toll. Less than 3 months after he left office, he died at his home in Nashville.

Zachary Taylor

TWELFTH PRESIDENT   1849–50

"Old Rough and Ready" Zachary Taylor, who at the time of his election was a national hero for his recent Mexican War service, was the first professional soldier to occupy the White House and the first Chief Executive to lack elective political experience. Although a southerner and a slaveholder, during his brief 16 months in office he fought against the extension of slavery into the newly acquired Southwest and, eschewing compromise, threatened the use of military force against secessionists to preserve the Union.

Taylor, the third son in a large family, was born into the Virginia planter class at Orange County in 1784. His parents soon moved to the outskirts of Louisville, Ky., where in a few years they built Springfield as their residence. Tutors provided Taylor with an elementary education. In his late teens, he joined the Kentucky militia, and in 1808 entered the Regular Army and served as an infantry lieutenant at New Orleans. Two years later, on leave at home, he married Margaret Mackall Smith. Two of their five daughters were to die as children and one was to wed Jefferson Davis; their only son, Richard, was to become a Confederate general. A few months after his marriage, Zachary won a captaincy.

Next based at Forts Knox and Harrison, in Indiana Territory, Taylor took part in William Henry Harrison's campaign against the Indians and moved up to brevet major. During the War of 1812, he served mainly in the same area, though he spent a few months in present Iowa and Illinois, and became a major. In 1815, irked by a peacetime reduction in rank to captain, he resigned from the Army, but the next year he was reappointed as a major.

Long years of garrison duty followed. For some time he was stationed principally in the Mississippi Valley at posts scattered from Minnesota to the Gulf of Mexico. He saw action in the Black Hawk War (1832), and advanced to a colonel. His next major

The Mexican War victories of General Taylor, pictured here with some of his staff at Monterrey, propelled him into the White House.

assignment was in Florida, in the years 1837-40, where his role in the Second Seminole War gained him a brevet brigadier generalcy. From 1840 to 1844, while headquartered at Baton Rouge, La., near which he purchased property, he served for a time at Fort Smith, Ark., and Fort Gibson, Okla.; established Fort Washita, Okla.; and then assumed command of Fort Jesup, La.

In 1845 while Taylor was commanding the First Department of the Army at the latter fort, President Polk ordered him to prepare to defend Texas against a possible Mexican invasion, and he concentrated an army at Corpus Christi. The following January, Polk directed him to advance into the area between the Nueces River and the Rio Grande, which was disputed with Mexico.

Following the outbreak of hostilities there in the spring, before the United States declared war against Mexico, he won quick victories and the rank of brevet major general in battles at Palo Alto and Resaca de la Palma. He subsequently crossed the Rio Grande and scored another success at Monterrey, shortly before which he became a major general in the Regular establishment.

But President Polk, dissatisfied with his independent manner of command and aware of his growing popularity with the public and his potential as a Presidential candidate for the Whigs, ordered him to remain in northern Mexico and sent Gen. Winfield Scott to capture Mexico City. Meantime, Taylor had triumphed again, at Buena Vista in early 1847, though Polk had already stripped him of most of his Regulars. Near the end of that year, his request to be relieved was granted. He returned home to a hero's welcome and the Presidency.

Although many Whigs had opposed the war, Taylor was attractive for a variety of reasons. His military record made him a certain vote getter in all parts of the country. As a southerner who owned a slave-operated plantation, he would strengthen the ticket of a party that was strongest in the North. Finally, essentially apolitical, he had not taken firm stands on any of the troublesome issues of the day.

The Whigs, however, had to expend considerable energy to enlist Taylor as their standard bearer. He disliked politics, had never even voted in a Presidential election, and was aware of his inexperience in statecraft. Even when a Whig faction induced him to make the race, only a couple of months before the 1848 convention, he asserted that he would be a national rather than a partisan President and that principle would prevail over party and politics.

The prime election issue, an explosive one, was the extension of slavery into the Southwest, newly acquired from Mexico. The Whigs avoided this issue and touted Taylor's military record. The Democratic Party, represented by Lewis Cass, straddled the fence by advocating popular sovereignty, or letting the residents of new areas decide for themselves whether or not they wanted slavery.

Many antislavery Democrats and some dissident Whigs defected to the Free Soil Party. Its candidate, ex-President Martin Van Buren, took a strong stand against the expansion of slavery. In the close election, aided by the divisive influence of the Free Soilers, the Whigs triumphed.

Taylor's most urgent problem was the status of California and New Mexico. The rush generated by the discovery of gold in California in 1848 had created conditions that the new U.S.

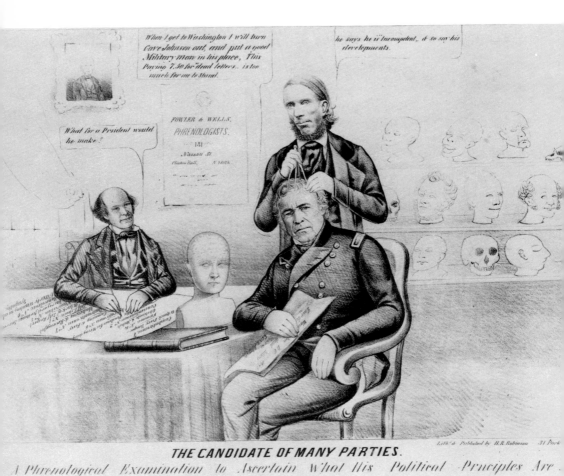

THE CANDIDATE OF MANY PARTIES.
A Phrenological Examination to Ascertain What His Political Principles Are.

General Taylor, the Whig candidate in 1848, failed to take a position on the complex and troublesome issues of the day. This cartoon reflects the resultant public uncertainty.

ORIGINAL PICTORIAL
ROUGH AND READY MELODIES,
No. 3.

UNCLE SAM.—You look very pretty, Mr. Cass, but you can't come in ; I've had so many of your sort already that I hardly know my own farm.

OLD ZACK TAYLOR IS THE MAN!

TUNE—"*Yankee Doodle.*"

Old ZACK TAYLOR is the man,
  His countrymen select him,
To fill the chair of Washington ;
  And surely they'll elect him.

Chorus—Old ZACK TAYLOR ! keep him up !
  Honest, Rough and Ready !
We've a voucher in his life
  He's good as he is steady.

When Uncle Sam last let his farm,
  Right sorry soon he'd done it,
He saw them knock his fences down,
  And *poke*-weeds overrun it.

Chorus—Old ZACK TAYLOR ! keep him up, &c.

But once again in careful hands,
  The right sort will be growing ;
As Uncle Sam found out one day,
  A Taylor apt at *sow*-ing.

Chorus—Old ZACK TAYLOR, &c.

The politicians now must learn
  'Tis not for them to reap all ;
Though *they* may mark out party lines,
  We've none for the whole people.

Chorus—Old ZACK TAYLOR is the man, &c.

Polk thought when first the war began
  How grand *he'd* be in story !
He little dream'd how Zack would rise,
  And carry off the glory.

Chorus—Old ZACK TAYLOR, &c.

In politics' mysterious ways
  Good often comes from evil ;
So Polk's ascendancy has brought
  His party to the ——— !

Chorus—Old ZACK TAYLOR, &c.

In ZACK we know we've chosen well—
  The noble, the undaunted—
One who's "no private ends to serve,"
  Is one we long have wanted.

Chorus—Old ZACK TAYLOR, &c.

Good cheer to every patriot's heart—
  The field is to the trusty—
"When thieves fall out, then honest men"—
  The proverb 's old and musty.

Chorus—Old ZACK TAYLOR, &c.

So gassy Cass, why you must pass—
  You shifting, sly pretender—
We've tried the tricksters long enough—
  We'll try our flag's defender.

Chorus—Old ZACK TAYLOR, &c.

NEW-YORK : Published by Horton & Co. Engravers and Publishers, 60 Nassau Street.
Entered according to Act of Congress, in the year 1848, by T. Horton, in the Clerk's Office of the District Court of the United States for the Southern District of New-York.

Song sheets captioned "Old Zach Taylor is the Man!" were disseminated during the 1848 election on behalf of "Old Rough and Ready."

military government was unable to control. New Mexican and Texan contention over a strip of land between the Pecos River and Rio Grande threatened to erupt into a full-blown war. Inhibited by the inflammatory slavery issue, Polk had been unable to push Territorial bills for California and New Mexico through Congress, so Taylor inherited the task.

To the surprise of many people, Taylor soon demonstrated the political independence he had stressed in his campaign. Despite his southern background, his long military experience had made him an ardent nationalist. He rejected a congressional compromise on the slavery extension issue espoused by Whig leaders and attempted to end the legislative dispute once and for all. To avoid the crisis lengthy debates over the status of slavery in Federal Territories would create, he sought to bring California and New Mexico into the Union as States as soon as possible. In an echo of the Democratic platform, he sent word to residents of the two areas that they should decide the slavery issue for themselves. They should then bypass the Territorial stage, and draw up "republican" constitutions for admittance as States.

Congress, which felt it should make such a decision, was offended, as were also most southerners and Democratic leaders, who knew the two areas would prepare constitutions banning slavery. Some leading northern Whigs wanted to compromise, and the southern proslavery Whigs were incensed. Nevertheless, Taylor stuck to his position. He reacted to threats of secession by vowing to use military force if necessary to preserve the Union. Furthermore, he let it be known that, though he did not favor the Wilmot Proviso, which would exclude slavery from the entire territory acquired from Mexico, he would sign it if Congress passed it. He managed to irritate southern opinion further by opposing an expedition being organized to conquer Cuba. Even moderate southern Whigs began to desert him.

Early in 1850 Taylor, averting the possibility of armed conflict with Great Britain, negotiated the Clayton-Bulwer Treaty. This instrument attempted to resolve American and British disagreements in Central America and to neutralize the region pending the construction of a transoceanic canal.

Taylor was stricken suddenly on Independence Day 1850 at the White House, shortly after attending a ceremony at the Washington Monument, and died a few days later at the age of 65. Congress soon compromised on the slavery issue. But, as he had foreseen, a confrontation between the forces of union and disunion was inevitable.

Millard Fillmore

THIRTEENTH PRESIDENT   1850-53

Fillmore, who succeeded to the Presidency on the death of Taylor, inherited the controversy over the extension of slavery into the Southwest that had divided his predecessor and Congress. Fillmore's conciliatory policies spurred passage of the Compromise of 1850. Although this proposal was unpopular with many elements in both the South and North and represented only a temporary and uneasy sectional truce, it helped delay the outbreak of civil war. Fillmore also made notable achievements in foreign affairs, particularly in Latin America and the Far East.

Fillmore's beginnings were humble. The first son and second child in a family of nine, he enjoyed few advantages in his youth. He was born in 1800 at Cayuga County, in the Finger Lakes region on the central New York frontier, shortly after his parents had moved there from Vermont. He received only limited primary education at local schools, and worked on his father's farm. In his mid-teens he served as an apprentice for a short time in the cloth trade and apparently worked in a store for awhile.

When Fillmore was about 18 years of age, he became acquainted with a young teacher, Abigail Powers, who tutored him. He soon also started to read law with a county judge, and instructed in a rural school. His family moved west to the East Aurora area, near Buffalo, N.Y., about 1819, and Millard followed them, probably 2 years later. He continued his legal study in Buffalo, and was admitted to the bar in 1823. Three years later, he married Abigail; they subsequently had a son and a daughter. The year they wed, the couple built a home in East Aurora. He, as well as his wife, taught there, and he practiced law.

Fillmore began his political career by helping to organize the Antimasonic Party, and as a protégé of party boss Thurlow Weed entered the State legislature (1829-31). In 1830 he moved to Buffalo, his home for the rest of his life except while serving in Congress and as President. During the years 1833-35 and 1837-43 he sat in

the U.S. House of Representatives, and eventually chaired the powerful Ways and Means Committee. In 1834 he followed Weed into the Whig Party and became a leader of its antislavery wing. In 1843 he returned to Buffalo and practiced law.

In 1844 Fillmore unsuccessfully sought his party's nomination for Vice President and was narrowly defeated in a bid for the governorship of New York. In 1847, however, he won election as State comptroller. The next year, thanks largely to the backing of the Clay faction, he was elected as Vice President under Taylor. Although the latter kept him isolated from policymaking and patronage, he judiciously chaired the increasingly vociferous debate over slavery in the Senate.

But, when Taylor died in July 1850, Fillmore inherited responsibility for dealing with the conflict. Civil war seemed imminent, but the absence of Taylor's opposition to passage of Clay's Compromise of 1850, which had created a deadlock with a divided Congress, brought a new climate. Fillmore, who still personally disliked slavery but was determined to be President of the whole country, threw his power behind the compromise. He quickly replaced all Cabinet members, and joined forces with the moderate Whigs who favored the compromise. It was an omnibus of bills that sought a middle ground between northern abolitionists and southern secessionists to save the Union.

The congressional deadlock was broken when Democratic Senator Stephen A. Douglas of Illinois took over management of the compromise from the aged, ill, and exhausted Clay. This bipartisan approach, coupled with Douglas' wise division of the compromise into a series of separate bills, eased its path.

Passed piecemeal in September 1850, the compromise admitted California as a free State; founded Utah and New Mexico Territories, whose residents were to choose whether or not slavery would prevail in their State constitutions; settled the Texas-New Mexico boundary dispute; abolished the slave trade (but not slavery) in the District of Columbia; and created a strong Federal fugitive slave law.

Although supporters of the compromise congratulated themselves that they had avoided civil strife, their work was fragile. The measure was a compromise on an issue that could not be compromised and did not settle the slavery controversy. Some provisions offended the North; others, the South. The conflict had not been solved; it would burst forth again.

WASHINGTON, D. C.

TUESDAY, FEBRUARY 26, 1856.

VESPASIAN ELLIS, } Editors.
SAMUEL C. BUSEY, }

FOR PRESIDENT,
MILLARD FILLMORE,
OF NEW YORK.
FOR VICE PRESIDENT,
ANDREW JACKSON DONELSON,
OF TENNESSEE,
THE PEOPLE'S CANDIDATES,
NOMINATED BY ACCLAMATION.

AMERICANS WILL RULE AMERICA !

When Fillmore sought to regain the Presidency in 1856 on the American, or "Know Nothing" Party ticket, he was paired with Andrew Jackson's nephew. Here a party newspaper announces their candidacy.

THE RIGHT MAN FOR THE RIGHT PLACE.

Unlike his opponents, abolitionist Republican Fremont (left) and pro-South Democrat Buchanan (right), during the 1856 campaign Fillmore failed to take a stand on the major issue of the day, the extension of slavery. Because of the division of his "Know Nothing" supporters on that issue, he was soundly defeated.

Congress and the Nation calmed, Fillmore turned his attention to other matters. He aided Senator Douglas' efforts to obtain Federal grants for railroad construction. Fillmore also exerted initiative in foreign relations. Trying to overcome the loss of good will in Latin America generated by the Mexican War, he restored diplomatic peace with Mexico; facilitated the negotiations whereby an American company undertook to dig a transoceanic canal through Nicaragua; and sought to deter filibusterers, including Americans, who tried to overthrow the Spanish colonial government in Cuba.

In 1852 Fillmore dispatched Commodore Matthew C. Perry to Japan to establish trade and diplomatic relations, a mission he was to complete during the Pierce administration. Fillmore also refused to yield to entreaties of the King of Hawaii, threatened by French

Despite the drubbing of the Fillmore-Donelson ticket in 1856, the American National Council, the governing body of the American Party, met at Louisville the next June to map future strategy.

domination, for U.S. annexation. But, pledged to protect Hawaii's independence, Fillmore warned Napoleon III to abandon his imperialistic plans there.

Northern Whigs, angered by Fillmore's support of the Compromise of 1850, prevailed at the contentious convention of 1852 and blocked his renomination. The next year, his wife caught cold at Pierce's inauguration and died in Washington within weeks. The bereaved widower went back to Buffalo. His sorrow soon increased when his daughter died.

Despite the disintegration of the Whig Party, Fillmore refused to join the Republicans. Instead, in 1856, while on an extensive tour of Europe and the Mideast, he accepted the Presidential nomination of the American, or "Know Nothing," Party. He campaigned more on the need for national unity than on the party's anti-Catholic and anti-foreign platform, but met overwhelming defeat. He never again sought public office, but later backed the Democratic Party.

In 1858 Fillmore remarried, to widow Caroline Carmichael McIntosh; she was to be childless. They honeymooned in Europe. Back in Buffalo, Fillmore continued to play a leading role in its philanthropic, civic, and cultural life. During the Civil War, he was loyal to the Union, but opposed many of Lincoln's policies and his reelection. After Lincoln's assassination, Fillmore supported Johnson's conciliatory stance toward the South. In 1866 Fillmore again visited Europe. Reaching the age of 74, he lived until 1874 and was buried in Buffalo's Forest Lawn Cemetery.

Franklin Pierce

FOURTEENTH PRESIDENT   1853-57

New Englander Pierce, a "dark-horse" candidate, entered office during a period of relative and deceptive calm on the slavery issue. Yet, though he evoked a nationalistic vision of territorial expansion and economic prosperity, his pro-southern policies alienated many northerners and raised sectional passions to a new pitch. The Kansas-Nebraska Act, which he supported, sparked a tragic turn of events in "bleeding Kansas." His expansionist schemes, except for the Gadsden Purchase, came to naught but served to further inflame discontent over the extension of slavery. Denied renomination, he retired to New Hampshire after a single term and lived out his years in restless disillusionment.

Born in 1804 at Hillsboro (Hillsborough), N.H., Pierce was the first President to see the light of life in the 19th century. His father was a farmer, tavernkeeper, militia leader, and politician. Young Pierce, the fourth son from his father's second marriage, attended a local elementary school and then academies at nearby Hancock and Francestown. In 1824 he graduated from Bowdoin College, Brunswick, Maine. After a winter back home, he read law at Portsmouth, N.H., Northampton, Mass., and Amherst, N.H.

Winning admission to the bar and returning to Hillsboro in 1827, the same year his father attained the governorship, Pierce began to practice. Two years later, at the age of 24, he was elected to the lower house of the State legislature (1829-33) and rose to the position of Speaker. Next came service in the U.S. House of Representatives (1833-37) and the Senate (1837-42), where when elected he was the youngest Member. In Congress he won a reputation as a solid Democrat.

In 1834 Pierce had married Jane Means Appleton of Amherst, N.H.; they were to have three sons, none of whom reached adulthood. About the time of his marriage, he bought a home in Hillsboro, but in 1838 changed his residence to Concord, N.H.

Pierce resigned from the Senate in 1842 for a variety of personal reasons. He went back to the practice of law, and later served as

Federal District Attorney for New Hampshire (1845-46). Also taking an active part in State political affairs, he opposed the abolition movement because he felt it contributed to national divisiveness. In 1845 he turned down an offer by the Governor to fill out the unexpired portion of a U.S. Senator's term; and the next year rejected the position of U.S. Attorney General, proffered by Polk.

Upon the outbreak of the Mexican War (1846-48), Pierce enlisted in a New Hampshire regiment as a private, but his political prominence quickly won him the rank of brigadier general under Gen. Winfield Scott, under whom he served in Mexico. Back in Concord, in 1848 Pierce rejected the Democratic gubernatorial nomination and continued his legal and political pursuits. He labored on behalf of the Compromise of 1850, and served as president of the State constitutional convention (1850), where he opposed anti-Catholic proposals.

In 1852 Pierce, then a youthful 48, won the Presidential nomination. After 49 ballots, the convention turned to him when it was unable to agree on one of four major candidates. His landslide victory over his former commander, the aging Whig Winfield Scott, is mainly attributable to his party's stronger stand on the Compromise of 1850, Scott's lack of popularity in the South, and defections from the Whig Party on both sides of the slavery issue.

Tragedy marred the election triumph. Not long before assuming office, Pierce, his wife, and last surviving child, an 11-year-old son, were in a train wreck and the youngster perished before his parents' eyes. As a result, Pierce entered the Presidency in a state of grief and nervous exhaustion, and his spouse was unable to attend the inauguration.

Pierce appointed an intersectional Cabinet and tried to apportion patronage among the different factions in his party, but relied heavily on the advice of pro-southerners. His expansionism in foreign affairs further incensed northerners, who resented his attempts to extend slavery by means of territorial acquisition or diplomatic maneuver. They were particularly upset when he persuaded the British to reduce their involvement in Central America and recognized the apparently proslavery government set up in Nicaragua by an American soldier of fortune. By one means or another, Pierce sought to acquire Hawaii, Santo Domingo, and Alaska.

Boyhood home and possibly the birthplace of Pierce, in New Hampshire.

But by far Pierce's strongest quest was the purchase of Cuba from Spain. This not only failed but also seriously embarrassed him after a secret memorandum of a discussion on the subject among U.S. diplomats in Europe, drafted by Minister to Britain James Buchanan, leaked out. Known as the Ostend Manifesto, it advocated the use of force if necessary to take over Cuba and stressed its importance as a base to revivify slavery. The administration renounced the document.

Also unsettling to the North—though the apparent rationale was to facilitate construction of a transcontinental railroad along a southern route—was Pierce's sponsorship of the Gadsden Purchase (1853), ceded by Mexico for $10 million. It consisted of the southern strips of present Arizona and New Mexico. Minister James Gadsden had sought but failed to acquire a far larger part of northern Mexico.

The event that spelled the doom of the temporary sectional truce, however, was the Kansas-Nebraska Act (1854). Senator Stephen A. Douglas introduced it, but the President vigorously championed it. This measure divided the relatively unsettled central portion of the Louisiana Purchase into Kansas and Nebraska Territories. One aim of the legislation may have been to aid construction of a transcontinental railroad, this one from Douglas' home State, Illinois, along a central route to the Pacific. Mindful of southern Democratic congressional sentiment, he added to the bill the provision that the settlers in the new Territories should decide for themselves, by the process of popular sovereignty, their position on slavery.

TERRIBLE ROUT & TOTAL DESTRUCTION OF THE WHIG PARTY.
IN SALT RIVER.

Satirization of Pierce's landslide defeat of Whig candidate Gen. Winfield Scott in 1852. The latter leads his party into the Salt River (political oblivion) while Pierce and the victorious Democrats occupy dry land.

Pierce supported and signed the bill in the hope that, if Kansas were admitted as a slave and Nebraska as a free State, both sides would be mollified. But the act reopened the question of slavery in the West. A storm of protest ensued from the North because, by permitting slavery north of 36°30′ North Latitude, the legislation virtually repealed the Missouri Compromise (1820). Pierce's assent to the bill was followed by dramatic antislavery gains in the Congress.

Meanwhile, pro- and anti-slavery settlers poured into Kansas hoping to influence the outcome. Sporadic guerrilla warfare, during which John Brown gained his first taste of fame, broke out between the two factions—a prelude to the Civil War. Many elections were also fraudulently conducted and violently disputed. Acrid debates occurred in Congress and in the Nation. In late 1856 Pierce created temporary peace by sending in Federal troops and appointing a new Governor.

The national political ramifications of the Kansas controversy were far reaching. Antislavery Democrats deserted in droves. A

Levee at the White House during Pierce's administration.

new and powerful northern sectional party, the Republican, opposed the extension of slavery into the western Territories. The Democratic convention scorned both Pierce and Douglas and nominated less controversial James Buchanan.

In the spring of 1857, Pierce returned to New Hampshire, but in November left on a leisurely tour of Europe that lasted until the summer of 1859. He also spent the first half of the next year in Nassau. But, back in Concord, he spent his last years in bitterness, still believing in the validity of his policies as President.

In 1861, disturbed by the imminence of war, Pierce sought but failed to arrange a meeting of the five living ex-Presidents (himself, Van Buren, Tyler, Fillmore, and Buchanan) to try to stem the tide. He still fiercely resented the abolitionists and the rise of antislavery militance in the North. During the war, his denunciation of the Emancipation Proclamation and outspoken criticism of what he felt were Lincoln's invasions of personal and property rights brought him excoriation, even in his own State and community.

Because of this, the death of his wife in 1863 as well as that of his lifelong friend, author Nathaniel Hawthorne, the following year, and ill health, Pierce suffered severe depression. He succumbed at Concord in 1869 at the age of 64, and was buried there in the Old North Cemetery.

James Buchanan

FIFTEENTH PRESIDENT   1857-61

The last in a line of three northern Presidents who futilely sought to resolve the virtually irreconcilable decades-old slavery clash between the North and South with a series of legal and political compromises, Buchanan was sorely tried but powerless to heal the rift. Instead, he was forced to preside forlornly over the disintegration of the Union as the Southern States began to secede following the election of 1860. His Presidency represented the culmination of four decades in public life—as Secretary of State, diplomat, legislator, and lawyer. He was the only Chief Executive who never married and he was one of the oldest, aged 65, at the time of his inauguration.

Buchanan, the first son and second child in a family of 10, was born in a log cabin just outside of Mercersburg, Pa., at Cove Gap (Stony Batter) in 1791. His father was a storekeeper and farmer who in time was to gain modest wealth. In 1796 the family moved into town. After attending a local elementary school and an academy, young Buchanan matriculated at Dickinson College, in Carlisle, Pa., as a junior and graduated in 1809. He then read law at Lancaster, where he was to maintain his home for the rest of his life. In 1812 he was admitted to the bar and began a highly successful legal career. Volunteering in a dragoon unit during the War of 1812 (1812-14), he saw brief service as an enlisted man in 1814, including participation in the defense of Baltimore.

Late that same year, as a Federalist, Buchanan entered the lower house of the Pennsylvania legislature (1814-16), after which he resumed his law practice. He next won a seat in the U.S. House of Representatives (1821-31). Following the demise of the Federalist Party, he switched to the Democrats and in 1828 supported Andrew Jackson for President.

Buchanan's reward was appointment as Minister to Russia (1832-33). He then began a long tour in the U.S. Senate (1834-45), including duty as chairman of the Foreign Relations Committee.

During these years, he declined appointment as U.S. Attorney General and a seat on the Supreme Court. In 1844 he lost the Presidential nomination to James K. Polk, but then supported his candidacy. The latter designated him as Secretary of State (1845-49). He handled the difficult negotiations preceding and ending the Mexican War (1846-48), and settled the Oregon question with Britain in 1846.

Buchanan made two more unsuccessful bids for the Presidential nomination, in 1848 and 1852. He threw his weight behind the Compromise of 1850. He served as Minister to Great Britain (1853-56) under President Pierce. His close association with the proslavery Ostend Manifesto, concerning the acquisition of Cuba from Spain, brought him popularity in the South and scorn in the North. Nevertheless, his absence from the country during the turbulent controversy over the Kansas-Nebraska Act and his reputation as a compromiser made him a more acceptable candidate in 1856 than either Pierce or Stephen A. Douglas.

Mainly because of his solid showing in the South, Buchanan won a substantial plurality over Republican John C. Frémont; and ex-President Fillmore, the American ("Know Nothing") Party standard bearer, ran a distant third. The regional strength of the Republicans in the North, however, coupled with the virtual disappearance of the Whigs, showed clearly the breakdown in the old party system—to be further demonstrated by the split of the Democrats during Buchanan's administration into northern and southern wings.

Despite all his legislative, diplomatic, and legal experience, Buchanan, a Unionist, proved unable to soothe sectional passions. He brought to the Presidency a long-held conviction that slavery might be morally wrong but that the Federal Government lacked the right to interfere with it. He opposed regionally based parties, resented northern and abolitionist agitation on slavery, and felt the North and South should be tolerant of each other. Hoping to achieve compromise, he appointed a Cabinet representing all parts of the country.

Buchanan felt that a Supreme Court ruling on what he believed was an abstract question of the rights of slaveholders in the West would end the acrimony. Only 2 days after he took office, the Court handed down the Dred Scott decision, which he favored and may have earlier influenced. It gave slaveholders the right to take their

Buchanan probably sat for this portrait in the 1830's or 1840's during his long congressional tour of duty.

human property wherever they chose, outlawed the Missouri Compromise, and implied that Congress lacked the power to make decisions concerning slavery in the Territories. In other words, they were all open to slavery and could exclude it only when they attained statehood. The Court's dictum obviously pleased the South and inflamed many elements of opinion in the North.

Turning to the still touchy issue of the status of Kansas Territory, in 1858 Buchanan, yielding to southern pressures, urged Congress to accept the proslavery Lecompton constitution and admit Kansas as a slave State—though the proslavery men in the Territory were heavily outnumbered. Buchanan hoped the admission of Kansas with or without slavery would remove the issue from public attention and calm Congress. But this proposal angered the Republicans and offended many of his own party; Congress rejected it. As a result, the South was enraged, and Kansas did not

President Pierce greets Buchanan as he arrives at the White House for his inauguration.

become a State until 1861. Until then, it remained a bloody symbol of the factionalism that was destroying the Nation.

By 1858 Buchanan's administration was near paralysis. The Republicans and anti-Lecompton Democrats scored heavily in the congressional elections and won a majority in the House; the Democratic Party divided into northern and southern elements. Southern votes in the Senate and Presidential vetoes doomed practically all House legislation. Government approached stalemate. Slow recovery from the Panic of 1857 produced gloom in the North. And in 1859 John Brown's antislavery raid on the Federal ordnance installation at Harpers Ferry, Va., reinflamed national emotions.

The Presidential election of 1860 brought the crisis to a head. Buchanan's refusal to be considered for renomination helped to split his party. Four candidates—one each from the northern (Stephen A. Douglas) and southern (John C. Breckinridge) wings of the Democratic Party, John Bell from the Constitutional Union Party, and Lincoln from the Republican Party—entered the campaign. Lincoln was elected, though with far less than a popular majority. Rejecting the prospect of a Republican administration, the Southern States began to secede and seize Federal installations within their borders. Buchanan, who thought secession violated the Constitution but felt the Government could not legally prevent it, watched in anguish.

During Buchanan's remaining months in office, he at first made repeated but unfruitful efforts to compromise with the secessionists. He urged Congress to exercise its constitutional prerogatives and address the issue. He also backed proposals for a national convention and constitutional amendment.

Early in 1861, however, "lame-duck" Buchanan finally took stronger measures against the secessionists. Promising to uphold Federal authority, he sent reinforcements and supplies in the unarmed merchant ship *Star of the West* to the beleaguered garrison at Fort Sumter, in Charleston Harbor, S.C. When South Carolina batteries drove the ship away, he refused to evacuate the fort, though he made no further efforts to resupply it. The outbreak of war was thus averted, but only temporarily.

Another thorny problem for Buchanan besides slavery was the Mormon-dominated Territory of Utah. Congress had ignored its requests for statehood, and the Mormons opposed Federal officials,

Buchanan and his Cabinet about 1859. Left to right: Secretary of the Interior Jacob Thompson, Secretary of State Lewis Cass, Secretary of War John B. Floyd, Buchanan, Secretary of the Treasury Howell Cobb, Secretary of the Navy Isaac Toucey, Postmaster General Joseph Holt, and Attorney General Jeremiah S. Black.

who were unsympathetic toward them. Buchanan replaced Brigham Young as Governor and dispatched a 2,500-man army to maintain law and order. The Mormons interpreted this as an invasion, and the short-lived and bloodless Mormon War (1857-58) broke out. Buchanan, sending a special representative, finally calmed the situation.

Despite his preoccupation with the domestic slavery crisis, Buchanan also expended much effort on diplomacy. He clarified with Great Britain interpretation of the Clayton-Bulwer Treaty

(1850), which called for nonintervention in Central America by either country. Although frowning on filibustering, he also expanded U.S. influence in Central and South America and discouraged intervention by European powers who were enticed by recurring political instability there. Like his predecessors Polk and Pierce, he continued southern-spawned efforts to purchase Cuba from Spain. In 1860 he received the first Japanese diplomatic mission to the United States.

After a public career that spanned the era from the War of 1812 to the Civil War—from the demise of the Federalists to the ascendancy of the Republicans—Buchanan lived out his remaining years of life at his Wheatland, Pa., estate. He retained his interest in politics and supported the Union during the Civil War, but its tragedy affected him deeply. He also did some writing and aided charitable causes. His death occurred in 1868 at the age of 77.

Abraham Lincoln

SIXTEENTH PRESIDENT   1861-65

**Although less famous and politically experienced
than his leading rivals for the Presidency, Lincoln
demonstrated remarkable maturity and statesmanship
in the office and immeasurably broadened its scope.
Unwaveringly devoted to preservation of the Union,
he led the North through a long, fratricidal war with
the Confederacy—the most perilous days the country
has ever faced. Once victory was imminent, he
adopted a conciliatory approach toward the South.
But his assassination on the eve of peace, the first of
a U.S. President, ushered in the recriminatory
Reconstruction Era.**

Born near present Hodgenville, Ky., in 1809, Lincoln was the first President whose birthplace was west of the Appalachians. His parents, already progenitors of a daughter named Sarah, had both come to Kentucky from Virginia as children. The father was a humble but ambitious farmer-carpenter. In 1816, when Abraham was 7 years old, after relocation to another nearby farm and a series of land-title disputes, the family moved to Indiana and settled near present Gentryville. Two years later, Mrs. Lincoln succumbed during an epidemic. The next year, her erstwhile husband traveled back to Elizabethtown, Ky., where he married a widow with three children, and returned to Indiana. Abraham's stepmother treated him and Sarah kindly.

Lincoln's 14 years in Indiana were formative ones. Determined to avoid the hardships of frontier life in the future, he read as many books as he could find time for after he had finished the farm chores or his work as a handyman. Altogether he managed to obtain less than a year of formal education. Occasionally he visited neighboring counties on family business, and in 1828-29 worked on a flatboat that journeyed down the Ohio and Mississippi to New Orleans. About that same time, he became interested in law, probably began its study, and attended court sessions.

In 1830, some 2 years after Lincoln's sister Sarah died in childbirth, the family moved to Macon County, Ill. The next year,

the 22-year-old Lincoln left home. He made another flatboat trip to New Orleans, and later in the year took positions as a clerk in a general store and millhand at New Salem, Ill. He continued to read voraciously and study law. In 1832 he served briefly in the State militia. Although he experienced no combat, as a private and for a short period as a captain he campaigned in northern Illinois and southern Wisconsin during the Black Hawk War.

That same year, back in New Salem, Lincoln, an admirer of Henry Clay, unsuccessfully ran as a Whig for a seat in the lower house of the State legislature. Before the year was out, he and a friend formed a partnership and operated a store for a short time, while he continued to study law. The business foundered, but he eventually paid off the debts. In 1833-36 he served as postmaster of New Salem; and in 1834-36, based on nighttime study of the subject, performed surveying jobs in the region.

Lincoln won a seat in the legislature in 1834 and began the serious study of law. He served until 1841 and in time took over legislative leadership of his party. Meanwhile, in 1837, the year after he was admitted to the bar, he had changed his residence from New Salem to Springfield, to which the capital moved in 1839 from Vandalia.

His position on slavery, like that of his party, was ambivalent. Although he deemed it unjust, he contended that abolitionist agitation tended to increase its evils; he held that the Federal Government could not constitutionally interfere with slavery in any State but could abolish it in the District of Columbia, especially if the residents so requested.

While a legislator, Lincoln prospered as an attorney and circuit lawyer. In 1842, the year after he left the legislature and concentrated on his practice and politics, he married socially prominent Mary Todd of Lexington, Ky. They were to have four sons, only one of whom, the eldest, Robert Todd, reached maturity. In 1844 Lincoln purchased a residence in Springfield that he occupied, except during congressional service, until he became President in 1861.

Lincoln was elected in 1846 to the U.S. House of Representatives, where he was the only Whig among the seven Members from heavily Democratic Illinois. His antagonism toward President Polk's expansionist policies and his querulous attitude on the constitutionality of the Mexican War shocked many of his

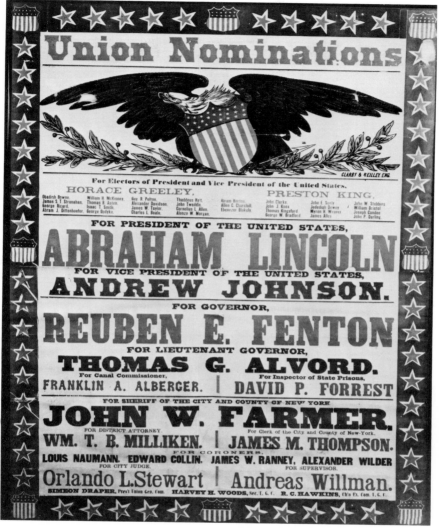

New York campaign poster in 1864.

constituents. He consistently favored the exclusion of slavery from the territory ceded by Mexico, but opposed Federal interference with it where it already existed. He announced he would not seek reelection in 1848 and became an early booster of Whig Presidential candidate Zachary Taylor.

Lincoln left Congress in 1849. Disappointed when Taylor did not appoint him to the position he sought as commissioner of the General Land Office, he rejected a proffered Federal post in Oregon Territory and resumed his legal activities in Illinois. Touring his judicial circuit in the central part of the State and practicing before Federal and State courts, he became a leading lawyer. His reaction to the Kansas-Nebraska Act, which in effect opened up the Louisiana Purchase area to slavery, brought him back again into the legislature in 1854, but he soon resigned to seek election to the U.S. Senate. This effort failed.

In 1856 Lincoln joined the Republican Party, a coalition of antislavery groups that had been organized 2 years earlier, and that year ranked second in its balloting for the Vice-Presidential nomination. While campaigning strenuously for Presidential candidate John C. Fremont, he enhanced his reputation in his own State and became a national leader of his party. In 1857 he attacked Illinois Democratic Senator Stephen A. Douglas for his defensive position on the Dred Scott decision, and criticized the institution of slavery.

In 1858, during his campaign for the Senate seat of incumbent Douglas, Lincoln gained nationwide recognition in a series of debates around the State. He denounced Douglas' doctrine of popular sovereignty as the answer to the extension of slavery into the Territories, and emerged as a spokesman for moderate Republicans. Lincoln lost the election in the legislature, though by only a close margin.

Nevertheless, Lincoln had drawn countrywide attention that aided him in obtaining the 1860 Presidential nomination because many in his party were seeking a moderate who could carry the West. Further enhancing his position and bolstering his prestige vis-a-vis his main opponent, William H. Seward, was a headline-generating speech he delivered a few months before the convention at New York City's Cooper Union. The subject was the attitude of the signers of the Constitution toward the extension of slavery. In this speech and subsequently in his Presidential campaign, he favored the exclusion of slavery from the Territories, but urged conciliation with the South, and, rejecting either secessionist or abolitionist extremism, denounced efforts to destroy the Union.

Lincoln won a clear majority of the electoral votes, all from the free States, but received a plurality of less than 40 percent of the

Lincoln, accompanied by a detective (left), meets with Gen. Lew Wallace at Antietam in September 1862.

popular vote over his three opponents—Northern Democrat Douglas, Southern Democrat John C. Breckinridge, and Constitutional Unionist John Bell.

The new President inherited a tense situation, which Buchanan had been unable to resolve. The Southern States, convinced that Lincoln would destroy them economically and politically, had begun seceding. The Federal garrison at Fort Sumter, S.C., was beleaguered, and the Confederates already held many other Federal installations in the South. Yet in his inaugural address the President was conciliatory, though firm, toward the South. Maintaining that secession was illegal, he was determined to enforce national laws and protect Government property in the South. The Civil War erupted on April 12, 1861, when the Confederates opened fire on Fort Sumter.

Blending statesmanship and political acumen, Lincoln provided dynamic leadership to the North and assumed unprecedented Presidential power. To still critics of the war or the Government and sympathizers with the Confederacy, he sometimes resorted to extra-constitutional measures, which he justified by the national emergency. Although the tragedy of the conflict weighed heavily on him, as it stretched out year after year and casualty lists mounted, he tried with his speeches and public statements to bolster public morale. Until he found consistently effective generals such as Grant, he took an active part in formulating overall military strategy and conducting individual campaigns.

Lincoln was unable to silence either the abolitionists, some of whom sought an all-out war on slavery as well as unconditional surrender and occupation of the Confederacy, or the Copperheads and other defeatists, who demanded a negotiated peace. Nor was he able to correct inefficiencies in the War Department or obtain the full cooperation of certain Democratic Governors. Yet early in the war he deterred several of the Border States from joining the Confederacy. Throughout the conflict he adroitly controlled his Cabinet, made up of a contentious and personally ambitious but able group of men, three of whom had contested with him for the 1860 Presidential nomination. His issuance of the Emancipation Proclamation, which declared the freedom of slaves in areas still in rebellion, won sympathy for the Union abroad and strengthened northern morale.

Lincoln's foreign policy, shaped by the requirements of the home front, was guided by his erstwhile opponent Seward, whom he had named Secretary of State. The administration succeeded in substantially isolating the Confederacy diplomatically and in counteracting European opinion favorable to the South, especially in Great Britain and France. European intervention in Latin America, however, particularly that of the French in Mexico, could not be countered during the war.

For purposes of the election of 1864, the Republicans, in an appeal to Democrats and Unionists of all stripes, reconstituted themselves into the National Union Party. They renominated Lincoln and, as his Vice President, chose Andrew Johnson, a pro-Union Democrat from Tennessee. While military victories were auguring the end of hostilities, the voters reelected Lincoln over a general he had relieved 2 years earlier, George B. McClellan.

By the President of the United States of America.

A Proclamation.

I, Abraham Lincoln, President of the United States of America, and Commander-in-Chief of the Army and Navy thereof, do hereby proclaim and declare that hereafter, as heretofore, the war will be prosecuted for the object of practically restoring the constitutional relation between the United States, and each of the States, and the people thereof, in which States that relation is, or may be, suspended or disturbed.

That it is my purpose, upon the next meeting of Congress to again recommend the adoption of a practical measure tendering pecuniary aid to the free acceptance or rejection of all slave States, so called, the people whereof may not then be in rebellion against the United States and which States may then have voluntarily adopted, or thereafter may voluntarily adopt, immediate or gradual abolishment of slavery within their respective limits; and that the effort

First page of the Emancipation Proclamation (January 1, 1863), in Lincoln's hand.

In his second inaugural address, Lincoln addressed the problem that he expected to be central to his next term: reconciliation of the North and South once the war was over. Guided by a philosophy of "malice toward none, with charity for all," as expressed in that address, he outlined a moderate Reconstruction program for the South.

But Lincoln did not live long enough to put it into effect. On April 14, 1865, only 5 days after Lee's surrender at Appomattox, a bullet struck him down while he was enjoying a play at Ford's Theatre, in Washington, and he died the next morning.

Andrew Johnson

SEVENTEENTH PRESIDENT   1865-69

Johnson, a southerner whose first loyalty was always to the Union, almost lost his life while trying to prevent his home State, Tennessee, from seceding. A tailor by trade, he rose by dint of self-education and the exercise of his political talent and courage to high office. Succeeding the martyred Lincoln, he faced the critical problem of "reconstructing" the South. But his policies clashed with the program of the dominant Radical Republicans in Congress. As a result, he suffered impeachment, the only President ever to do so, and barely escaped being removed from office.

The second of two sons, Johnson was born amid humble circumstances at Raleigh, N.C., in 1808. His father, a janitor-porter-laborer, died in an accident when he was only 3 years old, after which his mother was impoverished, even subsequent to her remarriage in 1814. As a result, Johnson never attended school nor received any sort of formal education, though in adolescence he did learn to read.

In 1822 his mother apprenticed Andrew and his brother to a tailor. Two years later, when the former was 15 years old, they both ran away from their master, first to Carthage, N.C., and then to Laurens, S.C., where they operated tailor shops. In 1826 they returned to Raleigh, but that same year the family moved westward to Greeneville, Tenn.

At first unable to find employment there, Andrew spent a few months in Rutledge, Tenn., and possibly other cities working at his craft. Early the next year, he went back to Greeneville and opened his own shop. Later that same year, he married Eliza McCardle, who tutored him in reading and taught him to write. In time, she was to bear three sons and two daughters.

Johnson achieved modest prosperity in business, took part in local debates, and became active in civic and political affairs. He held the positions of alderman (1828-30), mayor (1830-33), State legislator (1835-37 and 1839-41), State senator (1841-43), U.S. Representative (1843-53), Governor of Tennessee (1853-57), and U.S. Senator (1857-62).

During all these years, though a Jacksonian Democrat, Johnson often pursued an independent course and was never a party loyalist. Always favoring the cause of the common man and opposing the plantation aristocracy in Congress, to no avail he persistently advocated enactment of a homestead bill to provide free land to the poor.

Because of Johnson's close southern ties, secession created a personal crisis for him. His home was in the South. He had been born and raised there. He owned eight household slaves. And he accepted the existence of slavery, which he felt was a unique institution beyond the control of Congress. Yet, reflecting the strong Unionist sentiment in eastern Tennessee and believing secession to be unconstitutional, he chose to fight for preservation of the Union.

To prevent his State from seceding, right after Lincoln's inauguration on March 4, 1861, Johnson made a desperate trip back home from Washington to plead his case—despite threats to his life. En route, in Virginia, he almost lost his life to a lynch mob. In the eastern part of his State, for he dared not appear in the pro-secessionist western part, he met favor from some groups and hostility from others. Faced with the wrath of his opponents and possible capture by Confederate troops following the outbreak of war, he finally headed back to Washington via Kentucky. After Tennessee seceded in June 1861, he was the only Senator from the South who stayed in his chair. This brought him instant applause in the North and scorn in the South.

In 1862, after Union forces captured Nashville and a portion of western Tennessee, Lincoln appointed Johnson as military governor of the State. Two years later, Johnson was nominated as Lincoln's running mate on the victorious ticket of the National Union Party, the wartime label used by the Republicans, who were seeking to win the allegiance of prowar Democrats.

When Lincoln was assassinated in April 1865, Johnson took over a task virtually as onerous as conduct of the war: Reconstruction of the South, or the restoration into the Union of the seceded States and the establishment of satisfactory social and economic relationships between whites and the newly freed slaves. He adopted what he believed would have been Lincoln's moderate program, which was based on faith in the people of the South.

Included would be the pardon of all ex-Confederates who took an oath of allegiance except for former leaders and men of wealth, who

Andrew Johnson reviews the Union Army at the end of the Civil War. This parade, which followed Pennsylvania Avenue, lasted two days (May 23-24, 1865).

could be pardoned only by the President; and bringing the seceded States back into the fold as quickly as possible on condition that they forswear secession and ratify the 13th amendment (1865) to the Constitution, which abolished slavery. Standing behind Johnson on Reconstruction were most northern Democrats and moderate Republicans.

Johnson inevitably clashed with the Radical Republicans, led by Thaddeus Stevens in the House and Benjamin Wade in the Senate. They sought what Johnson regarded as a punitive peace, involving land confiscation and redistribution to blacks; disenfranchisement of ex-Confederates; and full suffrage and legal equality for blacks, as well as economic and educational opportunities for them.

The Radicals, who were motivated by a combination of morals and politics, believed their program represented realization of the major aim of the war, the abolition of slavery and the guaranteeing of full citizenship privileges to the freedmen. On the other hand, the Radicals surely also recognized that such policies would insure Republican influence in the South. Other northerners, who resented the return of many prewar southern leaders to key posts, including Congress, and the imposition by southern legislators of many restrictions on blacks, tended to go along with the Radicals. Furthermore, most northerners were in no mood to relinquish economic gains made during and as a result of the war.

Cartoon criticizing Johnson's veto of the New Freedmen's Bureau Bill (1866), which sought to protect the freedom of black men in the South. He is pictured as a drunkard who takes bribes to pardon ex-Confederates. Lincoln, "the Great and Good," looks on scornfully.

As time went on, the conflict between the President and the Congress mounted in intensity. Veto followed veto, usually based on Johnson's feeling that the rights of the States were being violated. Vituperation followed vituperation. As the Radicals gained in strength, they passed one act after another over the Presidential veto and made abortive attempts to impeach him. They refused to seat southern Senators and Representatives; passed measures restricting the powers of the Presidency; and created legislation, including the 14th and 15th amendments, that emphatically stated the legal equality of blacks, guaranteed their civil liberties, and forbade discrimination against them.

Johnson executed the letter, if not the spirit, of these laws. In an unprecedented attempt to gain public backing for his position, in the summer of 1866 he toured the East and Middle West, but the Radicals won overwhelmingly in the fall congressional elections. The next March, they placed the Southern States under military rule until they met certain conditions, including approval of the 14th amendment.

Facsimile of ticket to Johnson's impeachment proceedings.

Finally, when Johnson tried to dismiss Secretary of War Edwin M. Stanton, who sided with the Radicals, the House impeached Johnson, largely on the basis of his alleged violation of the Tenure of Office Act. Amid exceptional controversy—the real issue being whether Congress or the President would direct Reconstruction—the Senate tried him in the spring of 1868. He was acquitted by only one vote. After the trial, the Radicals continued their legislative efforts but ultimately secured neither equal rights for blacks nor Republican control of the South. Johnson resisted the Radicals throughout the remainder of his term, but his power and reputation were seriously impaired.

While Johnson was preoccupied with the Reconstruction turmoil, his able Secretary of State William H. Seward made notable gains. In 1866, reasserting the Monroe Doctrine and bolstered by the dispatch of 50,000 troops under Gen. Philip H. Sheridan to the Mexican border, he soon helped persuade the French to withdraw from Mexico, where they had installed a monarch.

The next year, Seward purchased Alaska from Russia—an action that had also been contemplated in the Polk, Pierce, and Buchanan administrations. For the sum of $7,200,000, the United States acquired a vast territory, rich in natural resources, but many people initially reacted by referring to it as "Seward's folly." The Senate quickly ratified the purchase. Other expansionistic projects proposed by Seward came to naught.

Johnson did not seriously seek renomination by either the Democrats or Republicans, and at the end of his term retired to Tennessee. He nevertheless kept active in political affairs. In 1875 he took a seat in the U.S. Senate, where he was greeted with applause. But, serving only a few months, he died at the age of 66 while visiting the rural home of one of his daughters, about 40 miles from Greeneville.

Ulysses S. Grant

EIGHTEENTH PRESIDENT 1869-77

Although Grant was the preeminent military hero of the victorious North in the Civil War, he was handicapped as President by his lack of political and governmental experience, as well as the corruption and incompetence of cronies and wealthy men he appointed to office. Nevertheless, he scored some achievements in foreign affairs, and won two terms in the White House. Until Theodore Roosevelt he was the youngest Chief Executive, aged 46, at the time of his first election.

Grant was born in 1822 along the banks of the Ohio River at Point Pleasant, Ohio. He was christened as Hiram Ulysses, but he apparently later reversed the name. His father was a farmer-tanner who had immigrated from Kentucky. The year after Ulysses' birth, the family, in which he was the first of six children, moved to nearby Georgetown.

There, Grant spent his boyhood, experiencing neither wealth nor poverty. He helped his parents on the farm or at the tannery, performed odd jobs, and earned a reputation as a horse trainer. Besides studying at local schools, he also briefly matriculated at academies in Maysville, Ky., and Ripley, Ohio.

In 1839 Grant received an appointment to the United States Military Academy, but he entertained no plans for a military career and entered reluctantly. Because of an error, he was registered as Ulysses Simpson Grant, which he was to retain, though his friends always called him "Sam." He excelled in horsemanship, but was not too interested in his studies except for mathematics and received a number of demerits. Gradually, however, he came to enjoy West Point. He graduated 21st in a class of 39.

Disappointed at not being detailed to the cavalry upon his graduation in 1843, Grant was assigned to the infantry at Jefferson Barracks, Mo., near St. Louis. While at that place, he met and became engaged to Julia Dent, sister of an academy classmate. The next year, he was reassigned to the Fort Jesup, La., area, and then joined Gen. Zachary Taylor's forces in Texas (1845-46). During the

Mexican War (1846-48), though he considered it a needless conquest, he fought with distinction under Taylor and Gen. Winfield Scott in most of the major battles and emerged a first lieutenant. In 1848 he married Miss Dent; they were to raise three sons and one daughter.

In the years 1848-52, other tours of duty followed at Madison Barracks, in Sackets Harbor, N.Y., and at Fort Wayne, in Detroit. Then, unaccompanied by his wife and infant son, Grant traveled across the continent to serve at Fort Vancouver, Wash. (1852-53) and Fort Humboldt, Calif. (1853-54). Although he gained a captaincy at the first of these posts, at both of them the lonely young officer, also bored and disenchanted with the Army, drank too much. Finally, after a dispute with his commanding officer, he resigned from the military service.

A difficult 7 years followed—years of privation, menial pursuits, ignominy, limited prospects, and despondence—though Grant was reunited with his family and aided by his in-laws. Between 1854 and 1860, in the St. Louis, Mo., area he tried his hand at farming, selling firewood, real estate, and bill collecting, but prospered in none. In 1860 he moved to Galena, Ill., to work as a clerk in a tannery-leather store owned by his family.

Although the Civil War (1861-65) brought tragedy to the Nation, it created opportunity for some men, such as Grant. It catapulted him into national fame and the Presidency. Rising quickly through the ranks from captain to lieutenant general and from leader of an Illinois volunteer company to the top Union command, he displayed remarkable aggressiveness and incisiveness, as well as an excellent mastery of organization and strategy.

Grant first gained renown for his campaigns in the Mississippi River Valley. They culminated in the capture of Vicksburg, Miss., which split the Confederacy. Later, after Grant's victory at Chattanooga, Lincoln placed him in command of the Union armies, and he established his headquarters with the Army of the Potomac. Taking advantage of his superior resources in men and materiel, he perfected plans for destroying the Confederacy by a coordinated offensive on all fronts. The war ended soon after the capitulation of Gen. Robert E. Lee's Army of Northern Virginia to Grant at Appomattox Court House, Va., in April 1865.

When hostilities ended, Grant remained at the head of the Army; and won the title of General of the Army. Grateful citizens in the

North presented him with homes in several cities and substantial cash gifts. Second in public esteem only to Lincoln, he was mobbed by crowds of people wherever he went. He escaped possible assassination at Ford's Theatre only because he and his wife declined the President's invitation to attend the performance.

Grant's great popularity and the seeming inevitability of his capture of the Presidential nomination in 1868 created friction with President Andrew Johnson. When the latter tried to arrest General Lee for treason, contrary to the terms of Appomattox, Grant threatened to take his case to the people and forced Johnson to back down. Yet on most political matters the general tried to maintain a neutral position—even during Johnson's impeachment trial. When the President had dismissed Secretary of War Stanton in 1867, Grant had accepted the position on an *ad interim* basis, but resigned when Congress refused to permit the dismissal. Both parties seriously considered Grant for the Presidential nomination in 1868. Although he had never affiliated with any party, he came to identify with the Radical Republicans.

After Grant resigned from the Army in 1854, he spent 7 frustrating years in the St. Louis area. During this time, he jumped from job to job, including real estate agent.

Grant in 1864.

Nominated easily, he defeated Democrat Horatio Seymour, who made a surprisingly good showing despite his party's failing fortunes. For his second term, in 1872, Grant, the magic of his military reputation still persuasive, triumphed by a much larger margin over Horace Greeley, nominee of the Liberal Republicans and the Democrats.

Grant was well trained to be a general, but ill prepared for the White House. Interpreting executive power narrowly, he looked to Congress or his advisers for guidance and offered no significant legislative program. Above all, he was unable to satisfy the need for a surcease from the turmoil of the previous decade. A key national issue was Reconstruction of the South. Ostensibly committed to Radical policy, Grant sometimes used military force to carry out the laws of Congress, which reflected Republican aims. On the other hand, he allowed southern white supremacists, the "Redeemers," to take gradual control of the governments of State after State in the former Confederacy. By the end of his second term, Reconstruction had largely ended.

The problems of the Grant administration reflected the loose political and business morality of the period. Business interests frequently sought to dictate political policy while resisting governmental intervention in their practices; and party bosses gained inordinate influence through management of patronage and Federal disbursements.

Grant naively introduced into his Cabinet and staff and took as confidants friends and wealthy men, many of whom turned out to be incompetent or corrupt. As a result, though Grant himself was personally honest, a series of scandals rocked his administration, particularly during his second term, including the Crédit Mobilier and the Whisky Ring. His private secretary, several members of his Cabinet, and some of those in his party in Congress were involved in highly illegal or improper acts.

Although Grant took steps to control inflation, restore public credit, and stabilize the currency, he proved unable to manage the speculation, overexpanded credit, and wild business expansion of the era. These conditions helped create the Panic of 1873, when unemployment soared and many businesses failed. Profiting from the dismal economic picture and the administration scandals, the Democrats won the House in the following year, for the first time since 1856.

Responding to eastern reformers who objected to the brutality of the Battle of the Washita, Okla. (1868), and other mistreatment of the Indians, in 1869 Grant inaugurated his Peace Policy. Hoping to end corruption on the reservations and to provide the natives with examples of morality, he appointed church-nominated men, predominantly Quakers, as Indian agents. Military interference was forbidden on the reservations unless they requested it. But the program proved ineffective. Among other factors, the Indians resisted attempts to turn them into farmers and often made forays off the reservations, which inflamed settlers. At the same time, the Government proved unable to keep whites off the reservations.

Grant achieved notable successes in foreign policy, executed by his capable Secretary of State, Hamilton Fish. The Treaty of Washington (D.C.) (1871) settled a series of controversies with Britain, the most prominent of which was the *Alabama* claims. By these, the United States sought reparations for damages inflicted on northern ships by Confederate raiders, which had outfitted in British ports. Grant and Fish also ignored provocations and avoided war with Spain during her suppression of a rebellion in Cuba. Grant tried to annex the Dominican Republic, but the Senate refused assent. A treaty of commercial reciprocity was negotiated with Hawaii that included a stipulation banning disposal of any of its territory to a third power.

In the grave constitutional crisis and attendant threats of serious domestic strife that followed the disputed Hayes-Tilden election of 1876, Grant resolutely sought a solution that would preserve our constitutional form of Government, and turned over the reins of Government intact to his successor.

About 6 weeks after leaving office, Grant, his wife, and his youngest son departed on a worldwide tour that lasted more than 2 years (1877-79), during which they enjoyed regal treatment and met many world leaders. Within the next few years, after returning to the United States and settling in New York City, Grant visited the West Indies and made three trips to Mexico, on personal, business, and governmental ventures. Meantime, in 1880, he had again sought the Republican Presidential nomination but lost it to James A. Garfield. Two years later, Grant entered a partnership in a financial firm at New York, but the enterprise failed in 1884. About that time, he suffered other economic reverses.

While thus penniless and humiliated, Grant was stricken with cancer of the throat. To help his family, in a race against death, he frantically wrote his memoirs, a classic in their field that were to earn his heirs almost half a million dollars in royalties. In 1885, a few days after laying down his pen, he died in the summer cottage of a friend at Mount McGregor, N.Y., in the Adirondacks. He was 63 years old.

Grant, his wife, daughter Nellie (left), and sons Jesse (left) and Fred (right) with their wives and children in 1885. This photograph was taken at the cottage in the Adirondacks where the retired President spent about 6 weeks before his death.

Rutherford B. Hayes

In one of the most bitterly contested elections in U.S. history, Hayes won the Presidency by only one electoral vote. Despite this onus and strong opposition in his own party, he carried out a program of moderate reform, particularly in the civil service. In terminating the role Federal troops had played in governing the South, he virtually ended Reconstruction and dampened the lingering hostility between the North and South. Before rising to the Presidency, he had served as a general in the Civil War, U.S. Representative, and Governor of Ohio. Throughout his life, but especially in retirement, he devoted himself to humanitarian causes.

Hayes, the youngest of five children, was born at Delaware, Ohio, in 1822. His father, a storekeeper and farmer, died before his birth. An uncle, Sardis Birchard, served as his guardian. After attending local schools, Hayes studied at academies in Norwalk, Ohio, and Middletown, Conn., and in 1842 graduated from Kenyon College, Ohio. He read law for a year at Columbus, and in 1845 completed Harvard Law School. He then took up practice at Lower Sandusky (present Fremont), Ohio.

In 1849 Hayes moved to Cincinnati. There, he gained attention as a criminal lawyer as well as a defender of fugitive slaves, and became active in the Whig Party. In 1852 he married Lucy Ware Webb, who would be the first wife of a President to be a college graduate. They were to have seven sons and a daughter.

After the demise of the Whig Party, in 1855 Hayes became a moderate Republican. He was willing to compromise on slavery to avoid war but sought to contain its extension. His first political office, held in the years 1858-61, was as city solicitor of Cincinnati.

When hostilities flared between the North and South, Hayes was appointed a major in the Ohio Volunteer Infantry. He was wounded several times and rose to the rank of brevet major general. While still in the Army, in 1864, he was elected to the U.S. House of Representatives (1865-67), where he unenthusiastically supported

Radical Republican programs. He resigned in the latter year to run for Governor of Ohio.

Between 1868 and 1872 Hayes served two terms as Governor. In the latter year, he tried for a seat in the U.S. House of Representatives, but failed to obtain it. The next year, he moved back to Fremont, and took up residence at Spiegel Grove estate. He was reelected Governor in 1875.

Hayes received the Republican Presidential nomination in 1876. A compromise candidate, he was acceptable because of his integrity, excellent war record, loyalty to the party, and moderate liberalism. He ran against Democrat Samuel J. Tilden, Governor of New York. An unprecedented and intricate election dispute followed, during which both sides at first claimed victory. Tilden was clearly ahead in the popular vote, but lacked one electoral vote for victory; Hayes went to bed on election night believing he had been defeated. But the remaining votes were disputed and the electoral contest was far from over. For months, the Government and country were in a quandary. The complication was that a few States each submitted two different sets of electoral votes. Tilden needed to win only one vote; Hayes needed all the disputed ones to win.

To settle the impasse, Congress created a special commission of 15 members. It consisted of five from each House of Congress and five from the Supreme Court. The commission finally accepted the returns favoring Hayes by a partisan vote of 8 to 7. The issue was resolved only 2 days before the inauguration. To prevent a Democratic filibuster from frustrating the decision, the Republicans—though Hayes was apparently not personally involved—promised southern Democrats at least one Cabinet post, railroad subsidies, Federal patronage, and discontinuation of the role of Federal troops in Reconstruction.

Whatever Hayes' part in the affair, this "bargain" created special difficulties for him. For one thing, though he insisted on merit in his Cabinet appointments and designated some highly competent individuals representing diverse factions, he did choose an ex-Confederate. This not only raised the question of a "bargain," but also infuriated many Republicans.

Secondly, Hayes almost immediately withdrew troops from the two Southern States where they remained, after obtaining promises from the would-be Democratic governments that they

Hayes and his Cabinet. Left to right: Hayes, Secretary of the Treasury John Sherman, Secretary of the Navy Richard W. Thompson, Attorney General Charles Devens, Secretary of State William M. Evarts, Secretary of the Interior Carl Schurz, Secretary of War George W. McCrary, and Postmaster General David M. Key.

would protect the constitutional privileges of all citizens. He justified this action on the grounds that no State governments could be legally maintained in power by force of arms. Yet he also apparently believed—mistakenly—that this step offered the hope that the Republicans could make gains in the South by attracting white southerners, especially businessmen and conservatives.

Hayes' power was sapped not only by the circumstances of his election and charges of his participation in the "bargain," but also by his pledge, made in advance of his election, to serve only one term. Because of his determination not to relinquish to Congress any of his prerogatives, he clashed repeatedly with members of his

Hayes receives Chun Lan-pin, the first Chinese Minister to the United States, in the Blue Room of the White House in 1878.

Hayes meets with Indian chiefs in the White House.

own divided party on appointment matters and with the resurgent Democrats on Presidential authority to deploy Federal troops in supervision of elections. The Democrats, during the first half of his term, controlled the lower House of Congress; during the last half, both Houses.

Nevertheless, Hayes managed to effect a modest reform program that possibly was at least partially motivated by a desire to counter the Stalwart-Radical element in his own party, which dubbed Hayes' supporters as "Half-Breeds." His major point of focus was the civil service. In the most famous episode of his crusade, during which he freed various jobs from partisan control and struggled bitterly with his own party, he removed Chester A. Arthur from the collectorship of customs at New York City. He was unable, however, to obtain the creation of a Civil Service Commission.

A fiscal conservative, Hayes was a foe of inflationary policies—in a day when much of the public clamored for the free coinage of silver and the proliferation of paper money. The Bland-Allison Act (1878), which permitted the limited coinage of silver, passed only over his veto.

Hayes faced other serious problems. The first great national strikes occurred during his administration. In the summer of 1877, for the third time in as many years, the railroads slashed wages. Strikes and riots ensued. Even though Hayes sympathized with the plight of the workers, he sent Federal troops to restore order in certain areas.

In 1879, despite vehement opposition in California, where Chinese labor forced down wages, Hayes vetoed a congressional bill that prohibited Chinese immigration. He contended it violated treaty obligations. Later, however, he obtained a modification of the treaty allowing the United States to restrict immigration. Other diplomatic activities were limited during the Hayes administration, though Hayes did arbitrate a boundary dispute between Argentina and Paraguay.

In 1881 Hayes returned to Spiegel Grove. Except for a visit to Bermuda, frequent speaking tours, and trips to Civil War reunions, he dwelt there until his death in 1893. Writing extensively and making many public addresses, he continued active in a variety of humanitarian causes, especially black education and prison reform. He came to view with alarm the increasing concentration of wealth and power in the hands of a few, and grew closer to the common people.

James A. Garfield

TWENTIETH PRESIDENT   1881

**The second President to be assassinated, Garfield
died only a few months after his term had begun. Yet,
within that short time, his assaults on political
patronage and Post Office corruption promised a
vigorous administration. But his death ended his
hopes of reuniting the Republican Party, reforming
the civil service, and fighting inflation. En route to the
Presidency, he had surmounted poverty, and made
notable achievements as educator, orator, soldier,
and U.S. Representative.**

Of New England ancestry, Garfield was born in 1831 at Orange
Township in Cuyahoga County, Ohio. His father, a canal worker
turned farmer who had already sired four children, died before
Garfield was 2 years old and left his widow impoverished. She and
her offspring continued to work the farm. James, however,
attended elementary school during the winter months. As a
teenager, he drove boat teams on the Ohio and Erie Canal, and
dreamed of a life at sea. But the farthest he traveled, in 1848, was to
Pittsburgh. That same year, he returned home to recuperate from
an illness.

In the spring of 1849, Garfield matriculated at Geauga Academy,
a denominational institution in Chester, Ohio, and that fall and
winter taught at a district school, after which he continued at
Geauga. In 1851 he entered Western Reserve Eclectic Institute
(Hiram College after 1867) at nearby Hiram. For 3 years, he studied
and taught at the institute, instructed on the elementary level, and
held various odd jobs. Saving sufficient money, he then enrolled at
Williams College, in Williamstown, Mass., as a junior. He excelled
in the classics and public speaking and learned German.

After graduating in 1856, Garfield rejoined the faculty at Western
Reserve. The prestige of an eastern college degree contributed to his
elevation in 1857 to the presidency of the institute, whose staff
consisted of five teachers. In addition, he became an accomplished
lay preacher-evangelist. In 1858 he married childhood friend
Lucretia Rudolph, who subsequently bore five sons and two
daughters.

Representative Garfield and his daughter Mary ("Molly") a few years before he assumed the Presidency.

Garfield soon received local acclaim in a debate with a pre-Darwin evolutionary theorist and made a statewide lecture tour on the subject. In 1859, as a Republican, he won a seat in the State senate (1860-61). He also studied enough law to be admitted to the bar a year or so later, and set up practice in Hiram.

During the secession crisis, Garfield, a rapidly emerging State leader of his party, advocated coercion to assure the continuity of the Union. Upon the outbreak of the war in 1861, he was commissioned in the Ohio Volunteer Infantry, becoming a lieutenant colonel and then colonel. In January 1862, commanding a brigade, he won a minor victory—a rare Union success at the time—at Middle Creek, Ky. As a result, at the youthful age of 31 he became a brigadier general, but before long illness forced him to take leave.

Meantime, the Republicans in his home district had nominated the absent general for the U.S. House of Representatives. Nevertheless, after his election in 1862, he made good his campaign promise to return to the battlefield. Early the next year, he was appointed as chief of staff in Gen. William Rosecrans' Army of the Cumberland, then in middle Tennessee. With the support of Garfield but the disapproval of many other officers, Rosecrans made plans to drive Gen. Braxton Bragg's forces out of the State. Although this goal was achieved, the failure of the second phase of the Union offensive at Chickamauga, Ga., resulted in the discrediting of Rosecrans. Nevertheless, Garfield gained credit for his courageous leadership and won promotion to the rank of major general.

In late 1863 Garfield resigned from the Army to take his seat in the U.S. House of Representatives, to which he was to be reelected eight times and occupy until 1880. Early in his congressional career, Garfield's belief in a stern Reconstruction policy and conservative economic attitude sometimes led him to disagree with President Lincoln's policies. Yet he supported his renomination and deeply mourned his assassination. In its wake, he dissuaded a vindictive mob in New York City, where he was visiting, from burning the offices of a Democratic newspaper.

Along with James G. Blaine, Garfield came to be a major ally of Radical Republican leader Thaddeus Stevens. Garfield, reflecting his party's position, staunchly rejected the inflationary "green-back" program for the issuance of paper money and advocated deflationary "sound-money" policies. On the other hand, he was lukewarm in his advocacy of the party's protective tariff program.

After Stevens died in 1868, Garfield and Blaine captained House Republicans during the stormy and scandal-ridden Grant adminis-tration. Garfield was peripherally involved in the Crédit Mobilier as well as in a lesser charge of corruption with a construction contractor, but he emerged relatively untainted.

After Blaine's election to the Senate in 1876, Garfield became the House Minority Leader. When the disputed Presidential election of that year came to the Congress, he helped frame the legislation for

Garfield "cuts a swath" to the White House in this 1880 campaign poster.

and served on the commission that settled the issue of disputed electoral votes. As a result, Hayes, whom he had campaigned for, went to the White House.

In 1880 the Republican-controlled Ohio legislature elected Garfield to the U.S. Senate, but he never served there because he soon won his party's Presidential nomination—by a circuitous route. After the convention hopelessly deadlocked over three candidates, Garfield triumphed as a "dark horse" on the 36th ballot.

Despite attempts to appease the party's "Stalwart" wing with the choice of Chester A. Arthur for Vice President, the Republicans remained disunited against Gen. Winfield S. Hancock and eked out only a narrow victory. Garfield conducted a good share of the campaign from the "front porch" of his Lawnfield estate in Mentor, Ohio.

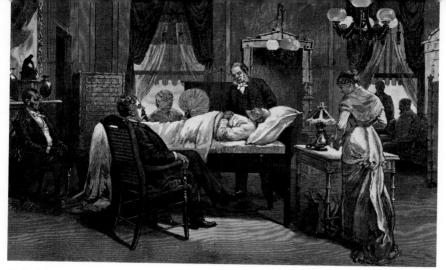

Felled by an assassin's bullet, President Garfield lies stricken in the White House. He later died at Elberon, New Jersey.

In hopes of reuniting his party, Garfield appointed a Cabinet representing various Republican factions. But harmony did not prevail because he clashed repeatedly with the New York-based Stalwarts on political appointments and patronage at the New York City Customs House. To compound the problem, his Postmaster General soon discovered that Republicans in his department were engaged in extensive corruption. Certain contractors had been awarded rural delivery (star) routes on the basis of favoritism, and had reaped unjust gains. Over the objections of implicated politicians, Garfield backed his appointee's well-publicized investigation. His bold actions on such matters won the acclaim of reform leaders.

During the few months he was in office, Garfield announced to England his desire to revise the Clayton-Bulwer Treaty of 1850, and his Secretary of State, Blaine, called a conference of American republics to be held in Washington in 1882. This meeting did not take place as scheduled partially because of the President's assassination.

On July 2, 1881, when vacation-bound Garfield arrived at Washington's Baltimore and Potomac Railroad Station, a disgruntled officeseeker shot the President twice in the back. Undergoing numerous medical treatments, including Alexander Graham Bell's attempts to find the bullet with his newly invented induction balance electrical device, Garfield lingered on for more than 2 months, at first in the White House and then at a seaside retreat in Elberon, N.J. He died there on September 19.

Chester A. Arthur

TWENTY-FIRST PRESIDENT   1881–85

Arthur, an erstwhile machine politician who became President upon the death of Garfield and had never held elective office except for the Vice-Presidency, seemed unsuited for the role of Chief Executive. Yet he gained major stature in that position. Abandoning the spoilsmanship with which he had long been associated and gaining many enemies in his own party, he championed bipartisan civil service reform. This cost him all chance for renomination.

The eldest son in a large family sired by a Baptist minister who had immigrated from Ireland via Canada, Arthur was born in 1830 near the Canadian border at Fairfield or Waterville, Vt. During his first decade of life, his father moved to a series of parishes, predominantly in the Vermont-New York border area. The youth attended schools in various localities until his father settled for 5 years in Union Village (present Greenwich), N.Y. In 1844 the family relocated to Schenectady, N.Y. Arthur studied at the Lyceum School for a year and then Union College, partially financing himself by teaching and graduating with honors in 1848.

For the next 5 years, Arthur continued to teach, mainly in the Pownal, Vt., area, and attained the rank of principal. Meantime, he had read law. In 1853 he intensified his studies with a New York City firm managed by family friends, was admitted to the bar that same year, and joined them. Because of his antislavery views, the young lawyer associated himself with the emerging Republican Party at its first State convention, provided legal services for fugitive slaves, and in one case dealt a legal blow against segregated public transportation in Brooklyn.

In 1859 Arthur married Ellen Lewis Herndon of Fredericksburg, Va., daughter of a prominent naval officer. She was to bear one daughter and two sons. In 1857 Arthur had joined the State militia as a judge advocate. During the Civil War, temporarily discontinuing his legal practice, he went on active duty. He ably served in a variety of administrative posts on the home front: engineer-in-chief, quartermaster general, and inspector general.

In 1863 Arthur resumed his law practice and renewed his interest in Republican politics. Five years later, he directed election strategy for the Central Grant Club of New York. The next year, he was named counsel for the New York City Tax Commission. In 1871 President Grant, rewarding him for his party loyalty, appointed him as collector of customs of the Port of New York.

Arthur, again proving to be an efficient administrator, hired most of his 1,000 employees on the basis of merit. But he also subscribed to the spoils system, hired more personnel than were needed, and expected them to support the party—particularly U.S. Senator Roscoe Conkling's Stalwart Republican machine. President Hayes, a Republican reformer who was at odds with the Stalwarts, removed Arthur in 1878.

Arthur returned to his law practice, and aided the revengeful attempts of Conkling's faction to win a third term for Grant at the 1880 convention. This effort failed, but Arthur received the Vice-Presidential nomination under James Garfield. Once in office, Arthur remained a Conkling loyalist, even when the latter clashed with President Garfield over patronage.

Arthur, still grieving over the loss of his wife the previous year, assumed the Presidency in 1881 upon the assassination of Garfield by a disgruntled job seeker. To the dismay of Conkling and his followers, Arthur rose above partisanship. He abandoned his presumed loyalty to the Stalwarts, attempted to unify his party, and became an ardent reformer.

Pursuing efforts initiated under Hayes and Garfield, Arthur pushed prosecution of a series of fraud cases in the Post Office Department, and reformed the civil service. Political party affiliation instead of merit had long determined Federal job appointments. Arthur prodded Congress to action. The Pendleton Act of 1883 prohibited assessment of salary kickbacks from public employees, as well as their removal for political reasons. Moreover, it established a bipartisan Civil Service Commission, which was charged with classification of Federal jobs and the administration of competitive examinations to fill them. Only a fraction of all positions were filled by merit at first, but the new act laid the foundations for a tenured and nonpolitical civil service.

Arthur met less success in his attempts to lower tariff rates. Although he recognized the need to protect fledgling native industries from cheaper foreign goods, he believed that the existing

Arthur at his desk in the White House.

high customs duties and taxes and the resultant Treasury surpluses fostered reckless "pork-barrel" appropriations by Congress. He created a commission, which included protectionists, to study tariff revision. Despite its advice to cut the duties, in the Tariff Act of 1883 Congress continued the protectionist policy, though it reduced some rates.

Although Arthur signed the bill under protest, many westerners and southerners, who felt high tariffs contributed to the high cost of manufactured goods and low prices for their farm and other products, turned to the Democratic Party for redress. Arthur did manage to reduce the Treasury surplus by applying about $400 million of it toward payment of the national debt. Then, too, he vetoed but failed to block an 1882 bill that included "pork-barrel" items.

President Arthur registers to vote in New York City.

Arthur also vetoed an act suspending Chinese immigration for 10 years but Congress overrode him. In 1883, at a time when only 24 outdated naval ships were in commission, the President approved legislation to build four modern steel warships. The next year, he signed a bill creating a rudimentary government for Alaska. Highlights in foreign affairs included: acquisition of the right to

Chief Executive Arthur rides down Bellevue Avenue while vacationing at Newport, Rhode Island, in 1884.

construct nautical coaling and repair stations in Hawaii, ratification of a pact of friendship and commerce with Korea, and Senate rejection of a treaty negotiated by Arthur to build a canal through Nicaragua.

In the waning days of his term, Arthur took part in two symbolic ceremonies. Marking the beginning of the electrical age, in December 1884 he pressed a button at the White House that set machinery in motion at a New Orleans exhibition. In February 1885 he dedicated the Washington Monument.

Although Arthur was a respected and popular President, he had made too many enemies within his party. Despite a spirited effort in 1884, he lost his place on the ticket to James G. Blaine. The following year, he even failed to win a nomination for the U.S. Senate from New York.

After the expiration of his Presidential term, Arthur retired to New York City and died less than 2 years later.

Grover Cleveland

TWENTY-SECOND PRESIDENT   1885-89
TWENTY-FOURTH PRESIDENT   1893-97

Cleveland, who had been a prominent upstate New York lawyer and politician, was the first Democratic Chief Executive after the Civil War and the only one ever elected to nonconsecutive terms. Disdaining paternalism for either the powerful or the weak, he vetoed more bills than any previous President. He rejected governmental interference with the economy, fought protective tariffs and inflationary monetary schemes, and continued the reform programs of his immediate predecessors. A severe economic depression and industry-labor strife plagued his second term.

Born in 1837 at Caldwell, N.J., Cleveland was christened as Stephen Grover, but stopped using his first name early in his life. He was the fifth of nine children sired by a Presbyterian pastor. In 1841 a ministerial reassignment resulted in a family move to Fayetteville, in central New York. There, the boy received an education at home and in village schools until he was 13 years old.

At that time, his father's failing health and financial problems forced Grover to work as a clerk in a local store. When his father took a job as district secretary of a missionary society and moved in 1850 to nearby Clinton, N.Y., the youth briefly enrolled at a college preparatory academy there, but soon had to return to his clerk position at Fayetteville. The death of his father in 1853, shortly after taking a parsonage in Holland Patent, N.Y., ended the young man's hopes of going to college.

After teaching in 1853-54 at Gotham's New York Institution for the Blind, Cleveland headed west to seek better economic opportunity. By the spring of 1855, however, he had ventured only as far as the stock farm of his uncle, Lewis F. Allen, near Buffalo, N.Y. After a summer of assisting in compiling *Allen's American Shorthorn Herd Book,* Cleveland entered a Buffalo law office as an apprentice clerk. In 1859 he was admitted to the bar and began practice. Lacking a martial spirit and still burdened by family financial responsibilities, during the Civil War (1861-65) he hired a substitute, as did many others, to perform his military service.

Cleveland had shown a predilection for Democratic politics as early as 1858, and first worked for the local party organization. Four years later, he was elected as a city ward supervisor, and the following year was appointed as assistant district attorney of Erie County, which included Buffalo. In 1865 he lost a race for district attorney. For the next 5 years, he devoted himself to his law practice. Then he was elected as county sheriff (1871-73), after which he resumed his legal activities. By the mid-1870's, he had attained recognition as one of the leading lawyers in the western part of the State. In 1881 he was elected as mayor of Buffalo, in which position he launched attacks on machine politics that irritated even his own party.

This untainted record helped Cleveland win the Democratic gubernatorial nomination in 1882 and a record plurality over a Republican machine candidate. The new Governor exhibited a bipartisan independence in office that gained him national recognition, but his resolute exercise of the veto to curb corruption and patronage angered New York City's Tammany Hall Democratic organization. Aided by Republican assemblyman Theodore Roosevelt, he also passed municipal reform legislation. On the other hand, he blocked reformers' attempts to lower rates of the privately owned New York City commuter railway because he felt they violated the company's right of contract.

Cleveland gained the Presidential nomination in 1884 without Tammany support. The campaign was close, and much mud was slung. Some Republicans claimed Cleveland had fathered an illegitimate son. The Democrats, who were backed by a splinter group of antimachine Republicans, charged James G. Blaine, the Republican candidate, with corruption because of his implication in the Crédit Mobilier scandal. He also lost some of the Catholic vote by not repudiating a supporter's charge that the Democrats were the party of "rum, Romanism, and rebellion."

Cleveland entered office firmly convinced he should only administer, execute, and react to congressional laws, but before long chose to exert leadership. Throughout his two terms, he opposed favoritism, no matter on whose behalf it was instigated. He opened thousands of acres of land to homesteaders that the railroads had falsely claimed had been granted to them. He

This 1888 broadside pictures Cleveland, his wife, and Vice-Presidential candidate Allen G. Thurman. Benjamin Harrison won the election.

"Deadeye Dick" (Senator Richard P.) Bland and other mutinous "sailors" in his own party try to force gold-standard-supporter Cleveland to walk the "Free Silver" plank of the ship *Democracy*.

appointed unbiased and able men to the first Federal commission to regulate railroads, created by the Interstate Commerce Act of 1887. He also returned to the Indians almost 500,000 acres of reservation land that President Arthur's administration had opened to settlement.

Moreover, Cleveland vetoed numerous bills granting pensions to individual Union Civil War veterans and their dependents, as well as a Grand Army of the Republic-sponsored act designed to compensate ex-Union soldiers for non-service incurred disabilities or old age. He championed legislation to lower tariffs, which he felt unduly benefited industry and harmed farmers and workers, but he was unable to get the legislation he wanted through Congress during either of his stints in office.

Fellow Democrats hounded Cleveland for appointments. Although he replaced two-thirds of the Federal bureaucracy in his first term, he irritated machine politicians by urging repeal of the Tenure-of-Office Act (1867), which had enhanced senatorial control over Presidential removals of previously confirmed officeholders. His strong support of the Civil Service Commission led to a doubling of the number of merit positions, but failed to satisfy all the civil service reformers.

In 1886 Cleveland married 21-year-old Frances Folsom, daughter of a former law partner who on his death had left her as Cleveland's ward. This was the only wedding of a President that has ever been held in the White House, and the bride was the youngest of all First Ladies. She was to bear two sons and three daughters. Met one son, Francis, at Tamworth, N. H.

Business opposition to his tariff position and intraparty squabbles over patronage probably cost Cleveland reelection in 1888. Although he captured a plurality of the popular vote, he lost the decisive electoral votes of New York and Indiana that he had carried in 1884 to Republican Benjamin Harrison.

After spending 4 years practicing law in New York City, in 1892 Cleveland was easily reelected over Harrison and the Populist, or "People's Party," candidate James B. Weaver. The year Cleveland reentered office, the Panic of 1893 hit the country. Companies went bankrupt, Treasury gold reserves fell, some 500 banks failed, mortgages were foreclosed, and unemployment rose drastically. Advocating deflationary gold-standard policies to insure business confidence and restore prosperity, he led the congressional fight for

Cleveland's second inauguration, March 4, 1893.

Spent one of two years with his son of same name, at Bedford School, near Bedford, N.J.

repeal of the mildly inflationary Sherman Silver Purchase Act
(1890). In 1895 he bolstered Treasury reserves and strengthened the
gold standard by obtaining a governmental loan from Wall Street
tycoons J.P. Morgan and <u>August Belmont</u>.

Meanwhile, growing unemployment, low wages, and excessively
long working hours had created domestic turmoil. In the spring of
1894, Jacob S. Coxey and his "army" marched from Ohio to
Washington, D.C., to petition for unemployment relief. Cleveland
approved Attorney General Richard Olney's use of police to
disperse the protesters.

Late that same year, the American Railway Union, led by
Eugene V. Debs, boycotted the cars of the Chicago-based Pullman
Palace Car Company, whose workers were striking over wage cuts

and the company's paternalistic policies. Olney appointed a small army of special deputies to continue railroad operations. After violence erupted, in a bitterly controversial move Cleveland ignored the objections of Illinois Gov. John P. Altgeld, and sent Federal troops to restore order. An injunction against labor to insure mail deliveries and prevent interference with interstate commerce brought an end to the strike and resulted in the imprisonment of Debs.

Conservation-minded like Harrison, in 1897 Cleveland created a number of additional forest reserves containing more than 21 million acres. Three years earlier, he had also signed the first Federal legislation designed to protect wildlife on Government lands, the Yellowstone Act. *not the Yellowstone N. Park Act of 1872.*

Foreign affairs claimed a share of Cleveland's attention. He reached agreement with Great Britain and Canada over fishing rights in waters adjacent to the latter. He favored Samoan autonomy over British, German, and even American intervention and control. He scuttled the treaty Harrison had negotiated for the annexation of Hawaii and checked further attempts in that direction. When rebellion broke out in Cuba against Spain, beginning in 1895, Cleveland, against rising public sentiment and the provocative actions of U.S.-based arms dealers and volunteer expeditions, maintained official neutrality. During a boundary dispute between Venezuela and Great Britain over the boundary of British Guiana, he invoked the Monroe Doctrine and convinced the parties to submit the issue to arbitration.

Cleveland's conservative economic policies failed to end the depression and alienated many Democrats, especially in the South and West. In 1894 the Republicans won landslide victories in the congressional elections. Two years later, the Democratic convention repudiated Cleveland's administration and nominated silverite William Jennings Bryan, whom the Populists also endorsed.

Cleveland spent an active retirement at Westland, his recently purchased home in Princeton, N.J. He sat on the board of trustees of the university and the Equitable Life Assurance Society. Although President Theodore Roosevelt appointed him as chairman of a coal strike commission in 1902, the body never met. *Presidential Problems,* a collection of his speeches, was published 2 years later. He also wrote various magazine articles and authored *Fishing and Shooting Sketches* (1906). In 1908 he passed away at Princeton.

Benjamin Harrison

TWENTY-THIRD PRESIDENT   1889-93

Benjamin Harrison was the great-grandson and namesake of a signer of the Declaration of Independence and the grandson of President William Henry Harrison. Benjamin earned fame as lawyer, soldier, and politician. He won the Presidency from Cleveland only by electoral vote. In domestic affairs, Harrison tried to avoid conflicts with his party's positions, but his moderate stance on such issues as civil service reform, the tariff, labor unrest, and monetary policy alienated reformers as well as machine politicians. On the other hand, he pursued a vigorous foreign policy.

Harrison was born in 1833 at North Bend, Ohio, at the estate of his grandfather, William Henry Harrison, who became President 7 years later. Benjamin was the second son of 10 children from the second marriage of his father. The latter was a well-to-do farmer who resided near William Henry and who was to be a Member of the U.S. House of Representatives (1853-57). Private tutors, mainly, educated the scholarly youth.

In 1847 Harrison enrolled at Farmers' College in nearby Cincinnati. Three years later, he transferred to Miami University, at Oxford, Ohio, and in 1852 graduated with distinction. The next year, he married college acquaintance Caroline L. Scott. She later gave birth to a son and a daughter.

From 1852 until 1854 Harrison read law with a prestigious Cincinnati firm. After being admitted to the bar, in 1854 he moved to Indianapolis and established a practice. The next year, he was appointed as commissioner for the Federal district court of claims. By 1856 he was one of the city's leading attorneys.

Harrison's aversion to slavery guided him to the Republican Party. In 1858 he took over the secretaryship of its State central committee. From 1857 until 1861, he held the elective position of Indianapolis city attorney, and in 1860 won the office of reporter of decisions of the State supreme court (1861-62). Eventually, he compiled *Indiana Reports,* a multivolume collection of State court proceedings.

In 1862, the year after the Civil War began, Harrison helped raise a regiment of volunteer infantry, and quickly rose to the rank of colonel. His strict discipline made him an unpopular brigade commander. For 18 months, his unit guarded sections of the Louisville and Nashville and Nashville and Chattanooga Railroads in Kentucky and Tennessee. In 1864 he ably led his men during Sherman's Atlanta campaign.

After the city's capture, Harrison took leave and returned to Indiana at Gov. Oliver P. Morton's bidding to counter Copperhead, or antiwar, sentiment in the 1864 election. Harrison was also again elected as reporter of the State supreme court (1864-68). He nevertheless returned to service in 1865, was promoted to brevet brigadier general, and rejoined his brigade in the Carolinas after its march through Georgia.

After the war, Harrison resumed his law practice in Indianapolis and adopted Radical Republicanism. In the 1870's he fought against his party's adoption of greenback ideas. He also participated in philanthropic and religious activities. In 1872 he failed to win the nomination for Governor. Four years later, however, because of his excellent reputation, he replaced the party's nominee, who had left the campaign amid charges of corruption, but narrowly lost the race.

During the national railroad strike of 1877, Harrison was appointed to the Indianapolis strike settlement committee, and commanded the militia in the city. The next year, he chaired the Republican State convention. In 1880 he headed the delegation to the national convention, where he played a major role in nominating James A. Garfield. Refusing a Cabinet post, Harrison accepted a seat in the U.S. Senate (1881-87), but was not reelected because the Democrats controlled the Indiana legislature.

In 1888 Harrison obtained the Presidential nomination. Despite powerful business opposition to Democratic attempts to lower tariff rates, incumbent Cleveland received a plurality. But Harrison, utilizing a "front porch" campaign, carried the key States of New York and Indiana, and won the Presidency with a majority of the electoral votes.

Because of the frequent illness of Secretary of State James G. Blaine, Harrison personally shaped much foreign policy. In 1889 Blaine's long-awaited first Pan-American Conference met in Washington and formed an informational organization, later

Benjamin Harrison as a college student.

This poster helped push Harrison into the White House in 1888.

named the Pan-American Union. Faced with German intervention in Samoa, to which the British had acquiesced, Harrison arranged with the two nations for a three-power protectorate. He also obtained an agreement with Britain regarding sealing rights in the Bering Sea.

During Chile's civil war in 1891, a mob attacked some American sailors as a reprisal for detention of a rebel ship in the United States, and in 1892 Harrison demanded and received a Chilean apology and an indemnity. After an 1893 coup, led by former Americans and abetted by U.S. officials and troops, overthrew the Hawaiian Queen, Harrison backed an annexation treaty, late in his term, but new President Cleveland was to withdraw the treaty before Senate ratification.

In domestic affairs, Harrison followed party positions and largely deferred leadership to congressional spokesmen. He believed in civil service reform, but pressure for patronage proved strong. He awarded the Postmaster Generalship to a major campaign contributor, who made wholesale appointments of Republican postmasters. To the chagrin of reformers, Harrison briefly removed civil service guidelines, initiated by Cleveland, to replace Democratic officeholders. Yet, Harrison's extension of the number of classified jobs and appointment of the vocal Theodore Roosevelt to the Civil Service Commission angered many powerful party regulars.

Many of the national controversies during the Harrison administration were linked to Republican championing of the protective tariff and disposition of the resultant large Treasury surpluses. In 1890 Harrison signed the McKinley Tariff, which raised duties an average of 48 percent. The President insisted, however, on adding reciprocity bargaining provisions for foreign nations that provided tariff reductions for U.S. exports.

Congress, while appropriating the first peacetime billion dollar budget, to the dismay of Harrison who favored reduction of taxes, expended the Treasury surplus in the following ways: liberalization of pensions for Union Civil War veterans, their widows, orphans, and dependent parents; heavy expenditures for river and harbor improvements; inauguration of free rural mail delivery; and, partly because of foreign policy considerations, the strengthening of the Navy and the merchant marine, as well as the construction of seacoast fortifications.

Harrison's victory in the State in 1888 was hailed in Madison Square by the New York City *Herald*.

Farmer and laborer grievances—expressed by such organizations as the Knights of Labor, the American Federation of Labor, and the Farmers' Alliances—grew rampant during the Harrison administration. The Sherman Antitrust Act of 1890, which he signed, partially responded to their demands for regulation of monopolies and trusts. But it was not strenuously enforced during this period, and was even effectively used against labor organizations.

The Sherman Silver Purchase Act of 1890, which Harrison approved, attempted to placate the calls of inflationist debtor groups, like the Farmers' Alliances, for free and unlimited silver coinage. But the bill's compromise requirement for modest monthly Treasury purchases of silver proved to be only mildly inflationary. Although creating business and financial apprehension that the weakened gold standard would be abandoned, the bill also did not satisfy those who urged a bimetallic system to check deflation.

In 1889 Harrison opened the Oklahoma District to clamoring homesteaders. Heralding the modern conservation movement, the next year he approved legislation creating several national parks, and the following year set aside more than 13 million acres of public domain for national forest preserves. During his administration, a record number of six States were admitted to the Union. Largely because of the high McKinley Tariff, the Republicans lost control of Congress in 1890, which hurt Harrison's programs. Despite intraparty disputes, 2 years later he was renominated, but Cleveland defeated him and Populist Party candidate James B. Weaver.

Two weeks before the election, Harrison's wife died. After leaving office, he returned to his Indianapolis law practice. He continued to write and speak, including a lecture series at Stanford University in 1894. Several of his speeches were collected in *Views of an Ex-President* (1901), and some of his magazine articles in *This Country of Ours* (1897). He also remained active in his party. In 1896 he married widow Mary Scott Lord Dimmick, a niece of his first wife. This marriage produced one daughter. In 1898-99 Harrison traveled to Europe as chief counsel for Venezuela in its dispute with Great Britain over the boundary of British Guiana. Increasingly, he spoke out on the duties of the wealthy and the evils of imperialistic extremes. He died in 1901.

William McKinley

TWENTY-FIFTH PRESIDENT   1897-1901

A former lawyer, Governor of Ohio, and Congressman, McKinley was the last Civil War veteran to be elected as President. Responding to the clamor of the press and expansionists, he led the Nation through the Spanish-American War and the acquisition of vast overseas territories. Domestically, he espoused high protective tariffs and defended the gold standard. About 6 months into his second term, he became the third Chief Executive to be assassinated.

McKinley, the seventh of nine children, was born in 1843 at Niles, Ohio. Nine years later, his father, an ironmaker, moved to nearby Poland. The youth was educated at local schools and Poland Academy. In 1860 he enrolled at Allegheny College, in Meadville, Pa., but illness and family financial problems forced him to return home after only one term. He then taught at a rural school and clerked in the post office.

In 1861 McKinley enlisted as a private in an Ohio infantry regiment that was to be commanded by Col. and future-President Rutherford B. Hayes. McKinley participated in several battles and by war's end had achieved the rank of brevet major. Upon his return to Ohio, he read law with a Youngstown firm, and in the fall of 1866 entered Albany (N.Y.) Law School. Before graduating, however, the following spring he went back to Ohio. Admitted to the bar later that year, he established a practice in Canton.

McKinley, a Republican, campaigned for his Army friend Hayes in his successful gubernatorial race, and won election as prosecuting attorney of Stark County (1869-71). In the latter year, he married Ida Saxton, daughter of a local banker. Following the early deaths of two daughters, Ida, who suffered from epilepsy after 1873, was to become a semi-invalid and remain so for the rest of her life.

From 1871 to 1875 McKinley practiced law and aided the Republican cause. Service in the U.S. House of Representatives

McKinley conducts "front-porch" campaign at Canton, Ohio, in 1896.

(1877-84 and 1885-91) ensued. During this long tour of duty, McKinley won prominence in State and National party affairs.

Although McKinley was a possible compromise Presidential candidate in the 1888 Republican convention, he resolutely backed Ohio Senator John Sherman, who lost to Benjamin Harrison. During the convention, McKinley caught the attention of Marcus A. Hanna, a wealthy Cleveland businessman who was to become his friend, political mentor, and manager. In 1889 McKinley failed to win the speakership of the U.S. House of Representatives. But he became chairman of the Ways and Means Committee, where he spearheaded the highly protective McKinley Tariff of 1890.

A Democratic gerrymander in Ohio in 1890 cost McKinley reelection, and nationally the Republicans suffered a landslide defeat in the House elections, largely because of their tariff position. But McKinley readily won two terms as Governor (1892-96). In 1892 he chaired the Republican national convention, at

McKinley and his wife, Ida (right), visit his political mentor, Mark Hanna (right, standing), in Thomasville, Georgia. The other people are unidentified.

which he received a considerable number of votes though he lost the nomination to incumbent President Harrison.

In 1896 McKinley easily gained nomination. In a fierce contest on the heels of a depression, Democrat William Jennings Bryan, endorsed by the Populists and renegade Republicans, advocated inflationary silverite policies. Defending the gold standard in a "front porch" campaign, McKinley addressed select delegations at his home in Canton while Hanna directed the nationwide offensive.

Despite Bryan's strength in the West and the South, economic recovery reduced debtor enthusiasm for his inflationary programs, and antisilver Democrats, such as retiring President Cleveland, refused their endorsement. McKinley had the first popular vote majority since 1872, and the Republicans continued the congressional dominance they had gained in 1894 and were not to lose until the elections of 1910.

Postponing monetary reform, McKinley called Congress into special session to enact the Dingley Tariff (1897), which established the highest duties to that date. Although McKinley warned of the danger to the public good from trusts, the number of new ones increased markedly during his administration.

Foreign affairs were McKinley's paramount concern. In 1895 Cuba renewed its sporadic revolt against Spain. Publicizing incidents of Spanish repression, the American "yellow press" and expansionist leaders fostered public sentiment for intervention. At first, backed by some leading businessmen and other anti-imperialists, McKinley sought a diplomatic solution. But early in 1898 negotiations suffered a setback when Spanish Minister Don Enrique Dupuy de Lôme resigned after the newspapers printed a copy of one of his private letters in which he characterized McKinley as weak and vacillating.

About the same time, the U.S. battleship *Maine,* on a courtesy call to Havana, mysteriously exploded and took the lives of 260 men. Blaming Spain, interventionists cried "Remember the Maine." Although Madrid made some concessions on Cuba, McKinley bowed to practically irresistible public and congressional pressure and demanded independence for the island. On April 25, 1898, Congress declared war.

U.S. sea and land invasions of Cuba, Puerto Rico, Guam, and the Philippines quickly brought Spain to her knees. The Treaty of Paris recognized Cuba's independence, and granted Puerto Rico, Guam, and the Philippines to the United States. Countering those people who contended these acquisitions were contrary to national principles and interests, McKinley justified them with economic, military, and humanitarian arguments.

Under McKinley's leadership, in 1898 the United States also annexed Hawaii and occupied Wake Island, and the next year partitioned the Samoan Islands with Germany. Beginning in 1899, Filipino revolutionaries engaged U.S. forces in a bloody but futile guerrilla war for independence. In 1900 McKinley appointed William Howard Taft (later U.S. Chief Executive) as head of a commission that was to set up civil rule for the Philippines.

As the major powers intensified their scramble for influence in China, in 1899 Secretary of State John M. Hay achieved recognition of an "Open Door" policy in that nation. This granted equal trading rights to all countries. During China's Boxer Rebellion (1900), which sought to expel foreigners, McKinley

Republican campaign poster in 1900.

assigned 5,000 U.S. troops to an international expeditionary force that lifted the siege on the Peking Legation Quarter.

In the Caribbean, McKinley established civil government in Puerto Rico under the provisions of the Foraker Act (1900). He encouraged Cuba's beginnings in self-rule while restricting her sovereignty by imposing U.S. rights of intervention.

At home, McKinley's approval of the fiscally conservative Gold Standard Act of 1900 briefly revived the monetary debate. In the Presidential campaign that year, Democrat Bryan spoke out again for free silver and railed against imperialism. But the majority of voters opted for McKinley's "full dinner pail" and a major role in world affairs. He defeated Bryan even more decisively than in 1896.

During his second term, McKinley seemed likely to continue strong overseas involvement. He encouraged Secretary of State Hay's negotiations with Great Britain to terminate restrictions on Central American canal construction set by the Clayton-Bulwer Treaty (1850). In domestic affairs, he hinted at changes in tariff and trust policy. But on September 6, 1901, at the Pan-American Exposition in Buffalo, N.Y., an anarchist shot him. He died 8 days later.

Theodore Roosevelt

Venturesome in spirit as well as intellect, flamboyant in personality, and physically energetic, Roosevelt won the warm affection of the American people and immeasurably expanded Presidential powers. When he took office at the age of 42 upon the assassination of McKinley, he became the youngest Chief Executive in history, and he later decisively gained election to a term of his own. Wielding a "big stick," he exerted U.S. influence in global affairs. His domestic reform program emphasized regulation of business and trusts, protection of the rights of consumers and labor, and advancement of conservation.

The first son and second child of four, Roosevelt was born in 1858 in lower Manhattan. His father was a well-to-do glass importer, merchant, and banker; his mother was of aristocratic Georgian stock. Asthmatic in childhood and always nearsighted, the frail boy was carefully supervised and received private tutoring. Nevertheless, he traveled extensively with his parents, who summered at fashionable Atlantic coast resorts and frequently visited Europe.

Roosevelt early demonstrated interest in reading and natural science. On the other hand, building his body through sports, exercise, and eventually rugged outdoor activity, he became a lifelong champion of physical fitness and devotee of the "strenuous life."

Roosevelt graduated from Harvard University (1876-80), where he was a dedicated student, won membership in Phi Beta Kappa, and participated in boxing. During his senior year, he started *The Naval War of 1812* (1882)—the first of some 40 books and many articles he was to write in the fields of history, politics, and adventure.

The year he graduated, Roosevelt married Alice Hathaway Lee of Boston. They established their home in New York City, though they spent the next summer and fall honeymooning in Europe, during which time he climbed Switzerland's Matterhorn. Meantime, after leaving Harvard, he had attended Columbia Law School for a short while.

Deciding on a political career and gaining the support of various local Republican leaders, Roosevelt next won a seat in the State legislature (1882-84). His independence and zeal for industrial and governmental reform annoyed old-guard politicians, but attracted the attention of newsmen. While heading the New York delegation to the Republican national convention in 1884, he further demonstrated his dislike of machine politics by backing the abortive candidacy of reformer George F. Edmunds. Roosevelt, however, unlike a group of disgruntled "Mugwumps," refused to bolt the party when James G. Blaine was victorious.

Earlier in the year and only hours after his mother's death, Roosevelt's wife had died shortly after the birth of their only child, a daughter. To conquer his sorrow, within a few months he headed back to the Badlands of Dakota Territory, which he had first visited the previous year and where he had invested in a cattle ranch. From then until 1898, he was to reside periodically in the area and expand his landholdings. Living the life of a cowboy, he gained inspiration for several books, such as his multivolume *The Winning of the West* (1889-96).

In 1886 Roosevelt ran third in the New York City mayoralty election—a race he recognized he had almost no chance of winning. Later that year, he traveled to London to marry Edith Kermit Carow, a childhood friend. They established their permanent residence at Sagamore Hill, which he had recently constructed near Oyster Bay, L.I. Edith was to give birth to four sons and one daughter.

Following a 3-year period of writing, part-time residence in Dakota, and political activity, during the years 1889-95, under Presidents Benjamin Harrison and Grover Cleveland, Roosevelt sat on the U.S. Civil Service Commission. Ever a reformer, he figured prominently in expanding the merit system through such means as competitive examinations. He also angered spoils politicians by attacking campaign assessments of public employees. As president of the New York City Board of Police Commissioners (1895-97), he cracked down on police corruption, inaugurated a merit system, and backed social-welfare measures.

Aided by his friend U.S. Senator Henry Cabot Lodge's influence with President McKinley, Roosevelt next served as Assistant

Secretary of the Navy (1897-98), in which office he espoused a strong Navy and manifested an imperialistic attitude. At the outbreak of the Spanish-American War (1898), he resigned to accept a lieutenant-colonelcy in a national volunteer cavalry regiment, the "Rough Riders," which he had helped organize. In Cuba, his bravery vaulted him into the national limelight. Promoted to colonel, he came home a hero.

In the fall of 1898, New York Republican leaders chose Roosevelt as their candidate for the governorship, which he won by a slim margin. But, resenting his reform and social-welfare programs, the State hierarchy maneuvered him into accepting the Vice-Presidential nomination in 1900. He contributed significantly to the heavy Republican victory, and later took over the Presidency upon McKinley's assassination in 1901. Three years hence, he was triumphantly elected over conservative Democrat Alton B. Parker.

Believing the President should be limited only by specific constitutional prohibitions, Roosevelt inaugurated an extensive

This cartoon satirizes the aggressive role played in world affairs by President Theodore Roosevelt, who had earlier headed the New York City Board of Police Commissioners.

reform program that promised a "Square Deal" for labor, capital, and the general public. He initiated many suits against trusts, though he distinguished between "good" and "bad" ones, and encouraged legislation to speed up prosecution.

Reacting to "muck-raking" denunciations of business abuses, Roosevelt was instrumental in enactment of the Pure Food and Drug Act (1906); signed legislation for the inspection of stockyards and packinghouses; and backed the Hepburn Act (1906), which expanded Interstate Commerce Commission control over railroads, express companies, and terminal facilities.

During a coal strike in 1902, Roosevelt made unprecedented use of Presidential influence to pressure mineowners into arbitration with labor. He also forced the railroads to comply with published rate schedules. In 1903 he convinced Congress to establish the Department of Commerce and Labor. When he entertained Booker T. Washington at a White House dinner, the first black man to be accorded this privilege, Roosevelt was roundly criticized in the South. Nevertheless, at Washington's behest, he appointed a few black officeholders.

Despite opposition from business interests and many westerners, Roosevelt also pushed the cause of conservation. His National Conservation Conference (1908) focused the public's attention on problems in this field and resulted in several beneficial programs. He also added about 150 million acres to the national forests, set aside extensive coal reserves and land for potential public dam sites, supported irrigation projects, founded many wildlife preserves, and expanded the number of national parks and monuments.

In international affairs, Roosevelt followed the principle "Speak softly and carry a big stick." He viewed the Navy as a key to imperial power, and in 1907-9 sent a fleet on a world cruise to impress Congress and foreign nations. To quicken naval movements, he obtained Senate approval of the second Hay-Pauncefote Treaty (1901). It removed earlier British-United States restrictions on unilateral construction of a Central American canal, but required that all nations enjoy equal access to it and pay equal tolls.

Two years later, Roosevelt aided a rebellion in Colombia that created the Republic of Panama and led to U.S. control of the Panama Canal Zone. He also began construction of the canal

Roosevelt delivering a speech in New Castle, Wyoming, probably in 1903.

(1904-14) under the Army Corps of Engineers. While inspecting its early stages, he became the first President to leave U.S. soil while in office.

In response to the threat of armed intervention by various European nations on behalf of their creditors in Venezuela and the Dominican Republic, the President enunciated the Roosevelt Corollary (1904) to the Monroe Doctrine. It asserted the right of the United States to intervene in the affairs of other hemispheric countries.

President Theodore Roosevelt with Russian and Japanese envoys on board the Presidential yacht, the *Mayflower,* at Portsmouth, New Hampshire, in 1905. This mediation, for which he was to win the Nobel Peace Prize, ended the Russo-Japanese War.

Roosevelt also spurred settlement in 1903 of British, Canadian, and United States boundary claims in Alaska. For his role in negotiating the Treaty of Portsmouth (1905), which concluded the Russo-Japanese War, he became the first American recipient of the Nobel Peace Prize (1906). That year, he induced France to participate in a 13-nation conference that discussed the role of various European powers in Morocco; and appointed a provisional governor of Cuba, who helped that country resolve civil strife.

To ease strained relations with Japan, in 1907 Roosevelt convinced a San Francisco school board to abandon its newly inaugurated policy of segregating Oriental children. The next year, he won Japanese agreement to U.S. immigration restrictions and to an "Open Door" pact in China.

Pledged to leave office after his second term, Roosevelt backed William Howard Taft as his successor. In 1909-10 Roosevelt went on an African safari, toured Europe, lectured at the Sorbonne and Oxford University, represented the United States at the funeral of King Edward VII of Britain, and returned to a triumphal parade in New York City. At Sagamore Hill, Roosevelt continued writing.

Feeling that President Taft had abandoned his policies, Roosevelt sought the Presidential nomination in 1912. When Taft became the candidate, after a bitter pre-convention struggle, Roosevelt bolted the party and ran on the Progressive, or "Bull Moose," ticket. Surviving an assassination attempt in Milwaukee, he gained more votes than Taft, but the Republican split gave the election to Democrat Woodrow Wilson.

In 1912 Roosevelt was named as president of the American Historical Association. Illness forced him to return home from an exploration (1913-14) of a branch of the Amazon River in Brazil. He criticized Wilson's neutrality at the outbreak of World War I (1914-18). Convinced that the Progressive Party lacked a future, in 1916 Roosevelt refused its Presidential nomination. He supported Republican Charles Evans Hughes, but Wilson was reelected.

When the United States entered the war in 1917, Roosevelt volunteered to raise a regiment, but Wilson refused his offer. Although bitter, Roosevelt joined Liberty Loan drives. After the war, in which one of his sons died and two were badly wounded, he opposed the League of Nations. While some Republicans were discussing the possibility of his Presidential candidacy in 1920, he died in his 61st year in 1919.

William Howard Taft

TWENTY-SEVENTH PRESIDENT   1909-13

Although he lacked the charisma of Theodore Roosevelt, who had handpicked him for the office, President Taft scored many solid domestic gains. But, always more a jurist than a politician, in time he alienated his mentor and the "progressive" element in the Republican Party. This cost him reelection. Achieving a lifelong dream, he was later appointed as Chief Justice of the United States, the only Chief Executive ever to sit on the Supreme Court. Before becoming President, he had served as Governor-General of the Philippines and as Secretary of War.

Taft was born in 1857 at Mount Auburn (now part of Cincinnati), Ohio. His father, Alphonso, was a well-to-do lawyer-judge who was to serve under President Grant as Secretary of War and Attorney General; and under Arthur as Minister to Austria-Hungary and Russia. Young Taft was the third son in a family of six.

William Howard was educated in the public schools, and graduated second in his class from Woodward High School (1870-74). He won similar distinction at Yale (1874-78), where he was class salutatorian. The summer of his graduation, he read law with his father's firm, and in the fall enrolled at Cincinnati Law School. He soon also took a job as court reporter for the Cincinnati *Commercial.* In 1880 he took his degree and was admitted to the bar.

About this time, Taft began to take part in Republican activities. As a reward, he was appointed as assistant prosecutor of Hamilton County (1881-82). President Arthur then designated him as district collector of internal revenue (1882-83). During the summer and fall of 1883, he visited his diplomat parents in Vienna and traveled about Europe.

From late 1883 until 1887, Taft practiced law, after 1885 serving as assistant county solicitor; and participated in politics. In 1886 he married Helen Herron, daughter of a leading State Republican. The couple were to have two sons and one daughter. The year after his marriage, Taft was named to a vacancy on the Ohio superior

court. The following year, retaining his seat, he won the only election he ever took part in except for the Presidency. He held the judgeship until 1890.

Taft next served as U.S. Solicitor General (1890-92) and briefly as Acting Attorney General under President Benjamin Harrison. At this time, he became acquainted with Civil Service Commissioner Theodore Roosevelt. During the period 1892-1900, Taft was Federal judge for the Sixth Circuit (Ohio, Kentucky, Michigan, and Tennessee). Although he often ruled in favor of labor and against industry, he gained an antilabor reputation because of antistrike injunctions he issued. While on the bench, he also taught part time at and was dean of the Cincinnati Law School (1896-1900).

After President McKinley promised him a seat on the Supreme Court when a vacancy occurred, in 1900 Taft headed a civilian governmental commission in the Philippines, which the United States had acquired at the end of the Spanish-American War (1898). Although originally averse to annexation, he believed the Filipinos required training before independence and that this could not be accomplished until all insurrection ceased. As the islands' Governor-General (1901-4), he encouraged limited self-government; reformed the court system; built roads, harbors, and schools; improved the economy; and fostered land reform. Feeling responsible for the inhabitants, he twice unselfishly refused President Roosevelt's offer of a Supreme Court appointment.

Early in 1904 Taft became Secretary of War, though he continued his patronage of the Philippines. A talented administrator and conciliator, he also handled many special assignments for Roosevelt. Taft superintended early construction of the Panama Canal; went on a diplomatic mission to Tokyo; and, as provisional governor of Cuba, helped that country end internal strife.

Although Taft undoubtedly preferred a Supreme Court judgeship, in 1908 his family and President Roosevelt persuaded him to accept the Republican Presidential nomination. Taft disliked campaigning and did not possess Roosevelt's magnetism, but his conservative judicial style appealed to many voters, and he defeated William Jennings Bryan by more than a million votes.

During his single term, Taft initiated more antitrust suits than Roosevelt, and was also active in conservation. Taft obtained legislation removing millions of acres of Federal land from public sale; rescinded his predecessor's order to reserve certain lands as

Campaign poster, election of 1908.

possible public dam sites, but ordered a study to determine what acreage should be protected; formed a Bureau of Mines in the Department of the Interior to safeguard mineral deposits; and supported a bond issue to undertake irrigation projects.

Furthermore, Taft backed extension of Interstate Commerce Commission power over the communications industry and in establishment of railroad rates; supported a modest tax on corporate earnings; advocated economy in Government; formed a commission to study Federal finances; signed campaign reform legislation; extended the Civil Service merit system; created the parcel post and postal savings systems; and oversaw creation of a Children's Bureau in the Department of Commerce and Labor. He also urged and saw passage of the 16th amendment to the Constitution, which authorized a Federal tax on personal income. Arizona and New Mexico, the last of the 48 contiguous States, were admitted to the Union during his administration.

Flanked by Secret Service men, President and Mrs. Taft ride back from the Capitol to the White House on March 4, 1909.

Despite these accomplishments, Taft's legalistic concept of his office and his increasing reliance on Republican congressional leadership soon alienated reformers. He hoped for compromise to reduce tariffs, but defended the Payne-Aldrich Tariff (1909). This outraged progressives who sought rate reductions as a further challenge to the trusts. Taft was accused of being anticonservationist because he dismissed Forest Service chief Gifford Pinchot, a Roosevelt ally, after Pinchot had quarreled publicly on policy matters with him and Secretary of the Interior Richard A. Ballinger.

Taft's conduct of foreign affairs was also criticized. Included were his "dollar diplomacy" in the Far East and Latin America, U.S. inaction in the face of Japanese and Russian penetration in Manchuria, and American intervention to insure political and financial order in Nicaragua. Then, too, Taft suffered some stunning diplomatic setbacks. He pushed a tariff reciprocity treaty with Canada through Congress, but Canadians rejected the measure, at least partly because they feared annexation. With France and Great Britain, he negotiated agreements to arbitrate international disputes, but the Senate amended the treaties to such a degree that the embarrassed Taft rescinded them.

In 1912, contrary to the amicable spirit indicated by this cartoon, the estranged Roosevelt and Taft contested bitterly for delegates prior to the party convention. Taft was victorious.

Accusing Taft of abandoning meaningful reform, Theodore Roosevelt sought to regain the Republican nomination in 1912, but lost to Taft. Roosevelt left the party and became the Progressive ("Bull Moose") candidate. This schism assured the election of Woodrow Wilson.

Taft returned to his legal career. From 1913 until 1921, he held a chair in constitutional law at Yale University. When the World War broke out in Europe in 1914, he at first favored neutrality. In 1916 he backed Republican candidate Charles Evans Hughes. Later, Taft aided the U.S. war effort as cochairman of the National War Labor Board (1918-19). With certain reservations, he supported President Wilson on the League of Nations.

Taft also served as an official of various philanthropic and educational institutions, including the American Red Cross, Yale University, and Hampton Institute. His writings and lectures were published in books, magazines, and newspapers.

In 1921 President Harding fulfilled Taft's long-cherished ambition by designating him as Chief Justice of the Supreme Court (1921-30), in which position he served industriously and expedited the flow of Court business. In 1930, a month after he retired, he died in Washington, D.C.

Woodrow Wilson

TWENTY-EIGHTH PRESIDENT   1913-21

An idealistic former educator and Governor,
President Wilson considered himself the steward of
the people. Toward that end, he proposed a reform-
oriented "New Freedom" domestic program, but he
soon faced serious international problems. During his
second term, he reluctantly abandoned neutrality in
World War I, but then led the United States into the
conflict on a crusade to "make the world safe for
democracy," and figured prominently in the
peacemaking. Yet the Senate refused to ratify the
Treaty of Versailles, which included provisions for a
League of Nations. And Wilson, afflicted with a
stroke, was incapacitated for his last 17 months in
office.

The eldest son and third child in a family of four, (Thomas)
Woodrow Wilson was born in 1856 at the manse of the First
Presbyterian Church, Staunton, Va., where his father was pastor.
During Woodrow's boyhood, Reverend Wilson held several posts in
the South. Shortly after the youth's first birthday, the family
moved to Augusta, Ga. In 1870 his father began teaching at a
seminary in Columbia, S.C., and for the next few years also held a
nearby pastorate. Parents, tutors, and local schools provided
Woodrow with his early education.

In 1873 Wilson matriculated at Davidson (N.C.) College, a small
Presbyterian institution. The following year, illness forced him to
rejoin his family at their new home in Wilmington, N.C. He next
won a B.A. at the College of New Jersey (present Princeton
University), which he attended during the period 1875-79. He was
not only a serious student, but also an able orator and debater.

Upon graduation, Wilson entered the University of Virginia Law
School. Late in 1880, however, ill health once again forced him to
go back to Wilmington, where he carried on his study. In 1882 he
received his degree, was admitted to the Georgia bar, and set up a
law practice with a friend in Atlanta. Before long, however, he lost
interest in the profession.

In the fall of 1883, Wilson enrolled at the graduate school of Johns Hopkins University in Baltimore. Two years later, his first book, *Congressional Government,* was published. That same year, he married Ellen L. Axson, daughter of a Presbyterian minister. She was to bear three daughters.

From 1885 until 1888, Wilson held a professorship of history at Bryn Mawr (Pa.) College. During this time, in 1886, he won his Ph. D. in political science from Johns Hopkins. He next taught history and political economy (1888–90) at Wesleyan University, Middletown, Conn. He then became professor of jurisprudence and political economy at the College of New Jersey (Princeton University after 1896). By 1902, he had authored nine books and 32 articles. During the interim, he had refused three offers of the University of Virginia presidency.

In 1902 Princeton's board of trustees unanimously chose Wilson as president. His fight to "democratize" the institution met with opposition from many faculty and alumni, but brought him some national recognition and encouraged an interest in politics. In 1907 State Democratic leaders considered him as a U.S. Senate nominee, but he withdrew after reformers attacked him as a machine spokesman.

Identifying himself with moderate progressivism, in the fall of 1909 Wilson was elected as head of the Short Ballot Association, a national organization dedicated to improving local government. Further broadening his reputation, he also began to speak out against trusts and high Republican-inspired tariffs.

In 1910 Wilson resigned from Princeton to become the Democratic gubernatorial candidate. Asserting his independence of party leaders and refusing to make patronage pledges, he campaigned as a reformer and won election by a wide margin. The Democrats also won enough votes to control the legislature. Wilson blocked the legislative selection of a party-backed candidate to the U.S. Senate, and pushed through significant measures. Included were those dealing with direct primary and other election reforms, regulation of utilities, pure food protection, woman and child labor restrictions, and employers' liability. When Republicans took over the legislature in 1912, Wilson refused to compromise and vetoed 57 bills.

In pursuit of the Presidential nomination, late in 1911 Wilson began a nationwide series of speeches. The national convention

Wilson (standing foreground, third from right) and members of the Alligator Club while he was a student at Princeton.

deadlocked the next year and nominated him on the 46th ballot. He then stumped the country and expounded his "New Freedom." This program emphasized restoration of the Government to the people through control of special-privilege groups by the initiation of various reforms, especially in the fields of tariff revision and the regulation of trusts and banks. Benefiting from the split between Republican William Howard Taft and Progressive Theodore Roosevelt, Wilson won only 42 percent of the popular vote but carried 40 of the 48 States.

As President, Wilson felt he needed to exert strong leadership to fulfill his self-conceived role as a direct representative of the people. He became the first Chief Executive since John Adams to address

Governor Wilson and family, probably during the Presidential campaign of 1912. Left to right: Margaret, Mrs. Ellen L. Wilson, Eleanor, Jessie, and Wilson.

joint congressional sessions; inaugurated regularly scheduled press conferences; championed substantially lowered rates in the Underwood Tariff (1913), which included the first constitutional Federal income tax; fought for the Federal Reserve Act (1913) to stabilize and regulate currency through regional governmental banks controlled by a board of Presidential appointees; established the Federal Trade Commission (1914) to prevent unfair business practices; strengthened antitrust legislation; and recognized the legality of labor unions and their right to strike.

Meanwhile, in 1914, Wilson's wife had died. The next year, he married widow Edith Bolling Galt. The couple had no children.

Before the 1916 election, Wilson signed bills for farm loans, the welfare of seamen, an 8-hour day for railroad workers, and child labor restrictions, though the Supreme Court later declared some of this legislation to be unconstitutional.

Wilson had not been in office too long before Latin American and European affairs captured his attention. In 1914, after incidents at Tampico and Veracruz, Mexico, he sent in troops that captured the latter city, but mediators prevented the outbreak of a full-scale war. Two years later, he dispatched a military expedition into Mexico in retaliation against raids that revolutionary Pancho Villa had made into Texas and New Mexico.

In the Caribbean, Wilson continued the traditional American role of intervention. Mainly to quell revolutionary strife and protect U.S. interests, in 1915 and 1916 he deployed military forces to Haiti and the Dominican Republic, respectively, and established virtual protectorates. In 1917 he acquired the Virgin Islands from Denmark.

The situation in Europe was far more serious. After the outbreak of World War I in 1914, Wilson proclaimed U.S. neutrality. It proved to be difficult to maintain. The President protested to Great Britain over her blockade against nonbelligerent maritime trade. But Germany's actions were even more alarming. To halt the flow of materiel to France and Britain, beginning early in 1915 her submarines (U-boats) sank neutral ships without warning. Wilson's complaints went unheeded. After the sinking of the *Lusitania,* a British liner carrying many Americans, Wilson further protested and Germany relented. Following another similar episode, in the spring of 1916 he threatened to break off diplomatic relations and Germany again backed down.

During the 1916 election campaign, defending his domestic program and employing the slogan "He kept us out of war," Wilson eked out a narrow victory in the electoral college over Republican Charles Evans Hughes.

In an attempt at mediation, early in 1917 Wilson proposed to the European powers a "peace without victory" plan that he felt would insure a just and equitable end to the conflict, but both sides were reluctant to negotiate. Meantime, most Americans had become convinced that Germany and her allies were the aggressors. Events soon underscored this position. The Germans launched an unrestricted submarine offensive in late January 1917 on the gamble that it would crush the Allies before the expected United States entry could affect the outcome.

After Wilson severed diplomatic relations the next month, anti-German feeling in the country increased because of the publication of the Zimmermann Note, a secret proposal for an alliance of Mexico, Japan, and Germany against the United States. Following the sinking of more American vessels, in April 1917 Congress declared war. Wilson, who viewed it as a moral crusade to preserve freedom and democracy against German autocracy, directed the

President Wilson, leader of the U.S. delegation, receives a tumultuous welcome as he arrives in Paris on December 14, 1918, to attend the Peace Conference that ended World War I. Next to him is French President Raymond Poincaré.

mobilization of the Armed Forces and the production of military materiel that helped bring Allied victory in November 1918.

Earlier that same year, distressed by Bolshevik, or Red (Communist), advances in the Russian civil war among other reasons, Wilson had supported Allied military intervention to aid pro-democratic Russians. It lasted until 1920.

The World War I armistice was partly based on Wilson's "Fourteen Points," which he had proposed early in 1918 as the basis for a lasting peace. Applauded by many Europeans, late that same year Wilson and his mostly Democratic delegation arrived at the Paris Peace Conference. Although he was forced to compromise on parts of his plan, he obtained European commitments to a League of Nations, which he trusted would resolve future international differences. Provisions for the league were incorporated into the Treaty of Versailles. These efforts were to win Wilson the Nobel Peace Prize in 1919.

That summer, Wilson presented the treaty to the Senate for ratification. Even though he faced a Republican majority there following the 1918 elections, he adamantly advocated unconditional adoption of the treaty and the league. In September he launched a "whistle-stop" tour to build up public support for ratification. Yet the Senate never ratified the treaty, and it was not until President Harding took over from Wilson that a joint congressional resolution formally ended the war. The latter's uncompromising stance was not the only reason for the Senate's lack of cooperation. Also involved were partisanship and the return of isolationist sentiment.

In October 1919 a stroke incapacitated Wilson, and he remained under the protective care of his wife until Harding took over the reins of Government in March 1921.

Before Wilson was stricken, he and the Nation had become fearful of the rise of domestic Communism as well as the outbreak of labor unrest and political agitation. As a result, Attorney General A. Mitchell Palmer arrested many "radicals" and deported some of them.

In 1920 Republican Warren G. Harding swamped James M. Cox, who supported the League of Nations. During retirement, Wilson never recovered his health. His wife ministered to him at their recently purchased home in Washington, D.C. Although he joined a law firm, he never practiced. He died in 1924.

Warren G. Harding

TWENTY-NINTH PRESIDENT   1921-23

Harding, the only newspaper editor who ever rose to the Presidency, closely allied himself with the conservatives in his party. In foreign affairs, he rejected U.S. membership in the League of Nations, but hosted the international Washington Conference, which fostered naval disarmament. Domestically, to ease the social and economic dislocations created by the end of World War I, he advocated "normalcy"—a return to the simplicity and quietude of an earlier America. But the corruption of a number of his appointees tarnished his administration. Feeling perplexed and betrayed, he died in the middle of his term before the scandals were fully exposed.

Harding was born in 1865 on a farm at Corsica (Blooming Grove Township), a rural town in north-central Ohio, the region that was to be his home until he entered national politics. Five years later, the family moved to Caledonia. There, Warren's father, who had been a teacher as well as a farmer, practiced homeopathic medicine. The youth, who was the eldest of eight children, attended public schools. His employment included work as a printer's devil for the *Argus.*

Harding won his B.S. degree from Ohio Central College at Iberia (1879-82). During these years, besides holding temporary jobs, he edited the school newspaper and yearbook, played in the band, and participated in debates. In 1882 his parents moved to Marion, where he soon joined them. He taught one term at a rural school, briefly studied law, sold insurance, and then went to work as a reporter and general assistant at the weekly *Democratic Mirror.* In 1884 he and two partners purchased for $300 the *Star,* a four-page weekly that was close to bankruptcy. Inside of 2 years, Harding bought out his associates.

At first, Harding participated in all phases of newspaper production. But, as his paper turned into a daily and circulation grew along with the town, he became a prosperous publisher and influential civic leader. He held directorships in a bank, lumber

company, and telephone exchange; served as trustee of a Baptist church; and figured prominently in local charities and fraternal organizations.

In 1891 Harding married Florence Kling DeWolfe, the divorced daughter of a local banker. They moved into a home they had constructed the year before in anticipation of their marriage, which proved to be childless. About this time, Harding became seriously interested in politics and joined the Republican Party. In 1892 the voters rejected him as county auditor, but 3 years later awarded him the office. He next sat in the State senate (1899-1903), where he became floor leader, and then held the position of Lieutenant Governor (1904-6).

For the next 4 years, Harding concentrated mainly on his newspaper business. In 1910, by a wide margin, he lost a bid for the governorship. Two years later, he presented the nominating speech for President Taft at the Republican national convention. Harding next served in the U.S. Senate (1915-21). In 1916 he chaired the Republican convention and delivered the keynote address.

When the 1920 convention deadlocked, party leaders picked Harding, who was backed by Ohio politician-lobbyist Harry M. Daugherty, as the compromise Presidential nominee. Conducting essentially a "front-porch" campaign, he offered voters a soothing formula for a return to "normalcy" and the restoration of peace and prosperity from the tumult of World War I and the 1920 economic panic. Democrat James M. Cox crusaded for U.S. participation in the League of Nations, but Harding's vague pronouncements on the subject could appeal to both its supporters and enemies. He and running mate Calvin Coolidge won more than 60 percent of the popular vote.

Many administration programs were directed by Republican congressional spokesmen and such able Cabinet members as Secretaries of State, Commerce, and Treasury, Charles Evans Hughes, Herbert C. Hoover, and Andrew W. Mellon. Unfortunately, some of Harding's Cabinet appointees and other officials proved to be corrupt. He signed measures that ended wartime economic controls; cut taxes, particularly for corporations; created the Bureau of the Budget and Veterans' Bureau; reimposed protective tariffs; and strictly limited immigration.

In international affairs, Harding and Secretary of State Hughes viewed his election as a mandate against membership in the

During the 1920 Presidential election, Democrat James M. Cox waged a vigorous campaign, while Harding used basically a "front-porch" approach.

League of Nations or European collective security arrangements. Yet, in response to a Senate resolution urging an international disarmament meeting, Harding convened the Washington (D.C.) Conference (1921-22). Five of the major powers in attendance—the United States, Great Britain, Japan, Italy, and France—set a ratio of capital warships, restricted their tonnage and armament, and limited the use of submarines. Other agreements reached among representatives of the various Nations present outlawed gas warfare, affirmed territorial claims in the Pacific, and guaranteed the "Open Door" policy in China and her territorial integrity and independence.

President Harding (just right of rear center) picnics with Thomas Edison (second to left of Harding), Henry Ford (second to right of Harding), and other notables.

By 1923, though many people praised Harding for these diplomatic achievements and for reviving prosperity, his administration faced mounting difficulties. Democratic gains in the 1922 midterm elections and Republican party schism cost him effective control of the Congress. Worse, insistent rumors that high officeholders were using their positions for personal enrichment began to spread. These complaints eventually centered on graft in the Veterans' Bureau and in the Office of Alien Property Custodian; and Interior Secretary Albert B. Fall's leasing of naval

One of the highlights of foreign affairs in Harding's administration was the Washington Conference (1921-22). He is shown here addressing the delegates.

oil reserves at Teapot Dome, Wyo., and Elk Hills, Calif., to private interests.

Harding apparently felt responsible for the wrongdoings of his appointees, but he died before the full extent of the scandals became public knowledge. During a tour of the West in 1923, he received information detailing the magnitude of the corruption. But he became ill in Alaska and passed away at San Francisco on the return trip. Later, several key administration figures were fined, imprisoned, or forced to resign.

Calvin Coolidge

THIRTIETH PRESIDENT   1923-29

**Sworn in as President upon Harding's death,
Coolidge continued on for a full elected term in his
own right. A New Englander who embodied the
legendary Yankee qualities of honesty, thrift,
solemnity, and taciturnity, he restored confidence in
Government after the exposure of the Harding
scandals and symbolized stability during a period of
drastic social and economic changes. He held that
any increase in Federal governmental activities would
endanger the prosperity that prevailed and destroy
individual freedom and initiative.**

Born on Independence Day 1872 in Plymouth (Plymouth Notch), Vt., John Calvin Coolidge, Jr., was the only son and the eldest of two children from the first marriage of his father, a storekeeper, postmaster, notary public, and justice of the peace. Young Coolidge eventually dropped his first name and the "Jr." suffix. When he was 12 years old, his mother died. About 7 years later, his father remarried.

Calvin attended a district elementary school and graduated from high school, the private Black River Academy in nearby Ludlow, in 1890. After illness delayed his plans for college, in the spring of 1891 he studied at St. Johnsbury (Vt.) Academy. That fall, he entered Amherst (Mass.) College and 4 years later took a B.A. degree with honors. He then read law in Northampton, Mass. After being admitted to the bar in 1897, he established a practice there.

Before long, Coolidge became active in politics on behalf of the Republican Party, which he came to serve as a local official. During the period 1899-1904, he held the city offices of councilman, solicitor, and court clerk. The next year, he married Grace A. Goodhue, another former Vermonter, who taught at a Northampton school for the deaf. The couple were to have two sons.

In 1907-8 Coolidge served in the lower house of the State legislature. The following year, he returned to his law practice. He was mayor of Northampton in 1910-11. From 1912 until 1915 he sat in the upper house of the legislature, where he rose to the

Governor Coolidge, his wife, and two sons, Calvin (left) and John (right).

presidency. Three consecutive terms as Lieutenant Governor (1916-18) followed. In 1918 Coolidge won the governorship. During the Boston police strike of 1919, the same year he abandoned his law practice, he gained nationwide recognition when he deployed the National Guard to control crime and maintain order. That fall, he was reelected as Governor by a large margin.

The next year, the Republican national convention nominated Coolidge as Vice President on the soon-to-be victorious Harding ticket. When the latter passed away in 1923, Coolidge was visiting his family in Vermont. His father administered the oath of office to him in the home where he had passed his boyhood.

As the scandals of the Harding administration surfaced, Coolidge encouraged governmental prosecution of offenders. This action and his personal integrity restored public confidence in the Presidency and the Republican Party. He was nominated for reelection in 1924 and won with the promise of a continuation of

Campaign song in 1924.

"Coolidge prosperity." He captured more than 54 percent of the popular vote in defeating Democrat John W. Davis and Progressive Robert M. La Follette.

Coolidge's emphasis on traditional moral and economic precepts reassured people in a time of social flux. Although affluence was unprecedented, the Ku Klux Klan perpetrated acts of violence, prohibition violations were common, and some segments of the population frowned on traditional morality.

Coolidge sent few pieces of legislation to Congress, maintained that Federal programs threatened individual freedom and initiative, and pledged maintenance of the *status quo*. He vetoed a proposed Federal power project at Muscle Shoals on the Tennessee River; slowed antitrust actions; blocked plans to subsidize farmers, who had suffered from a depression since the beginning of the decade; and advocated tax cuts, governmental economy, and high protective tariffs. In 1924 he signed a bill that set strict quotas on immigration, which favored entry from Northern Europe.

In the realm of foreign policy, Coolidge opposed international agreements to cancel foreign debts, stabilize currency, and reduce tariffs—though he usually deferred to his Secretaries of State, Charles Evans Hughes and Frank B. Kellogg. The latter sponsored the Kellogg-Briand Pact (1928), a multinational agreement to outlaw war. On the other hand, though Coolidge and Congress favored U.S. participation in the World Court, they imposed restrictions that ruled out formal American membership. At the invitation of the President of Cuba, Coolidge addressed the Sixth Inter-American Conference (1928), in Havana.

A reluctant conversationalist, Coolidge sometimes seemed remote. Yet, demonstrating his accessibility, he was the last President who held regular White House receptions for the general citizenry. Seeming to enjoy the ceremonial and symbolic aspects of office, he posed for a multitude of photographs with diverse groups, delivered many speeches, and received scores of delegations.

Despite Coolidge's continued popularity, he chose not to run for reelection in 1928 and retired to Northampton the next year—just a few months before the Wall Street Crash and the start of the Great Depression. In 1929 his autobiography appeared serially in a magazine and in book form. From 1930 to 1931, in a daily syndicated newspaper column, he attacked governmental economic interference and defended self-reliance. He also served as

President Coolidge signs the Kellogg-Briand Peace Pact in January 1929. One of its progenitors was Secretary of State Frank B. Kellogg, sitting to the right of Coolidge.

director of the New York Life Insurance Company, chairman of the Nonpartisan Railroad Commission, trustee of Amherst College and the National Geographic Society, president of the American Antiquarian Society, and honorary head of the Foundation for the Blind. He died in 1933 at Northampton.

Herbert C. Hoover

THIRTY-FIRST PRESIDENT 1929-33

An international mining engineer-businessman who had been Secretary of Commerce and won acclaim for his humanitarian efforts during World War I, Chief Executive Hoover faced the severe domestic problems created by a worldwide economic depression. Usually frowning on direct Federal relief projects, which he argued would endanger private initiative, he made unprecedented use of governmental powers to achieve economic recovery. Nevertheless, the worsening depression doomed his reelection. In retirement, he continued his humanitarian endeavors, and chaired commissions that formulated major Government reorganizations.

The second child in a family of three, Hoover was born in 1874 at West Branch, Iowa. Six years later, his father, a blacksmith and farm implement salesman, died. For 8 months beginning in the summer of 1881, Herbert stayed with an uncle, Laban Miles, an Indian agent in Indian Territory (present Oklahoma). In 1884 Mrs. Hoover, a Quaker minister, died, and relatives agreed to raise her orphaned children separately. Herbert briefly resided with an uncle, Allen Hoover, who farmed nearby.

In 1885 Herbert moved to Newberg, Oreg., to live with another uncle, Dr. Henry J. Minthorn, a physician and businessman. Hoover briefly attended public school and then enrolled in the first class of the Pacific Academy (present George Fox College), where his uncle was superintendent. Three years later, in 1888, Hoover graduated. That same year, the Minthorns moved to Salem, Oreg. Herbert served as office boy for his uncle, who ran a land business; learned to type and keep books; and attended business school at night.

In 1891, when Hoover was not quite 17 years of age, he matriculated at the newly opened Stanford University, Palo Alto, Calif. While specializing in geology and mining engineering, he managed the baseball and football teams and held various part-time jobs, including two summers of work for the U.S. Geological

Survey. In 1895 he was awarded a B.A. degree, and spent the summer again working for the survey.

That fall, unable to procure a professional position, Hoover worked as a miner in Nevada. Early the following year, he went to San Francisco and managed to find a job as an aide in a mining engineering firm. In 1897 his employers, who were impressed with his technical competence and budding executive skills, recommended him for a position in western Australia. In 1897-98 he managed gold extraction operations there for a British firm.

Hoover next arranged to enter the employ of the Chinese Government as a mining engineer-consultant. Before going to China, early in 1899 he returned to California and married his university sweetheart, Lou Henry, daughter of a Monterey, Calif., banker, who was to bear two sons. The couple sailed the next day. For the next two decades, they were to share an adventurous life on several continents.

In 1900, during China's Boxer Rebellion, directed primarily against foreigners, Hoover received his first taste of war and relief activities. He helped Tientsin's besieged defenders by taking charge of barricade construction and the distribution of food and water. He subsequently worked briefly for a private concern in China. In 1901 he headed back to the United States.

During the early 1900's, Hoover gained international renown for developing mines and managing other industrial projects in at least a dozen countries. From 1901 until 1908 he held a junior partnership in the firm he had earlier worked for in Australia, and from the latter year until 1914 operated his own mining consultant business. By the age of 40 he was a multimillionaire.

Upon the outbreak of World War I in 1914, Hoover, who was then visiting England, at the request of the U.S. Ambassador voluntarily headed the American Relief Committee (1914-15), which helped Americans stranded in Europe by the war. To distribute food, clothing, and medicine to war-ravaged Belgian and French civilians, he directed the Commission for Relief in Belgium (1915-18), and arranged with Allied and German officials to distribute these supplies on both sides of the lines.

When the United States entered the war in 1917, President Wilson called Hoover home to manage the Food Administration (1914-19). He increased production and, in order to allocate American food surpluses to Europe, persuaded the public to cut

Herbert Hoover (standing, left) in Wilson's War Council during World War I. President Wilson is seated (center). James Garfield (standing, right) was the son and namesake of another Chief Executive.

consumption through voluntary rationing, known as "Hooverizing."

After the fighting ended, Hoover attended the Paris Peace Conference (1919) as an economic adviser to the U.S. delegation, and once again oversaw relief and reconstruction efforts in many nations, at first through official aid programs and later through voluntary agencies. These efforts were notable in Central and Eastern Europe, including the Soviet Union.

While Hoover was spending much of his time in Europe, in 1919-21, his wife supervised construction of a home near the Stanford campus. He had been appointed to its board of trustees in 1912, and was to maintain a lifelong interest in its affairs. His collection of wartime documents and other archival materials became the basis of the school's Hoover Institution on War, Revolution, and Peace.

Hoover's unselfish services in Europe endeared him to both parties, but in 1919 he committed himself to the Republicans. The next year, at the national convention he received a few votes for the Presidential nomination. He next served as Secretary of Commerce (1921-28) in the Harding and Coolidge administrations.

In 1928, after Coolidge refused to seek renomination, the national convention nominated Hoover for President on the first ballot. Pledging to continue prosperity and enforce prohibition, he competed against Democrat Alfred E. Smith, the first Roman Catholic candidate chosen by a major party. In a decisive victory that carried him into his first public elective office, Hoover carried much of the traditionally Democratic South. He was the first Chief Executive born west of the Mississippi and the first elected from California.

Hoover immediately called a special session of Congress to deal with tariff revision and the economic hardships that had been plaguing farmers for a decade. To guard home markets from foreign competition, Congress passed and Hoover unhappily signed the highly protective Hawley-Smoot Tariff (1930). Rejecting farm subsidies, instead in 1929 he convinced Congress to establish the Federal Farm Board. It sought to encourage price stabilization through agricultural cooperatives, the purchase by Government corporations of various produce, and the enhancement of marketing efficiency.

Hoover soon faced a far graver crisis—an economic depression. In 1929 the Wall Street stock market crashed, and the economy quickly collapsed. To prevent further decline, Hoover called on labor to hold down wages and on industry to maintain payrolls as well as production. Along with calling on Congress to balance the Federal budget, he urged it to enact a tax cut and make larger allocations for public building programs.

By 1931 the continuance of international economic distress had intensified the situation in the United States. As a way to ease European ills, Hoover through diplomatic channels arranged for a 1-year moratorium on the payment of reparations and inter-Allied war debts.

The Hoover administration was beset with many problems, foremost of which was the economic depression.

A proponent of individualism and self-reliance, Hoover argued that massive Federal public doles would undermine the country's moral fiber. He believed that relief for the indigent and unemployed should mainly come from volunteer charities and State and local governments. As the crisis worsened, he and Congress undertook a broad Federal program to stimulate business recovery. They established the Reconstruction Finance Corporation (1932) to grant loans to financial institutions and businesses, set up a home loan bank system, awarded funds to States and localities for relief and public works, authorized the Federal Reserve System to make loans to businesses and industrial concerns, and fostered governmental economy.

Hoover was a dedicated humanitarian throughout his life. Polish youngsters greet him in 1946 during his post-World War II survey of Europe as Chairman of President Truman's famine emergency committee.

Despite these measures, Congress, especially after heavy Democratic gains in 1930, disparaged Hoover's leadership, and many people blamed him personally for the deepening of the depression. He was also criticized for his forceful dispersal of the 1932 "Bonus Army" of unemployed military veterans who encamped in Washington, D.C., and demanded immediate payment of compensation for their wartime service.

Foreign affairs captured less public attention during the Hoover era than the domestic. He sent a delegation to discuss arms reduction at the London Naval Conference (1930), and continued to advance disarmament proposals during the remainder of his term. Secretary of State Henry L. Stimson denounced Japanese intervention in Manchuria as a flagrant breach of the traditional Open Door policy and various treaties. As President-elect, Hoover journeyed to South America to herald a "Good Neighbor" policy with Latin America. As evidence of this, in office he withdrew U.S. Marines from Nicaragua.

In 1932 Hoover was renominated, but met ignominious defeat at the hands of Democrat Franklin D. Roosevelt. The next year, Hoover retired from the Presidency. From 1933 until 1944, he maintained his Palo Alto home, but after his wife's death in the latter year he permanently lived in New York City, which since 1934 had served as his second residence.

During his long and active retirement, Hoover wrote extensively on history and politics, including his memoirs. President Truman summoned Hoover in 1946 to coordinate post-World War II relief planning. During the Truman and Eisenhower administrations, he chaired bipartisan Federal study commissions to improve the efficiency of the Executive Branch. He also participated in several civic organizations, and received numerous awards, medals, and honorary degrees. He died in 1964 at New York City.

Franklin D. Roosevelt

THIRTY-SECOND PRESIDENT   1933-45

**When Roosevelt came to office, the Great Depression
had brought the Nation to its knees, and forces were
at work that were to generate the cataclysm of World
War II. During his unprecedented 12-year-term, he
greatly expanded Presidential authority, widened
governmental functions, strove to restore economic
vigor, launched an unparalleled program of social
welfare, and helped lead the country and its allies
toward victory over the Axis powers. Shortly before
the war ended in 1945, he died not long after he had
begun a record fourth term.**

Franklin Delano Roosevelt was born in 1882 on a Hudson River
estate at Hyde Park, N.Y., that was to be his lifelong permanent
home. The second son of James Roosevelt, a lawyer, financier, and
railroad executive, Franklin was the only child from his father's
second marriage, to Sara Delano. The parents and private tutors
provided the youth with almost all his formative education, which
was enhanced by frequent travel and some study in Europe, where
he learned to speak French and German. He also attended Groton
(1896-1900), a prestigious preparatory school in Massachusetts. He
was an excellent student and enjoyed many sports.

Roosevelt won a B.A. degree in history at Harvard in only 3 years
(1900-03), even though his extracurricular activities tended to
overshadow his classroom accomplishments. An admirer of his
fifth cousin Theodore Roosevelt, he temporarily abandoned his
family's Democratic loyalties and became active in the school's
Republican Club. He also participated in football, crew, and glee
club; served as managing editor-president of the student newspaper, *The Crimson;* and was elected as class chairman. After
graduation, he stayed on for a year of postgraduate study.

Roosevelt next pursued law at New York City's Columbia
University. When he passed his bar examination after 3 years of
study, in 1907, he left school without taking a degree. Two years
earlier, he had wed (Anna) Eleanor Roosevelt, a distant cousin. Her
uncle, President Theodore Roosevelt, gave her away. She was to
give birth to one daughter and five sons.

From 1907 until 1910, Franklin practiced with a prominent New York City legal firm. The latter year, he was a delegate to the State Democratic convention and won election to the State senate from his traditionally Republican home district. In 1912 he was reelected, and fought for Woodrow Wilson's Presidential candidacy at the national convention.

In 1913 Wilson appointed Roosevelt as Assistant Secretary of the Navy. The following year, the latter lost a bid for nomination to the U.S. Senate. Continuing at his naval post throughout World War I, he proved to be a tireless and efficient administrator.

At the national convention in 1920, Roosevelt was picked as the running mate of Presidential candidate James M. Cox. During the campaign, in which the duo strongly advocated the League of Nations, Roosevelt gained national stature, but Republican Warren G. Harding achieved a landslide victory. The next year, Roosevelt entered into a New York City law partnership, and became vice president of Fidelity and Deposit Company of Maryland (1921-28).

While at the family's vacation home off the Maine coast on Campobello Island, N.B., Canada, in 1921, Roosevelt was stricken with poliomyelitis (infantile paralysis). This set off a courageous, lifetime fight to overcome the ravages of the disease. While building up his chest, neck, and arm muscles, he regained partial use of his legs, particularly by swimming periodically in the healing waters at Warm Springs, Ga., beginning in 1924. In time, he established a foundation there to help other polio victims, and inspired as well as directed the March of Dimes program that eventually funded an effective vaccine.

Meanwhile, encouraged by his wife and associates, Roosevelt had reentered public life. In 1924, he resumed his legal career, and at the Democratic national convention made a dramatic appearance on crutches to place Alfred ("Al") Smith in nomination for the Presidency—though John W. Davis became the candidate.

In 1928 Roosevelt again nominated Smith, who was successful this time and subsequently arranged for his protégé to replace him on the New York gubernatorial ticket. Despite a vigorous campaign, Roosevelt narrowly won, but Smith lost the State and the national election to Republican Herbert Hoover. In 1930 Roosevelt was overwhelmingly reelected and served for 3 more years. Although the Republicans controlled the legislature, he gained nationwide recognition for the bold program he pushed

Franklin D. Roosevelt delivering a speech at Topeka, Kansas, in 1932, during his first campaign for the Presidency.

through to allay the effects of the depression and to promote social welfare.

After a determined preconvention effort, in 1932 Roosevelt won the Democratic Presidential nomination on the fourth ballot. Breaking precedent by delivering an acceptance speech at the convention, he pledged a "New Deal," devoted to relief, recovery, and reform. While later touring the Nation, he attacked irresponsible business interests, and advocated a loosely defined and sometimes contradictory program of unemployment compensation, the end of prohibition, Government spending cuts, tariff reductions, and protection of U.S. industry. President Herbert Hoover, the Republican candidate, argued that Roosevelt's proposals endangered individualism, the basis of American political and economic strength. Nevertheless, the electorate swept Roosevelt into office.

During the 4-month period preceding Roosevelt's inauguration, the depression worsened. Industrial production plummeted; the pace of factory closings accelerated; unemployment soared; breadlines lengthened; and, as depositors panicked, bank failures increased.

To reaffirm public confidence, Roosevelt made huge strides as soon as he assumed office. He immediately summoned Congress into special session. Working together, during the first "100 Days" they passed a mass of legislation, the extent and implications of which have probably never been matched in any other similar brief span of U.S. history. Roosevelt formed a "brain trust" of advisers, who included many ex-professors; and appointed a distinguished Cabinet, including Secretary of Labor Frances Perkins, the first woman member of that body.

Seeking to buttress the financial and business structure, Roosevelt at once ordered a 4-day closing of banks to halt depositor panic, cut governmental expenditures, and abandoned the gold standard as an inflationary means to provide economic impetus. To calm the public, he began a series of radio "fireside chats" that he was to continue as a means of explaining his programs and gaining public support.

Legislation passed during the "100 Days" was far reaching in scope and significance. The Federal Deposit Insurance Corporation (FDIC) safeguarded bank deposits. The Home Owners' Loan Corporation (HOLC) provided direct Government loans for mortgages to home owners and farmers. The Civilian Conservation Corps (CCC) put thousands of young men to work on conservation projects. The Federal Emergency Relief Act (FERA) granted funds to States and municipalities for aid to the unemployed.

Hoping to boost prices for agricultural products, the Agricultural Adjustment Act (AAA) paid subsidies to farmers for curtailing production of certain livestock and crops and guaranteed parity prices for them. The Tennessee Valley Authority (TVA) put the Government into the power business in a major way and marked the beginning of intensified regional planning.

The omnibus National Industrial Recovery Act (NIRA) created the National Recovery Administration (NRA) and the Public Works Administration (PWA). Respectively, these agencies promulgated voluntary business and industrial codes geared toward increasing wages and maintaining prices and reducing unemployment; and employed laborers on newly created construction projects. The NIRA also guaranteed labor's right to organize and bargain collectively.

Once the "100 Days" had passed, during the rest of 1933 and in 1934 legislation slackened, but Congress and the administration devoted considerable effort to amending and refining earlier bills.

The New Deal did not win the favor of all the populace, particularly businessmen and bankers. Especially concerned with what they considered to be excessive governmental expenditures and the effects of inflation, they and other critics charged that Roosevelt's programs were "socialistic" and would endanger capitalism and democracy. The salutary effects of the New Deal were also questioned. Yet in 1934, indicative of the support of much of the electorate and contrary to tradition, the Democrats, the party in power, gained rather than lost seats in the midterm elections.

During 1935, in the "Second New Deal," another flurry of legislation was enacted. The Works Progress Administration (WPA) (after 1939 the Works Projects Administration), a program similar to the Public Works Administration (PWA), provided Federal jobs mainly for laborers, but also for artists, writers, musicians, and actors. The allied National Youth Administration (NYA) provided students and other youths with employment.

The Rural Electrification Administration (REA) furnished electricity to rural areas not adequately served by private utilities. And the National Labor Relations Act (NLRA), which created a

President Roosevelt and some of his advisers enjoy "chow" with members of the Civilian Conservation Corps (CCC) in 1933.

National Labor Relations Board (NLRB), assured the protection of labor's rights. The Social Security Act primarily set up a system of cooperative Federal-State unemployment compensation and a Federal program of old-age and survivors' benefits. In 1935 Roosevelt also obtained legislation increasing taxes on corporate and personal incomes, especially those in the higher brackets.

In 1936 Roosevelt easily defeated Republican Alfred M. Landon, and by lesser margins would beat Republican candidates Wendell L. Willkie in 1940 and Thomas E. Dewey in 1944. The only President known to a generation of young Americans, Roosevelt shattered the two-term tradition, being elected to four terms and serving an unprecedented tenure of more than 12 years.

Meantime, in 1935 and 1936, the Supreme Court had declared some key New Deal legislation unconstitutional by narrow margins. Early in 1937 Roosevelt proposed to add new justices, but many people contended this was an attempt to "pack" the Court and undermine the separation of powers. Roosevelt met his first major legislative defeat on this proposal, but before long the Supreme Court began to render decisions more favorable to his legislation.

In 1938 Roosevelt won additional measures, like higher farm price subsidies, and the Fair Labor Standards Act to set minimum wages, limit hours, and ban child labor in production of interstate goods. But by 1939, after Republicans and conservative Democrats made gains in the 1938 elections, the burst of legislation had subsided. The ills of the depression did not fully abate until the Nation mobilized for World War II.

In foreign policy, Roosevelt made one major shift, in 1933, by granting diplomatic recognition to the Soviet Union. He also amplified the "Good Neighbor" policy Hoover had initiated to restore solidarity in the Western Hemisphere. Under this new approach, the concept expressed in the Monroe Doctrine and its Roosevelt (Theodore) Corollary was modified to one of American cooperation with Latin American nations instead of intervention in their affairs. Accordingly, Roosevelt completed the withdrawal of U.S. Marines from Haiti. He also applied a new spirit of amity in diplomatic negotiations, which included numerous reciprocal trade agreements. By treaty, he renounced the right of intervention in Cuba and Panama.

Elsewhere on the globe, menacing forces were on the rise. During the late 1930's, the accelerating expansionism of Hitler and Mussolini in Europe and Africa, continuation of Japanese warfare against China, and the Axis alliance formed by Germany, Italy, and Japan, presaged the outbreak of World War II, which began in 1939.

As the conflict loomed on the horizon and then one country after

Roosevelt delivering one of his "fireside chats" in September 1941, just prior to U.S. entry into World War II. The mourning band was occasioned by the recent death of his mother.

another fell under Axis control, Roosevelt pursued defensive rearmament, despite a considerable body of isolationist sentiment in the Nation. He followed a course of official neutrality, though he obtained legislation and negotiated treaties as well as other agreements that strengthened America's defensive posture and aided the anti-Fascist countries, with whose cause he and most Americans sympathized. After the collapse of France in 1940 and

We were present at the dedication of the new Jefferson memorial in Washington.

the onset of the Nazi onslaught against Great Britain, in early 1941 Roosevelt launched an extensive lend-lease program on behalf of the Allies, which included Britain, Free France, China, and the Soviet Union.

Within days of the surprise Japanese attack on Pearl Harbor on December 7, 1941, the United States declared war on the Axis powers and began an all-out global effort to defeat them. Roosevelt mobilized the Nation, defined war aims, conferred with other Allied heads of state, stressed the need for unconditional surrender, and from the wartime alliance strove to forge a lasting peace through creation of a United Nations organization. At home, in 1941 he created a Fair Employment Practices Committee (FEPC) to prevent racial discrimination in defense projects.

Roosevelt was cheered as the tide of war shifted decisively in favor of the Allies. But he did not witness the final victory. Only weeks before the war ended in Europe, he died in April 1945 at his Warm Springs retreat.

With this space on the final page of the Roosevelt story, why is there no mention of the Yalta conference between the president and Stalin, in which Roosevelt agreed to give Russia the eastern half of Germany and half of Berlin?

Harry S Truman

THIRTY-THIRD PRESIDENT   1945–1953

Thrust into the Presidency by the sudden death of Roosevelt, Truman entered office at an extraordinary time: the complex and turbulent era ushered in by the conclusion of World War II. He employed the atomic bomb against Japan to terminate the war, contained the spread of Communism through collective security alliances and extensive economic aid to war-ravaged and developing countries, launched a massive airlift that defeated the Soviet Union's blockade of West Berlin, and militarily resisted North Korea's invasion of South Korea. Truman also helped guide the Nation's economy back into peacetime channels.

Born in 1884 at Lamar, Mo., Truman was the eldest of three children. In 1890 his father, a farmer and livestock dealer, moved his family from his father-in-law's farm at Grandview to the first of a series of residences in nearby Independence. From his earliest public school days, Truman wore thick eyeglasses, which restricted his participation in athletics. As a consequence, he learned to play the piano and became an avid reader, acquiring a lifelong interest in history and biography.

Financial problems kept Truman out of college, and his poor eyesight caused West Point to reject him. From 1901, when he graduated from high school, until 1906, mainly in Kansas City, he held a variety of clerical jobs: railroad timekeeper, newspaper mailroom worker, bank clerk, and bookkeeper.

In 1906 Truman, at the request of his father who was suffering financial difficulties, rejoined him at Grandview, where the family had returned 3 years earlier, and helped him work the farm. Harry continued to operate it after his father died in 1914.

Truman had joined the National Guard in 1905. After U.S. entry into World War I, in 1917, he was commissioned a first lieutenant in the field artillery and served with distinction in France. He took part in the Vosges, St. Mihiel, and Meuse-Argonne campaigns.

Mustered out as a major in 1919, Truman returned to Independence and married Elizabeth V. ("Bess") Wallace, his childhood sweetheart. They moved into his widowed mother-in-law's home, which they were to maintain as their permanent residence for the rest of their married lives. Bess was to bear one daughter, (Mary) Margaret.

Just after his discharge, Truman and an Army friend opened a haberdashery in Kansas City, but it failed in 1922. Truman, however, avoided bankruptcy and insisted on paying off his debts.

Backed by fellow war veterans and endorsed by local politician Thomas J. Pendergast, Truman was elected as judge for the eastern district of Jackson County (1922-24), a post similar to that of county commissioner. He failed to win reelection partly because of Ku Klux Klan opposition. Meanwhile, in 1923-25, he had attended night classes at Kansas City Law School, but never graduated. From 1924 until 1926 he was a partner in a savings and loan association and also sold memberships for the Automobile Club of Missouri.

During the next 8 years, Truman held two 4-year terms as presiding judge of the Jackson County Court, where he earned repute for his honest and efficient administration. In 1934, endorsed by Pendergast, he won a U.S. Senate seat. Despite the exposure of corruption in the Pendergast organization, in 1940 Truman was reelected, though narrowly, partially on the strength of his personal integrity and loyalty to President Roosevelt's "New Deal." During Truman's second Senate term, his chairing of an investigation of war profiteering, military expenditures, and defense production brought him national recognition.

Following an intraparty fight, in 1944 Truman replaced Henry A. Wallace as Roosevelt's running mate. As Vice President after January 1945, Truman fulfilled mostly ceremonial duties and rarely enjoyed the opportunity to discuss crucial national matters with the President, who was away from the Capital much of the time or busily engaged in the war effort. When Roosevelt died in April, Truman was confronted with a series of major decisions that required extensive briefings on military strategy and peacemaking measures.

Ironically, it was in foreign affairs, the area where Truman enjoyed the least pre-Presidential experience, that he made an outstanding mark. V-E Day, on May 8, 1945, marked the end of fighting in Europe. Less than 2 months later, Truman witnessed the signing of the United Nations (U.N.) charter in San Francisco. That summer, he also met with Britain's Winston S. Churchill and

President Truman confers in 1951 with his Secretary of Defense and former Secretary of State George C. Marshall, who had just returned from a visit to the war front in Korea.

Clement R. Attlee as well as the Soviet Union's Joseph V. Stalin at the Potsdam (Germany) Conference. Stalin's recalcitrance on postwar issues there helped lay the basis of the future Cold War.

During this meeting, Truman received a message that reported a secret U.S. test explosion of the first atomic bomb. Agreeing with his advisers that it would obviate the need for a long and bloody invasion of Japan to force her surrender, he authorized its use. Within a matter of days following destruction of the cities of Hiroshima and Nagasaki, World War II ended, on August 14, 1945 (V-J Day).

By 1947 the Cold War with the Soviet Union, which grew out of conflicts and misunderstandings that followed World War II, had begun. The "Truman Doctrine" advocated the containment of Communism through collective security alliances and direct military and economic aid to friendly nations.

The North Atlantic Treaty Organization (NATO), organized in 1949 with Truman's strong backing, solidified the military defense of Western Europe. Two years earlier, to counter Soviet threats to Turkey and Communist guerrilla activity in Greece, he had convinced Congress to extend aid to both countries. Later that same year, he backed Secretary of State George C. Marshall's imaginative and massive program (Marshall Plan) to underwrite the economic rebuilding of Western Europe. Truman's "Point Four" program was a multibillion dollar economic and technical aid program for developing nations.

Truman also faced two major military confrontations. He directed a massive airlift (1948-49) that broke a Russian blockade of West Berlin. In 1950 Communist North Korean troops crossed the 38th parallel into South Korea. Truman immediately undertook to thwart the attack. The United Nations, during a Russian boycott of its meetings, voted to join the United States in defending South Korea. Insisting on a limited police action to contain aggression but also seeking to prevent a broader war with China and possibly even the Soviet Union, in 1951 Truman removed Gen. Douglas MacArthur as military commander for disagreeing with this strategy. By the end of Truman's administration, the war had stalemated near the old demarcation line, but no permanent peace had been reached.

As early as 1946, Truman had proposed international control of atomic energy and U.N. supervision of bomb stockpiles. Inside of 3 years, the Russians tested a nuclear device. The President then ordered creation of the more powerful hydrogen bomb, which was first exploded in 1952.

Domestically, Truman quickly put his own stamp on Rooseveltian policies. Within a few months of his inauguration in 1945, he appointed six new Cabinet members. And, that fall, he initiated his "Fair Deal" program. Although it retained Roosevelt's social-welfare orientation, it emphasized the conversion of the economy from a wartime to peacetime basis—one of Truman's major problems.

Truman elatedly displays newspaper erroneously proclaiming the election of Thomas E. Dewey in 1948. Truman's narrow victory, which only became apparent when the late returns were tallied, embarrassed pollsters and the press, who had predicted a Dewey landslide.

Toward that end, in 1946 Truman signed a bill stating the Government's goal of "full employment" and creating a Council of Economic Advisers, which would counsel the President on economic matters and issue an annual economic report. That same year, he backed establishment of the Atomic Energy Commission, whose mission was the peaceful development of nuclear energy. Both business and labor blocked his efforts to continue anti-inflationary wartime price controls.

During a wave of strikes in 1946, though sympathetic to the cause of labor, Truman boldly intervened in railroad and coal-mining disputes—as he was also to do in 1952 during a steel strike. On the other hand, after the 1946 midterm congressional elections gave control of both Houses to the Republicans for the first time since 1930, Congress overrode Truman's veto of the Taft-Hartley Act, which restricted union powers.

In his "whistle-stop" campaign for reelection in 1948 against Republican Thomas E. Dewey, Truman doggedly stumped against the "inaction" of the 80th Congress. Upsetting the predictions of most pollsters and many members of his own party of his landslide defeat, he won the election, though by only a slight margin in several key States, and control of Congress. "Dixiecrat" J. Strom Thurmond, who reflected southern opposition to Truman's civil-rights stance, and Progressive Henry A. Wallace drew just enough votes to deprive Truman of a popular majority.

Yet Congress still ignored or rejected many of Truman's "Fair Deal" recommendations, which included those to guarantee civil rights through a permanent Fair Employment Practices Committee and to grant Federal funds for education and national health insurance.

Truman also issued an Executive order decreeing the end of segregation and racial discrimination in the Armed Forces, and encouraged or supported congressional appropriations or programs in the following areas: increase of the minimum wage, slum clearance, public housing, conservation, expansion of Social Security, and continuation of farm price supports. Furthermore, he supervised various governmental reorganizations, including those recommended by the Hoover Commission, and unification of the various armed services under a new Department of Defense.

In 1950 Truman escaped assassination when two Puerto Rican nationalists stormed Blair House, across from the White House, where he and his family were residing during the mansion's rehabilitation. He was spared injury, but guard Leslie Coffelt died and two others were wounded; one of the attackers died, and the other was wounded. Truman subsequently commuted the latter's death sentence to life imprisonment.

Following a series of trials of Communists and their sympathizers, in 1950 Congress passed the anti-Communist McCarran Internal Security Act. Truman vetoed it on the grounds that existing legislation was adequate for the purpose, but the measure passed. About that same time, Senator Joseph R. McCarthy accused the State Department and other bureaus of harboring a number of alleged Communists or their supporters, among whom he also included former Secretary of State Marshall. Truman and other leading Americans hotly contested these charges, but they nevertheless became campaign issues in 1952.

Truman looks on as Secretary of State Edward R. Stettinius, Jr., signs the United Nations Charter at San Francisco in 1945.

Truman was also criticized for the existence of corruption and maladministration among his appointees in several executive agencies and on the White House staff. Although he initially came to their defense, he discharged many of them and took other corrective measures.

In 1952 Truman decided against seeking another term, and backed the Democratic convention's choice, Adlai E. Stevenson. Retiring to Independence, Truman assumed the role of elder statesman, continued to participate in party affairs, wrote his memoirs, and helped establish the Truman Presidential Library. He died in 1972. His widow and married daughter, Margaret Daniels, survived him.

Dwight D. Eisenhower

THIRTY-FOURTH PRESIDENT   1953-61

A popular military hero of World War II who had
enjoyed a distinguished Army career, Eisenhower
demonstrated strong leadership and administrative
abilities during his two terms. He negotiated an
armistice in Korea, furthered international
disarmament, reduced Cold War tensions, and
inaugurated the U.S. space program. His domestic
program of "Dynamic Conservatism" or "Modern
Republicanism" emphasized governmental economy
and decentralization of Federal projects through
cooperation with State and local governments as well
as private enterprise.

Dwight David Eisenhower was born in 1890 at Denison, Tex. The
next year, his family, in which he was the third of seven sons,
moved to Abilene, Kans. There, his father worked as a mechanic in
a creamery. The youth's pacifistic and devout parents provided him
with strong religious training, but he received a public education.
In high school, from which he graduated at the age of 19, he was an
average student, and played football and baseball.

For the next 3 years, Eisenhower worked in the creamery with his
father. Encouraged by a friend, he applied for admittance to both
military academies, but the Navy rejected him for being barely
overage. In 1911 he accepted a nomination to West Point, where he
excelled academically and played on the football team until he
broke his knee. He graduated in 1915 among the top third of his
class.

While posted as a second lieutenant at Fort Sam Houston, San
Antonio, Tex., Eisenhower met Mary G. ("Mamie") Doud of
Denver. They married in 1916. She was to bear two sons, the first of
whom died as an infant.

Eisenhower remained in the United States during World War I,
and established as well as commanded the tank training center at
Camp Colt, Gettysburg, Pa. During peacetime, he gained a
reputation for his staff and planning work and held a series of
overseas and stateside assignments, including service under Gens.

John J. Pershing and Douglas MacArthur. Eisenhower also graduated from the Command and General Staff School and Army War College. In 1941 he bolstered his career when he helped engineer a victory in the Louisiana war games, and achieved the temporary rank of brigadier general.

In 1942, shortly after the United States entered World War II, Gen. George C. Marshall named Eisenhower as Assistant Chief of Staff. In this position, he earned respect for his strategic and organizational talents. Later the same year, he was chosen to command the European Theater of Operations. His direction of the invasions of North Africa, Sicily, and Italy brought him international fame.

In late 1943 Eisenhower was appointed the Supreme Allied Commander in Europe. Inspiring Allied unity, he led the D-Day invasion of France (June 6, 1944). Late that year, he was awarded the newly created rank of General of the Army. After Germany surrendered, in 1945 Eisenhower returned to the United States to serve as Army Chief of Staff. During the next 3 years, he supervised

David and Ida Eisenhower and their six sons in 1902. Rear, standing: Dwight D., Edgar, Earl, Arthur, and Roy. Middle front: Milton.

demobilization and the integration of his branch of the service into the newly formed Department of Defense.

Popularly known by his high school nickname of "Ike" and beloved for his distinctive grin, Eisenhower became a national hero. Publication of his military memoirs, *Crusade in Europe* (1948), added to his public recognition. That same year, discouraging Presidential draft movements by both major parties, he left the Army and took over the presidency of Columbia University. Upon President Truman's request, late in 1950 he took a leave of absence and returned to active duty to command the North Atlantic Treaty Organization (NATO), which had been formed the year before.

In 1952, after deciding to cast his lot with the Republicans, Eisenhower returned to the United States and won nomination on the first ballot. His running mate was Richard M. Nixon. Winning the first national G.O.P. victory in 24 years, Eisenhower easily defeated Democrat Adlai E. Stevenson. Four years later, though in the interim Eisenhower had suffered a heart attack and an ileitis operation, he beat Stevenson by an even wider margin. Late in 1957, Eisenhower was temporarily hospitalized with a mild stroke.

Eisenhower labeled his domestic program as "Dynamic Conservatism" or "Modern Republicanism." Working with majority Democratic Congresses except for the first 2 years, he emphasized a balanced budget, but favored expansion of social-welfare legislation while also encouraging the decentralization of Federal projects through cooperation with business and State and local governments.

Eisenhower signed bills that broadened Social Security coverage and increased the minimum wage; oversaw an agreement with Canada to construct the St. Lawrence Seaway, completed in 1959; supported Federal aid for local health assistance, school construction, and educational programs, particularly in science; pushed the massive funding of a new system of interstate highways; established a "soil bank," which paid farmers to withdraw lands from production in the interest of maintaining food prices and conserving agricultural resources; distributed farm surpluses at home and abroad in the form of school lunches and foreign aid; hailed a labor-relations act that required management and union leaders to report dealings affecting the public and rank-and-file workers; and took various steps to relieve the recessions of 1954 and 1957-58.

Supreme Allied Commander Eisenhower and British Prime Minister Winston Churchill in 1944.

On the other hand, Eisenhower sought to minimize Government activity. His administration lowered individual and corporate taxes, abolished the Reconstruction Finance Corporation, stressed reduction of the national budget, rejected proposals for public utility dam projects, and welcomed the admittance of Alaska and Hawaii as States.

After the school desegregation decision of the Supreme Court in 1954, Eisenhower enforced specific judicial orders in this field, notably in Little Rock, Ark. He deployed Federal troops there in

1957 to insure enrollment of blacks at a local high school. That same year, he approved formation of a Civil Rights Commission as part of the first significant Federal legislation in this area in more than eight decades. In 1960 he sponsored another bill providing voting registration protection for blacks. Finally, he furthered the elimination of segregation in the Armed Forces.

Foreign affairs, which were administered by Secretary of State John Foster Dulles until 1959, attracted most of Eisenhower's attention. While maintaining a strong defensive military posture, he sought to mitigate Cold War tensions. In 1953, fulfilling a campaign promise, he concluded an armistice ending the Korean conflict. The following year, the United States joined the South East Asia Treaty Organization (SEATO), a collective security arrangement among anti-Communist governments.

Stalin's death in 1953 and Eisenhower's initiatives led to a gradual easing of East-West tensions. The new Russian leaders agreed with the three other occupying powers (France, Great Britain, and the United States) to a treaty creating an independent Austria, and spoke of "peaceful co-existence" between capitalism and Communism. Because of growing United States and Russian nuclear capability, the search for peace became ever more urgent.

Throughout Eisenhower's tenure, he tried to obtain Soviet agreement to limit nuclear arms and halt their testing. In 1953 he proposed to the United Nations "Atoms for Peace," a program for the peaceful use of atomic energy in developing countries. This proposal eventually led to creation of the International Atomic Energy Agency.

Eisenhower met in 1955 with French, British, and Russian heads of state in a summit conference at Geneva, Switzerland—the first since Potsdam. Although the Soviets rejected his "Open Skies" disarmament proposal for the interchange of military installation blueprints and mutual rights of aerial reconnaissance and inspection, the conference briefly relaxed relations between Russia and the Free World.

The "spirit of Geneva" soon evaporated, however. In 1956 the Russians put down a revolt in Hungary, and the United States offered the refugees asylum. In the fall of 1957, the Soviets launched the first earth satellite. In response, Eisenhower created the National Aeronautics and Space Administration (1958), expanded U.S. military might, and increased foreign aid.

Summit meeting in 1955 at Geneva, Switzerland. Left to right: Soviet Premier Nikolai A. Bulganin, President Eisenhower, French Premier Edgar Faure, and British Prime Minister Sir Anthony Eden.

Meanwhile, late in 1956, Eisenhower had joined the Soviet Union and the United Nations in criticizing the joint French, British, and Israeli attack on Egypt to force it to reopen the Suez Canal. The next year, he promulgated the "Eisenhower Doctrine," which committed the United States to help Middle Eastern countries resist Communism. Under this doctrine, in 1958 U.S. forces briefly intervened in Lebanon at the request of its President. That same year, Eisenhower, fulfilling a 1954 commitment to Nationalist China, backed her resistance to Chinese Communist bombardment of the offshore islands of Quemoy and Matsu.

Seeking further détente through personal diplomacy, Eisenhower invited Soviet Premier Nikita S. Khrushchev to tour the United States. During his visit (1959), Eisenhower discussed various issues with him at Camp David, Md.

But international hostility resumed in many parts of the world. In 1960, after an American U-2 reconnaissance jet was shot down inside Russia, Khrushchev abruptly ended a Paris summit meeting and cancelled Eisenhower's planned trip to his country. That same year, grave tensions arose on three continents. Conflict between political factions in Laos flared up; in the Congo (present Zaire) secessionist and revolutionary elements emerged just after independence was achieved; and disagreements between the United States and Cuba, which allied more and more closely with the Soviet bloc, led to a rupture in diplomatic relations.

Out of office in 1961 and in retirement at his Gettysburg farm, Eisenhower advised his successors, wrote his memoirs, and handled private business matters. He died in 1969 at Walter Reed Army Medical Center, D.C. His widow and son, John S., survived him.

John F. Kennedy

THIRTY-FIFTH PRESIDENT   1961-63

The youthful Kennedy brought to office a promising vigor, intellect, and style. He urged people to participate in Government and commit themselves to the solution of contemporary problems, inaugurated his "New Frontier" program of domestic reforms, defended minority rights, and met stern Cold War challenges. But a bullet struck him down before he completed his term and could realize many of his aims. He was the youngest elected President, the first born in the 20th century, the first Roman Catholic, the fourth to be assassinated, and the youngest at death.

John Fitzgerald Kennedy was born in 1917 at Brookline, Mass., a Boston suburb. He was the second child and second son of nine children. Both parents were well-educated members of prominent, prosperous, and politically active Irish-American families. The father, Joseph P., was to build a multimillion dollar fortune in business and finance, as well as serve as Franklin D. Roosevelt's chairman of the Securities and Exchange Commission (1934-35) and Ambassador to Great Britain (1937-40).

In 1927, by which time Joseph had achieved considerable wealth, the family moved to the New York City area. He soon acquired a winter home at Palm Beach, Fla., and a summer retreat at Hyannis Port, Mass. Young Kennedy received most of his early education at private schools. After graduation from Choate (1931-35), a prestigious college preparatory institution in Wallingford, Conn., he decided to enroll at Princeton University. But, while studying for the summer at the London School of Economics in England, he was stricken with jaundice. This delayed for a few weeks his entry at Princeton. During the winter, his illness recurred, and he was forced to leave school.

Kennedy entered Harvard University in 1936. During the second half of his junior year, he joined his Ambassador-father in England and traveled around Europe. In 1940 he took his B.S. degree from Harvard with honors in political science. His senior thesis, on the appeasement of Hitler, published under the title of *Why England*

Slept, became a bestseller. Later that same year, he enrolled in Stanford (Calif.) University Business School, but only attended for 6 months, after which he toured South America.

During the fall of 1941, Kennedy was appointed as an ensign in the Navy and assigned to Washington, D.C., and then to Charleston, S.C. Just after Japan attacked Pearl Harbor in December, his request for sea duty was granted. After appropriate training in Rhode Island, in 1943, as a lieutenant (jg), he commanded a motor-torpedo patrol boat (PT-109) in the Solomon Islands region of the South Pacific. A Japanese destroyer rammed and sank his craft. Despite a chronic back condition, he helped his crew reach safety. He was awarded the Purple Heart and the Navy and Marine Corps Medal. Finishing his military career in hospitals and as a training instructor, he was discharged early in 1945 with the rank of lieutenant.

Later that same year, employed by the Hearst newspapers, Kennedy reported on the formation of the United Nations at San Francisco, the Potsdam Conference, and the British elections. This activity whetted his interest in politics.

In 1946, after receiving a substantial plurality in the Democratic primary, he was elected to the U.S. House of Representatives from a Massachusetts district that included parts of Boston. In 1948 and 1950 he easily won reelection. Two years later, following a highly organized and energetic campaign, he defeated incumbent U.S. Senator Henry Cabot Lodge, Jr., though the Republican Presidential ticket carried the State.

The next year, Kennedy married Jacqueline Lee Bouvier. She was to bear one daughter, Caroline B., and two sons, John F., Jr., and Patrick B., the latter of whom died shortly after birth.

While convalescing from two critical spinal operations in 1954-55, Kennedy wrote *Profiles in Courage* (1956), a study of eight U.S. Senators who adhered to principle above political popularity. The book won the Pulitzer Prize for biography.

In 1956 Kennedy narrowly lost a bid for the Democratic Vice-Presidential nomination. Two years later, he was overwhelmingly reelected to the Senate. Before long, he began to campaign for the Presidency. After carrying several early State primaries, he won decisively in West Virginia. The national convention selected him on the first ballot. His major rival, Senate Majority Leader Lyndon B. Johnson, accepted the Vice-Presidential nomination.

John F. Kennedy and his wife, Jacqueline, in a 1960 campaign motorcade along Broadway, New York City.

After a campaign that featured four nationally televised debates between Kennedy and the Republican nominee, Vice President Richard Nixon—a historical first—Kennedy achieved an extremely narrow victory in the general election. Republican claims of fraudulent returns in Texas and Illinois were not pressed.

Kennedy exerted boldness in foreign affairs, which were marked during his administration by sharp intensification of the Cold War. Soon after his inauguration, in 1961, he allowed a force of anti-Communist Cuban exiles, who had been equipped and trained with U.S. assistance, to invade their homeland at the Bay of Pigs. This

President Kennedy confers with Soviet Premier Nikita S. Khrushchev at
Vienna in 1961.

attempt to overthrow Premier Fidel Castro failed dismally, and
Kennedy publicly accepted responsibility.

That same year, the President launched the Peace Corps and his
hemispheric Alliance for Progress to aid developing nations. He
also held talks on a variety of topics with Soviet Premier
Khrushchev in Vienna, but, especially in the wake of the Cuban
affair, these were ineffective. International rapport further declined
when East Germany constructed a wall to isolate West Berlin from
the Communist or eastern sector. In retaliation, Kennedy augment-
ed U.S. forces in Europe, and 2 years later delivered his "*Ich bin ein
Berliner*" ("I am a Berliner") speech at the wall. Meanwhile, both
Russia and the United States had enlarged their military budgets
and resumed nuclear testing.

Kennedy addressing the United Nations General Assembly in New York City, September 25, 1961.

Responding to pro-Communist revolutionary activity in Southeast Asia, in 1962 Kennedy helped arrange a negotiated settlement of the longstanding political turmoil in Laos. That same year, he began augmenting the military advisers President Eisenhower had sent to South Viet-Nam with special forces.

In October 1962 a major crisis arose over Cuba. Kennedy obtained aerial reconnaissance photographs proving that the Soviet Union had placed there intermediate-range missiles capable of striking the U.S. mainland. In an emergency telecast to the

Nation, Kennedy stated that the U.S. Navy would quarantine arms shipments to the island until the offensive weapons were withdrawn. Nuclear war seemed imminent, but the confrontation ended when Khrushchev agreed to remove the missiles.

Kennedy soon sought new understanding in Russian-American relations. In 1963 he signed the first arms-control treaty of the Cold War with the Soviet Union and Great Britain; it banned aboveground nuclear testing. He also agreed to the installation of a "hot line" for instant communication between the White House and the Kremlin, and approved the sale of surplus wheat to Russia.

Kennedy's "New Frontier" domestic program was only partially successful in Congress, which passed legislation in the fields of reciprocal international trade, aid to higher education, urban renewal, a higher minimum wage, relief of economically distressed areas, liberalization of Social Security procedures and benefits, grants to States for community mental health centers, and improvement of water quality. Civil-rights and tax-reduction measures he recommended were enacted after his death. Congress rejected his proposals for a Cabinet-level Department of Urban Affairs, medical care for the aged, general Federal assistance for public schools, and stronger regulation of farm production.

But Kennedy made notable gains in civil rights. He appointed many blacks to Federal posts, legally ended religious and racial discrimination in housing built or purchased with Federal funds; strengthened equal job opportunity in Government contract work; and backed the extensive program of his brother, Attorney General Robert F. Kennedy, for the registration of black voters.

To foster school integration, Kennedy sent U.S. marshals and troops to Oxford, Miss., to insure enrollment of the University of Mississippi's first black student, James H. Meredith. He also dispatched Federal forces to the University of Alabama for similar purposes. And he endorsed Martin Luther King, Jr.'s massive civil-rights march on Washington, D.C. (1963).

Kennedy proved to be forceful in other areas, too. After the first U.S. suborbital space flight in 1961, he imaginatively established as a national goal the landing of a man on the moon by the end of the decade. In 1962 he personally intervened to stop proposed steel price increases, which he feared would be inflationary.

During the fall of 1963, Kennedy visited various areas of the Nation to build support for administration programs and his reelection. While touring Texas, on November 22, 1963, to the shock of the world, he was shot from ambush as his motorcade passed through downtown Dallas. He never regained consciousness. His widow, daughter Caroline, and son John, Jr., survived him.

Lyndon B. Johnson

THIRTY-SIXTH PRESIDENT   1963-69

Johnson, who ascended to the Presidency upon Kennedy's assassination and won his own term of office by an unprecedented popular majority, enjoyed more Federal legislative experience than any former Chief Executive. He was also the first since Andrew Johnson to have come to office from the South. Seeking to build a "Great Society" at home while maintaining the Nation's role abroad, he made giant strides in civil rights and social welfare. Nevertheless, the eruption of urban black riots and repeated demonstrations against U.S. participation in the Viet-Nam War signaled deep-rooted social and racial discontent that burdened him and seared the national psyche.

The first of five children, Johnson was born in 1908 at a farm along the banks of the Pedernales River in the Texas hill country near Stonewall. His mother's father had been a State legislator and official. His paternal grandfather was a rancher-drover and Confederate Army veteran whose kin had founded nearby Johnson City.

In 1913 the father moved his wife and children there and followed careers in real estate, newspaper work, and State politics. Meanwhile, young Johnson continued his education at the local schools. In 1920 the family rented their home and returned to the farm, but 2 years later they sold it and headed back to their Johnson City residence.

The year before, Lyndon had briefly boarded with relatives to begin his freshman year at Johnson City High School. A good student, he held various part-time jobs, and participated in such extracurricular activities as public speaking, debate, and baseball. When he graduated in 1924, he headed west for California. There, he worked as an elevator operator, carwasher, fieldhand, and cafe worker. The next year, he trekked back to his Texas home, and for 2 more years again drifted from job to job.

Encouraged by his parents to continue his education, in 1927 Johnson entered closeby Southwest Texas State Teachers College

(later Southwest Texas College) at San Marcos. He majored in history and social science, excelled in debates, and edited the campus newspaper. To help pay for his schooling, he worked as a janitor, salesman, and secretary to the college president. In 1928 he received his elementary teacher's certificate, and left school to become principal and teacher at Cotulla. The following year, he returned to San Marcos and in 1930 won his B.S. degree.

In 1930-31 Johnson taught public speaking and coached the debating team at a Houston high school. About this time, he began to take part in State Democratic politics, and beginning in late 1931 worked for 4 years in Washington, D.C., as secretary to Texas Congressman Richard M. Kleberg. During this period, Johnson attended Georgetown (D.C.) University Law School for a few months.

In 1934 Johnson married Claudia Alta ("Lady Bird") Taylor, daughter of a well-to-do planter-merchant of Marshall, Tex. She was to bear two daughters. During the 1935-37 period, Johnson directed the National Youth Administration (NYA) in Texas and won praise for organizing a model program.

The voters sent Johnson to fill a vacant seat in the U.S. House of Representatives in 1937. Reelected to five more terms, he sat in that body until 1948, learned the intricacies of the legislative process, and became a protégé of Majority Leader (later Speaker) Sam Rayburn and President Franklin D. Roosevelt. During the 1940 elections, he chaired the Democratic Congressional Campaign Committee. In 1941 he was narrowly defeated in a special election for the U.S. Senate.

For 7 months after Pearl Harbor, Johnson served as a lieutenant commander in the Navy. When President Roosevelt recalled all Congressmen from active duty, in 1942 he returned to Washington and energetically championed the war effort.

Johnson ran again for the U.S. Senate in 1948. He won the runoff Democratic primary by a small and disputed margin, but in the general election handily defeated his opponent. A master of organization and detail, Johnson rose rapidly, and within 3 years was chosen as Majority Whip. The 44-year-old legislator was elected in 1953 as Minority Leader—the youngest in history. In 1954 the Democrats regained control of Congress; Johnson himself won reelection, and the next January was named as Senate Majority Leader.

Lyndon B. Johnson campaigns for the U.S. Senate in 1941.

That year, Johnson suffered a severe heart attack, but he recovered rapidly. During Eisenhower's Republican administration, he won acclaim for avoiding doctrinaire positions on White House proposals. He frequently cooperated with the President to win passage of important legislation, including national security measures and the first major civil rights acts in more than eight decades, the Civil Rights Acts of 1957 and 1960.

In 1960 Johnson seriously contended for the Presidential nomination. After John F. Kennedy became the party's candidate,

Johnson accepted the Vice-Presidential spot. His strenuous campaign in his native South contributed significantly to the ticket's narrow victory.

An active Vice President, Johnson represented the United States on missions abroad; participated in Cabinet and National Security Council sessions; and chaired the National Aeronautics and Space Council, the Peace Corps Advisory Council, and the President's Committee on Equal Employment Opportunity.

Sworn into the Presidency aboard the Presidential jet in Dallas, just hours after Kennedy's assassination in November 1963, Johnson soon brought his legislative skills to bear upon Congress, broke up the logjam of stymied Kennedy initiatives, and evolved a

President Johnson consults in the White House with civil-rights leader Martin Luther King.

domestic program he called the "Great Society." During his first 2 years in office, he signed a record number of significant pieces of legislation. Congress quickly approved his proposals for substantial foreign aid appropriations, reduced taxes, a major wilderness preservation system, funding of mass transit systems, and wheat and cotton price supports.

Johnson led the fight for the Civil Rights Act of 1964, which outlawed segregation in public accommodations and promoted fair employment practices. His antipoverty program provided for a food stamp system, established the Job Corps to train unemployed youth, created community action agencies to improve health services as well as to fulfill other local needs, and formed the Office of Economic Opportunity as a coordinating agency.

In seeking a full term as President in 1964, Johnson overwhelmed Republican Senator Barry M. Goldwater. Johnson subsequently pushed through additional legislation. It assisted education; attacked pollution; financed Medicare for the aged; aided depressed regions in Appalachia; created the new Cabinet-level offices of Department of Housing and Urban Development and the Department of Transportation; promoted urban renewal, public housing, historic preservation, and highway beautification; abolished immigration quotas; authorized the use of Federal registrars to safeguard black voting rights; and increased Social Security payments.

Johnson also espoused ratification of the Constitution's 25th amendment, governing the transfer of executive powers at times of Presidential incapacitation, resignation, or impeachment. He also oversaw spectacular American advances in space exploration—capped late in 1968 by an orbital flight around the moon.

Despite these accomplishments, Johnson faced mounting difficulties at home and abroad. In 1965 he sent U.S. Marines into the Dominican Republic to end a revolt, which he viewed as a Communist threat to the Caribbean but which also provoked some public criticism. Later that same year, he accelerated participation in the Viet-Nam War, and during the next 3 years steadily increased the flow of troops and materiel to counter Viet Cong and North Vietnamese attacks. Debate over this undeclared war came to divide the United States. Antiwar demonstrations took place across the country, and Johnson became the focal point of much of the controversy.

Soviet Premier Aleksei N. Kosygin and President Johnson during their meeting at Glassboro, New Jersey, in 1967.

But this did not end his woes—or those of the Nation. During the mid and late 1960's, the calm of the cities was shattered by a series of riots as many black people vented their anger at a host of social and economic grievances and the assassination of Martin Luther King, Jr.

During the Mideast crisis caused by the Six-Day War (1967), the administration took a position of neutrality, and urged Israeli-

Arab negotiations. That same year, Johnson and Soviet Premier Aleksei N. Kosygin discussed international affairs at Glassboro, N.J. In Viet-Nam Johnson continued United States involvement. In March 1968 he announced limitations on the bombing of North Viet-Nam, invited the Communists to negotiate, and made a surprise declaration that he would not be a candidate for reelection.

Retiring in 1969, Johnson returned to the LBJ Ranch in Texas, where he wrote his memoirs. He died there in 1973. His wife and two married daughters, Lynda Bird Robb and Luci Baines Nugent, survived him.

Richard Nixon

THIRTY-SEVENTH PRESIDENT 1969-74

Nixon's political career was meteoric and filled with vicissitudes. After service in the House of Representatives and Senate and two terms as Vice President, he barely lost the Presidential race in 1960 and failed to win the California governorship 2 years later. In 1968, however, he won the office of U.S. Chief Executive, though by a narrow margin. Four years later, he captured a record number of popular votes. Yet, despite notable achievements, particularly in international relations, the so-called "Watergate Affair" brought him to the brink of impeachment and forced him to resign—the first President ever to do so.

Reared by industrious Quaker parents, Richard Milhous Nixon was the second of five sons, two of whom died at early ages. He was born in 1913 at Yorba Linda, Calif. His father, who had worked at various jobs, earned a modest income by raising citrus crops. In 1922 the family moved to nearby Whittier. There, the senior Nixon, aided by his sons, operated a gas station-grocery.

Richard early showed interest in public speaking and drama, and took piano and violin lessons. He was a good student; participated in school debates, athletics, and politics; and played in the orchestra. In 1930 the youth graduated from Whittier Union High. In the fall, he entered Whittier College, a Quaker institution, but worked part time in his father's business to help finance his education. He majored in history, compiled an excellent academic record, was a member of the football squad, excelled in debating, and won the presidency of the student body. Ranking second in his class, in 1934 he received a B.A. degree. That same year, Nixon won a scholarship to Duke University Law School, in Durham, N.C. He was elected as president of the student bar association, and graduated with honors in 1937.

Returning to Whittier, later in the year Nixon was admitted to the bar and began practicing with a local firm. In 1938 he registered as a Republican, and 2 years later supported Presidential candidate Wendell Willkie. By 1941 Nixon had become assistant city attorney, a trustee of Whittier College, and president of two of his college alumni organizations. He also found time to organize a company that sought to freeze and market fresh orange juice, but despite his energetic management the business failed after 18 months. While acting in an amateur theater group, he met (Thelma C.) Patricia ("Pat") Ryan, a high-school business teacher. They married in 1940, and were to raise two daughters, Julie and "Tricia" (Patricia).

In 1942, not long after the outbreak of World War II, Nixon moved to Washington, D.C., to work for the tire-rationing section of the Office of Price Administration. That summer, though his religion made him eligible for conscientious-objector status, he enlisted in the Navy and was commissioned as a lieutenant junior grade. He held a variety of assignments, including those in supply and legal services. The highlight of these years, during which he attained the rank of lieutenant commander, was a 14-month tour of duty in the Pacific.

Back home from the war, in 1946 Nixon ran for the U.S. House of Representatives, and in a hard-fought campaign defeated a powerful Democratic opponent who had held office for a decade. During his two terms, Nixon served on the Committee on Education and Labor, where he helped draft the Taft-Hartley Labor Relations Act of 1947; and won recognition as an anti-Communist crusader on the Committee on Un-American Activities. In 1950, after another bitter election battle, he won a seat in the U.S. Senate by a wide margin.

Dwight D. Eisenhower, Republican candidate for President in 1952, chose Nixon as his running mate. During the campaign, Nixon was accused of using political contributions for personal purposes, but his televised "Checkers" speech convinced Eisenhower and most citizens of his innocence. Inaugurated to the first of two terms as Vice President at the age of 40, Nixon was the second youngest man ever to hold the office.

When President Eisenhower was hospitalized on several occasions, Nixon chaired meetings of the Cabinet and National Security Council. He also represented the United States on good-will trips to Latin America, the Soviet Union, and other places. In 1960 his party's national convention picked him to succeed Eisenhower, but in the first defeat of his political career he lost the general election to Democrat John F. Kennedy by a narrow margin.

Nixon during his successful campaign for the U.S. Senate in 1950.

Vice President Nixon and Soviet leader Nikita S. Khrushchev in 1959 at Moscow.

The following year, Nixon moved back to California. Not long thereafter his *Six Crises,* which detailed decisive events in his career, was published. In 1962 he lost a bid for the governorship of his native State. The next year, he relocated to New York City and joined a distinguished law firm. Still campaigning for Republican causes, he remained a party leader, though he did not actively seek the Presidential nomination in 1964.

Four years later though, after being victorious in various primaries, Nixon was again nominated. He chose as his running mate Spiro T. Agnew, Governor of Maryland. Nixon narrowly defeated Democrat Hubert H. Humphrey and independent candidate George C. Wallace. Running for reelection in 1972 against Democratic Senator George McGovern, Nixon won the largest number of popular votes in the Nation's history.

Domestically, Nixon advocated a more powerful role for local government in his "New Federalism." His revenue-sharing system allocated a greater share of Federal funds to States and cities. Confronting balance of payments deficits in international trade and high rates of inflation, he instituted mandatory wage and price controls; entered into international monetary negotiations; devalued the dollar; and took steps to counter the energy crisis, which intensified late in 1973 when the Arab nations placed an embargo on oil. He also declared a "war" against crime and narcotics, opposed compulsory busing to desegregate schools, made four appointments to the Supreme Court, and ended the military draft while converting the armed services to an all-volunteer basis. A spectacular event early in his administration was the landing of American astronauts on the moon.

Aided by his chief international affairs adviser and later Secretary of State Henry A. Kissinger, Nixon pursued a vigorous foreign policy. In Viet-Nam he gradually reduced U.S. commitments while seeking to "Vietnamize" the conflict. In conjunction with the Saigon government of South Viet-Nam, he continued aerial and naval assaults on the North Vietnamese and their Indochinese allies and made incursions against their strongholds in Cambodia and Laos. He finally succeeded in disengaging U.S. forces and arranging for the release of American prisoners-of-war held by North Viet-Nam and the Viet Cong. These latter actions played an important part in ending large-scale demonstrations in the United States against participation in the war.

Outstanding among Nixon's travels to many parts of the world was his historic journey in 1972 to the People's Republic of China, the first high-level contact between the two nations in decades. He was the first President to visit that country while in office. The result was establishment of limited diplomatic contact between the two nations and creation of a spirit of amity. Later that same year and in 1974, the President traveled to the Soviet Union, where in a spirit of detente he signed a treaty to limit strategic nuclear weapons and discussed such other matters as cooperation in outer space, trade, and international affairs. In the Middle East, which he toured in 1974, he helped reduce tensions and the associated threat of world conflict.

Nixon's tenure was cut short by a series of scandals. These began with press revelations of political espionage involving certain members of his own special reelection committee. During June 1972 their agents had broken into the offices of the national committee of the Democratic Party at Washington's Watergate office building. As time went on, the "Watergate Affair" came to be associated with a wide variety of questionable activities on the part of the President and some of his Cabinet members, key aides, and campaign advisers. Congressional investigations and judicial proceedings resulted in the conviction of a number of them.

In a separate matter, in October 1973 Vice President Agnew resigned, after pleading "no contest" to tax fraud. Utilizing the untried procedures of the 25th amendment to the Constitution, Nixon nominated and Congress confirmed the appointment of Gerald R. Ford to the Vice-Presidency.

One of the major discoveries made during the televised hearings of the Senate Select Committee on Presidential Campaign Activities was the existence of a tape-recording system in the White House. Ultimately, in one of the gravest constitutional crises in our history, the Supreme Court unanimously overruled Nixon's assertion of executive privilege to resist the subpoenas of Watergate prosecutors and ordered him to produce tapes and documents relevant to court proceedings.

Late in July 1974 the House Judiciary Committee publicly debated over television the charges against the President in preparation for full House impeachment. The committee finally recommended three articles: obstruction of justice, abuse of power, and contempt of Congress.

President Nixon confers with Chinese leader Mao Tse-tung in Peking during Nixon's 1972 visit to the People's Republic of China.

Under pressure from his own legal counsel, on August 5, 1974, Nixon surrendered three transcripts of conversations recorded in the White House a few days after the Watergate break-in. The implications of Nixon's involvement quickly eroded his remaining congressional support, and Republican leaders urged that he step down. On August 9, 1974, stating that he wished to spare the Nation further stress, Nixon resigned and retired to his home in San Clemente. He subsequently was given a full Presidential pardon.

Gerald R. Ford

THIRTY-EIGHTH PRESIDENT   1974–77

**Assuming office following President Nixon's
resignation and quickly restoring public confidence,
Ford regenerated the spirit of national unity. After
serving 25 years in the House of Representatives, he
had been appointed as Vice President under the 25th
amendment to the Constitution. Although the first
Chief Executive who had never been a candidate in a
nationwide election, he was the first to undergo an
exhaustive congressional investigation into his
qualifications. His prime domestic concern was
invigoration of the recessive economy. Abroad, he
improved relations with the Soviet Union as well as
China and spearheaded peacekeeping efforts in the
Middle East and southern Africa.**

Ford was born in 1913 at Omaha, Nebr. He was christened Leslie
L. King, Jr., after his father, a wool dealer. About 2 years later, his
parents divorced. His mother, Dorothy Gardner, took the infant to
her family home in Grand Rapids, Mich. The following year, she
remarried. Her new husband, Gerald R. Ford, a paint salesman,
adopted the child and gave him his own name. Along with three
younger half-brothers, Ford, Jr., learned the value of hard work and
community involvement.

Ford studied at public primary and secondary schools. At South
High, he starred in football as center and team captain. By 1929 his
stepfather had organized a small paint-manufacturing company,
where Gerald worked during vacations. For 3 years while in high
school, he was employed part time in a restaurant.

After graduation in 1931, Ford enrolled at the University of
Michigan and concentrated in economics. Working year round to
help support himself, he held such jobs as busboy at the university
hospital and dishwasher in a fraternity house. Despite this
schedule and the attainment of a "B" average, he also managed to
play football and was backup center on the school's national
championship teams of 1932 and 1933. The next year, he made the
first squad and was named as the team's "Most Valuable Player."

In 1935 he took part in the College All-Star Game. That same year, he won his B.A. degree.

Rejecting bids to play professional football, Ford joined the athletic staff of Yale University. While serving as an assistant football and boxing coach, he attended law school, where he ranked in the top third of his class. During the summer of 1936, he worked as a seasonal ranger at Yellowstone National Park. In 1941 he was awarded an LL.B. degree.

Before the year was out, Ford gained admittance to the Michigan bar and began practicing at Grand Rapids. Shortly after Pearl Harbor, he enlisted in the Navy as an ensign. He spent a substantial part of his tour of duty as an operations officer on the aircraft carrier U.S.S. *Monterey* in the Pacific. Early in 1946 he was separated as a lieutenant commander.

Returning to Grand Rapids, Ford resumed his law career. His participation in civic organizations earned him two major awards for community service. In 1948 he married Elizabeth Bloomer Warren, a department-store fashion coordinator. They were to have three sons and one daughter, Michael, John, Steven, and Susan.

Meanwhile, Ford's stepfather, a local Republican leader, and Michigan's Senator Arthur H. Vandenberg, nationally known spokesman for a bipartisan internationalist foreign policy, had encouraged Ford in 1948 to challenge the district's incumbent U.S. Representative, an isolationist. After winning the Republican primary in a sweeping upset, Ford easily carried the general election.

In 12 subsequent bids for the same office, Ford regularly obtained more than 60 percent of the vote. During 25 years of service in the House of Representatives (1949-73), the last 8 years of which he functioned as Minority Leader, he advanced Republican policies, figured prominently in party affairs, played a key role on the Defense Appropriations Subcommittee, and aspired to the House speakership. As a member of the Warren Commission, he helped investigate the assassination of President Kennedy.

During the autumn of 1973, in the first application of the 25th amendment to the Constitution, President Nixon nominated Ford as Vice President to replace Spiro T. Agnew, who had resigned. After extensive hearings, both branches of Congress overwhelmingly confirmed the appointment.

On August 9, 1974, Nixon left office and Ford was inaugurated as the 38th President. One of his first actions, designed to contribute

Ford as a seasonal ranger at Yellowstone National Park during the summer of 1936.

President and Mrs. Ford shortly after his inauguration in 1974.

to national reconciliation in the wake of Watergate, was the pardon of his predecessor. Ford also nominated former New York Governor Nelson A. Rockefeller as his Vice President.

Ford's major domestic problem was the economy. Ailing since 1973, it had been weakened by soaring inflation, mounting unemployment, and a worsening energy crisis. Ford first focused on inflation. But, by the end of 1974, the unemployment rate had become critical and demanded his primary attention. From then on, his proposals met considerable opposition from the Democratic-controlled Congress—despite his long service there and his personal popularity among its Members.

Neither that body nor the President, who held fundamentally different economic philosophies, was able to forge anti-recession policies acceptable to the other. Ford, stressing economic restraint by the Government, favored indirect stimulation of the private business-industrial sector by such incentives as accelerated tax writeoffs for plant expansion in high unemployment areas. For this reason, he vetoed or threatened to veto a series of emergency job and public-works projects that Congress passed. On the other hand, Congress supported few of his legislative initiatives.

Nevertheless, Ford's veto power did help him exact compromises on several key issues, including emergency unemployment programs, housing subsidies, and energy policy. He also managed to obtain a congressional ceiling on Federal expenditures in exchange for his approval of an economic-stimulus bill authorizing income-tax reductions.

Ford's fiscal conservatism was further demonstrated by his refusal to sign legislation extending special monetary aid to financially troubled New York City until it and the State took more substantive remedial steps of their own.

In the area of energy, Ford espoused a policy of marketplace pricing and increased use of alternative energy sources, especially nuclear power. Congress rejected his proposals to lift controls on oil prices and deregulate natural-gas rates, and forced him to remove fees he had imposed on imported crude oil as a means of encouraging domestic production and conservation. Yet Congress was unable to devise energy measures Ford would approve.

To encourage the self-sufficiency of farmers and to prevent the imposition of undue governmental controls, Ford advocated an open agricultural market and low crop-support prices. His embargo on

U.S. grain shipments to the Soviet Union, an anti-inflationary step to lower food prices, caused considerable resentment in the farm States.

Ford's most joyful domestic activity was presiding over the Nation's Bicentennial celebration, which culminated on July 4, 1976, with festivities across the land.

The President retained Henry A. Kissinger as Secretary of State, and stressed loyalty to traditional U.S. alliances and overseas commitments. On his three trips to Europe, he pledged to maintain support for the North Atlantic Treaty Organization (NATO); signed, at Helsinki, a multilateral agreement that among other things confirmed certain post-World War II boundary changes; and participated in an economic conference of the major Western powers held at Rambouillet, France. He later hosted a similar meeting in Puerto Rico.

Ford journeyed twice to Asia as well. He was the first American President to visit Japan while in office and reaffirmed U.S. friendship with that nation. He also conferred in Peking with Mao Tse-tung of the People's Republic of China.

A keystone of Ford's foreign policy was improvement of relations with the Soviet Union. Meeting at Vladivostok in 1974, he and Russian leader Leonid I. Brezhnev concurred on certain quantitative limitations on strategic nuclear arms. Two years later, the two powers agreed to limit underground nuclear tests.

In the Mideast, following arduous negotiations that Kissinger conducted as an intermediary, the administration scored a signal success in the disengagement of Israeli-Egyptian forces in the Sinai and Israeli-Syrian armies on the Golan Heights.

Ford strove early in his term to find means of preserving the anti-Communist governments of Cambodia and Viet-Nam. Congress rejected his proposals to increase military aid to these regimes, though it approved humanitarian assistance. Events rendered the disagreement moot, for in the spring of 1975 Communist-backed forces triumphed in both countries. The United States extended refuge to many thousands of exiles.

The Ford administration subsequently demonstrated strong concern over the fate of missing American prisoners-of-war, and vetoed Viet-Nam's admission to the United Nations. After the new Cambodian Government detained a U.S. merchant vessel, the *Mayaguez,* the President took stiff military action to gain her release.

Ford at his desk in the White House.

Because of the state of affairs in southern Africa during Ford's last year in office, he sought to mediate a lessening of tensions. Limited aid to pro-Western forces in Angola's civil war proved unavailing, and Congress refused to approve more substantial sums the President recommended. Conflict between the government of Rhodesia and its antagonists also mounted, and civil unrest grew in South Africa.

Ford fought an uphill battle in his attempt to win reelection. Within the Republican Party, he was seriously challenged from the right, by ex-Governor of California Ronald Reagan. Smoothing Ford's path, late in 1975 Vice President Nelson A. Rockefeller, who had been a target of party conservatives, announced he would not be a candidate for another term. Nevertheless, Ford's race with Reagan was a close one through the primaries, and he did not triumph until the convention. He chose Kansas Senator Robert J. Dole as his running mate.

In his clash with Democrat Jimmy Carter, Ford upset early public-opinion polls that pointed to a Carter sweep and nearly won the election.

Ford rendered maximum assistance to the President-elect during the transition and won praise in Carter's inaugural address for what he had done to heal the Nation. The Fords retired to Palm Springs, Calif.

Jimmy Carter

THIRTY-NINTH PRESIDENT   1977–

Carter, who was inaugurated as the Nation began its third century, invoked a "new spirit" for the country—one based on trust and rooted in basic and enduring American principles. Because he was the first Chief Executive to come to office directly from the Deep South since well before the Civil War, his election heralded a major reconciliation between the North and South. Although his only previous elective experience consisted of the governorship of his native Georgia and service in its legislature, his vigorous Presidential campaign had dramatically propelled him into national prominence and the White House.

Born in 1924 at Plains, Ga., James Earl ("Jimmy") Carter, Jr., was the first child of a farmer-storekeeper and a registered nurse-housewife. They later raised another son and two daughters. When Jimmy was 4 years old, the family moved to nearby Archery. He helped his father, who was also active in local and county affairs, on the farm and in the store.

Carter attended the local public school, which was in Plains. There, one of his teachers, Miss Julia Coleman, whom he quoted in his Presidential inaugural address, inspired him in intellectual and cultural endeavors. He graduated from high school in 1941.

After a year of study at Georgia Southwestern College in nearby Americus, Carter entered the Georgia Institute of Technology ("Georgia Tech") at Atlanta in 1942 as a naval ROTC student. The next year, he fulfilled a childhood ambition by entering the U.S. Naval Academy, in Annapolis, Md. His class, in which he stood in the top tenth, graduated in 1946 on an accelerated schedule because of the exigencies of World War II (1939–45). Shortly after graduation, he married Rosalynn Smith of Plains. They have four children—three sons and a daughter.

During Carter's subsequent naval career (1946–53), he rose from ensign to lieutenant. His wife accompanied him to his home ports. These included Norfolk, Va.; New London, Conn.; Pearl Harbor, Hawaii; San Diego, Calif.; and Schenectady, N.Y. He first served at sea on board experimental radar and gunnery vessels as well as submarines. The highlight of his service was participation in the nuclear submarine construction program, which was directed by Capt. (later Adm.) Hyman G. Rickover. During this time, Carter took courses in nuclear physics and reactor technology at Union College, Schenectady, N.Y.

Midshipman Carter in 1946, shortly before his graduation from the United States Naval Academy.

In 1953, following the death of his father, who among his other activities had been sitting in the State legislature, Carter resigned his commission. He and his family returned to Plains and took over his father's farm and agricultural supply business. After some lean years, they built up a prosperous peanut production and processing enterprise.

Although Carter also involved himself in civic, church, and fraternal affairs, he steadfastly refused to join the local segregationist White Citizens' Council. He served on the county school, library, and hospital boards; and participated in local and State economic planning organizations.

In 1962 Carter, a lifelong Democrat, entered the political arena. After a strenuous contest, he won a seat in the State senate and held it for two terms (1963–67). He demonstrated a special interest in election reform and improvement of the educational system.

Carter had planned to run for the U.S. House of Representatives in 1966, but decided to seek the governorship after the leading candidate in his party withdrew. Although he failed to win the nomination then, he did so 4 years later, and then won the general election.

During his single term (1971–75), while stressing economy and tightening budget procedures, Carter thoroughly reorganized the State government. He also displayed strong interest in conservation and attracted national attention for his moderate stance on civil rights. He capped his gubernatorial years by helping direct the 1974 Democratic national campaign.

Late that year, Carter announced his candidacy for the Presidency. In succeeding months, he, his family, and other backers crisscrossed the country to build up grassroots strength. After his success in Iowa's Democratic caucuses early in 1976, he won victories in several key primary elections. His phenomenal rise confounded political experts, who had regarded his quest as hopeless.

Carter's support mounted so steadily that several other leading contenders withdrew. Even before the convention, he gained virtual assurance of the nomination and, in a departure from tradition, announced in advance his Vice-Presidential choice, Senator Walter F. Mondale of Minnesota.

The contest between Carter and incumbent Chief Executive Ford, the first Presidential campaign conducted with substantial amounts of public funds, featured a series of three televised debates sponsored by the League of Women Voters. These were the first since those in 1960, but the television debate between Vice-Presidential candidates Mondale and Republican Senator Robert J. Dole set a precedent.

Carter won by a relatively narrow but conclusive margin over Ford in both popular and electoral votes—the popular margin exceeding that of Kennedy in 1960 and Nixon in 1968. Carter scored heavily among blacks and with labor, showed special strength in his native South, and ran well in the Northeast. He was the first President from Georgia and the first elected directly from the Deep South since Zachary Taylor in 1848.

Following his triumph, President-elect Carter vacationed at St. Simons Island, Ga. From there and his home in Plains, though he made a few trips to Washington, he directed preparations for the assumption of power. In naming his Cabinet, he stated that he

Campaigning in Oregon.

planned to emphasize its role in Government. The transition, which enjoyed the full cooperation of Ford, was conducted smoothly and amicably.

Dramatizing his intention to remain close to the people and to disavow many of the trappings of the Presidency, after his inauguration at the Capitol Carter broke with custom and walked down Pennsylvania Avenue to the White House.

As Carter took office, he stressed his plans to stimulate the economy, reduce unemployment, attack inflation, balance the Federal budget, reorganize the executive branch, formulate a comprehensive energy program, and further racial and social justice. In foreign policy, he set as his guideposts the maintenance of global peace, reduction of armaments, demonstration of concern for human rights, and the enhancement of relations with all nations.

Departing from tradition, Carter walked from the Capitol to the White House following his inauguration. Members of his family accompanied him.

Part Three

The Presidents:
Survey of Historic Sites and Buildings

OUR Presidents are commemorated by scores of sites, ranging from the humble to the palatial: birthplaces, residences, other buildings, inaugural places, monuments, and tombs. Visits to them enhance understanding of the distinguished group of men who have led the Nation; their ways of life; family backgrounds; locales and regions in which they were born or resided; eras in which they lived; and the social, economic, and intellectual influences that molded them.

This volume includes all National Park System units and National Historic Landmarks associated with the Chief Executives except those that are principally of pertinence to their pre- and post-Presidential professional, business, political, and military careers and those relating to domestic and foreign policy aspects of the various administrations. These two categories are treated in the volumes of this series dealing with political and military affairs by period.

Represented in the following descriptions are at least one residence or building other than the White House for every President except McKinley, whose tomb-memorial is included, and Ford and Carter, for whom no residences or structures had been designated by the time this volume went to press. The sites are in 20 States as well as one in Canada (Roosevelt Campobello International Park). The District of Columbia, Massachusetts, New York, Ohio, and Virginia predominate. The greatest number, 14, are in the District of Columbia. Virginia contains 11. The only States in the trans-Mississippi West included are California, Iowa, Missouri, North Dakota, South Dakota, and Texas.

The historic places range from the White House, Pennsylvania Avenue National Historic Site, and St. John's Episcopal Church—which honor most of the Presidents—to a variety of structures and memorials commemorating individual Chief Executives. Of the 71 sites treated, almost half, or 30, are in the National Park System and the remainder are National Historic Landmarks. Most of them are excellently preserved, though some are restorations or reconstructions. The Landmarks are owned and administered by U.S. Government agencies, States, cities, various nongovernmental institutions, and private individuals. Many of these have made outstanding restoration and preservation efforts.

IN addition to the sites discussed in this book, numerous Other Sites Considered shed further light on the careers of the Presidents. These are places of State and local significance, nominated through appropriate channels by the various States, that the Advisory Board on National Parks, Historic Sites, Buildings, and Monuments has deemed to possess noteworthy historical value but not national significance.

Many Other Sites Considered in all phases of history are listed on the National Register of Historic Places, maintained by the National Park Service's Office of Archeology and Historic Preservation. The register also incorporates National Park System units and National Historic Landmarks. It is published periodically and distributed by the Superintendent of Documents, U.S. Government Printing Office, Washington, D.C. 20402.

ALSO not included in the following descriptions are two monuments in the Washington area, one that is pending and the other that is in the process of being established. The only existing memorial to Franklin D. Roosevelt is a simple one, as he had requested, at the corner of Ninth Street and Pennsylvania Avenue near the National Archives Building. Although in 1959 Congress had authorized a more substantial monument, by the time this volume went to press the U.S. Commission of Fine Arts had not yet accepted any of the designs that had been proposed.

Nearing completion when this book was sent to the printer was the Lyndon B. Johnson Memorial Grove, D.C. It is near the Pentagon in Lady Bird Johnson Park (formerly Columbia Island) between Arlington Memorial and Rochambeau (14th Street) Memorial Bridges and the Boundary Channel and the west bank of the Potomac. The 15-acre site, which is just off George Washington Memorial Parkway and offers a panoramic view of Washington across the river, consists of a grove of 500 white pine trees, shrubs, biker-hiker trails, and picnic facilities.

Many Presidential residences, especially birthplaces, no longer survive. One of these is the Hayes Birthplace, Delaware, Ohio, shown here in 1876, the year he ran for President, when it was being used as a furniture warehouse. Today, a service station occupies the site.

Megalith at the Lyndon B. Johnson Memorial Grove, D.C. The Washington Monument is visible in the distance across the Potomac.

The focus of the park, designed by landscape architect Meade Palmer, is a huge block of rough-hewn, red Texas granite, which came from a quarry near the LBJ Ranch and is being sculpted by Harold Vogel. On four sides of the megalith will be flat pink marble stones bearing well-known statements of the President, selected by Lady Bird, on education, civil rights, environment, and the Presidency. Construction of the memorial, authorized by Congress in 1973 and dedicated late in 1974, was funded by public subscriptions.

ALSO well worth visiting are the Presidential Libraries, which are operated by the National Archives and Records Service of the General Services Administration for most modern ex-Presidents beginning with Hoover. Open to the public, they provide interesting exhibits and audiovisual programs on the lives and times of individual Chief Executives and offer excellent research opportunities to historians and other scholars.

The Hoover Library is in West Branch, Iowa; Franklin D. Roosevelt, at Hyde Park, N.Y.; Truman, in Independence, Mo.; Eisenhower, at Abilene, Kans.; and Lyndon B. Johnson, at Austin, Tex. The Kennedy, Nixon, and Ford Presidential Libraries have not yet been permanently established, and none has yet been proposed for Carter.

OUR Presidents have also been honored in many other ways than by the designation and maintenance of structures, national memorials, and Presidential Libraries. This is particularly true in placenames—not only across the land but throughout the world. These range from the *Avenue du Président Wilson* in Paris and the *Departamento del Presidente Hayes* in Paraguay to the State of Washington and the city of Madison. Many cities besides Washington, D.C., as well as a variety of other places are also named after our first President. Other Chief Executives are commemorated in cities, counties, educational institutions, naval vessels, and the like.

Two are honored in Washington, D.C., in the John F. Kennedy Center for the Performing Arts and its Eisenhower Theater. Visible from one part of the Nation's Capital is the eternal flame of the Kennedy Gravesite, in Arlington National Cemetery, Va., where Taft is also buried. In addition to the numerous statues in the U.S.

The documentary resources and exhibits in the Presidential Libraries, which have been established for most modern Chief Executives, attract the general public as well as scholars. This is the Eisenhower Library, in Abilene, Kansas.

John F. Kennedy Center for the Performing Arts.

Capitol, various others are located throughout the city, notably the equestrian tributes to Jackson in Lafayette Park and Grant at the foot of Capitol Hill on the east end of the Mall.

George Washington Memorial Parkway runs along the Potomac in Virginia, the District of Columbia, and Maryland. Theodore Roosevelt Bridge links the District of Columbia and Virginia; and Woodrow Wilson Memorial Bridge, Virginia and Maryland, just south of the District of Columbia boundary.

THE major aim of the National Survey of Historic Sites and Buildings is to identify nationally important places that are not *National Park System Areas,* but no survey would be complete without including them. This is particularly true because many were designated as National Historic Landmarks before they became part of the Park System.

National Historic Landmarks are those sites judged by the Secretary of the Interior and/or the Advisory Board on National Parks, Historic Sites, Buildings, and Monuments to meet the criteria of national significance in commemorating the history of the United States *(see rear matter).* Owners of National Historic Landmarks may receive certificates and bronze plaques attesting to the distinction by applying to the Department of the Interior and agreeing to preserve the designated properties.

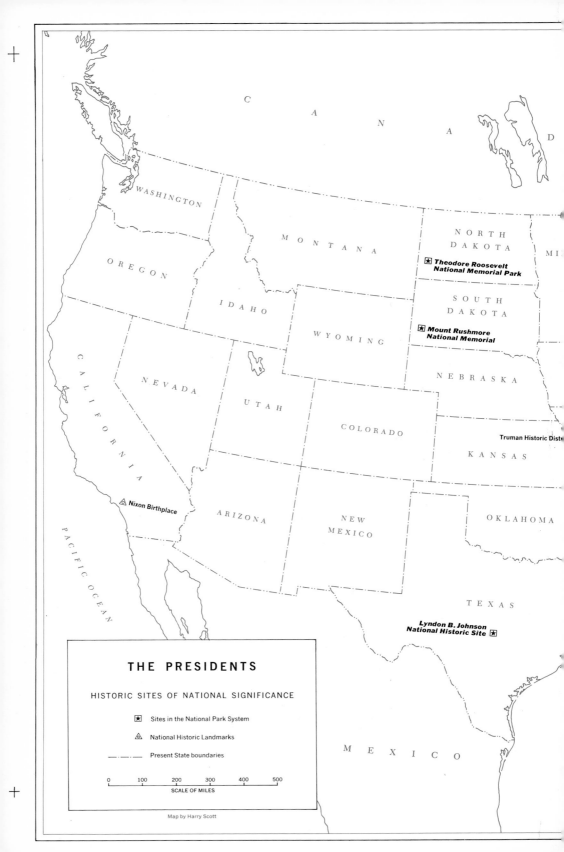

THE PRESIDENTS

HISTORIC SITES OF NATIONAL SIGNIFICANCE

★   Sites in the National Park System

⚠   National Historic Landmarks

—·—·—   Present State boundaries

0   100   200   300   400   500
SCALE OF MILES

Map by Harry Scott

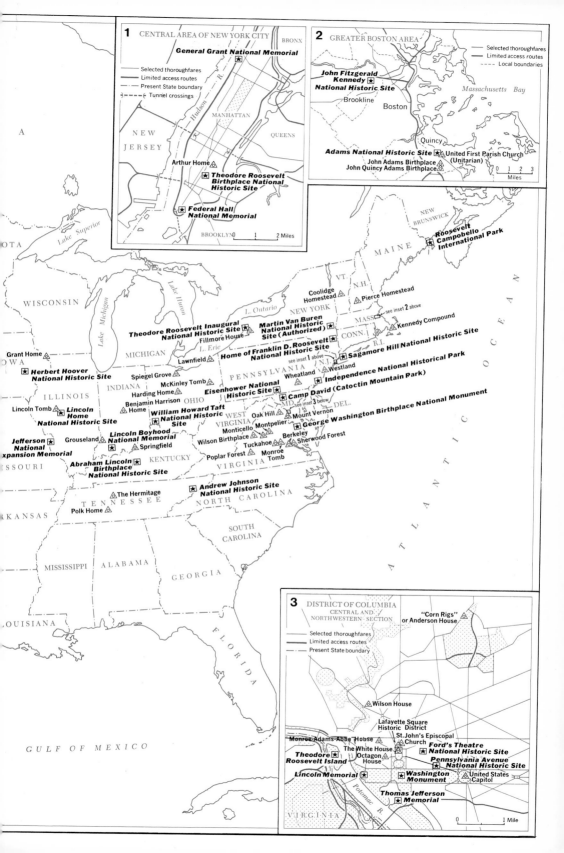

For the convenience of users of this volume, sites and buildings are listed alphabetically by State. The following code indicates site categories:

Site Categories

☒ NATIONAL PARK SYSTEM AREAS

⚠ NATIONAL HISTORIC LANDMARKS

NOTE: *Except where otherwise indicated, all the following sites are open to the public. Before visiting any of them, inquiry should be made to the owners or custodians concerning dates and hours of access and admission costs, usually nominal. Special permission should be obtained to visit privately owned sites.*

Nixon Birthplace, California ⚠

Orange County, 18061 Yorba Linda Boulevard, Yorba Linda.

On January 9, 1913, this modest framehouse was the birthplace of Richard M. Nixon, 37th President of the United States. His father, Frank Nixon, had come to California from Ohio in 1907 and worked at a variety of jobs before moving 5 years later to Yorba Linda. There, he constructed a residence and began raising citrus fruit for a living. The Nixons were active in the civic and religious life of the community. Mrs. Nixon was a charter member of the Women's Club, and both parents helped found the local Friends Church, where their children attended Sunday school. Richard began his education in the town and completed third grade in public school before the farming operation became unprofitable and the family moved in 1922 to closeby Whittier.

After the Nixons departed, the birthplace home passed through the hands of a series of owners. About 1948 the Yorba Linda School District, which held the adjacent property, acquired the structure as part of an expansion program. Subsequently, the house faced destruction several times. In 1959, however, the school board and citizens of Yorba Linda officially designated it as a historic site.

The residence stands in a small grove of trees at the top of a hill

Nixon Birthplace.

above Yorba Linda Boulevard. The main section of the structure is 1½ stories in height; a shed dormer is located on the north side of the gable roof, which is low pitched and covered with asphalt shingles. The front elevation features overhanging eaves and a shallow gabled vestibule. The rear of the house, probably created by enclosing a porch, is one story high with a flat roof. The clapboard siding is white and the window trim is green.

The structure, which has changed little during the past few decades, is utilized by the Yorba Linda School District and is not open to the general public. About 30 yards to the west is an elementary school that was recently renamed after President Nixon.

Roosevelt (Franklin D.) Campobello International Park, Canada ★

New Brunswick Province, on Campobello Island, about one-half mile northeast of the Franklin D. Roosevelt International Memorial Bridge, which connects the island with Lubec, Maine.

This international park, administered jointly by the United States and Canada and a symbol of friendship between the two nations,

The residence at Franklin D. Roosevelt Campobello International Park.

Franklin D. Roosevelt, his mother, and sons James (right) and Elliott (left) at Campobello in 1913.

commemorates the life of Franklin D. Roosevelt and preserves the summer home that frequently gave him respite during his youth and early political career.

About 1880 a group of New York and Boston entrepreneurs acquired Campobello Island, on Passamaquody Bay just east of the U.S.-Canadian boundary across Lubec Channel from Lubec, Maine, for development as a resort area. One of the first U.S. citizens who began spending his summers at the place was James Roosevelt. He first vacationed there in 1883, when his son Franklin was only a year old. The next year, James purchased 4 acres of waterfront land, and 2 years later completed construction of a cottage.

As a youth on the island, Franklin acquired a love for the sea and sailing that became a lifelong passion, hiked over the rugged terrain, and learned to play golf and tennis. After the death of his father in 1900, he continued to accompany his mother to the island. Following his marriage to Anna Eleanor Roosevelt in 1905, he brought his own family there for the greater part of each summer.

In 1910 Roosevelt acquired his own residence on the island. A two-story frame structure built in 1897 in the Dutch Colonial style, it was considerably larger than his father's cottage, to the north, which came to be known in the family as "Granny's House." In 1910-15 Roosevelt added a study onto the south end of his home. Crippled by an attack of polio he suffered on the island in 1921, when he was 39 years old, he did not return until 1933, while serving his first term as President. His final visits occurred in 1936 and 1939, though his family continued to use the residence until 1952, 7 years after his death, when his son Elliott sold it to the Hammer family.

In 1962 the dedication of Franklin D. Roosevelt International Memorial Bridge, between Lubec, Maine, and Campobello Island, made the island more accessible to the public. The next year, during a meeting with Prime Minister Lester B. Pearson of Canada, President John F. Kennedy suggested that the home be preserved as a memorial to Roosevelt and as an expression of international peace and good will between the two countries.

In 1963 the Hammers, who had furnished the residence with items appropriate to the time of Roosevelt's occupancy, donated the structure, its furnishings, outbuildings, and about 10½ acres of land to the Governments of the United States and Canada. The next year, the park was established. It is owned and administered by a joint Canada-United States commission. The house is in good condition today, and some of its 34 rooms are open to the public. "Granny's House" is no longer extant. The larger part of the 2,721½-acre park is kept in a natural state.

"Corn Rigs," or Anderson House (part of "Old Soldiers' Home"), District of Columbia △

Rock Creek Church Road and Upshur Street NW., Washington.

Known at various times as the United States Military Asylum and "Old Soldiers' Home" but officially designated today as the U.S. Soldiers' and Airmen's Home, the institution is primarily of importance as the only retirement domicile in the Nation for Regular Army and Air Force enlisted personnel, warrant officers, and disabled soldiers and airmen. Its origins, establishment by Congress in 1851, operation, financing, and evolution, as well as the building complex, are treated in other appropriate books in this series. Its pertinence to this volume, however, is the use of the original quarters—"Corn Rigs," or Anderson House—as a sort of early "Camp David," or Presidential retreat, by Buchanan, Lincoln, Hayes, and Arthur.

The soldiers' home opened on December 24, 1851, in a building on 17th Street NW., while the board of commissioners considered sites for a permanent location. That same year, they purchased from George W. Riggs, prominent Washington banker, his 200-acre estate near Rock Creek Church and an adjoining one of about 58 acres owned by Charles Scrivener. One of the highest points of land in the District of Columbia, its elevation is more than 300 feet.

Anderson House.

In June 1852 the home's occupants moved into a house on the Riggs property that he had constructed in 1842-43. It was called "Corn Rigs" from the estate's cornfields and the Scottish word for a ridge or furrow. Later, the building was renamed Anderson House, or Cottage, after Gen. Robert Anderson, of Fort Sumter renown, to commemorate his early advocacy of and part in creating the soldiers' home, whose founder was Gen. Winfield Scott.

In 1857, when the new Main (present Sherman South) Building was completed, the veterans moved into it. Beginning in that year and intermittently until 1884, with the approval of hospital authorities, the following Presidents and their families utilized Anderson House as a summer home to escape the heat of downtown Washington: Buchanan (1857-60), Lincoln (1861-64), Hayes (1877-80), and Arthur (1882-84). Possibly Grant occasionally occupied the residence; and Garfield apparently planned to move in during the summer of 1881, but he was assassinated before he could do so.

Lincoln, enjoying the peace and seclusion afforded by the house, reached many critical decisions there about the conduct of the Civil War and wrote the second, or final, draft of the preliminary Emancipation Proclamation (September 1862). Because of numerous threats to his life, a military guard escorted him back and forth to the White House. He was less cautious on July 12, 1864, when he became the only President to come under hostile fire while in office. On that occasion, he traveled 2 miles north from Anderson House to witness Gen. Jubal A. Early's attack on Fort Stevens, which culminated his 2-day thrust against Washington's defenses.

When Anderson House was vacant during the summer of 1866, the hospital of the soldiers' home was relocated there until the spring of 1876, when the Barnes Building, which houses the present hospital, was occupied. Beginning 10 years later and lasting for more than three decades, Anderson House served as quarters for the home's band members. From the early 1920's until the 1950's, the house reverted to its original use as a general barracks and until recently provided living quarters for women occupants. After they were switched into a dormitory in one of the new buildings in 1969, Anderson House was renovated and converted into a guesthouse and supervisors' lounge.

The building is a 2½-story, brick structure in the Gothic style. In 1897 the walls were coated with gray stucco. Bargeboards decorate the ends of the gabled roof. A wide, five-bay, one-story porch, whose roof is surrounded by a wrought-iron railing, extends across the front of the residence. The center and two southwestern bays protrude from the other two bays. The steps lead up the side of the center bay, which is decorated with a triangular pediment. Extensive white-colored latticework covers much of the porch.

The rooms are large and the ceilings high. The interior remained unchanged from the time of President Lincoln until 1923, when small squad rooms were constructed to accommodate the occupants. When the women were residing there, a small elevator was constructed on the southwest corner of the building to handle those who were disabled. Anderson House is not accessible to the public.

Ford's Theatre National Historic Site, District of Columbia ☒

Ford's Theatre, 511 - 10th Street NW.; and Petersen House, 516 - 10th Street NW., Washington.

This national historic site consists of two units: Ford's Theatre, the scene of one of the most tragic events in U.S. history—the assassination of President Abraham Lincoln; and the Petersen House, also known as the House Where Lincoln Died. Restored Ford's Theatre now offers regularly scheduled theatrical performances and serves as a museum and shrine to Lincoln. Complementing it across the street is the Petersen House, whose historical appearance has also been recreated.

In the spring of 1865 the Nation's future seemed promising. After 4 long years of devastating warfare, the Civil War had virtually come to an end. On April 9 Gen. Robert E. Lee, commanding the Confederate Army of Northern Virginia, surrendered to Gen. Ulysses S. Grant at Appomattox Court House, Va., and the capitulation of another large force under Gen. Joseph E. Johnston was imminent. In the South, the weary task of Reconstruction was already underway. In the North, many citizens, determined to forget the past, looked forward to national harmony.

For all these reasons, President Lincoln proclaimed April 14 as a day of thanksgiving. To conclude a long list of his scheduled activities on that date, he decided to attend Ford's Theatre, a popular entertainment center in Washington. The play to be presented was a light comedy, *Our American Cousin,* which starred the celebrated actress Laura Keene.

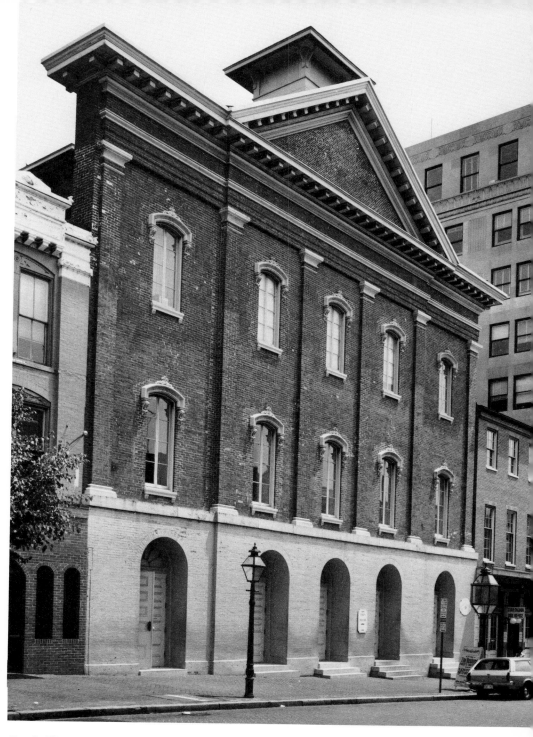

Ford's Theatre.

On the morning of April 14, a White House messenger informed the manager of the theatre of President and Mrs. Lincoln's plans to attend that evening's performance and that they would be accompanied by General and Mrs. Grant. Excitement mounted among Washingtonians as the news filtered out into the streets that the President and Grant were to be present. The theatre's manager prepared for a capacity crowd.

Stagehands scurried to make preparations for the Presidential party. For more spacious accommodations, they converted the two upper boxes at the south side of the stage into a single one by removing a partition between them. They flanked the box with two American flags on staffs and draped two others over the balustrade. At the front of the center pillar in the box, they hung an engraving of George Washington and suspended on a staff the blue regimental flag of the U.S. Treasury Guards. For the party's maximum comfort, a sofa and some chairs, including an uphol-stered rocker used by Lincoln on previous visits, were moved into the box.

During the afternoon, the Grants notified the President that they would be unable to attend the performance. In their place, Lincoln invited Miss Clara Harris, daughter of New York Senator Ira T. Harris, and her fiancé, Maj. Henry Rathbone. About 8:30 p.m., after the play had already begun, the Lincoln carriage arrived in front of the theatre. When the Presidential party entered the box, stage action ceased, the orchestra struck up "Hail to the Chief," and a full house rose and cheered. Lincoln moved forward, bowed to the audience, and then took a seat in the rocker at the front of the box. The play resumed.

At approximately 10:15, while one of the actors was delivering a monologue, Lincoln leaned slightly forward to peer into the audience below. Simultaneously, John Wilkes Booth, an actor who frequented the theatre and who knew its layout intimately, slipped silently though the unguarded door at the rear of the box and fired a pistol shot at close range into the back of Lincoln's head. He slumped forward unconscious. Instantly, Rathbone lunged at Booth, and the two men struggled. Booth dropped his pistol but managed to slash Rathbone with a knife he was carrying.

Handbill for the performance at Ford's Theatre during which Lincoln was assassinated.

FORD'S THEATRE

TENTH STREET, ABOVE E.

SEASON II..........WEEK XXXI..........NIGHT 196

WHOLE NUMBER OF NIGHTS, 495.

JOHN T. FORD.. PROPRIETOR AND MANAGER
(Also of Holliday St. Theatre, Baltimore, and Academy of Music, Phil'a.)
Stage Manager.. J. B. WRIGHT
Treasurer... ....H. CLAY FORD

Friday Evening, April 14th, 1865

BENEFIT!

—AND—

LAST NIGHT

OF MISS

LAURA KEENE

THE DISTINGUISHED MANAGERESS, AUTHORESS AND ACTRESS,.

Supported by

MR. JOHN DYOTT

AND

MR. HARRY HAWK.

TOM TAYLOR'S CELEBRATED ECCENTRIC COMEDY,

As originally produced in America by Miss Keene, and performed by her upwards of

ONE THOUSAND NIGHTS,

ENTITLED

OUR AMERICAN

COUSIN

FLORENCE TRENCHARD.......	MISS LAURA KEENE
(Her original character.)	
Abel Murcott, Clerk to Attorney..................	.............John Dyott
Asa Trenchard.....................................	............Harry Hawk
Sir Edward Trenchard.............................	.................T. C. GOURLAY
Lord Dundreary...................................	...............E. A. EMERSON
Mr. Coyle, Attorney..............................	............MATTHEWS
Lieutenant Vernon, R. N...........................	...........W. J. FERGUSON
Captain De Boots.................................	............C. BYRNES
Binney...	..............R. G. SPEAR
Buddicomb, a Valet...............................	...............J. H. EVANS
John Whicker, a gardener..........................	...........J. L. DE BONAY
Rasper, a groom..................................	
Bailiffs..	G. A. PARKHURST and L. JOHNSON
Mary Trenchard...................................	.................Miss J. GOURLAY
Mrs. Mountchessington............................	.....Mrs. H. MUZZY
Augusta..	............Miss H. TRUEMAN
Georgiana..	.............Miss M. HART
Sharpe...	.............Mrs. J. H. EVANS
Skillet...	.............Miss M. GOURLAY

SATURDAY EVENING, APRIL 15,

BENEFIT of Miss JENNIE GOURLAY

When will be presented BOURCICAULT'S Great Sensational Drama,

THE OCTOROON

Easter Monday, April 17, Engagement of the YOUNG AMERICAN TRAGEDIAN,

EDWIN ADAMS

FOR TWELVE NIGHTS ONLY

THE PRICES OF ADMISSION:

Orchestra..$1.00
Dress Circle and Parquette................................75
Family Circle..25
Private Boxes.................................. $6 and $10

J. R. FORD, Business Manager.

H. Polkinhorn & Son, Printers, D street, near 7th, Washington, D. C.

When the injured Rathbone broke his hold on Booth, the latter vaulted over the box balustrade. In doing so, he entangled the spur of one of his boots in a flag, lost his balance, and landed on the stage below in a kneeling position, fracturing his left leg. Regaining his balance within seconds, he hurried across the stage and through the wings to the back entrance of the theatre, mounted the horse he had left outside, and galloped away.

Meantime, the audience, many of whom thought that Booth's leap was part of the play, had reacted slowly. When they began to realize what had actually occurred, a stunned silence turned into pandemonium. Several doctors rushed to the Presidential box, examined the wound, and ordered that Lincoln be carried to the nearest bed, which happened to be across the street in the home of tailor William Petersen.

The assassination of Lincoln was part of a conspiracy organized by 26-year-old John Wilkes Booth, who as a youth had cultivated an intense admiration for the South and its institutions. Member of a prominent family of actors, but less successful than his father Junius Brutus or his brother Edwin, John Wilkes had occasionally performed at Ford's Theatre, once in Lincoln's presence. Talented, handsome, and popular though he was, throughout his life Booth had displayed signs of eccentricity, occasional erratic behavior, and a thirst for fame. During the Civil War, his hatred of the North and his love for the South became an obsession. Brooding over the sinking fortunes of the Confederacy, he had originally planned to kidnap Lincoln and hold him hostage, probably hoping to win the release of Confederate prisoners.

Abetting Booth in this scheme were several of his friends, with whom he often met and plotted in a boardinghouse on H Street, in Washington, D.C. It was operated by Mrs. Mary E. Surratt, the mother of John Surratt, who was a member of the group. Following an abortive attempt to abduct Lincoln in March 1865, they separated. Booth and several of them later reassembled and conceived an even more drastic plot: the assassination of Lincoln, Vice President Andrew Johnson, and Secretary of State William H. Seward.

When Booth visited Ford's Theatre at noon on April 14, he learned of Lincoln's plans to attend. Realizing that his moment of opportunity had come, he called together his accomplices and hastily devised a course of action. He was the only one of the conspirators who successfully carried out his mission. One other, Lewis Powell, also known as Lewis Payne, did gain entrance to Secretary of State Seward's quarters and stabbed him in the neck but not fatally. George A. Atzerodt, who was supposed to kill Johnson, lost his nerve and made no attempt. Within days, all the conspirators except Booth and John Surratt were rounded up, including a couple of men who had only been involved in the kidnapping plot.

On April 26 a cavalry detachment trapped Booth in a barn near Port Royal, Va. Shortly after the troops set fire to the barn, Booth suffered a fatal gunshot wound. Surratt, apprehended in Alexandria, Egypt, in 1866, was tried in civil court, but was released after the jury deadlocked. Also arrested were Mrs. Surratt, who was probably innocent; Dr. Samuel Mudd, who had set Booth's fractured leg during his flight; and Edman Spangler, a Ford's Theatre stagehand who was charged with aiding Booth to escape.

In one of the most sensational and irregular trials in U.S. history, they were all tried in the summer of 1865 by a military tribunal. Payne, Mrs. Surratt, and two others died on the gallows. Three, including Dr. Mudd, were sentenced to life imprisonment at Fort Jefferson, Fla. One of them died in an 1867 yellow-fever epidemic, and President Johnson pardoned the other two, as well as Spangler, who had received a 6-year sentence.

Interior of Ford's Theatre. Lincoln was sitting in the flag-draped mezzanine loge when he was shot.

AT the time of the assassination, Ford's Theatre, an imposing brick structure three stories high, was one of the finest and most modern in the Nation. In 1863 theatrical producer John T. Ford had built it to replace one on the same site that had burned the previous year. Shortly after the assassination, the War Department placed guards outside the theatre and cancelled all future productions. Ford planned to reopen it later in the year, but public opinion prevented him from doing so.

In 1866 Ford sold the theatre to the Federal Government, which fireproofed it by removing the woodwork and converted it into an office building. For years, the structure housed the Army Medical Museum and the records and pension office of the War Department. On June 9, 1893, tragedy struck once again when a section of the third floor collapsed, killing 22 Government employees and injuring 65 others. Thereafter, the edifice served as a storehouse for official records.

In 1932 the building became the Lincoln Museum, depository of the Lincoln Collection of Osborn H. Oldroyd. A private citizen who had acquired more than 3,000 items of Lincolniana over a period of 60 years, he had sold the collection to the Government in 1926. In 1933 the National Park Service took over administration of the museum. Following World War II, public interest in restoration of the theatre began to mount. In 1960 the National Park Service undertook an extensive program of historical and archeological research, and 4 years later Congress provided funds for a total restoration, completed in 1968.

Although the architectural plans of Ford's Theatre were not extant, the National Park Service restored its exterior through the use of original photographs and other records. At the front facade on 10th Street, five arched entranceways are on the first story, and brick pilasters on the second and third stories separate the bays. The gable roof ends in a triangular pediment above a false parapet.

Today, Ford's Theatre again offers live dramatic productions. When plays are not in progress, visitors may tour the theatre and witness a regularly scheduled sound-and-light program from the orchestra seats on the main floor. The program recreates the atmosphere of the Civil War era in Washington, relates the history of the theatre, and dramatically recounts the story of the assassination. The interior of the theatre is furnished with period pieces and authentic reproductions; the Presidential box appears exactly as it did on the night of April 14, 1865; and the stage is set for the scene in *Our American Cousin* during which the fatal shot was fired.

In the basement is the Lincoln Museum, the nucleus of which was the Oldroyd Collection. In the center of the room are three crescent-shaped display areas, containing objects associated with three phases of Lincoln's life: his youth, legal and public careers, and the Presidential years. Recorded messages explain the significance of the items. Numerous other Lincoln memorabilia occupy specially designed glass cases throughout the room. One alcove is devoted exclusively to items associated with the assassination. Also on display are the plaster casts of the hands and life mask of Lincoln. In a lounge at the east end of the room, visitors may hear recorded passages from some of his speeches.

THE Petersen House, across the street from the theatre, was built in 1849 by William Petersen, a tailor. A three-story brick rowhouse over a high basement, it contained more than enough space for Petersen, who rented out extra rooms to lodgers. On the night of April 14, 1865, as doctors were carrying Lincoln out of Ford's Theatre, an unidentified man, probably either Petersen or one of his lodgers, appeared on the landing of the house and beckoned to them. The doctors then carried the President across the street, up the curved steps to the first floor of the house, and placed him in a small bedroom at the rear of the entrance hall that was rented by a William Clark.

Throughout the night, the doctors maintained a solemn vigil over the dying President, while a continuous stream of Cabinet members, Congressmen, Army officers, and friends, as well as Vice President Andrew Johnson, paid their respects at the bedside. Mrs. Lincoln, who sat stricken with grief in the front parlor, wandered in periodically to gaze at her husband. At one point, she fell into a faint so prolonged that she was denied further access to the room. In the rear parlor, Secretary of War Edwin M. Stanton began an investigation of the assassination, conferred with Cabinet members, and carried on Government business. About 7:00 a.m., Dr. Robert K. Stone, the Lincoln family doctor, announced that death was near. Within a half hour, Lincoln passed away. Approaching the bedside, Stanton is said to have uttered the words "Now he belongs to the ages."

House Where Lincoln Died.

This is the most historically authentic of the many artistic renditions of Lincoln's deathbed scene. As Surgeon-General Joseph K. Barnes provides medical attention, Lincoln's son Robert Todd, personal secretary John M. Hay, and military and governmental officials look on.

THE Petersen House remained in the hands of the Petersen family until 1878, when newspaper editor Louis Schade purchased it. He used it as a residence and office for his newspaper, the *Washington Sentinel,* which he published for many years in the basement. Throughout the years, curious visitors desiring to see the room where Lincoln died became such a nuisance that in 1893 Schade moved out and rented the residence.

The new tenant was Osborn H. Oldroyd, who had been collecting Lincoln memorabilia for nearly three decades. He moved his collection into the house and opened it to the public as a museum. Three years later, the Federal Government purchased the building, but allowed him to continue to live in it and operate his museum. He died in 1930, or 4 years after the Government had purchased his collection. In 1932 the Oldroyd Collection was moved to Ford's Theatre to form the Lincoln Museum. At that time, several women's organizations refurnished the Petersen House. Under the jurisdiction of the National Park Service since the early 1930's, it has undergone only one major rehabilitation, in 1958-59.

A semicircular stairway, equipped with a wrought-iron railing, leads to the entrance of the first floor, the only section of the house open to the public. The first room to the left of the entrance hall is the front parlor, where Mary Todd Lincoln spent the night of April

The room where Lincoln died.

14-15 with her son Robert and friends. From this room, a double doorway leads to the back parlor, which features the marble-top center table that Secretary of War Stanton used on the same night. At the rear of the house and at the end of the hallway is the room where Lincoln died. Its furnishings approximate those of April 14-15, 1865, including replicas of the pictures hanging on the walls and similar wallpaper.

Jefferson Memorial, District of Columbia   ⊠

Directly south of the White House and the Washington Monument, on the southeast edge of the Tidal Basin, SW., Washington.

This memorial, a circular colonnaded structure in the classic style associated with Jefferson in this country, honors his contributions to the founding and growth of the Republic. Author of the Declaration of Independence and the Virginia Statute of Religious Freedom, the Nation's third President, and apostle of democratic government and freedoms, Jefferson served with distinction in many high offices. An opponent of tyranny and proponent of personal liberty, he believed in a simple democratic form of government, freedom of the press, freedom of speech, education of the populace, and the dignity of the common man.

The reflections of the memorial in the Tidal Basin enhance its beauty. More important factors than the purely esthetic, however, influenced selection of the site. Jefferson's position in the Nation's history demanded a memorial site of prominence in the central plan of the Capital and in relation to other national memorials already built. The Capitol, the White House, and the Mall had been located in accordance with the L'Enfant plan. The subsequent erection of the Washington Monument and Lincoln Memorial on the approximate west axis of the Capitol established the cardinal points of the city's plan. The lone remaining site in this cross-like scheme was the one selected for the Jefferson Memorial south of the Tidal Basin on a line with the south axis of the White House.

The significance of the classic architectural scheme of the memorial is apparent to even the casual student of Jefferson. One of the best-known characteristics of his genius was his many-sided ability and the remarkable practical application of his vast knowledge to many fields of activity. His outstanding ability as an architect can be seen in the design of the Virginia State Capitol, which was essentially his. His designs of the Rotunda at the University of Virginia and his home, Monticello, further indicate his preference for classical architecture.

The entrance to the memorial is from the plaza on the north, or Tidal Basin, side. The sculpture group above the entrance way, the work of Adolph A. Weinman of New York City, depicts Jefferson standing among the committee appointed by the Continental Congress to write the Declaration of Independence. To his left, as viewed from the steps, are Benjamin Franklin and John Adams,

Jefferson Memorial.

We were present at a ceremony in which F.D.R. gave a speech - in early 1941.

and seated on his right are Roger Sherman and Robert R. Livingston.

The interior of the memorial is dominated by a heroic statue of Jefferson. Rudulph Evans, the sculptor, was chosen from more than 100 who participated in a nationwide competition conducted by the Thomas Jefferson Memorial Commission. The statue is 19 feet high and stands in the center of the memorial room upon a 6-foot pedestal of black Minnesota granite. The statue, together with the wall inscriptions executed in bronze, is in pleasant contrast with the white Georgia marble of the interior, and the Indiana limestone of the dome, approximately 67 feet above the head of the statue. Through the four colonnaded openings of the memorial—two on the east-west axis and two on the north-south—the statue may be viewed from many angles and with varying light and shadows.

The exterior walls and dome of Danby Imperial Vermont marble reach approximately 96 feet above the entrance. In early spring, usually in April, when the hundreds of Japanese cherry trees bordering the Tidal Basin are in bloom, the memorial appears in its most beautiful setting. During this period, the annual Cherry Blossom Festival is staged near the Tidal Basin.

In 1934 Congress passed the act that provided for the building of a permanent memorial to Jefferson in the Capital City. The Thomas Jefferson Memorial Commission, created by this legislation, assumed responsibility for the planning and supervision of the project. The designers were John R. Pope, Otto R. Eggers, and Daniel P. Higgins. Ground-breaking ceremonies were held on December 15, 1938, and the cornerstone officially laid on November 15, 1939. On both these occasions, President Franklin D. Roosevelt and commission members took part. The memorial was dedicated on April 13, 1943, the 200th anniversary of Jefferson's birth.

Lafayette Square Historic District, District of Columbia ⚿

Directly across Pennsylvania Avenue from the White House and vicinity, NW., Washington.

Immediately surrounding and in the environs of Lafayette Square, or Lafayette Park as it is officially known, are a group of sites and buildings possessing unusual historical and architectural merit. They illustrate the growth of the Nation's Capital from its early years to the present day and reflect a variety of architectural trends and styles. Many prominent Americans have worked, lived, or visited in these places. Several of them bear a close association with the Presidency or with specific Presidents, and the park itself was once part of the White House grounds.

In architect-engineer Pierre L'Enfant's 1791 plan for the Capital, he included the present park, then a neglected, treeless common, in President's Park. This area, the original White House estate,

extended from present H Street between 15th and 17th Streets NW. to the Potomac River. President Jefferson, however, specified the boundaries of today's park and designated it as a public area. Workers constructing the White House lived there in temporary shelters.

A market later occupied the grounds. During the War of 1812, U.S. soldiers camped there. In 1824, under the direction of the U.S. Commissioner of Public Buildings, who was then responsible for the plot, the park was improved and the first walks laid out. It soon after began to be known as Lafayette Square, in honor of the Marquis de Lafayette, French hero of the War for Independence, who visited Washington while touring the United States in 1824-25.

The first plans for professional landscaping occurred in 1851, shortly after the newly formed U.S. Department of the Interior took over jurisdiction of the park. Noted landscape architect Andrew J. Downing was retained to lay out several city park areas. He completed a plan for Lafayette Park before he died in a boating accident the next year, but the national crises leading up to, during, and right after the Civil War (1861-65) delayed further progress.

The one major accomplishment during the period was erection in 1853 of the bronze, equestrian statue of Andrew Jackson that stands in the center of and dominates the park. Cast by sculptor Clark Mills from cannon captured by Jackson from the Spanish in Florida during the period 1812-19, it was one of the first major equestrian statues produced in the country. During the Civil War, troops who guarded the White House camped in the park.

In 1867 the U.S. Army Corps of Engineers assumed jurisdiction over the area. In 1872, generally adhering to the Downing plan, it carried out the first full-scale landscaping of the park. From then until the 1930's, when the National Park Service acquired jurisdiction, a pattern of routine maintenance was followed, except for the erection at each corner of the square of statues commemorating foreigners who fought alongside the Continental Army during the War for Independence. The first one, placed at the southeast corner in 1891, honors the Marquis de Lafayette. The

View along Jackson Place, on the west side of Lafayette Square. President Theodore Roosevelt resided in the building from which the flag is flying, 736 Jackson Place, during the White House renovation in 1902.

second, dedicated in 1902 at the southwest corner, commemorates the Comte de Rochambeau. The third, erected in 1910 at the northeast corner, is dedicated to Gen. Thaddeus Kosciuszko of Poland. The final statue, placed that same year at the northwest corner, pays tribute to Prussian military leader Baron Friedrich W. Von Steuben.

A second landscaping project, conducted in 1936-37 by the National Park Service and the Works Progress Administration, enhanced the beauty of the park and made it more accessible to the public. Since that time, except for the incorporation of some of the features of the Downing plan in the 1960's, it has remained essentially unchanged.

Over the years, Lafayette Park has become a center of community life and a public area of national significance. Administered by the National Park Service, it traditionally serves as a gathering place for civic and patriotic organizations as well as any group that wishes to make its views known to the Nation and to the Chief Executive. Special events include memorial tree plantings, wreath-laying ceremonies, and community cultural activities.

Despite extensive urban renewal and expansion elsewhere in Washington, D.C., the Lafayette Park vicinity retains much of its historical flavor and charm. A number of 19th- and early 20th-century buildings around or near the square are of major architectural or historical interest. Five that are associated with individual Presidents or the Presidency in general possess National Historic Landmark status. The first, St. John's Episcopal Church, known as the "Church of the Presidents" and located at the corner of 16th and H Streets, is described separately in this volume.

Another, the Decatur House, at 748 Jackson Place, was the home of Martin Van Buren in 1829-31 while he was serving as Secretary of State. A fine example of a Federal-period townhouse, it was built in 1818 by U.S. naval hero Commodore Stephen Decatur and was the first private home on the square. It has been the residence of several distinguished diplomats and political figures. In later years, during Gen. Edward F. Beale's ownership, President Grant was a frequent guest. Today, the National Trust for Historic Preservation operates the residence as a historic house museum.

The third structure, just west of the White House at the corner of

Blair-Lee House.

Pennsylvania Avenue and 17th Street, is the Executive Office Building, which is not open to the general public. An excellent example of French Second Empire architecture, it was built in 1871-88 to house the State, War, and Navy Departments. Presidents who have maintained temporary or part-time offices there include Hoover, Lyndon B. Johnson, and Nixon. Other Chief Executives who worked in the building earlier in their careers were Assistant Secretaries of the Navy Theodore and Franklin D. Roosevelt, Secretary of War Taft, and Vice Presidents Lyndon B.

State, War, and Navy Building (present Executive Office Building) about 1880. The occasion for which it was decorated cannot be ascertained.

Johnson and Ford. Today the structure accommodates some of the Office of Management and Budget, as well as part of the White House staff.

Blair House, also a Landmark, erected in 1824 by Dr. Joseph Lovell, Army Surgeon General, is at 1651 Pennsylvania Avenue. In 1837, the year after his death, noted newspaper editor Francis P. Blair acquired it and for more than a century his socially and politically prominent family owned it. During this time, close personal and political associates Presidents Jackson, Van Buren, Lincoln, and Taft often paid calls, as did some other Chief Executives on special occasions.

In 1942 the U.S. Government purchased the building for use as a guest residence for visiting dignitaries. Six years later, it was joined to the adjacent Lee House, just to the west at 1653 Pennsylvania Avenue, which had been acquired by the Government in 1941. Francis P. Blair had built the latter structure in the

1850's for his daughter and her husband, Samuel P. Lee. President Andrew Johnson occupied it briefly in 1865 while waiting for Mrs. Lincoln to leave the White House.

In the period 1948-52 President Truman and his family, who had also lived in Blair House temporarily upon his assumption of the Presidency in 1945, while Mrs. Roosevelt was vacating the White House, resided in the combined Blair-Lee House while the Executive Mansion was undergoing a major renovation. On November 1, 1950, two would-be assassins tried to shoot their way into the house to attack Truman, but White House guards repelled them. The impressive edifice is 3½ stories high over an elevated basement. The west (Lee) portion is painted brick; and the east (Blair), stucco-covered brick. The structure is not accessible to the public and continues to house official guests, especially foreign chiefs of state.

The fifth Landmark in the historic district that has a Presidential relationship is the Treasury Building (1836-69), which is open to the public. In present room 3434, President Andrew Johnson maintained offices from April 16 to June 8, 1865, immediately after Lincoln's assassination.

A few other buildings in the district have major Presidential associations. The Dolley Madison House, an unpretentious Federal-style structure at the southeast corner of Madison Place and H Street, was built in 1818-20 by Richard Cutts, Dolley's brother-in-law, who had borrowed money for the construction from James Madison. In 1829, after Cutts had lost most of his fortune in unsuccessful business ventures, ownership of the house reverted to Madison, who never lived in it. Upon his death in 1836, Dolley inherited it. During her residence, from 1837 until she succumbed in 1849, she advised various First Ladies and played a prominent role in Washington society. The restored building, now federally owned, is not open to public visitation.

During a renovation of the White House in the summer of 1902, President Theodore Roosevelt occupied an extant house at 736 Jackson Place. Another structure, at 716 Jackson Place, has been restored by the Federal Government for the official use of ex-Presidents. A four-story building dating from the late 1860's, it was once the home of Supreme Court Justice Oliver Wendell Holmes, Jr.

Many other structures in the district possess historical or

Decatur House.

architectural importance. Two of these are the U.S. Chamber of Commerce Building (1925) and Riggs National Bank (1898). The majority, however, are former private residences that are today owned and used by the Government. One, near the Dolley Madison House, is the Tayloe-Cameron House (1818), known as the "Little White House" during President McKinley's administration because Senator Mark ("Boss") Hanna lived in it.

In recent years, the Federal Government has restored many of the buildings in the district, demolished a few modern ones, and constructed several replicas in a style that harmonizes with the historical setting. As a result, the district now approximates its 19th-century appearance.

Lincoln Memorial.

Lincoln Memorial, District of Columbia ★

West Potomac Park, on Lincoln Memorial Circle, just west of the Reflecting Pool and directly east of Arlington Memorial Bridge and the Potomac River, Washington.

This memorial ranks with the Washington Monument and the Jefferson Memorial as one of the most beloved shrines in the Nation. Outstanding among the many sites and monuments honoring President Lincoln, it symbolizes his belief in the freedom and dignity of all men. The monument is also one of the most impressive examples of classical architecture in the United States.

The first major effort to commemorate Lincoln occurred on March 29, 1867, or 2 years after his death, when Congress incorporated the Lincoln Monument Association for the purpose of erecting an appropriate memorial. Despite some preliminary planning, the association failed to accomplish its objective. In subsequent years, several other organizations considered and abandoned similar projects. Finally, in February 1911, Congress created the Lincoln Memorial Commission, under whose auspices the present memorial was constructed.

Statue in Lincoln Memorial.

In 1912 the commission chose a site, at the west end of the Mall in West Potomac Park on the axis of the Capitol and the Washington Monument. The next year, Congress approved a design submitted by architect Henry Bacon. Workmen broke ground in 1914 and the following year laid the cornerstone. At the dedication ceremony, on Memorial Day, May 30, 1922, Chief Justice of the Supreme Court and former President William Howard Taft, who was also chairman of the Lincoln Memorial Commission, presented the structure to President Warren G. Harding, who accepted it on behalf of the people of the United States.

The memorial, constructed primarily of white Colorado-Yule marble, is of classical design and resembles the Parthenon, in Athens, Greece. The basic structure, rectangular in shape, is surrounded on all four sides by a colonnade of 36 Doric columns, one for each State at the time of Lincoln's death. Their names, separated by double wreaths of pine and laurel boughs, are carved into the frieze above the colonnade. Inscribed on the walls over the frieze are the names of the 48 States at the time of the dedication, linked together by a series of garlands broken at intervals by eagle wings. The date of admission to the Union appears in Roman numerals under the name of each State. An unusual architectural feature of the memorial is the tilting inward of the columns, the outer facade above them, and to a lesser degree the main walls to prevent an illusion, created by the size of the structure, that it is bulging at the top.

A long flight of steps rising from a landscaped terrace and circular driveway leads up to the entranceway, which faces eastward toward the Reflecting Pool and Washington Monument. Two tripods, each cut from a single block of pink Tennessee marble, flank the steps; and two columns behind the colonnade support the lintels over the entrance. The interior walls of the memorial chamber are constructed of Indiana limestone; the floor and wall base, of pink Tennessee marble. The ceiling features bronze girders ornamented with laurel and oak leaves. The panels between the girders are of Alabama marble saturated with paraffin to produce translucency.

Eight Ionic columns, arranged in two rows of four, divide the chamber into three sections. In the center section is the huge seated statue of Lincoln designed by sculptor Daniel C. French. It was carved over a period of 4 years from 28 blocks of Georgia white marble and rests on an oblong pedestal and platform of Tennessee marble. A large stone tablet inscribed with Lincoln's Second Inaugural Address adorns the wall of the north section of the chamber. A similar tablet on the wall of the south section contains the Gettysburg Address. Above each of these tablets is a mural painted by Jules Guerin. The murals, 60 feet long and 12 feet high, allegorically depict some of the principles espoused by Lincoln.

Monroe-Adams-Abbe House, District of Columbia ⚠

2017 I Street NW., Washington.

This distinguished early 19th-century townhouse, located about a block southeast of Washington Circle and a few blocks northwest of the White House, is also known as the Timothy Caldwell House, after its first owner. Ranking in historical significance with the Octagon and Decatur Houses, it is one of the oldest extant buildings in Washington and was the scene of many distinguished social events. For a time, it was the Nation's Executive Mansion, while the White House was being renovated after the British put it to the torch during the War of 1812; and later, ironically, headquarters of the British Legation. Besides President James Monroe, other prominent occupants included statesman Charles Francis Adams and scientist-meteorologist Cleveland Abbe, "father" of the United States Weather Bureau.

In 1802 Caldwell built what is essentially the present northwest rear wing, which apparently faced K Street. Three years later, he obtained more land and extended the structure by erecting the larger, main, front part. During the period 1808-13, ownership temporarily passed to Gideon Granger, U.S. Postmaster General. Caldwell, who may never have lived in the house, subsequently again held possession, until 1840, but apparently because of financial difficulties leased the residence to various tenants. One of these was Monroe, for at least part of the time while he served as Secretaries of State (1811-17) and War (1814-15) under Madison; and during the first 6 months of his own Presidency, from March 4 to September 17, 1817, while remodeling of the White House was being completed following its burning by British troops in 1814. The I Street home of the Monroes, who had acquired many fine furnishings during his service abroad as a diplomat, epitomized

Monroe-Adams-Abbe House.

tasteful and luxurious living. They entertained graciously, notably at a post-inaugural reception.

The next lessee was the British Legation, from 1821 or 1822 until 1831. During the tours of duty of Ministers Stratford Canning and Charles R. Vaughan, particularly, the house was a social center of the city. Subsequent occupants were the Baron de Mareschal, an Austrian diplomat; Charles Francis Adams, noted diplomat and son of John Quincy Adams; Silas Casey, a young officer who was later to gain renown during the Civil War; and a Mrs. Latimer, who operated a boardinghouse. In 1840 Caldwell sold the property to

Francis Markoe, Jr., a State Department official. Then, in 1877, Abbe acquired it and resided in it until his death in 1916. For a few months, the St. John's School for Girls utilized the structure, but its present owner, the Arts Club of Washington, then took title.

The Federal-style rowhouse is four bays wide and 3½ stories in height. The strong, rhythmical design and careful detailing of the street, or south, facade, as well as the spatial relationship of the entrance hall, stairway, and principal reception rooms on the second floor, typify an approach to urban architecture that achieved a high point in this type of house, whose architectural history is somewhat obscure.

The red brick is laid in Flemish bond, and the trim and two belt courses are of buff-colored stone. The gray slate gabled roof, which is edged by a simple wooden box cornice, is flanked by two end chimneys. The two dormers are gabled and fanlighted. Sills are stone; the flat arch lintels feature splayed voussoirs and keystones. First-floor shutters are paneled, and those on the upper two floors are louvered. The third-story windows are shorter in height than those on the two lower levels. The main entrance, in the west bay, is decorated with a semicircular fanlight and double-hung sash sidelights. Surmounting the fanlight is a molded steel arch, which is capped by a console-shaped keystone.

The rear of the house, including the three-story wing, which is three bays in length, is similar in detail to the front but the brick has been covered with stucco. A one-story, shed-roofed, enclosed porch is attached to the north, or rear, wall of the wing. A cast-iron balcony at the rear, second-floor level of the base of the ell overlooks a walled garden-patio.

A fire in 1963 and extensive alterations over the years, including the addition of modern plumbing and heating systems as well as structural strengthening, have vastly changed the interior, which has a side-hall plan. Except for the numerous six-panel doors, few features are original, though much of the decoration and detail is interesting, particularly the stairway and mantels. The plan is roughly the same on all floors: two large front rooms, one behind the other; and smaller rooms in the rear wing. Of particular interest on the second floor is the front drawing room, the largest room in the house. Behind it, adjacent to the stair hall, is a smaller reception room.

Still used by the Arts Club of Washington as a clubhouse, the building is not ordinarily open to the public. Honoring the occupancy of James Monroe, a small city park across the street is named after him.

Octagon House, District of Columbia ⚠

1799 New York Avenue NW., Washington.

Not only·is this building, erected by Col. John Tayloe, a superb example of Federal-style architecture, but President James Madison and his wife also temporarily resided in it for about a year while the White House was being rebuilt following its burning by British troops in 1814. In the second-floor, front study he held Cabinet meetings and signed the Treaty of Ghent.

Colonel Tayloe, a wealthy and influential planter whose main residence was at Mount Airy estate in Richmond County, Va., was apparently persuaded by his friend George Washington to build a townhouse in the new Capital City instead of in Philadelphia. In 1797 Tayloe purchased a triangular corner lot 2 blocks west of the newly rising President's House (White House), and obtained the architectural services of Dr. William Thornton, original architect of the Capitol. Work on the Tayloe home, one of the first to be put up in Washington after it was designated as the Capital, began in 1798 or 1799, and George Washington likely visited the site to observe construction progress.

Octagon House.

When completed in 1800, the year after his death and well before the White House was finished, the residence was one of the finest in the Nation. After the Tayloes moved in the next year, it became a gathering place for early Washington society and the scene of many notable social affairs. Guests over the years included Jefferson, Madison, Monroe, John Quincy Adams, Jackson, Decatur, Webster, Clay, Calhoun, the Marquis de Lafayette, and Baron Von Steuben.

On August 24-25, 1814, during the War of 1812, the British occupied Washington and set fire to the White House, Capitol, and other public buildings. Octagon House was likely spared only because the Tayloes had leased it temporarily to French Minister Louis Serrurier (Serurier), who flew the Tricolor from it. Offered the use of several local homes when they returned to the city, the President and his wife, Dolley, after living briefly at another residence, accepted the invitation of the Tayloes, who stayed at their Virginia plantation, and moved into Octagon House on September 8, 1814.

Presidential life quickly resumed a normal pace, though wartime anxieties cast a pall over social gatherings. The Madisons maintained their living quarters on the second floor, in the southeast suite, which consisted of a small vestibule, a large bedroom with a fireplace, and a smaller dressing room. The President used the adjoining circular tower room as a study and at least some of the time as a meetingplace for his Cabinet. There, on February 17, 1815, he signed the Treaty of Ghent concluding the war, after the Senate had unanimously ratified it. Later in 1815, for some reason the Madisons relocated to 1901 Pennsylvania Avenue, at the corner of Pennsylvania Avenue and 19th Street NW., in the "Seven Buildings." They lived there for the remainder of his Presidential term.

The Tayloes returned to Octagon House. After Colonel Tayloe died in 1828, his wife continued to occupy it until her death in 1855. Thereafter the building was leased for a variety of purposes and fell into disrepair. As early as 1889 the American Institute of Architects expressed interest in acquiring it from the Tayloe family for its national headquarters, and in 1897 agreed to rent it for 5 years and began rehabilitation. The institute took formal possession in 1899, and 3 years later effected the purchase.

The mansion, which has been carefully restored, is in excellent condition. Marking a new zenith in Federal architecture, as characterized by its spare though brilliant geometric forms and in the restrained yet elegant Adam-style decoration, it represents a major departure from the traditional late Georgian and early Federal styles that preceded it. The unusual plan, which combines a circle, a triangle, and two rectangles, ingeniously adapts the structure to the acute angle formed by the intersection of New York Avenue and 18th Street. Despite its name, Octagon House is actually an irregular hexagon broken by a dominant semicircular bay projecting from the front, or southwest, face. There are eight sides only if the front bay is counted as three.

Constructed of red brick laid in Flemish bond on the facade and in English bond on the rear, the building rises three stories over a raised stone basement. The only important structural change ever made was removal, sometime before 1830, of the original Adam-style, flat-deck roof and fronting high brick parapet. A low, hipped roof was added, and the present cornice was installed. Four tall, interior chimneys now pierce the roof.

The belt course marking the second floor, recessed rectangular panels below the third, and all the window sills are of Aquia sandstone. Small, elliptical, grilled-iron balconies accent the floor-to-ceiling windows of the second floor. Window lintels are rubbed brick jack arches without keystones. Stone steps, flanked by a grilled-iron handrail lead to the one-story, flat-roofed portico, which is supported by two Ionic columns and two pilasters. A leaded, glazed fanlight tops the six-paneled door.

The elaborate interior decoration, in the Adam style, includes molded baseboards and chair railings, plaster cornices and ceiling centerpieces, mahogany doors with brass knobs and locks, wide pine floorboards, several ornate mantels, and period furniture.

In the circular entrance hall, opposite the main doorway is a graceful classical archway, which has engaged, fluted Corinthian columns. Alongside it are two arched alcoves containing cast-iron stoves, which were once used for heating and which resemble classical urns on pedestals. The archway opens into a nearly oval stair hall, in the triangular portion of the house. The stairs have plain balusters and a sweeping, rounded handrail unhindered by any newel posts. The curved landings are lighted by the rear Palladian and semicircular windows. Arched statue niches decorate each side of the first landing. Underneath this level on the

Treaty Room, Octagon House.

main floor is the back entrance. West of the stairway are small, enclosed service stairs.

The two present rectangular reception rooms that angle off from the stair hall on the ground floor, one on each side, were originally the drawing room to the southeast and the dining area to the southwest. Both rooms feature handsome, artificial cast stone mantels made in 1799 in London by a Madame Coade.

Exhibited in President Madison's study, the front rotunda on the second floor, is the pivoted, circular table on which he signed the Treaty of Ghent. Displayed thereon is the small, leather-bound trunk in which the document was brought back from Europe. Off the upper stair hall are two exhibition galleries, which were originally partitioned into living quarters, including those used by the Madisons. Offices now occupy the third floor, which once consisted of five bedrooms. The restored kitchen, wine cellar, and other service rooms are in the basement.

The outbuildings once included a kitchen, carriage house, slave quarters, stable, and smokehouse; only the latter remains. Behind it and the restored garden is the new headquarters building of the American Institute of Architects, which was completed in 1973.

Pennsylvania Avenue National Historic Site, District of Columbia ★

The part of Pennsylvania Avenue and environs between Capitol Hill, on the east, and the White House, on the west, NW., Washington.

For more than a century and a half, the segment of Pennsylvania Avenue between the White House and the Capitol has symbolized the majesty and power of the American Republic and the achievements and travails of its people. Along this truly national thoroughfare have traveled most of our Presidents in the ritual procession following inauguration that allows the Nation to welcome them and marks the assumption of their official responsibilities. Along it in death, in state funeral processions that expressed the national sense of loss, have been borne the bodies of seven Presidents who died in office and those of other national leaders. In the vicinity, assassins' bullets struck down Lincoln and Garfield. Along the avenue, victory celebrations have signaled the close of four major wars; the public has acclaimed military and civil heroes; and the Nation has received foreign heads of state and visiting dignitaries.

Our statesmen have trod the ceremonial way not only in pageantry and death but also in their daily lives. Along the avenue and its adjacent streets, in hotels, boardinghouses, and restaurants, they lodged, dined, debated the issues of the day, and determined courses of action that affected national destiny. In the theaters and places of amusement, they sought release from the cares of office. In the markets and shops, they purchased necessities and frivolities. In the hostelries, they gathered for entertainments and celebrations, highlighted by the quadrennial Presidential inaugural balls. On the south side of the avenue, as time went on the commercial center of the Capital receded before the eastward advance of the Executive Branch of the Government that ultimately produced the Federal Triangle, which typifies the monumental architectural scale of modern Washington.

THE evolution of the avenue as a ceremonial route originated in Maj. Pierre L'Enfant's 1791 plan for the Capital City, in which he laid out the street as a direct link between the White House and Capitol. The widest thoroughfare in the city, it was also the first to be paved. In 1805, at the beginning of his second term in office, President Jefferson set the precedent for subsequent inaugural parades by riding to the Capitol on horseback, reciting his oath of

Modern view of Pennsylvania Avenue, dominated by the clock tower of the Old Post Office Building. The Capitol stands to the left in the distance.

office, and then returning to the White House along the avenue, accompanied by a group of Congressmen, other Government officials, and local residents.

As other Presidents followed Jefferson's pattern, the ritual acquired a symbolic significance: the manifestation of the formal assumption of the powers and duties of the Presidency. Except for those men who ascended to that office upon the death of an incumbent and were not elected to a second term—Tyler, Fillmore, Andrew Johnson, and Arthur—as well as Ford, who took office upon

President Johnson's grand review of the Union Army at the end of the Civil War was one of the greatest parades in the Nation's history. During a 2-day period (May 23-24, 1865), approximately 200,000 troops, led by Gen. George .G. Meade on the first day and Gen. William T. Sherman on the second, marched down Pennsylvania Avenue.

Nixon's resignation, all the Presidents since Jefferson have participated in inaugural parades. Theodore Roosevelt, Coolidge, Truman, and Lyndon B. Johnson, who also succeeded deceased Presidents but won reelection, were honored with parades at the inception of their second, full terms of office.

Just as Pennsylvania Avenue has traditionally provided the means for the American public to greet new Chief Executives, it has also allowed for the expression of sorrow over their deaths or those of other prominent people. Of the eight Presidents who died in office, the state funerals of seven—William Henry Harrison, Taylor, Lincoln, Garfield, McKinley, Harding, and Kennedy—have featured processions along the avenue. That of Franklin D. Roosevelt followed Constitution Avenue. Other individuals honored with funeral processions along Pennsylvania Avenue include ex-Presidents John Quincy Adams and Taft; Vice President George Clinton; Gens. Jacob Brown, Alexander Macomb, and Philip H.

Part of the Lincoln funeral procession moving along Pennsylvania Avenue in April 1865.

Sheridan; Adm. George Dewey; statesman Henry Clay; Chief Justice Salmon P. Chase; and Ambassador Adlai E. Stevenson.

Perhaps the most memorable funeral procession along the avenue, occurring in 1921, was that of the Unknown Soldier of World War I. Arriving at Washington Navy Yard from a burial ground in France aboard the cruiser *Olympia* on November 9, the body lay in state in the Capitol for 2 days, and was then taken via the avenue to Arlington National Cemetery for reburial. Participating in the procession were President Harding, Chief Justice Taft, General Pershing, and ex-President Wilson.

The tradition of welcoming foreign dignitaries and paying tribute to national heroes along the avenue probably began in 1824, when a huge military and civilian contingent escorted the Marquis

Harding funeral procession nearing the corner of Pennsylvania Avenue and 11th Street NW.

de Lafayette, hero of the War for Independence, from the Capitol to his lodgings at Franklin House on 21st Street. In more recent times, many world dignitaries have been honored by parades along the crowd-lined street. Military leaders who were individually acknowledged include Adm. George Dewey (1899), Gen. John J. Pershing (1919), and Gen. Dwight D. Eisenhower (1945); among the other individuals acclaimed in this manner were aviator Charles A. Lindbergh (1927) and astronaut John Glenn (1962).

The only formal victory celebration on Pennsylvania Avenue occurred in May 1865 at the end of the Civil War, when President Andrew Johnson, Congress, and the Supreme Court held a grand review of the Union Army. The greatest spectacle that has ever taken place in Washington, it lasted for 2 days and featured many of the prominent generals, as well as thousands of their troops. Spontaneous celebrations on a lesser scale followed the end of the Spanish-American War and World Wars I and II.

On other occasions, the avenue has served as a national platform for expressing dissatisfaction. One memorable example of such a demonstration occurred in the spring of 1894, when "General" Jacob S. Coxey led an "army" of unemployed workers from Massillon, Ohio, to Washington to protest the failure of the Government to alleviate the national depression following the Panic of 1893. About 500 strong, Coxey's "army" marched up Pennsylvania Avenue to the Capitol, where police officers arrested them, ostensibly for treading on the grass, and thus ended the march.

A far more significant demonstration took place in the summer of 1932. Some 60,000 to 80,000 unemployed World War I veterans, known as the "Bonus Expeditionary Force," descended upon Washington and engulfed the avenue, many of them camping in vacant buildings at the tip of the present Federal Triangle. On July 28 a force of cavalry and tanks, under the direction of Gen. Douglas MacArthur and Maj. Dwight D. Eisenhower, dispersed them. On other occasions, such varied groups as suffragist, civil rights, and peace demonstrators have utilized the avenue.

Throughout most of the 19th century, the environs of Pennsylvania Avenue consisted of a diverse assortment of business

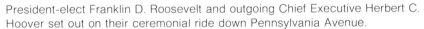

President-elect Franklin D. Roosevelt and outgoing Chief Executive Herbert C. Hoover set out on their ceremonial ride down Pennsylvania Avenue.

establishments, lodginghouses, and hotels to accommodate Government officials, relatively few of whom maintained permanent residences in the city. Most of these structures are no longer extant. Foremost among the hotels were such establishments as the National, Washington House (Gadsby's), Indian Queen, United States, St. Charles, Irving, St. James (Bunkers), Prescott House, Kirkwood, Globe, and Ebbitt. Many Presidents resided in one or more of these buildings at various times in their careers and several held inaugural balls in them. Vice Presidents John Tyler and Andrew Johnson, upon the deaths of Presidents William Henry Harrison and Abraham Lincoln, were inaugurated, respectively, in the Indian Queen and Kirkwood Hotels.

The most famous of all the Washington hotels was the elegant Willard's, at 14th Street and Pennsylvania Avenue. Known as the "Residence of Presidents" and a prominent social and political center, it was described by Nathaniel Hawthorne as the "center of Washington and the nation." The present structure, closed as a hotel in 1968 but still standing and a fine example of the French-inspired Beaux Arts style, was constructed in 1901 from the design of Henry Hardenbergh, who also created the Plaza Hotel in New York City. The 1901 building replaced an earlier hotel of the same name that dated from the 1830's. Along with such national notables as Buffalo Bill, Jenny Lind, Mark Twain, and Albert Einstein, Presidents Taylor, Fillmore, Pierce, Buchanan, Lincoln, Grant, Taft, Wilson, Harding, and Coolidge all lodged at Willard's on various occasions. On August 21, 1923, President Coolidge took his public oath of office in his suite there. And every President from Benjamin Harrison through Eisenhower attended the annual Gridiron dinners held by the press corps.

Four Presidents—Madison, John Quincy Adams, Buchanan, and Andrew Johnson—owned private residences within the boundaries of the national historic site; none of these are extant.

Another important aspect of the historical character of Pennsylvania Avenue was its role as a social and entertainment center for Presidents and other officials, as well as the general public. Until the construction of the Federal Triangle complex of buildings in the 20th century, the area within it between 11th and 12th Streets on C Street, on the south side of the avenue, traditionally housed entertainment facilities: the Washington Theater from 1805 until 1820, once attended by President Madison; and its successor,

Modern view of the Willard Hotel.

Carusi's Assembly Rooms, scene of several inaugural balls between 1825 and 1857.

Since 1835, six successive buildings at 13th and E Streets, on the north side of the avenue, have housed the National Theatre. Presidents, Congressmen, and other officials have attended performances there; in 1850 President Fillmore and his entire Cabinet were in the audience on the opening night concert of Jenny Lind, the "Swedish Nightingale." The one other major theater in the area, Ford's, on 10th Street between E and F Streets, was closed in 1865 after John Wilkes Booth assassinated President Lincoln during a performance. Today a unit of the National Park System, it is described elsewhere in this volume.

The site of President Garfield's assassination in 1881, at the Baltimore and Potomac Railroad depot at Sixth and B Streets, is now occupied by the National Gallery of Art.

PROBABLY the most historically notable buildings that are extant within the boundaries of the national historic site are the public structures, which represent about a century and a half of governmental architecture. Four of them that possess National Historic Landmark status are the U.S. Department of the Treasury Building (1836-69), along 15th Street just east of the White House; the Old Patent Office (1837-67), on F Street between Seventh and Ninth Streets, presently the National Portrait Gallery; City Hall (District of Columbia Court House) (1820-81), on Judiciary Square, where John Surratt was tried for his part in the conspiracy to assassinate President Lincoln and Charles Guiteau was convicted for the murder of President Garfield; and the General Post Office (Old Post Office) Building (U.S. Tariff Commission) (1839-69), occupying the block bounded by Seventh, Eighth, E, and F Streets.

Also of historical interest are the Old Pension Building (1882-85), on Judiciary Square; and the Federal Triangle (1928-39), a group of structures in the triangle formed by Pennsylvania and Constitution Avenues and 15th Street. They provide quarters for the Federal Trade and Interstate Commerce Commissions; National Archives; Internal Revenue Service; Federal Energy Administration; and Post Office, Justice, Labor, and Commerce Departments. Earlier structures left undisturbed when the triangle was built were the old Post Office Building, noted for its clock tower, and the U.S. Coast Guard and District Buildings. Since that time, the Coast Guard Building has been razed.

The remainder of the structures within the area of the national historic site, most of them on the northern side of the avenue, consist primarily of modern commercial and office buildings. Numerous statues and memorials enhance the street's beauty. One of them, an unembellished block of marble on a small plot of land at the juncture of the avenue and Ninth Street just behind the National Archives Building, commemorates President Franklin D. Roosevelt.

Memorial area at Theodore Roosevelt Island.

Roosevelt (Theodore) Island, District of Columbia ★

In the Potomac River, opposite the Kennedy Center for the Performing Arts, on the Washington shore, and the George Washington Memorial Parkway, on the Virginia shore, NW. Accessible only by a pedestrian causeway from the Virginia shore or by boat.

An 88-acre natural area in the Potomac River, this island serves as an appropriate tribute to the conservation activities and interests of President Theodore Roosevelt. Although primarily a plant and wildlife preserve, it is also the site of a monument honoring his Presidency and other accomplishments.

The first white men to explore the island called it "Anacostian" or "Analostan," derivations of a local Indian name. After 1632, when King Charles I of England granted it to Lord Baltimore as part of Maryland, it became known as "My Lord's Island." Capt. Randolph Brandt, who acquired it in 1681, renamed it "Barbadoes" after his home in the West Indies. The next purchaser, in 1717, was George Mason, father of the well-known Virginia constitutionalist of the same name. For more than a century, "Mason's Island" was one of the finest farming estates in the region. John Mason, grandson of the purchaser, built there a fine brick mansion, which no longer exists. Following construction of a causeway to the Virginia shore in 1805, stagnant water began to create unhealthful conditions, and about 1832 the Masons departed; later, floods washed away the causeway.

Subsequent owners included the Columbia Athletic Association, the Analostan Boat Club, and the Washington Gas Light Company. In 1931 the Theodore Roosevelt Memorial Association bought the island and offered it as a gift to the American public in memory of Roosevelt. The next year, Congress accepted the gift.

For many years, plans to erect a memorial on the island came to naught. Finally, however, in 1960 the National Park Service acquired funds for a monument, constructed between 1963 and 1967. Designed by Eric Gugler, it is in the center of the northern part of the island. It features a 17-foot-high bronze statue of Roosevelt, executed by Paul Manship, in front of a 30-foot-high granite shaft overlooking an oval sunken terrace. A water-filled moat, crossed by footbridges, surrounds the terrace. Rising from the latter are four 21-foot-high granite tablets inscribed with Roosevelt quotations.

To facilitate access to the island, the National Park Service has constructed a pedestrian causeway from the Virginia shore. Three natural environments—upland forest, swamp, and marsh—provide refuge for a variety of plants and wildlife, which may be observed via a 2½-mile network of trails.

St. John's Episcopal Church, District of Columbia ⚠

Corner of 16th and H Streets NW., Washington.

This "Church of Presidents," across from Lafayette Square, is an excellent example of Federal-style architecture and was one of the first buildings after the White House built around the square. It is today one of several surviving Federal-period structures in the vicinity, which also include the White House, Decatur House, Dolley Madison House, and the Tayloe-Cameron House. The church is included in Lafayette Square Historic District, a National Historic Landmark described elsewhere in this volume.

St. John's Episcopal Church.

The distinguished architect Benjamin H. Latrobe designed St. John's, constructed in 1815-16 in the form of a Greek cross. A lantern cupola sitting above a flat dome dominated the gabled roofline, which towered above the high sidewalls. At the intersections of the transepts were four massive pillars. Surrounding the interior was a graceful circular gallery, which had a railing and was supported by columns. The aisles were of brick and the pews high-backed. Within the chancel was a communion table, above which was a movable wine-glass pulpit, reached by a spiral staircase.

Four years after the completion of the church, workmen erected a major addition on the west side, fronted by a Doric-columned portico which became the new main entrance, and above which rose a high steeple. New flat-roofed vestibules, just behind and lower than the portico, created the form of a Latin instead of a Greek cross. In 1842 church officials replaced the old pews and subsequently made other minor modifications, but over the course of the years restored many original features.

At the time of the opening of the church, a pew was reserved for President Madison. He chose Number 28, later redesignated Number 54, and the next five Presidents—Monroe, John Quincy Adams, Jackson, Van Buren, and William Henry Harrison— occupied the pew. Since then, by tradition, pew 54 has been set aside for the President. Funeral services for William Henry Harrison and Taylor were conducted at the church. Recent Presidents who have attended include Franklin D. Roosevelt, Truman, Eisenhower, Kennedy, Lyndon B. Johnson, and Ford.

St. John's Church, in fine condition today, is still an active parish church. The basic structure, much the same as at the time of the original construction and subsequent major enlargement, is of brick and yellow stucco with white trim. Twenty-seven handsome memorial windows adorn the building. Many of the Presidents have autographed an 18th-century prayerbook, placed in the President's pew. A silver chalice donated by John Tayloe, builder of the Octagon House, and a solid gold communion chalice, encrusted with jewels, are among the many notable treasures of the church.

The White House, District of Columbia   ⚠

1600 Pennsylvania Avenue NW., Washington.

The official residence of our Presidents since 1800 and a national shrine that symbolizes the honor and dignity of the highest office in the land, the White House has not only been the scene of many historic events and brilliant social affairs but has also reflected the triumphs and tragedies of the Nation as well as the joys and agonies of the First Family.

Rear, or south, side of the White House in winter.

A home as much as the focus of national pride, the residence has reverberated with the pronouncements of statesmen and international dignitaries, the sounds of children at play, recitations of marriage vows, the sobs of mourners at state funerals, the gaiety of splendid balls. World leaders and ordinary people have trod the halls. The panorama of furnishings, decorations, portraits, other paintings, and art objects reveal the diverse careers and tastes of the occupants and portray the history of our country.

Like the Nation itself, the building and furnishings bear the influences of successive Chief Executives. Atlhough it has often been renovated and modernized, the original sandstone walls have been preserved to maintain the historical atmosphere, and the structure retains the simplicity and charm of its original appearance.

PRESIDENT Washington approved the plans, drawn by Irish-born James Hoban, winner of a prize competition, in which one of the participants, anonymously, had been Thomas Jefferson. Maj. Pierre Charles L'Enfant, the French architect-engineer, located the mansion in his plan of the Federal City, in which it and the Capitol were the first public buildings erected.

Guests arrive at the White House for a holiday reception given by President Cleveland in the first week of January 1886.

Construction began in 1792. Light gray sandstone from the Aquia Creek quarries, in Virginia, was used for the exterior walls. During the course of erection or soon thereafter, they were apparently painted white. The building was thus unofficially termed the "White House" from an early date, but for many years it was usually referred to as the "President's House" or the "President's Palace."

Hoban probably derived many of the architectural details from various European mansions, and the main facade resembles the Duke of Leinster's mansion in Dublin. Although the roof has subsequently been altered and is now flat, it was originally hipped. Hoban supervised the basic construction, the rebuilding after the burning by British forces in 1814, and erection of the north (front) and south porticoes some years later. Over the course of time, however, various architects, notably Benjamin H. Latrobe during and after the Jefferson administration, modified the original design. He added long, terrace-roofed arcades, which faced south, at the east and west ends of the building.

The John Adamses moved in during November 1800, late in his administration when the Government moved to Washington from Philadelphia. The White House was then unfinished, barely habitable, and offered few conveniences of the day. Many of the walls were still unplastered, the principal stairs had not been erected, and the roof leaked. Temporary wooden steps flanked the principal entrances, the grounds were untidy, and outbuildings were lacking. Abigail dried the family wash in the uncompleted East Room.

By the time Jefferson assumed the Presidency in 1801, the residence was still only partially finished. During the last years of his occupancy, he and Latrobe were so busy making it more livable and enhancing the exterior appearance that they found almost no time to decorate the interior. That task was partially accomplished with Latrobe's aid by Dolley Madison, who had often served as Jefferson's official hostess and who in 1809 became the new tenant with her husband. She introduced some of the elegance and glitter

Secretary of the Interior Carl Schurz entertains the Hayes family and guests at the White House.

of Old World courts into the social life of the White House until the War of 1812 struck home. In August 1814 British forces captured the city of Washington and set the White House, the Capitol, and other Government buildings to the torch in retaliation for the destruction by U.S. troops of some public structures in Canada. Before Mrs. Madison fled, she arranged for the removal of many valuable documents, objects, and the Gilbert Stuart portrait of Washington that now hangs in the East Room.

A torrential rain prevented total destruction of the edifice. Because of the fire, however, the decorations and furnishings, all of which perished, and the interior arrangement of rooms before that time are not precisely known. Only the partially damaged exterior walls and interior brickwork remained in the spring of 1815, when reconstruction under Hoban began. The Madisons lived out the remainder of his term in Octagon House and "Seven Buildings."

In September 1817 James Monroe, who had been renting a home on I Street NW. (the Monroe-Adams-Abbe House, described elsewhere in this book), was able to occupy the White House. Among its treasured possessions today are some of the furnishings

President Cleveland, shown here saying his vows with Frances Folsom in 1886, was the only Chief Executive who was wed in the White House.

The White House is the home as well as the official residence of our Chief Executives. Whether young or old, their children have had to adjust to the unique way of life there. Theodore Roosevelt's sons Archie and Quentin join the guards for morning rollcall.

he installed. During his second term, in 1824, builders completed the semicircular south portico; and in 1829, the first year of Jackson's tenancy, the front, square north portico. No other substantive changes were made in the exterior during the rest of the century, though the landscaping was improved and the garden and stable areas were reduced. President Buchanan replaced the west arcade with a greenhouse; and Grant razed the east one, which had become dilapidated.

The interior of the structure remained basically the same throughout the 19th century, but various new facilities were provided: gaslights (1848), furnace (1853), telephone (1877), elevator (1882), and electricity (1891). During the early 1880's, while widower President Arthur resided for a few months in the home of a friend on Capitol Hill, New York designer Louis C. Tiffany extensively redecorated the interior.

Late in the century, various individuals and organizations advanced proposals—practical and grandiose—for the renovation, enlargement, or replacement of the White House. One suggestion was that it be used only for state functions and that a new private residence be built for the President. At the root of these proposals was recognition that the interior had become a conglomeration of styles and periods representing the previous occupants, though it had remained sparsely furnished until the latter part of the century. Also, the use of the east end of the second floor for the Presidential and staff offices, a practice that had originated about 1850, not only made for crowded conditions but also interfered with the privacy of the First Family.

In 1902 Theodore Roosevelt, moving his family temporarily across the street to a privately owned residence on the west side of Lafayette Park at 736 Jackson Place, undertook a major restoration and expansion program. Rebuilding much of the interior, workmen enlarged the State Dining Room by removing the west stairway, altering the arrangement of the Cross Hall, and combining two smaller chambers, one of which had served as Jefferson's library and Cabinet Room. This created the present north-south orientation of the State Dining Room. Before that time, large dinners had required use of the Cross Hall or the East Room.

The main stairway was also rebuilt to open on the Cross Hall near the East Room instead of just off the north foyer, or main Entrance Hall. A solarium and guest annex were created by reconstructing the attic; a new basement was dug; and the old ground-floor rooms, which had been used for service purposes, were finished off. In addition, a new West Wing was erected to provide office space for the President and his staff, and Latrobe's east and west (replacing the greenhouse) terraces were rebuilt in gallery form. Finally, the first floor was redecorated and refurnished to conform essentially with its early 19th-century appearance.

Between 1903 and 1948 a series of alterations occurred. President Taft, the first Chief Executive to utilize automobiles, replaced the stable with a garage. In 1909 the West Wing was doubled in size by the addition of an Oval Office for the President and other offices. In 1927 a third floor was superimposed on the wing. That same year, the attic of the main building was converted into a full additional floor to provide more guestrooms, a new glassed-in sunroom, storage areas, and servants' quarters. During the renovation, the Coolidges first temporarily resided at 15 Dupont Circle, in a still-extant mansion loaned by the Patterson family, and then took an extended vacation in the Black Hills of South Dakota.

Improvements during the Franklin D. Roosevelt era (1933-45) were enlargement of the West Wing (1933-34), including a swimming pool, financed by private donations, which facilitated Roosevelt's recuperation from poliomyelitis; addition of a modern electric kitchen on the ground level of the main part of the residence (1936); erection of additional storerooms and service areas in the basement (1936); and construction of the two-story East Wing (1942), consisting of additional offices and an underground air-raid shelter.

In 1946 President Truman built a second-floor balcony inside the columns of the south portico, under which the year before Roosevelt for wartime security reasons had taken the formal oath of office for his fourth term. Later during the Truman period, in 1949-52, the White House underwent a major renovation, during which time the First Family lived at nearby Blair House, described elsewhere in this volume. Because examination had revealed that the main section of the building lacked adequate support, certain ceilings had dropped several inches, and the foundations were too weak to support the walls, the interior was dismantled and reconstructed. New concrete foundations and floors were laid, the wooden beams and interior brick supporting walls were replaced with steel framework, and new partitions were erected. The only basic change in the floor plan was the turning of the main stairway from the Cross Hall to the north foyer.

The walls and ceilings were plastered, woodwork installed, and the interior and exterior repainted. Third-floor alterations included the addition of bedrooms and a parlor, as well as enlargement of the sunroom. A new basement and mezzanine for service facilities and the placement of machinery and electrical equipment were also constructed.

Since that time, structural alterations and repairs have been minimal. President Nixon replaced the swimming pool in the West Wing with additional press facilities; and President Ford, an avid swimmer, constructed an outdoor pool, financed by private donations, behind the Oval Office.

THE White House represents the Adamesque-Federal style of architecture. The main structure is 11 bays wide and five deep, each Ionic-columned portico traversing three bays. The square front portico is gabled, whereas the semicircular rear one is flat-roofed. The large and alternately pedimented and hooded windows on the first floor and the smaller, plainly trimmed ones on the second level are the only embellishments in the regular mass and form. The center windows on the sides are Palladian on the first floor and arched, or lunette, on the second. Also providing symmetry are a crowning balustrade, the dentiled cornice, and the long east and west galleries and adjoining wings.

Because the galleries are scarcely visible from Pennsylvania Avenue, the front of the White House appears to be rectilinear in shape and its scope to be comparatively restricted. The extra ground-level story of the rear facade and the visual impact of the galleries and wings enhance the esthetic effect from that orientation, especially because the galleries give the impression of low colonnaded wings. The terraces above them provide spacious promenades at the first-floor level. Arcades, behind a series of rooms, lead under the terraces from the East and West Wings to the basement of the main structure.

The only floor open to the public is the first. Its furnishings and decorations are predominantly 19th century. Portraits of several Presidents and First Ladies hang in the foyer (Entrance Hall), main corridor (Cross Hall), and the various rooms. The main stairway to the second floor is just off the lobby on the east side of the Entrance Hall. The seals of the Thirteen Original States are carved on the marble sides of the stair archway. Six modified Classic columns separate the lobby from the main corridor. The columns and pilasters spaced along the latter's walls are of vari-colored Vermont marble; the floors are of gray and pink Tennessee marble.

The East, Green, Blue, and Red Rooms, as well as the State Dining Room, are used mainly for public functions. The East Room, which spans that end of the floor, is the largest chamber in the building and is used primarily for state receptions and balls. The dominant colors are white and gold. Decorative highlights include fluted pilasters, a cornice decorated with Greek palmettes, ceiling medallions, and parquet floors. On the east wall is the most notable portrait in the White House, Stuart's rendition of Washington that Dolley Madison removed as she fled from advancing British troops in 1814. It is said to be the only object that has been in the residence since the John Adamses first occupied it in 1800.

The East Room has other rich history. During the Civil War, troops guarding Lincoln occupied it. While the mansion was draped in mourning, the bodies of Presidents William Henry Harrison, Taylor, Lincoln, Garfield, McKinley, Harding, Franklin D. Roosevelt, and Kennedy—the first two of whom were the only Chief

Life in the White House has always reflected that of the Nation. To release men for military service, sheep served as "grass cutters" during World War I.

Executives to die in the White House—have lain in repose in the room. Married in it were Maria Monroe, Elizabeth Tyler, Nellie Grant, Alice Roosevelt, Jessie Wilson, and Lynda Bird Johnson. Because January 20, 1957, fell on Sunday, when it was considered inappropriate to take the oath of office publicly, Eisenhower took a preliminary one in the chamber before taking part in the formal ceremonies the next day at the Capitol. The second inauguration held in the room was that of Ford, who was formally sworn in there in 1974 after Nixon resigned.

The elliptically shaped Blue Room, a drawing room that was once used for diplomatic receptions, is opposite the Entrance Hall in a central position on the south side of the first floor. Furnished to represent the Monroe period, it is one of the most beautiful in the Executive Mansion. There the Chief Executive and First Lady receive guests at state dinners and receptions. The only wedding of a President in the White House took place in the Blue Room in 1886, when Grover Cleveland and Frances Folsom took their vows. Also married in the chamber were John Adams, son of John Quincy, in 1828; and Eleanor Wilson, in 1914. Franklin D. Roosevelt maintained his public office there during the summer of 1934 while the West Wing was being enlarged.

The Green Room, a parlor between the East Room and the Blue Room, also on the south side of the floor, once served as Jefferson's dining room. Restored in the Federal style, it now hosts informal receptions. The Red Room, another parlor, just west of the Blue Room, was once called the "Ladies' Drawing Room" and "Mrs. Madison's Parlor." It is decorated in the American Empire motif, and is now used for informal receptions, mainly by the First Lady. Heeding the Sabbath restriction on public oaths, on Sunday morning, March 4, 1877, Hayes first took his in the Red Room and then, the next day, repeated the words at the Capitol.

The State Dining Room, exceeded in size only by the East Room, is the southwest portion of the first floor. It is decorated in white and gold. Up to 140 guests can be accommodated at large dinners and luncheons. The Family Dining Room, just to the north, is furnished in the late 18th-century pattern, is decorated in yellow, and features a vaulted ceiling. The Presidential family dined there

President John F. Kennedy, his wife, Jacqueline, and Vice President Lyndon B. Johnson view television coverage of a space flight in 1961.

The body of ex-President John F. Kennedy lies in state in the East Room. President and Mrs. Lyndon B. Johnson exit at the left; former Chief Executive Dwight D. Eisenhower passes by the coffin, and Chief Justice Earl Warren stands bowed.

until 1961, when separate dining and kitchen facilities were created on the second floor. This freed the Family Dining Room for more intimate official functions.

The ground and upper three floors, as well as the East and West Wings, are reserved for the use of the First Family, staff, and guests. A corridor, whose ceiling is vaulted and whose walls are

President Lyndon B. Johnson welcomes King Faisal of Saudi Arabia on the rear lawn of the White House.

vari-colored Vermont marble, gives access to the ground floor. The oval Diplomatic Reception Room is below the Blue Room. Franklin D. Roosevelt delivered some of his "fireside chats" over the radio from this chamber. It is furnished with Classical Revival pieces and antique French wallpaper. The rug bears the seals of the 50 States. The China Room houses a collection of Presidential dishware. The Library contains a suite of rare Duncan Phyfe furniture. Other ground-floor rooms include the Curator's Office, Vermeil (Gold) Room, and the kitchens.

The President's private apartments occupy the west end of the second floor; the principal guest suites, the east. The Lincoln Bedroom, near the southeast end of that level, features items associated with Lincoln and is furnished in the Victorian style. It is now a guestroom, but was his Cabinet Room and he signed the Emancipation Proclamation there. Adjoining this chamber, in the southeast corner of the building, is the Lincoln Sitting Room, where various Presidents maintained their offices during the last half of the 19th century. Just west of the Lincoln Bedroom is the present

Treaty Room, which the President now uses for informal conferences. Lincoln used it as his office, and during the period 1865-1902 it accommodated the Cabinet Room. The Lincoln Sitting and Treaty Rooms are decorated basically in the Victorian motif.

The Rose Guest Room (Queens' Bedroom), near the northeast corner of the floor, is furnished as an elegant lady's bedchamber of the early 19th century. In the Yellow Oval Room, a Louis XVI salon directly over the Blue Room, the President and his lady receive visiting heads of state prior to official dinners and other functions in their honor.

The present Cabinet Room, which faces south to the Rose Garden, is in the West Wing. Truman took his oath of office there in 1945 upon the death of Franklin D. Roosevelt.

The natural beauty of the informally but carefully landscaped 18-acre grounds enhance the dignity of the White House. Particularly notable are the Rose Garden, begun by Mrs. Ellen Wilson in 1913 and the scene of Tricia Nixon's wedding in 1971, which is behind the West Wing; and the present Jacqueline Kennedy (formerly East) Garden, to the rear of the East Wing, which was dedicated to her by President and Mrs. Lyndon B. Johnson. The Chief Executives and members of their families have planted many of the trees on the grounds, which have other Presidential associations.

United States Capitol, District of Columbia ⚠
Capitol Hill, Washington.

An architectural masterpiece reminiscent of an ancient Roman temple, the Capitol sits on the crest of a knoll dominating the Capital City. It is not only a national shrine, but also a worldwide symbol of liberty and a monument to the hopes and aspirations of all mankind. Since 1800, except for a few short periods, it has been the seat of Congress; the flag flies over it day and night. Within its walls, political forces affecting the destiny of our land have recurrently and dramatically clashed. They have been resolved in the enactment of laws influencing the lives of all Americans.

THE Capitol and Congress are closely associated with the selection of the Presidents, the ceremonial aspects of their office, and their role in the Government. The Chief Executives are officially elected

View of the Capitol's east front, where most Presidents have been inaugurated.

in the Capitol. They take their oaths of office and deliver their inaugural addresses in public ceremonies at the east front. They deliver many speeches to the Congress. Most of them held congressional seats prior to their ascent to the higher office; and two even returned afterward for further service. In death, the Presidents are mourned in the rotunda.

Congress, in joint session, counts the electoral ballots to determine the President and Vice President. When no candidate receives a majority, the House of Representatives elects the President. This occurred with Jefferson in 1801, and with John Quincy Adams in 1825. The two Houses established a special commission to settle the disputed election of 1876, and Hayes emerged the winner. In the early years of the Republic, before

This daguerreotype by John C. Plumbe, Jr., taken about 1846, is the earliest known photographic image of the Capitol. This dome was later replaced, and the wings substantially extended.

national conventions were introduced, congressional caucuses nominated Presidential candidates.

Congress is also empowered under certain circumstances to remove the Chief Executive or to ascertain whether or not a disabled one should remain in power. In 1868 the House impeached

Andrew Johnson, and the Senate tried but acquitted him. In 1974 the House Judiciary Committee approved articles of impeachment for President Nixon, but he resigned before the full House could consider them.

Thomas Jefferson, in 1801, was the first Chief Executive to be inaugurated at the Capitol. He walked over from his nearby boardinghouse and took his oath of office in the Senate Chamber. Other subsequent early Presidents spoke their vows there or in the House Chamber. Beginning with Andrew Jackson, in 1829, they have customarily been sworn in during outdoor ceremonies at the east front, though in a few instances bad weather and other factors have dictated that they be held within the Capitol or elsewhere. For example, because of World War II security precautions, the fourth inaugural of Franklin D. Roosevelt was conducted at the White House.

In the Senate Chamber on May 16, 1868, Senator Edmund G. Ross of Kansas casts his decisive "not guilty" vote during the impeachment proceedings against President Andrew Johnson. Although the latter was not present, he was represented by counsel.

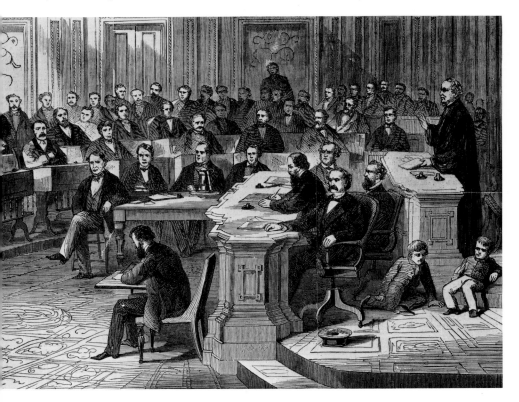

Vice Presidents succeeding to the Presidency upon the death or assassination of their predecessors have assumed office in more subdued ceremonies at a variety of locations. Only two of these ceremonies transpired at the Capitol: in 1850, when Millard Fillmore took his pledge of office in the House Chamber following Taylor's death; and in 1881, after Garfield's assassination, when Chester A. Arthur repeated, in the Vice President's Office, the oath he had earlier rendered in his New York City home.

John Adams, in 1800, was the first Chief Executive to address a joint session of Congress in the Capitol. Woodrow Wilson, in 1913, broke the custom initiated by Adams' successor, Jefferson, that the President should not appear there in person. Frequently since Wilson's time others have personally delivered State of the Union speeches and other communications to the Congress.

Many Chief Executives, earlier in their careers, served as Senators or Representatives. Several Vice Presidents, who presided over the Senate, subsequently rose to the highest office in the land. Two former occupants of that post, John Quincy Adams and Andrew Johnson, served in Congress. The former suffered a stroke in the House Chamber and died in a nearby room.

In the central rotunda, nine Presidents or ex-Presidents have lain in state—Lincoln, Garfield, McKinley, Harding, Taft, Hoover, Kennedy, Eisenhower, and Lyndon B. Johnson—as well as such notables as the Unknown Soldiers of World Wars I and II and Korea, Adm. George Dewey, and Gens. John J. Pershing and Douglas MacArthur. In 1835 Andrew Jackson, while President, escaped an assassination attempt in the rotunda while he was attending funeral services for a Congressman.

THE Capitol, which was positioned at the hub of Washington's streets by city planner Maj. Pierre Charles L'Enfant, sits on Capitol (originally Jenkins) Hill. In April 1793 Dr. William Thornton, a physician by profession but architect by avocation, won the design competition. George Washington laid the cornerstone in September. Work soon began, laborers using light gray sandstone from the quarries in Aquia, Va. But Thornton clashed with a series of professional architects who were supervising construction, some of whom wished to make major alterations in his design. He acquiesced, however, to changes that James Hoban, their supervisor and the White House architect, recommended.

When the Government moved from Philadelphia to Washington in 1800, Congress and the Supreme Court crowded into the newly finished north (Senate) wing, the first part of the structure to be completed. The next year, the House moved into a temporary building that was erected within the foundations of the south wing. In 1804 the progress of construction necessitated return of the House to the north one. The year before, Benjamin H. Latrobe had taken charge of the building. Four years later, the House Chamber was finished, and it was then connected with the Senate side by a covered wooden walkway.

During the War of 1812, in August 1814, British troops raided Washington and set fire to many buildings, including the unfinished Capitol. A heavy rainstorm and a small group of patriots quenched the flames and saved it from total destruction. Congress reconvened the next month in the Patent Office Building (formerly Blodgett's Hotel), the only Government structure to escape burning. From late the following year until 1819, sessions were held in a hastily erected structure, known as the Brick Capitol, which stood on part of the site of the present Supreme Court Building (1935); outside it, in 1817, James Monroe took his first Presidential oath.

Latrobe had undertaken restoration of the Capitol immediately following the war, but in 1817 Charles Bulfinch replaced him. Two years later, the Senate and House Chambers, somewhat modified

President McKinley delivering his second inaugural address at the east front of the Capitol, in 1901.

from the original plans, were finished. Meanwhile, construction of the projected central portion of the edifice, including its east and west fronts and rotunda, had begun. The latter, which was surmounted by a wooden, copper-covered dome, was essentially completed by 1824. But neither the Senate nor the House assumed any responsibility for it. For a few years, a multitude of hucksters invaded it and turned it into a marketplace; they sold everything from vegetables to ribbons and pianos.

The present House and Senate wings (1851-59), extensions of the old south and north ones, were constructed to provide more spacious quarters for Congress. Under the direction of Thomas U. Walter, they were built of Massachusetts and Maryland marble. Within a few years, the old House Chamber became Statuary Hall; and the Supreme Court, which had been meeting on the ground floor in the room underneath, took over the old Senate Chamber. It remained there until the present Supreme Court Building was finished in 1935. During the later part of this time, former President Taft held the Chief Justiceship. The Electoral Commission that decided the election of 1876 included some Justices and met in the old Senate Chamber.

To improve architectural proportions with the new Senate and House wings, the present and taller cast- and wrought–iron dome over the rotunda was designed to replace the wooden one. Begun in 1855, it was completed during the middle of the Civil War, late in 1863, when Thomas Crawford's bronze "Statue of Freedom" was hoisted into position atop the new dome. Simultaneously, fire from 12 fortifications surrounding the city echoed a 35-gun salute from Capitol Hill. During the war, the rotunda served as a barracks and hospital.

Although the porticoes and other exterior details were not finished until a few years later and various renovations have occurred over the course of time, the only major alteration since the Civil War has been the extension of the east facade (1958-62), a new marble front between the Senate and House Chambers that followed the design of the old sandstone one.

THE gleaming white Capitol rises majestically at the east end of the Mall. The gracefully landscaped grounds surrounding it on all sides have been greatly enlarged from the extent originally envisioned. Frederick Law Olmsted planned their present arrange-

President Wilson presents his war message to a joint session of Congress on April 2, 1917. During this speech, he employed the phrase "The world must be made safe for democracy."

ment, including the plaza to the east and the west, south, and north stone terraces, under which are offices. Just outside the west grounds are memorials to Grant and Garfield.

The vista from the west facade—down the Mall to the Washington Monument and Lincoln Memorial—is magnificent. Massive colonnaded porticoes project from this front and its two extended wings. The terraces, which stretch along this side and the flanks of the building on the ground-floor level, hide the basement, which is above ground, from the approaches.

Chief Justice and former Chief Executive William Howard Taft administers the oath to Calvin Coolidge on March 4, 1925.

The famed dome of the Capitol, modeled after European examples, springs from a drum-like base, which is surrounded by a peristyle colonnade of 36 fluted Corinthian columns. Inside the colonnade is a group of long semicircular windows; atop it is an exterior gallery. Above the peristyle, a clerestory features additional semicircular windows. A row of console brackets separates the clerestory from the ribbed surface of the cap of the dome. Medallion windows are set in the spaces between the ribs. A lantern decorated with a colonnade of 12 fluted Corinthian columns surmounts the cap, which is crowned by the Statue of Freedom.

The east front looks directly out over the broad open east plaza—a concourse of humanity on Inauguration Day—and across to the U.S. Supreme Court Building and the Library of Congress. Double porticoes of giant 30-foot Corinthian columns dominate the facades of the three main sections. Wide marble stairways lead up to each of the porticoes, the central portions of which are set forward and topped by sculptured pediments. The inaugural stand, a temporary structure, is erected quadrennially over the central steps in front of the entrance to the main rotunda.

Ex-President Kennedy's body lies in state in the rotunda of the Capitol.

The interior of the Capitol is divided into about 540 rooms, on five main levels. Besides the House and Senate Chambers, it includes a President's Room, an office for the Vice President, and various staff facilities. Senators and Representatives maintain their offices in the House and Senate Office Buildings, which are adjacent to their respective wings of the Capitol and connected to it by subways.

The Senate Chamber has changed little over the years, but contains modern lighting and acoustical facilities. The mahogany desks, arranged in a semicircular pattern, face the rostrum, where the Vice President presides. Visitor galleries are on the second level. The President's Room, near the Senate Chamber, is richly appointed. Chief Executives have sometimes utilized it to sign congressional bills. Woodrow Wilson took his oath of office privately there in 1917 because his inaugural fell on a Sunday. The next day, he was sworn in publicly on the east portico. The House Chamber is similar to the Senate in that its rows of seats, of walnut, are alined in a semicircle around the Speaker's rostrum and the galleries are above. It is, however, a much larger room and Congress uses it for joint sessions.

The Capitol's artwork honors the Presidents and other outstanding individuals and groups. The main rotunda features statues of Washington, Jefferson, Jackson, Lincoln, Grant, and Garfield. On the interior of the dome is the remarkable fresco "The Apotheosis of Washington," painted from scaffolds by Constantino Brumidi, much of whose work is also visible elsewhere within the structure. On this gigantic canopy in a prodigious feat of solitary workmanship, he employed his artistic powers to scale heroic figures to appear life size from below.

The frieze, circling the walls below the fresco and picturing events in U.S. history, is partially the work of Brumidi. He died in 1880, before he could complete it, a task accomplished by Allyn Cox. Below the frieze hang four large paintings by John Trumbull that commemorate the War for Independence and another four on different themes by other artists. Below the rotunda, on the basement floor, is the empty crypt intended as a tomb for George Washington, who preferred to be buried at Mount Vernon.

Other sections of the building consist of offices, committee rooms, and other facilities for Congressmen. Guided tours of some of the public rooms begin in the rotunda.

Washington Monument, District of Columbia ⊠

On the Mall, between the Capitol and the Lincoln Memorial, to the south of the White House, Washington.

This towering 555-foot-high obelisk, a striking monument to the "Father of Our Country" and one of the most famous in the world, is the dominating feature of the Capital. Built between 1848 and 1885 with funds from public subscriptions and Federal appropriations, it commemorates the achievements and unselfish devotion to public duty of our first President—peerless military leader of the War for Independence and wise statesman of the Republic.

Between 1783 and 1833 the Continental and U.S. Congresses considered several proposals to erect a monument in honor of Washington, but took no action on them. In the latter year, influential citizens of the Capital organized the Washington National Monument Society, a civic organization dedicated to building a memorial. Progress was slow at first, but by 1847 a substantial sum had been collected by popular subscription. Meantime, the society had selected a design submitted by architect Robert Mills, but later substantially revised it. On January 31, 1848, Congress granted authority for erection of the monument. About 5 months later, on July 4, Benjamin French, Grand Master of the Washington, D.C., Masonic Lodge, laid the cornerstone, using the trowel employed by Washington at the Capitol in 1793.

Work proceeded rapidly until 1854, when the Washington National Monument Society became involved in a political quarrel. Many citizens grew dissatisfied with the progress; the collection of funds lagged; and, because of the mounting disagreement between the North and South, which resulted in the Civil War, construction soon came to a halt. For more than 20 years, the monument stood incomplete at the height of about 156 feet. Finally, in 1876, President Grant approved an act calling for the Federal Government to complete the monument. The Corps of Engineers of the War Department took over the project.

In 1880 work resumed on the shaft. Practically all the marble with which the remainder of the monument is faced was obtained from the same vein as the stone used for the lower part. Because it came from a different stratum, however, and has weathered to a slightly different tone, a "ring" is noticeable on the memorial. On August 9, 1884, its walls reached the height of 500 feet and on

Washington Monument.

December 6 the capstone was set in place. On February 21, 1885, President Arthur dedicated the monument and on October 9, 1888, it was opened to the public.

The monument, a hollow shaft of Maryland marble and a few courses of Massachusetts granite, is without embellishment or decoration. It has little in common with Mills' original elaborate plan, which provided for a decorated obelisk 600 feet high and 70 feet square at the base. It was to rise from a circular colonnaded building 100 feet high and 250 feet in diameter, surrounded by 30 columns, each 12 feet in diameter and 45 feet high. This temple was to be an American pantheon, a repository for statues of Presidents and national heroes, containing a colossal statue of George Washington. The proportions of Mills' shaft, at variance with traditional dimensions of obelisks, were altered to conform to the classic conception. The result was a creation of grace and delicacy of outline.

The top may be reached by elevator or a stairway. The iron stairway consists of 50 landings and 898 steps. Inserted into the interior walls or otherwise displayed are 190 carved stones presented by individuals, societies, Territories, States, and nations of the world, including a stone from the ruins of ancient Carthage. The observation platform at the top of the monument affords a majestic view of the central buildings, monuments, and outlying areas of Washington. To the east, at one end of the wide vista of the Mall, is the Capitol. To the north is the White House; to the west, the Lincoln Memorial; to the south, the Thomas Jefferson Memorial. These memorials, along with the Washington Monument, are a national tribute to figures in our history who have made vital contributions to our independence, the preservation of the Union, and the concepts of liberty and democracy.

Wilson House, District of Columbia ⚠

2340 S Street NW., Washington.

Woodrow Wilson retired to this house at the end of his Presidency and lived in it until his death 3 years later. Late in 1920, as his second term neared an end, Edith Bolling Wilson began searching for a permanent residence in Washington. One day she happened to visit the house at 2340 S Street NW., which was for sale though it had been built only 5 years earlier. Delighted with it, she informed her husband that it would make an ideal retirement home. Not long thereafter, on December 14, he surprised her by presenting her with the deed, though he did not personally see the structure until the next day.

Before moving in, the Wilsons installed an elevator and a billiard room, rearranged some partitions, built stacks for Wilson's 8,000-volume library, constructed a one-story brick garage, and placed iron gates at the driveway entrance. The roof of the garage, just off

Wilson House.

Crippled ex-President Wilson, aided by an attendant, leaves his S Street home shortly before his death in 1924.

the second-floor dining room, was converted into a terrace so that Wilson could walk outside without the need to utilize steps. He and his wife occupied the house on inauguration day, March 4, 1921, following President Harding's swearing-in ceremony at the Capitol. On that occasion, as well as on many later ones, particularly Armistice Days and Wilson's birthdays, throngs of people gathered outside the home to greet the ex–President.

Wilson, partly paralyzed from a stroke he had suffered in 1919, spent his few remaining years in partial seclusion under the continuous care of his wife and servants. Except for a daily automobile ride and a weekly visit to the movies, he rarely left home or received guests, who did include Lloyd George of Britain and Georges Clemenceau of France. In the evenings, Mrs. Wilson played cards with or read aloud to him until he fell asleep. On two occasions, he attended state functions: the 1921 Armistice Day ceremony preceding the burial of the Unknown Soldier at Arlington National Cemetery, and President Harding's funeral in 1923. In the latter year, on the eve of Armistice Day, he broadcast a radio message to the public from his library. The following day, he spoke to a crowd that had gathered outside, his last public appearance. On February 3, 1924, he died in his upstairs bedroom and was laid to rest in Washington's National Cathedral.

Mrs. Wilson continued to live in the residence until her death in 1961. Prior to that time, she had donated it and many of the furnishings to the National Trust for Historic Preservation, which in 1963 opened it to the public.

The residence is a three-story, red-brick structure of neo-Georgian design. The front door opens to a marble-floored hallway, flanked by a small room on each side. From the hallway, steps lead to a main hall, behind which are the kitchen, servants' dining room, and billiard room. On the second floor, a front drawing room faces S Street, and a library, dining room, and solarium overlook a rear garden, which is surrounded by a brick wall. The third floor contains five bedrooms.

Among the furnishings Mrs. Wilson bequeathed to the National Trust are portraits, books, autographed photographs of prominent persons, a Gobelin tapestry, commemorative china, and furniture that had been in her family for many years. In the library, which is filled with volumes related to or dating from the Wilson era, is the leather chair he used at Cabinet meetings. The Bible on which he took the oath of office as Governor of New Jersey and twice as President is featured in the drawing room.

Grant Home, Illinois   ⚑

Jo Daviess County, 511 Bouthillier Street, Galena.

At the end of the Civil War, the citizens of Galena, Ill., to demonstrate their appreciation for the achievements of their hometown war hero, Gen. Ulysses S. Grant, presented him with this handsome residence. Because of official duties and his preference for various other homes he maintained in the East,

Grant Home.

however, he used it infrequently, most notably during his victorious first race for President in 1868.

In 1860 Grant, who had resigned from the Army and failed in farming and business ventures in and near St. Louis, went to work in a family-owned leather goods store in Galena. He lived a relatively quiet life there until the outbreak of the Civil War the next year, when he returned to active service as colonel of the 21st Illinois Volunteer Infantry. Earlier, he had acted as a drillmaster for local volunteers.

When Grant returned in triumph in 1865, the residents of the city awarded him this furnished home overlooking the Galena River and affording a commanding view of the city. A two-story, Italianate structure of brick, it had been built in 1859-60 by Galena's former city clerk Alexander J. Jackson. The house featured wide overhanging eaves supported by large wooden brackets, a low-pitched roof, white wood trim, and green shutters. A columned and balconied piazza adorned the main entrance, at the southeast corner. The kitchen was in a one-story, rear wing.

After completing his second term as President in 1877, Grant resided temporarily at Galena, but soon began an extensive world tour (1877-79), after which he again stayed for a short time in the residence. After settling permanently in New York City in 1880, the Grants rented it out until his death 5 years later.

In 1904, his son, Gen. Frederick Dent Grant, deeded the house to the city for preservation as a memorial to his father. In 1932 the State acquired the structure, by which time it had fallen into disrepair, and in 1955-57, utilizing the original plans, restored it to its historic appearance.

The home is furnished with period pieces and Grant family items. Among the latter are china and silver used in the White House, Grant's favorite armchair, military trophies, and souvenirs acquired on the world tour. Also exhibited is a carriage he used during his Presidency. A small brick building to the northeast of the residence contains additional exhibits; it was constructed at the time of the restoration. The property is a State memorial.

Lincoln Home National Historic Site, Illinois ★

Sangamon County, the area bounded by Capitol Avenue and Seventh, Edwards, and Ninth Streets, Springfield.

This national historic site preserves the only home Abraham Lincoln ever owned, as well as the surrounding 4 blocks, which contain several structures dating from his era. He lived in the residence for most of the period 1844-61, during which time he advanced from smalltown lawyer and local politician to President of the United States.

IN 1839 Rev. Charles Dresser, rector of St. Paul's Episcopal Church in Springfield, erected a modest, 1½-story, frame residence on the northeast corner of Eighth and Jackson Streets. Lincoln, who in 1837 had moved from New Salem to Springfield, designated the State capital that same year, and was living in rented quarters, purchased it in 1844, or 2 years after his marriage to Mary Todd and less than a year after the birth of his first son, Robert Todd. In the home, Mrs. Lincoln gave birth to three more sons, Edward,

Lincoln Home National Historic Site.

William, and Thomas; Edward died there in 1850 at the age of 4.

At the time he bought the house, Lincoln had already retired from the State legislature and was pursuing a thriving law practice. Party conflicts had caused him to give up politics for awhile, though he continued to harbor strong aspirations for public service. In 1846 he gained his first major political triumph when he won election to the U.S. House of Representatives. During the year's lapse before he was required to report to Washington, Lincoln decided to take his family with him. In October 1847 he leased out his home for a period of a year beginning on November 1.

By the time the Lincolns returned to Springfield the following October, between sessions of Congress, Lincoln had already decided not to make a bid for reelection. In December he departed once again for Washington, this time leaving his wife and children behind. Following the end of the session, in the spring of 1849, discouraged with politics, he came back to Springfield and turned his attention to the law.

In 1854 the controversy over slavery, arising from the repeal of the Missouri Compromise by the Kansas-Nebraska Act, brought Lincoln back into the political forum. At first, he limited his participation to speechmaking and campaigning for the Whig Party, but in 1855 he ran unsuccessfully for the U.S. Senate. The turning point in his career came in 1856, when he abandoned the floundering Whigs and joined the Republicans. They had organized 2 years earlier as a coalition of antislavery groups. Lincoln rapidly rose to a position of leadership in the party. During 1858, the year he campaigned for the U.S. Senate against Stephen A. Douglas, he

Lincoln and his sons William ("Willie") and Thomas ("Tad") in front of their Springfield residence during the early summer of 1860, about the time he became a Presidential candidate.

achieved national recognition. Although he lost the election, his performance in the Lincoln-Douglas debates, in which he steered a moderate course on the slavery issue, brought him acclaim from the masses and led to his candidacy for the Presidency.

Meantime, during these politically hectic years, Lincoln had found time to improve his home. In 1849-50 he had it repainted, remodeled, and repaired. In 1856 he enlarged it to two full stories, containing 12 rooms.

On May 19, 1860, in his parlor, Lincoln received official notification of his Presidential nomination from a committee of Republican officials. He conducted the campaign from his residence, leaving the traveling, speechmaking, and writing to others

Lincoln's home, which he had leased out 4 years earlier when he went to Washington to become President, draped in mourning after his assassination in 1865.

and maintaining communication with the party through correspondence and by receiving visitors. In the election, he received a clear majority of the electoral votes, though the combined popular vote of his three opponents far exceeded his own.

In February 1861, prior to their departure for Washington, the Lincolns sold much of their furniture at public auction and leased their house to Lucian A. Tilton, president of the Great Western Railroad, who also purchased much of the furniture. On the 6th, the Lincolns held a grand reception in the home that was attended by about 700 people. A move was then made to Chenery House, a hotel, where Lincoln packed up the family's personal belongings and addressed them to "A. Lincoln, The White House, Washington, D.C." At the train station on the morning of February 11 he bade farewell to a large crowd of friends, neighbors, and well-wishers. His departure marked the final time he would set eyes on Springfield, though in 1865 his remains would be brought there for burial.

The Tiltons resided in the house until 1869, when they moved to Chicago. In 1882, upon the death of Mary Todd Lincoln, her eldest and only surviving son, Robert Todd, inherited the residence. The next year, he rented it to Osborn H. Oldroyd, a longtime collector of Civil War mementos and Lincolniana, who converted it into a museum. Encouraged by Oldroyd, Robert Todd in 1887 donated the house to the State. Oldroyd served as the first custodian until 1893, when he moved his collection to the Petersen House, in Washington, D.C. The collection later became the nucleus of federally owned Lincoln Museum, currently a part of Ford's Theatre National Historic Site, described elsewhere in this volume.

AIDED by the Abraham Lincoln Association of Springfield and by the National Society of Colonial Dames in Illinois, the State restored the house as nearly as possible to its appearance at the time of Lincoln's occupancy. Restoration work included repainting the house brown, its color in 1860; reproducing the interior decor, including the wallpaper; and reconstructing outbuildings and fences. Most of the furnishings in the home are period pieces. Much of the Lincoln furniture that the Tiltons had taken with them in 1869 was lost in the 1871 Chicago fire. Other items passed into the hands of private collectors or museums, and the State eventually acquired some of them.

Parlor of the Lincoln Home.

In 1971 Congress authorized establishment of Lincoln Home National Historic Site. The National Park Service plans to restore or reconstruct the structures at the intersection of Eighth and Jackson Streets and the facades of nearby buildings on Eighth Street. The visitor center is on Seventh Street.

A number of buildings historically related to the Lincoln era are within the boundaries of the national historic site and are open to the public. The Ninian W. Edwards House, a privately owned reconstruction of the dwelling where Lincoln courted and married Mary Todd, stands on the southeastern corner of Eighth Street and Capitol Avenue. A museum, it contains historical exhibits, period costumes, and a series of dioramas depicting events in Lincoln's life. Another privately owned museum containing similar exhibits, the Abraham Lincoln Museum, is in a 19th-century structure across the street from the Lincoln home. The First Presbyterian Church, on the northwestern corner of Seventh Street and Capitol Avenue, preserves a pew once used by the Lincoln family in a church that no longer exists. The rest of the historic houses in the vicinity are unrestored and may not be visited.

Several buildings in Springfield possess Lincoln associations but are outside the boundaries of the national historic site. The most significant of these is the Old State Capitol, situated in the square bounded by Adams, Fifth, Washington, and Sixth Streets. A National Historic Landmark owned and administered by the State, it preserves the chambers where Lincoln attended the State legislature, the Superior Court where he pleaded many cases, the Governor's office, and several other historic rooms. It also houses the State Historical Library, which owns the second largest collection of Lincolniana in the Nation.

Privately owned structures, open to the public, include the Lincoln Depot, on 10th and Monroe Streets, where in February 1861 Lincoln delivered his "Farewell Address," today a museum; the Lincoln-Herndon Building, at Sixth and Adams Street, which contains the third-floor law office Lincoln shared with Stephen T. Logan and later with William H. Herndon, as well as the Federal District Court where Lincoln pled cases, and the old post office; and the Springfield Marine Bank, at 114 South Sixth Street, opened in 1851 and still an active bank today. It displays Lincoln's depositor's ledger.

The Governor's Mansion, between Jackson, Edwards, Fourth, and Fifth Streets, residence of the Governor since 1855 and open to the public on special occasions, was the scene of several social events the Lincolns attended. Another home they often visited was the Benjamin S. Edwards House, a gracious Victorian mansion at 700 North Fourth Street that was once owned by an in-law of Mrs. Lincoln. Today owned and administered by the Springfield Art Association, it is furnished with pre-Civil War items and is accessible to the public. The Illinois State Museum, at Spring and Edwards Streets, contains exhibits on State and local history, including some on Lincoln.

The Lincoln Tomb, in Oak Ridge Cemetery about 4 miles northwest of the Lincoln Home, is described immediately following.

Lincoln Tomb.

Lincoln Tomb, Illinois ⚠

Sangamon County, at the terminus of Monument Avenue, in Oak Ridge Cemetery, Springfield.

This impressive memorial—a showplace of Lincoln statuary and symbolic ornamentation—contains his tomb as well as those of his wife and three of their four sons.

On April 15, 1865, the day after President Lincoln's assassination, a group of Springfield citizens, learning that the body would be returned to Illinois for burial, formed the National Lincoln Monument Association and spearheaded a drive for funds to construct a memorial/tomb. Upon arrival of the corpse on May 3, it lay in state in the capitol for a night, and after the funeral the next day was placed in a receiving vault at Oak Ridge Cemetery, the site Mrs. Lincoln had requested for burial. In December her husband's remains were removed to a temporary vault not far from the proposed memorial site. In 1871, or 3 years after laborers had begun constructing the tomb, the body of Lincoln and those of the three youngest of his sons were placed in crypts in the unfinished structure.

In 1874, upon completion of the memorial, Lincoln's remains were interred in a marble sarcophagus in the center of a chamber known as the "catacombs," or burial room. In 1876, however, after two Chicago criminals failed in an attempt to steal Lincoln's body and hold it for ransom, the National Lincoln Monument Association hid it in another part of the memorial. When Mrs. Lincoln died in 1882, her remains were placed with those of Lincoln, but in 1887 both bodies were reburied in a brick vault beneath the floor of the burial room.

By 1895, the year the State acquired the memorial, it had fallen into disrepair. During a rebuilding and restoration program in 1899-1901, all five caskets were moved to a nearby subterranean vault. In the latter year, State officials returned them to the burial room and placed that of Lincoln in the sarcophagus it had occupied in 1874-76. Within a few months, however, at the request of Robert Todd Lincoln, the President's only surviving son, the body was moved to its final resting place, a cement vault 10 feet below the surface of the burial room. In 1930-31 the State reconstructed the interior of the memorial. Rededicated in the latter year by President Hoover, it has undergone little change since that time.

The tomb is in the center of a 12½-acre plot. Constructed of Massachusetts granite, it has a rectangular base surmounted by a 117-foot-high obelisk and a semicircular entrance way. A bronze reproduction of sculptor Gutzon Borglum's head of Lincoln in the U.S. Capitol rests on a pedestal in front of the entrance way. Four flights of balustraded stairs—two flanking the entrance at the front and two at the rear—lead to a level terrace. The balustrade extends around the terrace to form a parapet.

In the center of the terrace, a large and ornate base supports the obelisk. On the walls of the base are 37 ashlars, or hewn stones, cut to represent raised shields, each engraved with the name of a State at the time the tomb was built. Each shield is connected to another by two raised bands, and thus the group forms an unbroken chain encircling the base. Four bronze statues adorn the corners of the latter. They represent the infantry, navy, artillery, and cavalry of

Ceremony during Lincoln's initial burial in a temporary tomb.

the Civil War period. In front of the obelisk and above the entrance stands a full-length statue of Lincoln.

The interior of the memorial, constructed of marble from Minnesota, Missouri, Massachusetts, Arkansas, Utah, Italy, Spain, France, and Belgium, contains a rotunda, burial room, and connecting corridors. A replica of the Daniel C. French statue in the Lincoln Memorial, in Washington, D.C., dominates the entrance foyer. The walls of the rotunda are decorated with 16 marble pilasters, which are separated by marble panels. The pilasters symbolize Lincoln and the 15 Presidents who preceded him. The room also contains 36 bronze panels, one for each State at the time of Lincoln's death. The ceiling is of platinum leaf.

Corridors lead from the rotunda to the burial room at the rear of the memorial. Located in niches along the corridor walls are eight statues by prominent sculptors depicting various phases of Lincoln's life. Four bronze tablets on the walls are engraved with the Farewell Address, the Gettysburg Address, a portion of the Second Inaugural Address, and a biographical sketch. Large gold stars in sets of 12 at each corner of the memorial represent the 48 States in the Union at the time of its remodeling.

The burial room features black and white marble walls and a ceiling of gold leaf. At its center stands the cenotaph, a 7-ton block of reddish marble inscribed with Lincoln's name and the years he lived. It marks the approximate location of the burial vault. Nine flags are arranged in a semicircle around the cenotaph. Seven of them—the State flags of Massachusetts, New Jersey, Pennsylvania, Virginia, Kentucky, Indiana, and Illinois—commemorate the homes of Lincoln and his ancestors. The eighth and ninth are the Stars and Stripes and the Presidential flag. The inscription "Now he belongs to the ages," reputedly spoken by Secretary of War Edwin M. Stanton at the time of Lincoln's death, is inscribed in the wall above the U.S. Flag. Along the south wall of the burial room are five crypts containing the remains of Mrs. Lincoln, three of Lincoln's four sons, and a grandson.

The Lincoln tomb is owned and administered by the State of Illinois.

Grouseland, Indiana ⚠

Knox County, Scott and Park Streets, Vincennes.

This mansion, now surrounded by the city of Vincennes, preserves the memory of William Henry Harrison—Indian fighter, military leader in the War of 1812, Governor of Indiana Territory, and ninth President of the United States. He built Grouseland and lived in it during most of his term as Territorial Governor, when he helped bring peace to the old Northwest and opened to white settlement a vast territory between the Ohio River and the Great Lakes.

In 1800 Congress created Indiana Territory out of a part of the old Northwest Territory and President John Adams appointed Harrison, who had been serving as Secretary of and Delegate to Congress from the Northwest Territory, as Governor. Arriving in

Grouseland.

the small Territorial capital of Vincennes in January 1801, Harrison purchased a 300-acre tract just northeast of town, which he called Grouseland, and in 1803-4 built a mansion on it. As Territorial Governor, he sought to protect white settlers against Indian tribes blocking the tide of westward expansion. He negotiated a series of treaties with tribal leaders of the Northwest that provided for the cession of millions of acres of Indian lands. During a meeting with Harrison at Grouseland in 1810, Tecumseh, the Shawnee leader, warned that his people would fight white encroachment.

Apparently learning from Tecumseh that he was going south to seek allies, Harrison left Grouseland in September 1811 and traveled northward to the site of present Terre Haute, where his troops constructed Fort Harrison to serve as an advance base for an attack on the stronghold of the Shawnees and their allies at Tippecanoe Creek, near present Lafayette, Ind. Late in October, he resumed his march northward and at the Battle of Tippecanoe— precipitated by a premature attack on the whites led by Tecumseh's half brother, "The Prophet"—scattered Tecumseh's followers. Harrison suffered heavy losses and the victory was inconclusive, but the battle made him a national hero and helped him win the Presidency in 1840.

When the War of 1812 broke out, Harrison resigned as Governor of Indiana Territory, obtained a commission in the Army as brigadier general, and left Grouseland to command U.S. forces in the old Northwest. The next year, he became a major general. Harrison's forces finally drove the British and their Shawnee and other Indian allies into Canada and decisively defeated them at the Battle of the Thames (1813). After years of diplomatic struggle and frontier war, this victory assured U.S. domination of the old Northwest. In 1814, after resigning his commission, Harrison returned to a house that he had built at North Bend, Ohio, instead of to Grouseland.

The next occupant of Grouseland was Judge Benjamin Parke, who lived there until about 1819. John Harrison, William Henry's son and father of President Benjamin Harrison, Receiver of the Land Office in Vincennes, then resided in the mansion for about a decade. Subsequently it fell into disrepair and the city encroached upon it. By 1850 ownership had passed out of the Harrison family, and during the following decade the mansion served as a grain storehouse and a hotel. From 1860 to 1909, it was again a private residence. In 1909 the Vincennes Water Company purchased it and planned to raze it, but the Francis Vigo Chapter of the Daughters of the American Revolution collected enough money to acquire, furnish, restore, and open it as a historic house museum. This group still administers the property.

Grouseland is a 2½-story, brick Georgian house containing 26 rooms and 13 fireplaces. It resembles Berkeley, Harrison's birthplace and boyhood home in Virginia and may have been designed by him. To its rear is a one-story annex, joined by a covered passage. One of the most handsome rooms in the residence is the "Council Chamber," where Harrison held many of his meetings with Indian leaders and conducted much of his business as Governor. Features incorporated for protection against the

Indians include two false windows in the front of the house, a lookout in the attic, heavily barred basement windows, powder magazine, and basement well. All the rooms are furnished with period pieces. On display are articles associated with the Harrisons, as well as with Francis Vigo, fur trader and merchant of Vincennes who was friendly to the American cause during the War for Independence.

Adjoining Grouseland is the Indiana Territorial Capitol, where the first Indiana Territorial Legislature met. This building stood elsewhere in Vincennes until 1919, when it was moved to its present location.

Harrison (Benjamin) Home, Indiana ⚠

Marion County, 1230 N. Delaware Street, Indianapolis.

Benjamin Harrison, 23d President of the United States, lived in this house from the 1870's until his death in 1901. In 1854 he had moved from his home State, Ohio, to Indianapolis, the burgeoning capital of Indiana, to pursue a legal career. Through the years, as his law practice prospered, he lived in various residences, each one larger and more spacious than its predecessor. Finally, in 1867, he purchased a double lot on North Delaware Street, then on the outskirts of the town, as the site for a home. Constructed in the 1870's, the house was a red brick structure two stories high and contained 16 rooms. It was situated in a spacious yard full of elms, oaks, and a variety of plants and shrubbery.

In 1888 Harrison initiated a "front porch" Presidential campaign from his home, and often spoke to crowds of people assembled in the street. On one occasion, when the populace learned of his nomination, overenthusiastic admirers demolished and carried off the picket fence surrounding the yard. Defeated in his second bid for the Presidency in 1892, Harrison returned to Indianapolis and resumed his law career. About the time of his second marriage, in 1896, he renovated the house, installed electricity, and added the present Ionic-columned porch. His death occurred in 1901 in the master bedroom on the second floor of the home. He was buried in the city's Crown Hill Cemetery.

In 1937 Harrison's widow sold the house and most of its furnishings to the Arthur Jordan Foundation, which has restored

Harrison Home as restored.

Harrison Home about 1888, the year he became President.

10 of the 16 rooms and furnished them with Harrison items or appropriate period pieces. One of the most beautiful rooms, the front parlor, appears as it did when redecorated in 1896 for Harrison's new bride. Among its furnishings are cut-crystal chandeliers, an Aubusson rug, and gold-lacquered mirrors. Harrison's library, the room where he planned his 1888 campaign for the Presidency, features his massive hand-carved bookcase and numerous other mementos. His law office furniture occupies a second-floor room. The master bedroom contains a huge hand-carved bed, an exercise machine, and a cradle originally owned by William Henry Harrison, Benjamin's grandfather and ninth U.S. President.

Presently, the Arthur Jordan Foundation leases the Harrison house to the Benjamin Harrison Foundation, incorporated in 1966, which operates it as a historic house museum.

Lincoln Boyhood National Memorial, Indiana   ★

Spencer County, on Ind. 345, just north of its intersection with Ind. 162, about 4 miles south of Dale and 2 miles east of Gentryville.

This national memorial preserves the site of the farm where Abraham Lincoln grew to manhood and the traditional gravesite of his mother, Nancy Hanks Lincoln. Although none of the structures associated with the family are extant, an impressive memorial building commemorates its Indiana years and a typical frontier farm of the era is operated.

Early in the winter of 1816, Thomas Lincoln, embroiled in the last of several land-title disputes that had plagued his years in Kentucky, moved northwestward from his Knob Creek farm to Indiana to make a fresh start. Accompanying him were his wife, Nancy Hanks, his 9-year-old daughter Sarah, and his 7-year-old son Abraham. They probably crossed the Ohio River at Thompson's Ferry, near the mouth of the Anderson River, followed the Troy-Vincennes Road northward about 12 miles, and then turned westward a short distance to a tiny settlement along Little Pigeon Creek. Because harvesting had already been completed, the Lincolns endured a difficult first winter, living off wild game and corn and pork bartered from nearby settlers. Aided by their neighbors, however, the family soon completed a small log cabin and settled down to the slow and painstaking task of converting the surrounding forest to farmland.

In the fall of 1817, following his first harvest, Thomas traveled 60 miles northwestward to the land office at Vincennes, Ind., where he made a down payment on two 80-acre tracts in the Little Pigeon Creek region. A decade later, he gained full title to one of the tracts by relinquishing the other as a final payment. Meantime, he had acquired from a neighbor an adjacent 20 acres. A subsistence farmer, Lincoln cultivated at the most about 40 acres, deriving his cash income from carpentry.

The Indiana years brought about many changes in the family. In the fall of 1817, Nancy Lincoln's uncle and aunt, Thomas and Elizabeth Sparrow, and their nephew Dennis Hanks emigrated from Kentucky and settled on Thomas Lincoln's land. Less than a year later, the Sparrows and Nancy Lincoln died during a milk sickness epidemic. The grief-stricken Thomas took Dennis Hanks into his household, and for a time 11-year-old Sarah Lincoln assumed responsibility for the household chores, while Thomas and the two boys tended to the farming, hunting, and carpentry.

Late in 1819, Thomas trekked back to Kentucky, to Elizabethtown, and took a second wife, Sarah Bush Johnston, a widow with three children. Under her guidance, the two families merged easily, and she proved to be a kind and loving stepmother to Abraham and Sarah. Unfortunately, following her marriage, the latter died in childbirth in 1828.

During the 14 years Abraham Lincoln lived in Indiana, several factors combined to shape his destiny. Although he benefited physically from the demands of frontier life and nurtured an enduring respect for the hardy pioneers who tamed the wilderness, he grew to dislike the long hours of manual labor necessary for survival and determined early in life that he would not follow in his father's footsteps. Frustrated in his desire for learning because of the scarcity of schools, the lack of leisure time for studying, and the overcrowded conditions in the Lincoln cabin, he received only a minimum of formal education. Fortunately, he was blessed with an excellent memory, a sharp wit, and an inquisitive mind. Devouring all available books and seizing every opportunity to exchange ideas with neighbors or passersby, by dint of self-determination and tenacity, he educated himself to a degree that was exceptional for a person in his station of life.

Memorial building at Lincoln Boyhood National Memorial.

During these years, Lincoln seldom had the opportunity to view the world beyond Little Pigeon Creek. Occasionally, family business provided a welcome chance to visit neighboring counties. His first prolonged stay away from home came in 1826 at the age of 16, when he obtained employment for a few months as a hired hand on the Ohio River farm of James Taylor. His happiest hours there were spent operating Taylor's ferry across the river, during which time he conversed with passengers from all walks of life and from all sections of the United States. A further source of stimulation were encounters with steamboat passengers at the nearby town of Troy.

In 1828-29 merchant James Gentry, who was sending his son Allen with a flatboat of goods down the Ohio and Mississippi Rivers to New Orleans, hired Lincoln to go along and provided him with steamboat passage for the return trip. From that time on, he was discontented with frontier life and even considered seeking employment on a steamboat. One factor that may have influenced him not to do so was his growing fascination with the law. During his last few years in Indiana, whenever possible, he traveled to the county courthouse at Rockport or to those in nearby counties to hear lawyers pleading their cases. He may have borrowed lawbooks from area attorneys, but *The Revised Laws of Indiana* (1824) is the only one he is known to have read before moving to Illinois.

Sometime in late 1829, the Lincolns, spurred by glowing reports from a relative who had settled in Illinois, decided to move westward once again. Also, the husbands of Thomas Lincoln's two stepdaughters, one of whom was Dennis Hanks, had already determined to relocate, and Sarah Bush Lincoln was loath to break up the family. In March 1830, after a journey to Elizabethtown to dispose of Sarah's property there, Thomas sold his Indiana landholdings. The family, including 21-year-old Abraham, piled all its goods into three wagons, bade farewell to their longtime friends and neighbors, and proceeded via the Troy-Vincennes Road to Vincennes, where the Wabash River was crossed into Illinois.

With the passage of time, the Lincoln sites in Indiana disappeared. In 1879 a private citizen, using local tradition as a guide, marked the probable site of Nancy Hanks Lincoln's grave, and the owners donated the site to the commissioners of Spencer County. Subsequently, the State of Indiana, aided by various patriotic associations and commissions, especially the Indiana Lincoln Union, acquired the gravesite; purchased additional acreage, including part of Thomas Lincoln's landholdings; and marked the approximate location of the Lincoln cabin.

By 1932, two State-owned areas, comprising jointly more than 1,000 acres, had evolved. One, the Nancy Hanks Lincoln Memorial, containing the sites of the cabin, outbuildings, and grave, was already open to the public. The other, Lincoln State Park, which eventually incorporated the memorial, was being developed as a recreation and scenic area. In 1938 the State opened it to the public. Improvements between 1940 and 1944 included additional land acquisition, landscaping, and the construction of a limestone memorial building.

The memorial building consists of two low wings connected by a semicircular cloister and features a central courtyard. The west wing, Abraham Lincoln Hall, serves as a small chapel; the east wing, Nancy Hanks Lincoln Hall, designed and furnished to represent a frontier dwelling, is used as a meeting room and exhibit area. Five relief panels symbolizing events in Lincoln's life adorn the walls of the cloister facing the courtyard. North of the memorial structure, lies a grassy plaza and parking lot. From the latter, a mall extends through the woods to the gravesite, beyond which a trail leads to the cabin site.

In 1962 Congress authorized establishment of Lincoln Boyhood National Memorial. The following year, the State transferred more than 100 acres of the park, primarily the memorial area, to the National Park Service. Today, in addition to the memorial, a farm similar to those of the Lincoln era is operated. It consists of a log cabin and outbuildings, garden, orchard, cultivated fields, and livestock. The visitor center is at the memorial.

Hoover National Historic Site, Iowa ★

Cedar County, on the southwest edge of the town of West Branch.

The nucleus of this national historic site, a complex of structures in West Branch commemorating Herbert Hoover, is the tiny cottage where he was born and spent the first 5 years of his life. Another major building is the Friends (Quaker) Meeting House he attended. Also within the park area are the Herbert Hoover Presidential Library, operated by the General Services Administration, and his grave and that of his wife.

In 1853 Jesse Hoover, Herbert's great-grandfather, emigrated from Ohio to West Branch, Iowa, a predominantly Quaker community on the west branch of Wapsinonoc ("Sweet Water") Creek. In 1871 his grandson, a blacksmith of the same name, built a small cottage at the corner of Downey and Penn Streets as a residence for himself and his wife, Huldah Minthorn Hoover. Across Penn Street, he erected a blacksmith shop. On August 10, 1874, Mrs. Hoover gave birth to her second child, Herbert, nicknamed "Bertie."

In 1879, after the arrival of his third offspring, Jesse Hoover, who had decided to sell agricultural implements, disposed of both structures and moved into a larger residence on Downey Street, about a block to the south, no remains of which are extant. His premature death the next year and that of his wife in 1884 orphaned their three children. Herbert at first went to live with an

Hoover Birthplace.

uncle, Allen Hoover, on a farm just northeast of West Branch. In 1885, at the age of 11, however, he was sent to Newberg, Oreg., to reside with another uncle, Dr. Henry J. Minthorn.

The Hoover birthplace was a three-room frame cottage with small front and rear porches. The two main rooms were the bedroom, the birthplace of Hoover; and a combined living room, kitchen, and dining room. The third room, formed by an enclosed portion of the rear porch, served as a summer kitchen or spare sleeping room. The sidewalls of the cottage were constructed of wide vertical boards and battens closely fitted together. To keep out the cold, the cracks were taped with strips of cloth; they are now covered with board strips. In 1890 the owner of the cottage shifted it to a different direction on the same location and attached a large two-story structure on the side facing Downey Street.

About the time Hoover achieved the Presidency, in 1929, his family became interested in restoring the birthplace to its original appearance. In 1935 a son, Allan, purchased it, as well as several adjoining lots. Restoration work, begun by the family in 1938, was completed the next year by the Herbert Hoover Birthplace Society, an organization of West Branch citizens that had acquired the site that same year. The project included razing the front two stories of the altered structure and relocating the remaining section to its original position; painting the exterior and interior walls white; reconstructing the front and rear porches and a picket gate and board fence around the yard; and restoring the wooden pump at the rear of the cottage. The society furnished the house with period pieces, among them the original high chair, bureau, and kerosene lamp, plus a cupboard apparently built by Jesse Hoover at an earlier date. A short distance to the west of the birthplace, the society constructed a caretaker's house.

Throughout the years, as the society acquired additional land, the birthplace cottage became the nucleus of a 28-acre park. One of the major projects was the installation of a statue of Isis, Egyptian goddess of life, that had been presented to Hoover in the early 1920's by Belgian school children in appreciation for his relief work

Blacksmith shop of the Jesse Hoover era.

Hoover Presidential Library.

in Europe. Other improvements included picnic and camping grounds and landscaped areas. In 1956-57 the Herbert Hoover Birthplace Foundation, formed in 1954 to assist the Birthplace Society in administering the park, built adjacent to the birthplace a blacksmith shop typical of the era of Jesse Hoover. It is furnished with 19th-century tools and other historic objects.

In the late 1950's, the two organizations merged under the name of Herbert Hoover Birthplace Foundation, Inc. The major accomplishment of this realinement was the completion in 1962 of the Herbert Hoover Presidential Library, a storehouse of Hoover papers, books, and other memorabilia that is southwest of the birthplace.

In 1962, the year of the library dedication, in which Hoover and Truman participated, the foundation donated the entire park to the Federal Government. The General Services Administration operated it until 1965, the year Congress authorized it as a national historic site. At that time, the National Park Service assumed responsibility for all of the park except the library, which remained under the control of the General Services Administration. Meantime, in October 1964 Hoover had died and was buried on a hillside about one-quarter mile southwest of and overlooking the birthplace. That same month, the body of his wife, Lou Henry Hoover, who had been buried in California in 1944, was reinterred adjacent to that of her husband.

The national historic site has continued to expand and today includes about 148 acres, approximately 22 of which are in non-Federal ownership. Most of the increased acreage, to the south and west of the birthplace complex of structures, has been acquired to preserve the natural setting and to prevent commercial intrusions. Other acquisitions extending north and east of the birthplace into the town of West Branch contain various historic and modern structures. Some of the older buildings have been or are being restored and others have been removed as part of a long-range plan to recreate the 19th-century appearance of the southwestern portion of the town.

One of the major historic structures, the Friends meetinghouse in which Hoover worshipped with his parents, was restored in 1964-65 by the Herbert Hoover Birthplace Foundation, Inc. It had earlier been moved to its present location on the east side of Downey Street, opposite the Hoover Library and southeast of the birthplace. The meetinghouse had originally been on the west side of Downey Street north of Main. Subsequently, prior to the erection of a new place of worship, it was sold and moved directly across the street and used for a theater and garage before the Hoover Foundation acquired it and moved it to its present and third site.

The one-room West Branch elementary school that Hoover may have attended is on the corner of Penn and Poplar Streets. It was moved there in 1971 from the corner of Orange and Oliphant Streets, where it had been a residence for many years. The exterior has been restored.

Lincoln Birthplace National Historic Site, Kentucky   ★
Larue County, just off U.S. 31E-Ky. 61, about 3 miles south of Hodgenville.

This national historic site commemorates the humble beginnings of Abraham Lincoln, who was born in a crude log cabin on the Kentucky frontier. Preserved are most of the farmland that his father owned at the time of his birth; the traditional birthplace cabin; Sinking Spring, where the Lincolns obtained their water; and an ancient oak tree that was then a boundary landmark.

The Lincoln family moved westward from Virginia to Kentucky at the end of the War for Independence. About 1800 Thomas, Abraham's father, settled in Elizabethtown, where he pursued a

Memorial Building, which houses the traditional Lincoln Birthplace cabin.

living as a carpenter. In 1806 he married Nancy Hanks. Two years later, they purchased a 300-acre tract on the south fork of Nolin Creek, about 14 miles south of Elizabethtown and a few miles south of Hodgen's Mill, the site of present Hodgenville. Not long afterward, with their first child, a daughter named Sarah, they moved into a small, one-room log cabin on a section of the property near Sinking Spring. In that abode, which Thomas may have built, on February 12, 1809, Abraham was born. The Lincolns lived on the farm for 2 more years. Then, as a result of a land-title dispute, they moved to a new location, on Knob Creek about 6 miles northeast of Hodgenville. In later years, Abraham stated that this was the first home he could recall.

Traditional Lincoln Birthplace cabin.

In 1894 Alfred W. Dennett of New York, a restaurateur and philanthropist, purchased 110 acres of the property where Thomas Lincoln's farm once stood and shortly thereafter began to create a park known as "Lincoln Spring Farm" and "Lincoln Birthplace." In 1895 Dennett acquired an aging log cabin standing on nearby property and reerected it near Sinking Spring, on the approximate location of Thomas' cabin. According to Dennett and local opinion, the cabin incorporated some of the same logs that had been used in the Lincoln cabin, though the latter apparently had been moved and rebuilt after the departure of the Lincolns.

Apparently Dennett's plans to create a commercially successful park failed, for in 1897 he dismantled the cabin and transported it

Logs of the Lincoln Birthplace being loaded at College Point, New York, in 1906 for shipment to Kentucky. Five years later, after exhibition in Louisville, they were reassembled in the Memorial Building at the future Lincoln Birthplace National Historic Site.

to Nashville, where it was reassembled and displayed as part of the Nashville centennial celebration. He then placed the logs in storage in New York City until 1901, the year they were exhibited at the Pan-American Exposition in Buffalo. Subsequently, some of the logs were lost while being transported; the remainder lay untouched for several years in the basement of an old mansion on Long Island. During that time, Dennett lost title to them.

In 1906 the Lincoln Farm Association, incorporated 2 years earlier, acquired both the birthplace site and the logs. The association transported the latter to Louisville, where they were reassembled and exhibited in Central Park and then stored pending construction of a memorial shelter at the birthplace site. In a ceremony on February 12, 1909, on the centennial of Lincoln's birth, President Theodore Roosevelt laid the cornerstone for the shelter. Two years later, the association reassembled the birthplace in the completed building, a huge Greek Revival structure of Connecticut pink granite and Tennessee marble, designed by John R. Pope and erected with funds raised by popular subscription. President Taft took part in the dedication ceremony, held on November 9 of that year.

In 1916 Congress authorized Federal ownership of the birthplace site and placed it under the administration of the War Department. The National Park Service acquired it in 1933. Today, the national historic site, comprising 116½ acres of land, includes about 100 acres of the original Lincoln farm. The main feature is the memorial building, which houses the traditional birthplace cabin. Also of interest is nearby Sinking Spring, source of water for the Lincoln family, and the ancient oak tree that marks the boundary of the property. A visitor center houses exhibits on Lincoln and pioneer life and offers an audiovisual program.

Springfield, Kentucky ⚐

Jefferson County, 5608 Apache Road, Louisville.

Zachary Taylor lived at Springfield, his boyhood home, until the beginning of his military career in 1808, was married there 2 years later, and probably returned periodically until the death of his father in 1829.

In 1785, when Taylor was less than 1 year old, his father, Richard, moved from Orange County, Va., to a 400-acre farm on the Muddy Fork of Beargrass Creek, about 5 miles east of the village of Louisville. The family at first lived in a small log structure, but within a few years construction of Springfield began; it was erected in two stages, ca. 1790 and 1810-30. A brick house, more substantial than most on the frontier, it had 2½ stories and a basement. The basement provided quarters for servants; a large central hall divided the first floor into twin parlors on the east, and dining room and kitchen to the west; four bedrooms occupied the second floor; and quarters for coachmen comprised the third floor, an unfinished attic.

As a boy at Springfield, Taylor received minimal formal

Springfield, Kentucky, which is now being restored following storm damage.

education, but he was physically active. When not assisting his father in caring for the farm, he learned to ride, shoot, and hunt—skills that prepared him for a military career. By 1800 his father, who had become one of the more prosperous settlers in the vicinity, had increased his landholdings to 700 acres and owned 26 slaves.

Young Taylor lived at Springfield until 1808, when he received a commission as first lieutenant in the 7th U.S. Infantry. In 1810, while on leave, he was married in the home, which was also probably the birthplace of several of his children. In 1815 he retired from the Army and took up farming on a 324-acre tract on Beargrass Creek that had been given to him as a wedding present.

During that time, he may have resided at Springfield, but within a year returned to military life. Thereafter, he only visited it occasionally while on furlough.

In 1829 Richard Taylor died and Hancock Taylor, Zachary's eldest brother, either purchased or inherited the estate. Following Zachary's death in the White House in 1850, his body was brought back to Springfield and interred in the family burial ground, which later became the nucleus of Zachary Taylor National Cemetery.

Since passing out of the hands of the Taylor family, Springfield has had several owners. It now occupies a small plot that is surrounded by a housing development. Notable original features of the residence include the door locks and window glass. Each of the eight rooms is equipped with a fireplace. The walnut paneling and doors in the entrance hallway and dining room have been restored to their original finish. The two-story rear porch may date from the original construction or from the 19th century, when one-story side and front porches were added. The latter two porches have since been removed. A tornado in 1974 substantially damaged the house, which is not open to the public, and its private owners are now restoring it.

Camp David (Catoctin Mountain Park), Maryland   ★

Frederick County, near the center of Catoctin Mountain Park, whose main entrance is about 3 miles west of Thurmont.

Since the time of Franklin D. Roosevelt, when it was known as "Shangri-la," this isolated camp in the hills of western Maryland has served as an official Presidential retreat and has often been the site of conferences and decisions of national and international significance. Heavily guarded, it may not be visited by the public.

In March 1942 President Roosevelt directed the National Park Service to investigate locations reasonably close to the Washington area for use as a Presidential retreat. One of his reasons for desiring to establish it was the wartime necessity to remain close to the Capital at all times and to limit visits to his home at Hyde Park, N.Y. Also, for security reasons, naval officials had recommended that he discontinue weekend use of the Presidential yacht, the U.S.S. *Potomac.* Because of his aversion to air conditioning and the oppressive summer heat and humidity of Washington, his medical

Dwight D. Eisenhower's oil painting of one of the cottages at Camp David.

advisers recommended that he seek respite in a nearby region of high altitude.

After studying several locations, the National Park Service selected three tentative sites: one in Shenandoah National Park, in Virginia, and the other two in the Catoctin Recreational Demonstration Area, in Maryland. The President chose one of the latter two sites, known as Camp Number Three or Camp Hi-Catoctin. By using the existing buildings there, the retreat could be completed in the shortest possible time and at minimum cost. The camp also occupied a perfect location, atop Catoctin Mountain at an altitude of about 1,700 feet above sea level; experienced a consistently lower temperature than Washington; and was only about 70 miles, or a 2-hour drive, from the White House. The camp was one of three units the Federal Government had constructed between 1936 and 1939 as part of an experiment to establish public recreation facilities out of industrially depleted and worn-out lands. Although portions of the area had been opened to the public in 1937, the events leading up to World War II had ended the project prematurely.

In April 1942 Roosevelt visited the camp and chose as its nucleus and his personal residence an existing cabin, a one-room frame structure with a huge stone fireplace, an open porch, and an outside kitchen. Rebuilt by local laborers and the crew of the U.S.S. *Potomac*, which was transferred to the retreat in June, the completed structure, or lodge, contained a living-dining room, probably the original room; an enlarged, screened-in porch; a bedroom wing to the south; and a kitchen wing to the north. The exterior was constructed of local stone and hardwood; the interior, mainly of commercially obtained materials. A special feature of the lodge was a hinged wall that coud be used as an emergency exit ramp for the crippled President. Furnishings consisted of various items from the White House attic and Navy storage. Above the main entrance of the lodge, which looked out over a small, trout-stocked pond, workmen hung the Presidential seal.

Laborers also assembled a communications building out of three existing cabins; combined two others to form a guest lodge; altered another structure for use as servants' sleeping quarters; and constructed a log gatehouse to guard the access road. Landscaping included selective removal of trees and shrubbery to accommodate the eastward view; additional planting in the vicinity of the main lodge; some clearing to aid in construction; and the obliteration of old service roads. Labor in the swimming pool area involved landscaping, road improvement, and the erection of a frame platform and tent for use as a dressing room. Utility work included the installation of water, power, and telephone lines and an underground intercommunication system.

On July 5 the President inspected the retreat, which he had named "Shangri-la" in April. The secluded mountaintop setting of James Hilton's novel *Lost Horizon*, it had also been the code name for the secret starting point of James Doolittle's raid over Tokyo on April 18. Among the names Roosevelt applied to individual buildings were "The Bear's Den" (the main lodge), "The Soap Dish" (the laundry), "The Baker Street Urchins" (Secret Service building), and "Little Luzon" (Philippine stewards' cabin). Before his death in April 1945, he visited "Shangri-la" 22 more times. The

President Kennedy and his predecessor, Eisenhower, stroll at Camp David in April 1961.

most distinguished guests he entertained there were Prime Minister Winston Churchill of Great Britain on two occasions and the British Foreign Secretary Anthony Eden.

Roosevelt's successor, Harry S Truman, used the retreat only a few times. President Eisenhower, however, was a frequent visitor and renamed it Camp David in honor of his grandson. He also re-designated the main lodge as "Aspen." The Eisenhowers not only repaired, repainted, and refurnished most of the cabins, but they also added a large flagstone terrace and picnic and outdoor cooking facility in the area of the main lodge. The President also installed a golf green and several tees. Because they owned a farm near Gettysburg, Pa., only 20 miles to the north, the Eisenhowers found the retreat to be convenient, especially while they were erecting a residence at the farm. Their most famous guest, in 1959, was Premier Nikita Khrushchev of the Soviet Union.

Presidents Kennedy and Johnson rarely utilized Camp David, though in 1965 the latter conferred there with Lester Pearson, Prime Minister of Canada. It was President Nixon's favorite retreat when he was in Washington, not only for relaxing and meeting with foreign dignitaries, but also for working. President Ford seldom visited the retreat.

Extensive modernization of the facilities at the camp has occurred since Roosevelt's time, including installation of a helicopter pad, new figure-eight swimming pool, bowling alley, and skeet shooting range. There are now 11 residence cabins, including the main lodge, which is presently called "Laurel." The President utilizes a three-room cottage, named "Birch," as an office.

In 1954 the Federal Government created Catoctin Mountain Park, which surrounds Camp David, out of almost 6,000 acres of the old Catoctin Recreational Demonstration Area. The remainder of the area was transferred to the State of Maryland, which now operates it as Cunningham Falls State Park. Catoctin Mountain Park is primarily a wilderness and public recreational area that provides nature and hiking trails and picnicking and camping facilities.

Adams (John) Birthplace, Massachusetts

Norfolk County, 133 Franklin Street, Quincy.

This was the original homestead of the Adams family and the birthplace of John Adams. Although not architecturally impressive, it is historically notable as the place where John Adams grew to manhood. It is adjacent to the John Quincy Adams birthplace.

The original house, a typical New England saltbox structure of frame construction with a massive central chimney, was probably built about 1681. It consisted of two lower and two upper rooms. Extensive alterations were made over the years. The rear lean-to,

John Adams Birthplace.

built at some unknown date in the 18th century, added two downstairs rooms and two small upper ones, separated by a large attic.

In 1720 John Adams' father, "Deacon" John Adams, purchased the house, where in 1735 young John was born. He lived there until his marriage in 1764. He and his bride moved into a residence next door that he had inherited from his father in 1761 and 6 years later was to be the birthplace of his son John Quincy. In 1774 John

bought his birthplace home from his brother. His public duties and
legal business kept him away most of the time. By 1783, when he
and his family were in Europe, tenants resided in both the John
Adams and John Quincy Adams birthplaces. In 1788, when John
Adams sailed home, he settled at "Peacefield," or the "Old House,"
now Adams National Historic Site, in another part of Quincy. In
1803 he sold both birthplaces to his son John Quincy.

The John Adams birthplace remained in the possession of the
Adams family until 1940, when it was deeded to the city of Quincy.
In 1896 the Adamses had given the Adams Chapter, Daughters of
the American Revolution, permission to restore the residence,
which the next year was made accessible to the public. When the
Adams Chapter dissolved in 1950, the Quincy Historical Society
took over the administration. The house is in excellent condition
and still owned by the city.

Adams (John Quincy) Birthplace, Massachusetts ⚠
Norfolk County, 141 Franklin Street, Quincy.

This frame structure was John Adams' residence and law office
during the War for Independence and the birthplace of his son John
Quincy. In 1744 "Deacon" John Adams had acquired the residence,
the oldest part of which may date from 1663. In 1761 he bequeathed
it to young John. At the time of the latter's marriage 3 years later,
he moved into it from his neighboring birthplace so that he could
better accommodate his library and set up a law office. In 1767
John Quincy was born in the house.

Shortly thereafter, John's growing law practice and role in public affairs made it convenient for him to live in Boston most of the
time, but his wife and son remained in the Quincy home until after
the War for Independence. By 1783, when the family was in Europe,
tenants were occupying it. After coming back to the United States
in 1788, John Adams took up residence at "Peacefield," or the "Old
House," now Adams National Historic Site. In 1803 John Quincy
purchased both birthplaces from his father, and from 1805 to 1807
lived in his own birthplace.

The John Quincy Adams birthplace is well preserved. Like the
John Adams birthplace, it is of typical New England saltbox
design, originally comprised of two upper and two lower rooms

John Quincy Adams Birthplace.

arranged around a huge central chimney, and has been extensively altered. John Adams added a lean-to of two rooms at the back for use as a new kitchen during the time he used the original kitchen as a law office-library.

In 1897 the Quincy Historical Society, aided by Adams heirs, restored and opened the John Quincy Adams birthplace to the public. In 1940 the Adams family turned it over to the city of Quincy. It is administered by the Quincy Historical Society.

Adams National Historic Site.

Adams National Historic Site, Massachusetts   ⭐

Norfolk County, bounded by Adams Street, Furnace Brook Parkway, and Newport Avenue, Quincy.

Featuring the Adams Mansion, this site is a memorial to four generations of the distinguished Adams family, who resided in it from 1788 until 1927.

John Adams (1735-1826), signer of the Declaration of Independence, diplomat, the first Vice President, and the second President, founded a long line of men who were outstanding in politics and intellectual life, John Quincy (1767-1848), his son, won fame as a diplomat, U.S. Congressman, Secretary of State, and sixth President. Charles Francis Adams (1807-86), son of John Quincy, became a U.S. Congressman, diplomat, and author. His four sons—

John Quincy II (1833-94), Charles Francis, Jr. (1835-1915), Henry (1838-1918), and Brooks (1848-1927)—made notable marks in politics, literature, and historiography.

The Adams Mansion, named "Peacefield" by John Adams but known to some as the Vassall-Adams House and later to the Adams family as the "Old House," was dear and close to all of them. In 1730-31 Maj. Leonard Vassall, a wealthy West Indian sugar planter who had come to Massachusetts some 8 years before, built the oldest part of the building. Comprising the front western section of the present residence, it was a 2½-story frame structure of Georgian design with clapboarded walls and gambrel roof. The first floor contained two rooms separated by a central stair hall; the second floor, two bedrooms and center hall; and the dormered attic, three smaller chambers. The kitchen and servants' quarters were detached.

John Adams, while still Minister to Great Britain, bought the house in September 1787 from Vassall's grandson, Leonard Vassall Borland, and on his return the next year took possession. At that time, he apparently attached the 2½-story kitchen and servants' quarters to the rear, or northwest, corner of the main structure. In

"Peacefield" in 1798.

1800, near the end of his Presidency, he doubled the size of the residence by adding a large, 2½-story, L-shaped wing of frame at the eastern end. It was constructed in the same Georgian style as the original house and contained on the first floor a second entry hall and staircase and the "Long Room" to the east of the hall. Adams' large study-library was on the second floor.

Other additions were made in the 19th century. In 1836 John Quincy Adams built the passage along the back, or north, side of the structure connecting the two rear service ells. In 1869 Charles Francis added 30 feet to the kitchen ell for additional servants' quarters; the following year, a detached stone library overlooking the garden; and in 1873, the stone stable. Brooks constructed the present entrance gates in 1906.

After retiring from the Presidency in 1801, John Adams lived in the house year round until his death in 1826. Subsequently, until Brooks' death in 1927, other family members resided in it full time or spent their summers there. The furnishings, to which each generation contributed, reveal the continuity of life in the residence and the tastes of the Adams family.

In 1946 the Adams Memorial Society donated the property to the Federal Government. Consisting of almost 5 acres, it includes the well-maintained house, library, garden, and stables. It may be visited from the spring until fall.

Kennedy Compound, Massachusetts ⚠

Barnstable County, Irving and Marchant Avenues, Hyannis Port.

The Kennedy Compound consists of about 6 acres of waterfront property along Nantucket Sound. It contains the homes of Joseph P. Kennedy and two of his sons, Robert F. and John F. During the late 1950's and early 1960's, the latter utilized the compound as a base for his Presidential campaign and as a summer White House and Presidential retreat until his assassination in 1963.

In 1926 Joseph P. rented a summer cottage on Marchant Avenue in Hyannis Port. Three years later, he purchased the structure, which had been erected in 1904, and enlarged and remodeled it to suit his family's needs. In and around this house, the children spent their summers, acquiring a lifelong interest in sailing and other competitive activities. In 1956, or 3 years after his marriage,

Joseph P. Kennedy summer home.

John F. Kennedy residence at Hyannis Port.

John F. bought a smaller home of his own on Irving Avenue, not far from that of his father. Subsequently, Robert F. acquired a residence adjacent to the other two.

All three buildings, none of which are accessible to the public, are white frame clapboarded structures typical of vacation residences on Cape Cod. The Joseph P. Kennedy home, the largest and most impressive of the three, is surrounded by well-tended lawns and gardens and commands sweeping views of the ocean from its long porches. On the main floor are a living room, dining room, sun room, television room, the bedroom that President Kennedy used before he purchased his own house in the compound, the kitchen, and various pantries and utility rooms. On the second floor are six bedrooms, a sewing room, packing room, and four servants' bedrooms. The attic is a full one. The basement contains a motion-picture theater and sauna. On the grounds are an enclosed swimming pool, tennis court, and four-car garage. The house has changed little, either structurally or in furnishings, since John F. Kennedy's association with it.

Kennedy National Historic Site, Massachusetts ★
Norfolk County, 83 Beals Street, Brookline.

This national historic site preserves the birthplace and early boyhood home of President John F. Kennedy.

In 1914 young banker Joseph P. Kennedy purchased this modest, 2½-story residence in the Boston suburbs; moved into it with his bride, the former Rose Fitzgerald; began to raise a family; and soon achieved remarkable business success. These years were quiet ones and typical of young couples. The father went to work each day, and dined at home practically every evening. His wife oversaw the growing household, attended concerts and club meetings with other young women who shared her interests, and cared for her children. The Kennedys took their youngsters sledding in winter, entertained at small dinners, and took part in church activities.

Joseph, Jr., was born in Hull, Mass., but the other three of the couple's first four children (John, Rosemary, and Kathleen) were born in this house. Within a few years, the Kennedys outgrew the residence. In 1921, when John was only 4 years old, they moved to a

Kennedy National Historic Site.

Mrs. Rose F. Kennedy speaks at the dedication of the Kennedy National Historic Site. Her son Edward is seated on the porch.

larger residence only a few blocks away, at the corner of Naples and Abbottsford Roads.

Since that time, the birthplace home has had various owners. In 1961 the town of Brookline marked it with a commemorative plaque; 4 years later it was designated as a National Historic Landmark; and, the next year, the Kennedy family purchased it for preservation as a historic site. The President's mother supervised restoration and refurnishing of the first two floors to their 1917 appearance, and in 1967 the family donated the residence to the Federal Government.

A nine-room, clapboarded structure dating from 1907, the house has a gabled and dormered roof and a small front porch. The first floor contains a hall, living room, dining room, and kitchen; the second floor, a hall, study, guestroom, nursery, master bedroom (where John and the two other children were born), and bath. The furnishings of these two floors are either original or other Kennedy family items, period pieces, or reproductions. The recorded voice of the President's mother describes the significance of each room. The third floor, originally a servants' quarters, contains an administrative office and is not open to the public.

A few other structures associated with the Kennedys are within easy walking distance of the national historic site. Outstanding among them, at the northeast corner of Naples and Abbottsford Roads, is their residence from 1921 until 1927, when they moved to

Riverdale, a New York City suburb. Now privately owned, it is not open to the public. In this house, Mrs. Kennedy bore three more children (Eunice, Patricia, and Robert) and John spent his years from 4 to 10, during which time he first went to school, learned to love sports, and established a lifelong reading habit. Jean and Edward were born after the family moved to New York.

While they lived in Brookline, the Kennedys attended St. Aidan's Catholic Church, on Freeman Street, which has since been extensively altered. Joseph, Jr., and John were baptized there and served as altar boys. They also attended nearby Dexter School, a private, nonsectarian institution also on Freeman Street, but the school has moved to a new campus and the building in which they went to class no longer stands. Finally, on Harvard Avenue, is the public Edward Devotion School, which they attended for a short time before transferring to the Dexter School. In front of the former is the Edward Devotion House, a historic structure dating from the early 1700's. The Brookline Historical Society operates it as a museum.

United First Parish Church (Unitarian), Massachusetts   ⌂

Norfolk County, 1266 Hancock Street, Quincy.

This church, also known as the "Stone Temple" and "Church of the Presidents," contains the graves of two Presidents, John and John Quincy Adams. Architecturally one of the finest houses of worship in New England, it illustrates a transition in style from Georgian and Federal to Greek Revival.

Designed and built in 1827-28 by architect-engineer Alexander Parris and financed primarily by John Quincy Adams, the First Parish Church was constructed of blue granite from nearby quarries and represents one of the earliest uses of native granite as a building material in the United States. Parris altered the basic Georgian and Federal design by adding to the front a broad, pedimented portico supported by four massive Doric columns, a feature that augured the popularity of Greek Revival architecture. The columns, 25 feet long and weighing 25 tons each, were hauled by oxen teams from the quarries to the construction site.

In 1828 the remains of John Adams, who had died 2 years earlier, and of his wife Abigail, who had passed away before her husband,

United First Parish Church.

were removed from Hancock Cemetery and placed in a crypt beneath the vestibule in the basement of the church. In 1852 the bodies of John Quincy Adams, who had passed away 4 years before, and his wife, Louisa Catherine, who succumbed in 1852, were interred in the same crypt. The only other church in the Nation containing the tomb of a President, that of Woodrow Wilson, is the Washington Cathedral (Episcopal), in Washington, D.C.

The only major alteration throughout the years was the addition in 1889 of a one-story, five-sided stone wing on the east, or rear, elevation. In 1959 the church merged with the Wollaston Unitarian Society to become the United First Parish Church (Unitarian) in Quincy. Restored in 1961-64 and still an active place of worship today, it is in excellent condition.

The outstanding exterior features of the two-story, oblong-shaped structure are the huge Greek Revival portico at the front and the tower and the cupola on the roof. A broad flight of stone steps leads up to the pedimented portico, supported by the four monolithic Doric columns. Above and behind the pediment rises a stone tower in two stages. The first stage, broad and rectangular in shape, is unornamented. The second stage, stepped back and square, has a clock on each facade. The second stage is surmounted by a round, open, wooden cupola, which has eight columns and a dome. The north and south sidewalls of the building feature two-story high, round-headed windows with exterior louvered blinds. Extending across the west, or front, wall under the portico is a horizontal panel over three doorways. Double doors, topped by flat lintels, lead into a projecting porch, or vestibule.

Three more doors open from the vestibule into the interior of the church. Two longitudinal aisles divide the pews; and galleries extend around the north, south, and west sides of the room. A fine mahogany pulpit is located in the center of the east, or rear, wall. A magnificent plaster dome adorns the ceiling.

Jefferson National Expansion Memorial, Missouri ★

St. Louis, downtown.

This memorial celebrates the vision of President Thomas Jefferson, architect of westward expansion, as well as all aspects of that vital national movement.

Jefferson National Expansion Memorial.

St. Louis, "gateway to the West," was founded in 1764 by Frenchmen from New Orleans. It evolved into a center of French culture and Spanish governmental control. In 1803 the United States acquired it from France as part of the Louisiana Purchase, consummated during Jefferson's administration.

For many decades thereafter, the city was a key one on the western U.S. frontier. Conveniently located in relation to the mouths of the Ohio, Missouri, and other Mississippi tributaries, it became the hub of midcontinental commerce, transportation, and culture—the place where East met West and point of departure for the wilderness beyond. A base of operations for traders, travelers, scientists, explorers, military leaders, Indian agents, and missionaries, it was also headquarters of the western fur trade and focus of scientific and political thought in the West.

Along the waterfront, hulking steamboats from the East and South met the smaller river boats that served the frontier communities and outposts on the upper Mississippi and Missouri Rivers. At this major transfer point, a small but teeming city, mercantile establishments, boatyards, saloons, and lodginghouses accommodated and supplied the westbound settlers and other frontiersmen who congregated there before setting out across the Plains to Oregon, California, Santa Fe, and other points.

To dramatize westward expansion and the rich cultural, political, and economic benefits that accrued to the Nation from the Louisiana Purchase of 1803, the National Park Service and the Jefferson National Expansion Memorial Association, a nonprofit organization of public-spirited citizens, have undertaken an extensive development program for the memorial. As part of a broad urban renewal program, obsolescent industrial buildings occupying about 40 city blocks have been cleared away.

The dominant feature of the memorial—on the west bank of the Mississippi on the site of the original village of St. Louis—is a 630-foot-high stainless steel arch, designed by the noted architect Eero Saarinen and completed in 1965. It symbolizes the historic position of St. Louis as gateway to the West. A special elevator system carries visitors to an observatory at the top. Scaled to the heroic dimensions of such other structures as the Washington Monument, Eiffel Tower, and Statue of Liberty, the Gateway Arch ranks with them in size and grandeur.

A Museum of Westward Expansion, which is beneath the arch, presents the story of our western heritage in new dimensions.

Truman Historic District, Missouri ⚠

Jackson County, North Delaware Street and environs, Independence.

Harry S Truman was intimately associated with the town of Independence, Mo., from his youth until his death in 1972. His home for more than half a century is the main attraction of this historic district, which incorporates the neighborhood that best illustrates his life and career.

Truman's parents moved to Independence in 1890, when he was only 5 years old. About that time, he began attending Sunday school at the First Presbyterian Church, on North Pleasant Street.

Truman House.

There, he met Elizabeth ("Bess") Wallace, his future bride. The Trumans resided at various places in the town, where he grew up and completed high school. In 1903 the father, beset by financial difficulties, moved back to his father-in-law's farm at nearby Grandview, Mo., where the family had lived earlier. Truman, in his late teens, remained in Independence for awhile, living in rented quarters, and then took up residence in Kansas City, where he held various jobs.

In 1906, responding to his father's request for help, the youth rejoined his family and helped manage the Grandview farm, a grueling occupation that consumed about a decade of his life. Nonetheless, he frequently visited friends and relatives in Independence and courted Bess Wallace. Their marriage in 1919, following his overseas service as an artillery officer during World War I, marked the beginning of Truman's long residence at 219 North Delaware Street, where Bess had been living with her widowed mother and grandmother, who continued to reside in the house.

For about 18 years following his election to the U.S. Senate in 1934 and continuing through his Presidency (1945-53), the Trumans resided for extended periods in rented quarters, the White House, and the Blair-Lee House in Washington, D.C. In January 1953 they returned to Independence, where Truman died in December 1972.

The Truman house is one of the earliest and architecturally most interesting buildings in the historic district. The construction date is unknown, but George P. Gates, Bess Truman's maternal grandfather, purchased the lot in 1867. He may have begun constructing the structure at that time; architectural evidence suggests that it probably did not assume its present appearance until several years later. About 1903, after the death of her husband, Bess Truman's mother moved into her parents' residence. In 1924 she acquired full title to it. After her death in 1952, it became the property of the Trumans. Three years later, they refurbished and partially modernized the interior. In recent years, the slate roof was replaced with asbestos shingles.

The framehouse, asymmetrical in design and combining several mid-19th century architectural styles, is 2½ stories high and contains 14 rooms. A hip-and-gable roof, pierced by tall arched dormers, tops the structure. Dominant features of the west, or front, facade include the balustraded porch, which is bracketed and has elaborate wooden jigsaw trim; scroll gables; and the massive and highly ornamented bay that juts out from one side of the central doorway. The main porch extends from this bay around the north side of the house; a similar but smaller one is on the south side. Narrow sashes filled with colored glass flank the windows on the first two stories of the bay. Extending from the rear, or east, facade of the dwelling is a two-story ell housing the kitchen. A one-story porch resting on high brick piers and partially screened for use in the summer, surrounds the ell's eastern and southern sides. A wooden lattice conceals the south side of the storage area beneath the ell; the east end is open.

The broad lawn surrounding the house contains oak trees,

President and Mrs. Truman in front of their Delaware Street residence in 1952, while on a visit from Washington to Independence.

informally landscaped shrubbery, and flowerbeds. At its rear, a driveway provides access to a frame garage, formerly the carriage house, at the southeastern edge of the property. A tall iron fence, erected in 1947, protects the home from intruders. An antique-style gas lamp stands to the left of the entrance gate.

The Truman residence, still occupied by Mrs. Truman, is not accessible to the public.

The historic district centers around the Truman residence and forms a corridor leading north along North Delaware Street from the vicinity of the house to the Truman Library grounds, which adjoin the district on the northern side of U.S. 24. The upper section of the district, south of the library and north of College Avenue, has been altered by urban redevelopment and is relatively modern. The lower portion, south of College Avenue, remains largely unchanged since the time Truman was President or earlier. From the immediate vicinity of the house, the district boundaries extend to the south to incorporate portions of Pleasant Street, Truman Road, and Maple Avenue and preserve the environs on all sides. The district remains primarily residential, most of the structures dating from the mid-19th or early 20th centuries, and includes only a few public buildings.

Many sites and structures in the district are closely associated with the Trumans. Some of them were the homes of relatives; others, of friends or associates. A modern school building at the corner of Truman Road and Pleasant Street has replaced Central High School, attended by Mr. and Mrs. Truman. The World War Memorial Building, a civic auditorium erected in 1926 at the corner of Pleasant Street and Maple Avenue, was the place where Truman voted for years and the scene of at least one of his press conferences. Diagonally across the street at 100 North Pleasant Street, stands the First Presbyterian Church, a little-altered, simple, Midwest Gothic Revival structure dating from 1888. There, Truman met his future wife. The Chrisman School, at the corner of Maple Avenue and Union Street, was attended by their daughter, Margaret.

Outside the boundaries of the district are three of Truman's boyhood homes, none of which are open to the public. At 909 West Waldo Street, 619 South Crysler Street, and 902 North Liberty Street, they are still standing but are privately owned and have undergone numerous alterations. Other pertinent sites are the Jackson County Courthouse, bounded by Maple and Lexington Avenues and Liberty and Main Streets, which contains offices Truman used during his early public career; the Missouri Pacific Railroad Station, at 600 South Grand Street, the scene in 1953 of a welcome-home ceremony for the Trumans at the end of his Presidency; and Trinity Episcopal Church, at 409 North Liberty Street, site of the marriage ceremonies of the Trumans in 1919 and their daughter in 1956.

Just beyond the northern boundary of the district is the Truman Presidential Library, which houses about 5½ million documents, other items relating to his life, and various historical exhibits. He maintained an office there from the time of its construction until his death and was interred in the courtyard. Financed by private contributions, the library is administered by the General Services Administration.

Truman, retired, at his desk in the Presidential Library in 1960.

Pierce Homestead, New Hampshire ⚿

Hillsboro (Hillsborough) County, on N.H. 31 near its junction with N.H. 9, about 3 miles west of Hillsboro (Hillsborough).

This was the boyhood home and possibly the birthplace of Franklin Pierce. About the time of his birth in 1804, his father, Benjamin, built it and relocated his family there from a nearby log cabin. In addition to farming and participation in local politics, Benjamin operated a tavern in the structure, which became the

Pierce Homestead.

social center of Hillsboro. He also trained county militia in the upstairs ballroom.

During the years 1820-27, Franklin was often away from home, attending Bowdoin College, in Brunswick, Maine, and then studying law in Portsmouth, N.H., Northampton, Mass., and Amherst, N.H. In 1827, the year he returned home and established a law practice in a shed across the road from the homestead, his father became Governor of New Hampshire. Not long afterward, Franklin himself sought public office. In 1829 he entered the legislature, and 4 years later won election to the U.S. House of Representatives. About the time of his marriage in 1834, he purchased his own home in Hillsboro; 4 years later he moved to Concord, N.H.

The homestead remained in the Pierce family until 1925, at which time the State acquired it. Between 1945 and 1950, the New Hampshire Federation of Women's Clubs restored it. A handsome example of New Hampshire village architecture, it is a two-story frame structure that contains eight rooms. The roof is hipped. Furnishings include a few period pieces. The most outstanding room is the parlor, highlighted by mahogany furniture covered in horsehair cloth, a Brussels carpet, and French wallpaper decorated with scenes of Naples Bay. Stencilled decorations adorn the walls of other rooms. In the upstairs ballroom, which extends the length of the house, is a curved table that the State legislature used when Pierce held the speakership. A restored barn at the rear of the residence is connected to a kitchen and service ell that was added at a later date. The house is surrounded by fields and woodlands. It is owned and administered by the State.

Westland, New Jersey
Mercer County, 15 Hodge Road, Princeton.

Westland was the home of Grover Cleveland from the time of his retirement from the Presidency in 1897 until his death in 1908. During the last year of his second term in the White House, in 1896, he had decided to retire at Princeton, N.J. Mrs. Cleveland apparently selected the house, which had been built in the mid-19th century by Commodore Robert F. Stockton. Cleveland named it Westland in honor of a close friend and professor at Princeton University, Andrew F. West.

Cleveland enjoyed his retirement. Although he had never attended college, he took an active part in Princeton activities, maintained a brisk correspondence with friends, and kept socially and politically active. His favorite recreations were billiards and meetings of the Poverty Club, composed of a group of his comrades

Westland.

who played cards regularly at Westland. The students at Princeton University, who were fond of Cleveland, serenaded him on his birthdays. And, after football games, they led victory parades to his home. He died at Westland in 1908 and was buried in Princeton Cemetery. His <u>widow</u> continued to reside in the house for many years.

Westland was patterned after Morven, an elegant Georgian mansion built in Princeton in the 18th century by the prominent Stockton family and today a National Historic Landmark. A 2½-story, stone structure covered with stucco painted yellow, Westland

Grover Cleveland, his wife, <u>Frances</u>, and family at Westland in 1907, the year before he died. The children (left to right) are Esther, Francis, Marion, and Richard.

[Handwritten marginalia, top left, vertical:] Frances, a friend of my Aunt Laura Baker, came occasionally to Castle Howard Farm, northeast of Princeton on the right side of the Kingston Road, where I lived for several school years. I met Frances more than one occasion. There I also met her and husband (whose name I do not remember). The Clevelands offered to accompany me on a visit to Washington, D.C., about 1925, and I drove Aunt Laura's little Chrysler roadster. This was an exciting joint visit to the capital city. We were away for 2 days.

[Handwritten marginalia, middle:] Son Frances (see also page 201) in much later years, lived near Tamworth, N.H. Early in the spring, about 1939, I rented a car at Concord and drove to Tamworth. When the dirt roads were thawing out, we followed a road past the Cleveland house and

[Handwritten marginalia, right side, vertical:] just beyond got stuck in the mud. Walking back to the house, I knocked on the door. Frances came out, listened to my predicament, and drove his horse, attached to a tree and chain, and pulled out the car.

had twin parlors on the first floor, spacious rooms, high ceilings, and handsome marble mantelpieces. Shortly after moving into the house, Cleveland added a two-story, flat-roofed wing containing a billiard room on the first floor and some bedrooms on the second. Through the years, other additions became so numerous that the rear of the structure was later detached and moved back on the lot to form a separate residence. Westland, privately owned and in excellent condition, may not be visited by the public.

Arthur Home, New York ⚠

New York County, 123 Lexington Avenue, New York City.

Chester A. Arthur lived in this house for most of his adult life. In 1848, after graduating from Union College in Schenectady, N.Y., he taught school for awhile and about 1853 moved to New York City to practice law. At some unknown date, he acquired this residence.

In 1880 Arthur was elected Vice President on the Republican ticket with James Garfield. Less than a year later, on September 19, 1881, the latter died as a result of an assassin's attack the previous July. During the wee hours of the next morning, Arthur privately took the oath of office in his New York home and became the 21st President of the United States; 2 days later, he repeated the oath in the Vice President's Office at the U.S. Capitol. In 1885 Arthur retired from the Presidency and returned to New York City to resume his law practice. Illness soon enfeebled him, however, and he never recovered. He died in his New York home in November 1886 and his body was laid to rest at the Rural Cemetery in Albany.

The residence, a five-story, brownstone rowhouse, has been considerably altered throughout the years. The original entrance, once at the second-floor level and accessible by a flight of stone stairs, has disappeared. A grocery store occupies the front part of the first, or ground, floor; a beauty shop is on the second floor; and the remaining three floors have been divided into apartments. The exterior has been painted white; the interior is in poor condition. No Arthur furnishings remain in the structure.

On January 16, 1964, the 81st anniversary of the signing of the U.S. Civil Service Act by President Arthur, the Native New Yorkers Historical Association and the New York Life Insurance Company placed a bronze plaque on the building. Privately owned, it is not open to the public.

Arthur Home.

Early on the morning of September 20, 1881, a few hours after Garfield's death, Judge John R. Brady administered the oath of office to Chester A. Arthur in his New York City residence. Arthur later repeated the oath at the U.S. Capitol.

Federal Hall National Memorial, New York ★

New York County, at the corner of Wall and Nassau Streets, just off Broadway, New York City.

This memorial commemorates two earlier buildings on this site that were the scene of momentous events vital to American freedom and the formation of the Union, including the inauguration of George Washington as the first President. City Hall, the first structure, was a Capitol of the United States under the Articles of Confederation; enlarged and renamed Federal Hall, it was the first Capitol under the Constitution. The present edifice, erected in the period 1835-42, was designated as Federal Hall National Memorial in the 20th century.

Federal Hall National Memorial.

In City Hall the Continental Congress issued the call for the Constitutional Convention at Philadelphia; received, debated, and transmitted the Constitution to the States for ratification; and prepared for the transfer of power to the new Government. On the balcony of Federal Hall, George Washington took the oath of office as our first President. In its chambers, the First Congress created the original governmental departments as well as the Federal judiciary system, and drafted and submitted the Bill of Rights to the States for approval.

City Hall, begun about 1699 to replace an earlier structure on another site, the Dutch *Stadt Huys*, was completed and occupied in 1703 or 1704 and remodeled in 1763. In time, the building also accommodated the colonial and State governments.

In 1734 newspaper publisher John Peter Zenger, charged with publishing "seditious libels," was imprisoned by the colonial Governor in the garret of City Hall. The following year, he was tried in the hall. His attorney, Andrew Hamilton, won his acquittal, an important precedent for freedom of speech and the press. In October 1765 the Stamp Act Congress, consisting of delegates from 9 of the 13 Colonies, convened in the hall. Offering the first united colonial opposition to British policy, it sent an address to the King, petitioned Parliament, and draw up a Declaration of Rights and Grievances.

During the 1770's Philadelphia displaced New York as the prime meetingplace for intercolonial gatherings and hosted both the First and Second Continental Congresses. During the War for Independence, from 1776 to 1783, British forces and Loyalists controlled New York City. City Hall became a guardhouse and housed a military court.

In late 1784 the Continental Congress, meeting in Trenton, N.J., selected New York City as the seat of Government; and in January began meeting in City Hall, at the invitation of the city government. In February 1787 Congress approved the resolution of the Annapolis Convention that called for the convening of a Constitutional Convention in Philadelphia. During the Convention, some delegates journeyed to and from New York to sit in the Congress. During this period, it passed the Northwest Ordinance, which provided for the government of the Territory Northwest of the Ohio River. After the Convention, Congress received and forwarded the Constitution to the States for ratification.

View of Wall Street, including Federal Hall and Trinity Church, in 1789. That year, George Washington was inaugurated on the balcony of Federal Hall, where the First Congress met.

In September 1788 the Continental Congress designated New York City as the U.S. Capital under the Constitution. The city council promptly offered the continued use of City Hall, and hired Maj. Pierre Charles L'Enfant to renovate and enlarge it. The work was largely completed before Congress met the following spring. Filling in the space between the two front wings, which projected from a central block, L'Enfant erected an imposing second-floor balcony in the middle of the new front facade. Large extensions were also made at the rear of the building, and a new roof was built for the entire structure. In the repartitioned interior, spacious chambers were provided for both the House and Senate as well as an imposing office for the President. Inside and out, the building was ornately decorated to celebrate American freedom and Union.

In the new structure, renamed Federal Hall, the First Congress held its initial sessions early in April 1789, counted the electoral votes, and announced the election of George Washington as President and John Adams as Vice President. On the afternoon of April 30, a joint committee of Congress had arrived at his residence on Cherry Street and announced that Congress was ready to receive him for inauguration. In the procession, Washington rode along in a coach drawn by four horses, and other dignitaries rode in coaches drawn by two horses. Ahead of Washington were the Senators of the joint committee and a group of soldiers. Behind him, were the committee's Representatives, Washington's secretaries, the heads of Federal departments, Chancellor of the State of New York Robert R. Livingston, and a few eminent citizens. The procession, followed by a huge crowd of citizens and militia, proceeded to Broad Street. There, Washington and the others who were riding alighted and walked the remaining distance to Federal Hall.

On the front second-floor balcony, overlooking throngs of people at the intersection of Broad and Wall Streets, Livingston administered the Presidential oath. Upon the ceremony's conclusion, as the flag was raised on the cupola of the building, cheers filled the air, church bells rang out, and guns saluted from the harbor. Shortly thereafter, inside the building, from the dais of the Senate Chamber, Washington delivered his inaugural address to Congress and guests. The assemblage then adjourned to nearby St. Paul's Chapel, today a National Historic Landmark; listened to a sermon delivered by Rev. Samuel Provost, Episcopal Bishop of New York and Chaplain of Congress; and Washington was then escorted home.

Between July and September, Congress created the Supreme Court and other courts and the Departments of State, War, and Treasury, as well as the office of Attorney General; and adopted and transmitted the Bill of Rights to the States for ratification. One of Congress' last acts in this building, in July 1790, was selection of a 10-mile square tract along the Potomac as the site of a permanent national Capital, to be called the District of Columbia. In August 1790 the Federal Government moved from New York to Philadelphia, which was to serve as the interim Capital.

During the following two decades, Federal Hall was utilized only for State and city offices. In 1796 the legislature relocated to Albany, and in 1811 the city also vacated the deteriorating building. The following year, it was demolished. Commercial buildings were soon erected on the site. In 1816 or 1817 the Federal Government acquired or leased them for temporary use as a customhouse. The permanent New York City Custom House, built at the site in the period 1835-42, is an outstanding example of Greek Revival architecture. In 1862 it became the United States

Sub-Treasury. Later, it housed the Federal Reserve Bank of New York and a number of minor governmental offices. When most of these were relocated, local civic and patriotic organizations conceived the idea of preserving the structure as a memorial to the founding of our Federal form of Government. The building was designated as a national historic site in 1939 and became a national memorial in 1955.

Federal Hall National Memorial is administered by the National Park Service with the cooperation of the Federal Hall Memorial Associates, Inc. Extensive exhibits trace the historical events associated with the site.

Fillmore House, New York ⚠

Erie County, 24 Shearer Avenue, East Aurora.

In 1826 young lawyer-politician and bridegroom Millard Fillmore, while continuing his odyssey from log cabin to the White House, built the front part of this simple frame residence where his only son was to be born, and lived in it for 4 years before moving to Buffalo. Although his occupancy was brief, the history of the structure is obscure, and it has been relocated and extensively altered, this was the first home he owned and is the only extant one significantly associated with him except for the White House.

Fillmore erected his house across from his law office on Main Street. Little is known about the subsequent owners or tenants or the nature of any structural changes until 1930. In 1915, however, the residence had been moved back on the lot to make room for a movie theater, and for a long time it was unoccupied and underwent deterioration.

In 1930 the present owners moved the structure about a mile to its present location, placed it on a new cement-block foundation, proceeded to renovate it, and erected one-story additions at the rear. The plain, attenuated columns supporting the shed-roofed porch, which once had latticework along the sides, were replaced with fluted Doric columns. To create an artist's studio in the front section, the second floor was removed and a large window added on the north facade, as well as a small skylight in the roof.

The fireplace and chimney on the north side of the house were removed, and new ones built at the south end. Most of the old

Fillmore House.

windows, the plain interior woodwork, and some of the wide floorboards were retained. The building, the front and rear portions of which have gabled roofs, is painted white and the trim is black. Except for the front, which is covered with flushboard, the home is all clapboarded. A private residence, it is not open to the public.

Also of interest in East Aurora is the Millard Fillmore Museum, 644 Oakwood Street, which is operated by the Aurora Historical Society, Inc.

General Grant National Memorial, New York ★

New York County, Riverside Drive near its intersection with W. 122d Street, New York City.

This national memorial, popularly known as "Grant's Tomb," commemorates the life and career of Ulysses S. Grant and shelters the crypt containing his remains and those of his wife, Julia Dent Grant.

Shortly before his death, Grant conveyed to his son, Frederick D., a request that he be buried in New York City, where he had lived in

General Grant National Memorial.

retirement for several years. Frederick chose a picturesque location overlooking the Hudson River in newly created Riverside Park. When death came on July 23, 1885, at a cottage on Mount McGregor, near Saratoga, his father's body first lay in state at the capitol in Albany, and then was taken to New York City Hall. From there on August 8, a parade of thousands of Civil War veterans escorted it to a temporary vault in Riverside Park. The funeral, attended by the Nation's highest officials, was one of the most impressive ever held in the city.

Meantime, a group of prominent New Yorkers had formed the Grant Monument Association to raise funds for the construction of

Grant's temporary tomb about 1885, the year of his death.

a permanent memorial. The city donated a sizable plot of land in Riverside Park, not far from the temporary gravesite. Construction, delayed several years because of the lack of funds, began in 1891 and was completed in 1897. During this time, various financial and architectural problems caused the design of architect John H. Duncan of New York to undergo considerable alterations, resulting in a smaller and less elaborate structure than had been planned.

Ten days before the dedication ceremony, which occurred on April 27, 1897, the 75th anniversary of Grant's birth, his remains were transferred from the temporary vault to a sarcophagus in the memorial crypt. A vast crowd of citizens attended the dedication, which was highlighted by a military parade and an address by President McKinley. When Mrs. Grant died in 1902, her body was placed in a twin sarcophagus adjacent to that of her husband.

At the time of the dedication, the Grant Monument Association presented the memorial to the city. Not long afterward, the Board of Park Commissioners entered into an agreement with the association whereby the latter would administer it with municipal funds. This arrangement lasted for the next six decades, until 1956, when

Dedication ceremonies on April 27, 1897, at Grant's Tomb. Highlights were a military parade and an address by President McKinley.

the State legislature authorized the transfer of the memorial from the Grant Monument Association and the city to the Federal Government. In 1959, with the cooperation of the association, the National Park Service began administering it as General Grant National Memorial.

A 150-foot-high gray granite structure, the monument sits on a bluff overlooking the Hudson River. Its architecture, a combination of styles and motifs, is basically classical. The base is 90 feet square and 72 feet high. A portico, supported by 10 fluted Doric columns, projects from its southern facade and provides access to the interior. Rising from the base is a rotunda surrounded by Ionic columns and topped by a conical dome with a 5-ton capstone. Dominating the white-marble-lined interior is the open crypt containing the sarcophagi of Grant and his wife. Two trophy rooms at the rear of the crypt exhibit Union Army battle flags and mural maps outlining Civil War campaigns. Allegorical figures between the four arches in the rotunda represent phases of Grant's life. In niches around the walls of the crypt are heroic busts of five of his comrades in arms: Generals William T. Sherman, Philip H. Sheridan, George H. Thomas, Edward O.C. Ord, and James B. McPherson.

Home of Franklin D. Roosevelt National Historic Site, New York ⊠

Dutchess County, on U.S. 9 (New York-Albany Post Road), about 2 miles south of Hyde Park and 4 miles north of Poughkeepsie.

This rambling country house, overlooking the Hudson River, was the birthplace and lifelong home of Franklin D. Roosevelt. Although his law career and public service made it necessary for him to maintain several other residences throughout his life, he always considered Hyde Park his permanent home and returned to it as often as possible. His grave, as well as that of his wife, is on the grounds of the estate, as is also the Franklin D. Roosevelt Library.

From the time of his birth at Hyde Park in 1882, Roosevelt traveled extensively with his parents, James and Sara Delano Roosevelt. They maintained a winter apartment in New York City; a summer cottage on Campobello Island, in New Brunswick, Canada; and frequently toured Europe. Nonetheless, Franklin, who received his elementary education from governesses and tutors, spent considerable time at his birthplace home. These interludes diminished during the years 1896-1904 when he was away at Groton School, a private boarding establishment at Groton, Mass., and Harvard University.

Meantime, in 1900 James Roosevelt had died and his widow received lifetime use of the 500-acre estate, actually bequeathed to Franklin. In 1904 the latter entered law school at Columbia University, in New York City, where the next year he married his fifth cousin Eleanor. Thereafter, his career kept him away from Hyde Park for extended periods, especially after he became

Home of Franklin D. Roosevelt National Historic Site.

Assistant Secretary of the Navy in 1913. On several occasions he utilized it as a campaign headquarters. And it was an invaluable retreat for him following 1921, the year after he was defeated for the U.S. Vice-Presidency, when he was stricken with infantile paralysis, though beginning in 1924 he frequently visited Warm Springs, Ga.

As a "summer White House" during the Presidential years (1933-45), Hyde Park provided Roosevelt with respite from the turmoil of public life and was the scene of several conferences and events of national and international significance. Notables he entertained there include Winston Churchill, King George VI and Queen Elizabeth of Britain, and Queen Wilhelmina of the Netherlands.

In 1941, when Sara Delano Roosevelt died at the age of 87, Franklin assumed full jurisdiction over the estate. Three years earlier, he and his mother had offered it as a gift to the Federal Government provided that Eleanor Roosevelt and her children would retain the right to live out their lives there. In 1944, after appropriate congressional action, the Secretary of the Interior declared the property a national historic site. The next year, shortly after Franklin's death, his widow waived the family's residence rights. The following year, the National Park Service opened the house and grounds to the public.

The oldest portion of the house, incorporated into the front central section of the present structure, dates to the early 1800's. It was a modest, two-story Victorian residence, 46 feet long and 39 feet wide. The walls, constructed of vertical heavy timbers and crude brick filling, were covered with wide clapboards. Two tall end chimneys projected from the gable roof. The first floor contained an entrance hall and four rooms; the second floor, four rooms and a large closet. Josiah Wheeler, who occupied the house from 1845 until 1867, attached a three-story tower to its south side and a two-story service wing to the north. Other improvements included the addition of a garden, incorporating a greenhouse and grapery; a carriage house over a stable; and a gardener's cottage.

In 1867 James Roosevelt acquired this 116-acre estate, which he named Springwood. In 1887, or 7 years after his second marriage, to Sara Delano, he added a two-story bay to the rear of the central section. At one end of the bay, he attached a one-story, octagonal smoking room, later raised to two stories to provide a second-floor bedroom. In 1893 he extended an existing veranda from the front around the south end of the house to the dining room door at the rear, and in 1900 enlarged the service wing.

In 1915-16 Franklin and his mother renovated and enlarged the house, which at that time assumed its present H-shape. Laborers stripped off the clapboards and covered the exterior with gray stucco to match two, two-story stone wings that they constructed at the north and south ends of the structure; lowered the tower on the south side and added another on the north service wing to match it; raised the roof between the towers to provide an additional third-floor room; flattened the gable roof; and removed the veranda from the front and south end of the building. At the front of the main house, between the towers, a small Doric-columned portico and large balustraded stone terrace were constructed. As finished in 1916, the residence consisted of 35 rooms and 9 baths. Its facade

Franklin D. Roosevelt poses with his wife, mother, and family at Hyde Park on Christmas Day, 1932, shortly before he began his first term as President. Standing (left to right): James, Elliott, Franklin D., Jr., Elliott's wife, Curtis Dall (Anna's husband), and John. Seated on floor (left to right): James' wife and their daughter Sara, Anna Roosevelt Dall.

President Roosevelt relaxes with his wife, Eleanor, and his dog, Fala, at Hyde Park in 1941.

was Georgian. During subsequent years, the Roosevelts made no major structural alterations.

Today, the house, its furnishings, and the grounds appear essentially as they did at the time of Roosevelt's death. The main living areas on the first two floors are open to the public; servants' rooms, utility and work rooms, and the third floor are closed. Most of the furnishings date from the 1850's through the 1920's and only a few items postdate 1930. Portraits include those of various family members, and many of the paintings reflect Franklin's nautical interest.

The central section of the first floor contains a substantial entrance hall, and Dresden, dining, and smoking rooms. Between the main house and the south wing, which contains a huge living room-library that was added in 1916, is a hallway and small "snuggery," the sitting and writing room of Sara Roosevelt. Franklin presented several of his radio "fireside chats" from the living room-library. In the north wing are his study (the "summer White House"), the kitchen, servants' hall, and various utility rooms. In the study, in 1942, Roosevelt and Churchill decided to launch the research program that created the atomic bomb; and, from there, Roosevelt gave his last campaign speech of the 1944 Presidential campaign over the radio. The second floor is comprised of nine bedrooms (including the one where Roosevelt was born) and guestrooms, plus servants' quarters. Three additional bedrooms, a nursery, and a playroom are on the third floor.

Outbuildings include the coachhouse, built by James Roosevelt in 1886 to shelter riding and work horses; the stable-garage put up by Josiah Wheeler about 1850 to accommodate trotting horses and used by James Roosevelt for the same purpose, but after 1910 converted into a garage; a laundry erected about 1850; an equipment shed dating from 1911; a small icehouse built before 1867 and a larger one constructed in 1898; a greenhouse erected in 1906; and two cottages for servants. The graves of Franklin D. and Eleanor Roosevelt are a short distance to the northeast of the house in the rose garden, which is enclosed by a century-old hemlock hedge and assumed its present design in 1912.

Also on the grounds is the Franklin D. Roosevelt Library, built in 1939-40, the first such Presidential institution administered by the Federal Government. He used an office in it during the last few years of his life. The library not only houses thousands of books and papers relating to his era, but also provides public research facilities and serves as a museum of Roosevelt memorabilia. It is administered by the General Services Administration.

Roosevelt (Theodore) Birthplace National Historic Site, New York ★

New York County, 28 East 20th Street, New York City.

On this site stands a reconstruction of the four-story, brownstone townhouse where Theodore Roosevelt was born and spent the first 14 years of his life. During these formative years, he waged a victorious struggle against persistent childhood ailments and poor health; nurtured a passion for books and learning; and, with the help of exercise and a loving family, created a strong body and molded a vigorous personality.

Theodore Roosevelt Birthplace National Historic Site.

In 1854 Roosevelt's father, also named Theodore, brought his bride from Georgia to New York City and moved into a residence at No. 33 (later No. 28) East 20th Street. It had been built in 1848 either by or for the elder Theodore's brother, Robert Barnwell Roosevelt. After 1854, the former occupied the adjacent house to the west.

During the nearly two decades the Roosevelts lived in the house, all four of their children were born in it. Theodore, Jr., born in October 1858, suffered from poor health from the beginning of his life. Physically unable to attend school, he received some tutoring, but gained his education primarily on his own by extensive reading. When he was 10 years old, he accompanied his parents on a grand tour of Europe, a major ordeal for him because of illness, homesickness, and physical exhaustion. Two years later, his father installed gymnasium equipment off the nursery on the second-floor porch. From that time on, Theodore assiduously tried to better his health, which had improved considerably by the time the family made a second trip to Europe in 1872-73. In the latter year, when the Roosevelts arrived back in New York, they moved into another home, at 6 West 57th Street.

The birthplace house remained in the Roosevelt family until 1896. Gradually, however, as the surrounding neighborhood passed from a residential to a commercial area, it underwent a series of transformations that obliterated its original character. By 1919, shortly after Roosevelt's death, the newly organized Woman's Roosevelt Memorial Association purchased the site, then occupied by a two-story brick commercial structure, as well as the adjacent home, where Robert Barnwell Roosevelt had lived. In 1921-23, following a successful fund-raising drive, the association reconstructed the birthplace home and converted the adjoining building into a museum and office. At the same time, the two structures, which had only been connected by a door leading from one porch to the other on the second floor, were made into a single unit.

Except for a few bricks used in the cornerstone, the birthplace was totally rebuilt. Every effort, however, was made to duplicate the prototype house. The Roosevelt Memorial Association, incorporated in 1919, contributed sizable amounts of money to the project, and, at the invitation of the Woman's Association, placed its extensive collection of books, manuscripts, photographs, and other Roosevelt memorabilia in the two houses. In 1956 the two associations merged under the name of the Theodore Roosevelt Association; 7 years later, it donated to the U.S. Government the reconstructed birthplace home and Sagamore Hill, which is described elsewhere in this volume.

The basement of the combined buildings houses exhibit rooms and other public facilities. The first floor contains the restored parlor, library, and dining room, and a museum room. The second floor consists of a refurnished bedroom approximating the one in which Roosevelt was born, the nursery, porch on which Roosevelt's father installed gymnasium equipment, library, and study. Office facilities occupy the third floor. The fourth floor, which features an auditorium, projection booth, and dressing rooms, accommodates meetings, programs, and other activities. Furnishings in the restored portions of the present building include many original Roosevelt items, and the museum preserves thousands of objects, pictures, and documents relating to his personal and public life.

Roosevelt (Theodore) Inaugural National Historic Site, New York ★

Erie County, 641 Delaware Avenue, Buffalo.

This national historic site features the Ansley Wilcox House. There, on September 14, 1901, Vice President Theodore Roosevelt recited the Presidential oath of office following the death of President McKinley, who had been shot by an assassin a few days earlier. The residence is among the few inaugural sites outside of Washington. Also, as one of the oldest houses in the city of Buffalo, it possesses local historical and architectural significance.

The site on which the structure stands was originally part of the Holland Land Company's holdings in western New York. Ebenezer Walden, who acquired it in 1809, leased it to the Federal Government in 1838 for use as a military base. That year, three artillery companies established Poinsett Barracks on the site. A row of officers' quarters ran along present Delaware Avenue. One of these, a two-story, two-family, brick edifice whose huge portico faced the parade ground, became the nucleus of the Ansley Wilcox House. It is the only surviving building of the barracks, in whose social life Buffalo lawyer Millard Fillmore had frequently participated.

In 1847, after troops had abandoned the post, the structure

Theodore Roosevelt Inaugural National Historic Site.

passed into private hands. Attorney Albert P. Laning, who owned it from 1863 until 1881, added a 1½-story frame service wing and basement to its east (present rear) facade and dug a full basement under the main section. He also apparently moved the portico to the Delaware Avenue (front) facade and built a central doorway.

In 1883 Dexter P. Rumsey purchased the house as a wedding gift for his daughter Mary Grace and her husband, Ansley Wilcox, a prominent Buffalo lawyer. In the 1890's the latter hired local architect George Cary to effect a remodeling. Except for the construction of a bay window on the south side of the residence and the addition of some ornamented glass panels in the entrance way, Cary left the main section as it was. He tripled the size of the entire structure, however, by replacing the frame service wing with a 2½-story brick addition over a basement. The result was a stately mansion, which was flavored with Greek Revival and Adamesque styles and seasoned with 19th-century eclecticism.

One of Wilcox's close friends was Theodore Roosevelt, who called on him whenever he happened to be in Buffalo. Not long after he was inaugurated as Vice President, in May 1901 Roosevelt officiated at the opening there of the Pan-American Exposition. Later that year, on September 6 while visiting the exposition, President McKinley was shot by an assassin; he was moved to the Milburn House at 1168 Delaware Avenue, which is no longer extant.

Roosevelt, who was then in Vermont on a speaking trip, rushed by train to Buffalo, where members of the Cabinet had begun to assemble to carry on governmental affairs. After spending a few anxious days at the Wilcox House, on September 10, the condition of the President seemingly better after surgery, Roosevelt joined his family for an outing in the Adirondacks. Three days later, he learned by messenger that McKinley was close to death. By the time he arrived back in Buffalo the next afternoon, the President had passed away.

After paying his respects to Mrs. McKinley, Roosevelt met with several Cabinet members and Government officials in the library of the Wilcox House. There, at 3:15 p.m., on September 14, 1901, he took the Presidential oath of office. That same day, in another room he drafted his first official document, a proclamation announcing McKinley's death and designating September 19 as a day of national mourning.

The Wilcoxes continued to live in the house until their deaths in the 1930's. Subsequently, it served as a restaurant and underwent considerable interior alteration. In 1963, when the structure faced demolition, a group of Buffalo citizens formed a committee to save it. Under the committee's auspices, in 1964 the Liberty National Bank purchased the residence. Two years later, Congress designated it as a national historic site.

In 1969 the Theodore Roosevelt Inaugural Site Foundation, Inc., organized 2 years earlier, and the National Park Service entered into a cooperative agreement for the restoration and administration of the site. These organizations, aided by the New York Historic Trust, the Buffalo and Erie County Historical Society, and other groups in the area, have completed work on the exterior of the structure, the front hall and staircase, and the first-floor Library Room, where Roosevelt was inaugurated. Adjacent rooms will be used as orientation and exhibit areas; the remainder of the house will be made available to private organizations for activities compatible with the historic surroundings. Portions of the building are now open to the public.

Sagamore Hill.

Sagamore Hill National Historic Site, New York ⭐

Nassau County, on Cove Neck at the terminus of Cove Neck Road, about 2 miles northeast of the town of Oyster Bay, Long Island.

Sagamore Hill, overlooking Oyster Bay Harbor and Long Island Sound, was the home of Theodore Roosevelt for nearly four decades and is the site most closely associated with his life and career. During the period 1901-9, as a "summer White House," it was the focus of national attention and the scene of numerous major events and decisions. Today, the little-altered mansion, furnished with Roosevelt possessions, is one of the most authentically preserved historic sites in the Nation.

As a young man, Roosevelt acquired a lifelong attachment to the countryside in the vicinity of Oyster Bay, Long Island. By 1874, when he was 15 years of age, his grandfather, Cornelius Van Schaack Roosevelt, had been summering in the area for some time. That year, his father rented as a vacation retreat Tranquility, a residence about 2 miles southwest of the future site of the Sagamore Hill mansion. Young Roosevelt spent his summers exploring the fields and woodlands of nearby Cove Neck, a peninsula jutting out into the bay.

In 1880, not long after Roosevelt graduated from Harvard and married Alice Hathaway Lee, he purchased some property on Cove Neck, including a hill on which he planned to build a residence. At that time, only a barn stood there. In 1884, the year construction began and he ended 2 years of service in the State legislature, his mother and his wife died on the same day, the latter 2 days after childbirth. The child, a daughter named Alice, survived. By the time workers completed the residence, early in 1885, Roosevelt was spending much of his time in Dakota Territory, where 2 years earlier he had established a cattle ranch. His sister Anna moved into the new house to care for his infant daughter.

Roosevelt returned to the East in the fall of 1886 and ran unsuccessfully for mayor of New York City. He then traveled to London, where he married childhood friend Edith Kermit Carow, who was living with her mother in Europe, and embarked on an extended honeymoon tour of the Continent. In the spring of 1887, he brought his new wife home to the Cove Neck residence. About that time, he named it Sagamore Hill in honor of Mohannis, who had been the sagamore, or chief, of an Indian tribe that had once lived in the area.

For a few years, Roosevelt lived quietly at Sagamore Hill writing history. In 1889, however, President Benjamin Harrison appointed him to the U.S. Civil Service Commission, the first in a series of offices leading to the Presidency. These and military service in Cuba during the Spanish-American War (1898) were to keep him away from home for long periods. Yet, the Roosevelts returned as often as possible, especially in the summers. During these years, Alice grew to womanhood; Theodore, Jr., Kermit, and Ethel were born at Sagamore Hill; and Archibald and Quentin in Washington, D.C.

In 1900 Roosevelt was elected as Vice President under President McKinley. The following year, the assassination of McKinley catapulted him into the Presidency. From then until 1909, the year he retired from office, Sagamore Hill served as a "summer White House." During that time, it became the focus of national interest, and newspapers daily reported the activities of the six Roosevelt children, their 10 cousins, and "Teddy" himself. Notorious among his escapades during these years were his camping trips. At least once each summer, he and his older sons and nephews eluded Secret Service guards, newsmen, and everyone else; boated to a distant beach; and spent a rare, uninterrupted night in the wilderness.

But the President worked more than he played at Sagamore Hill. It was not only headquarters for the day-to-day administration of

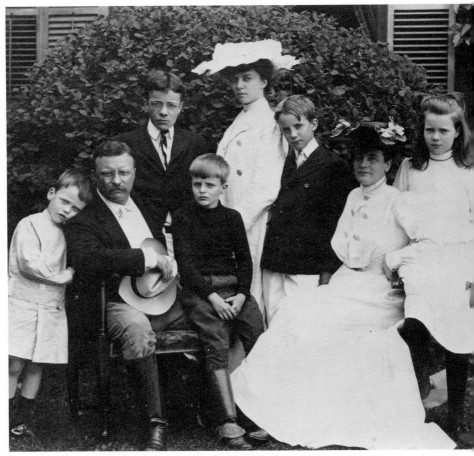

Roosevelt and family at Sagamore Hill. Left to right: Quentin, the President, Theodore, Jr., Archie, Alice, Kermit, Mrs. Roosevelt, Ethel.

the country, but was also the scene of events of international consequence. One of these occurred in August 1905 when Roosevelt conferred separately in the library with envoys from the warring countries of Russia and Japan. Subsequently he brought them face to face in New Hampshire for negotiations that led to the Treaty of Portsmouth (September 5, 1905), which ended the Russo-Japanese War.

Roosevelt found solace at Sagamore Hill between his long absences. He is pictured here while he was away leading the "Rough Riders."

After Roosevelt retired from public office in 1909, though he traveled extensively throughout the world, Sagamore Hill grew even dearer to him and his family. Politically, coming to differ with Taft and the Republican Party, his influence waned and in 1912 he met defeat as a Progressive in a new bid for the Presidency. When the United States entered World War I, which he had heartily advocated, all four of his sons sailed off to Europe. He suffered an irreparable blow when Theodore, Jr., and Archibald were seriously wounded and Quentin, his youngest son, lost his life. Despite failing health, at least partially brought on by his strenuous activities, Roosevelt was one of the leading contenders for the Republican nomination in 1920. But fate decreed otherwise. On January 6, 1919, at the age of 60, he died in his sleep at Sagamore Hill.

Mrs. Roosevelt continued to live on the estate until her death in 1948. Two years hence, the Roosevelt Memorial Association (later incorporated as the Theodore Roosevelt Association) purchased the house, its furnishings, and 83 acres of adjacent land. While maintaining the mansion's historical integrity, the association thoroughly renovated it by fireproofing the roof and providing other fire protection devices, repainting the exterior, redecorating the interior, and installing modern heating and electrical systems. The rooms were also refurnished with Roosevelt items to approximate their appearance during the first two decades of the century.

The mansion, a rambling frame and brick structure in the Queen Anne style, contains 22 rooms. On the first floor are a large center hall; the library, which served as Roosevelt's private office; dining room; Mrs. Roosevelt's drawing room; the kitchen; and the spacious north, or trophy, room, added in 1905. The latter, designed by Roosevelt's friend C. Grant LaFarge to receive distinguished guests and official emissaries, is one of the most interesting in the house. Built of fine American and Philippine woods, it is crammed with Roosevelt's most intimate possessions—trophies, animal skins, books and works of art, flags, and a variety of personal mementos.

The second floor contains family bedrooms, nursery, guestrooms, and dressing room. On the top floor are chambers once used by servants, currently exhibit rooms; the gunroom, where Roosevelt kept his extensive collection of weapons and retreated to write or to escape the bustle of his busy schedule; a sewing room; a

Parlor at Sagamore Hill.

schoolroom, where some of the children received tutoring; and the bedroom of Theodore, Jr.

The wide piazza on the south and west sides of the house figured prominently in daily life at the estate, but was also on three occasions the scene of notable historical events. On it, Roosevelt received official notification of his nominations for the governor-ship of New York in 1898, for Vice President in 1900, and for the Presidency in 1904.

In 1963 the Theodore Roosevelt Association donated Sagamore Hill and the Roosevelt Birthplace, in New York City, to the American public. The former gift included the mansion and about 83 acres of land, containing landscaped grounds and gardens and various outbuildings. Both sites are now administered by the National Park Service in cooperation with the association.

Sites of related interest within the vicinity of Sagamore Hill include the following: adjacent Old Orchard Museum, a handsome, two-story Georgian structure that was once the home of General Theodore, Jr., but is now a museum commemorating his father's contributions to conservation; Roosevelt's grave, at Oyster Bay Cove, about 1½ miles south of the mansion; the Audubon Bird Sanctuary and nature preserve, on Cove Neck Road, next to the gravesite; and Theodore Roosevelt Memorial Park, a bayside recreation area in the town of Oyster Bay.

Van Buren National Historic Site, New York   ★

Columbia County, on N.Y. 9H, about 2 miles south of Kinderhook.

The focus of this park is Lindenwald, the retirement home of Martin Van Buren from 1841 until his death in 1862. During these years, in 1844 he attempted to win the Democratic Presidential nomination, ran for President again in 1848 on the unsuccessful Free Soil ticket, and traveled extensively in Europe from 1853 to 1855.

Peter Van Ness, a prominent judge and local politician, built the residence in 1797. His son William, an associate and mentor of Van Buren, inherited it in 1804 and lived in it until the 1820's. One of his close friends was Washington Irving, who visited often, tutored the Van Ness children for awhile, and may have written some of his stories in the house. Another frequent guest was Aaron Burr, whom Van Ness supported for President in 1800. He also acted as Burr's second in his 1804 duel with Alexander Hamilton.

Van Buren, who had been born and raised in Kinderhook, decided in 1839, during his Presidency, to retire in that area. That same year, he purchased the Van Ness house and about 130 acres of land. By 1845 he had acquired 90 more acres. Meantime, 4 years earlier, after his defeat for a second term, he had retired to the residence, which he named Lindenwald after the linden groves on the property. He died there in 1862 and was buried in Kinderhook Cemetery.

Originally the building was a simple, two-story, Georgian structure built of red brick. The woodwork was white. In 1849 Van Buren hired architect Richard Upjohn to renovate the exterior and create a "Venetian villa" appearance. Dormers were installed to provide an additional half-story for servants' quarters; a four-room library wing, two kitchens and a four-story Italianesque tower added at the rear of the house overlooking the Hudson River; the eaves laced with Victorian trim; and a Victorian porch attached to

Van Buren National Historic Site.

the front. The red brick was plastered over and the house painted yellow. On the grounds, a semicircular driveway, ending in a carriage circle near the house, was laid out. Ornate gatehouses were erected at each of the two entrances.

Since Van Buren's time, Lindenwald has had several owners, but exterior alterations have been minimal. The main roof and tower are now covered with slate and the lower roofs are of sheet metal. Some of the Victorian trim has been removed, and a white-colonnaded portico added across the front of the house. One of the gatehouses and a shed from the time of Van Buren still stand; the garage is a later addition.

The interior arrangement remains much as it was in Van Buren's day. The entrance opens into a large central hall, once used as a banquet room. Two pairs of spacious rooms flank the hall. On the second floor are five rooms and a central hall. The attic contains three rooms, halls, and storage space. The basement houses servants' dining quarters, kitchen, vegetable room, wine and vinegar cellar, furnace room, and other chambers. In 1944 the owners of the house sold most of the Van Buren furniture, but a few historical items remain.

The National Park Service acquired the property in 1975, and eventually plans to open it to the public.

Roosevelt (Theodore) National Memorial Park, North Dakota ★

Consists of three units along the Little Missouri River between Watford City, in McKenzie County, on the north, and Medora, in Billings County, on the south. The visitor center and park headquarters are at Medora.

This park commemorates Roosevelt's contributions to conservation and his role in the growth of the open-range cattle industry on the northern Plains. From his experiences in North Dakota, he came to appreciate the country's natural resources and gained an awareness of the need to preserve them, a policy he championed as President. Within the boundaries of the park, topography, plants, and wildlife remain essentially unchanged from his time and the era when the open-range cattle industry flourished.

In the fall of 1883, Roosevelt, a young New York legislator, made

Maltese Cross Cabin.

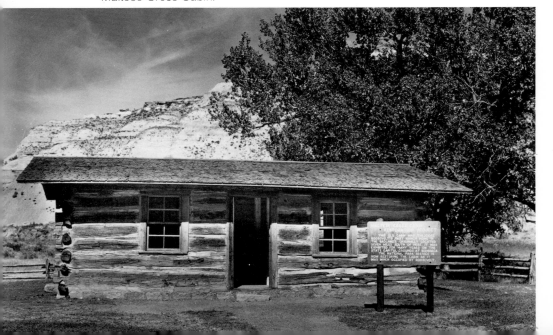

his first trip to the Badlands of North Dakota. His primary purpose was to hunt buffalo and other game. Not long after his arrival on September 7 in the tiny settlement of Little Missouri, on the west bank of the Little Missouri River opposite the newly founded cowtown of Medora, he hired a cowboy, Joe Ferris, as a guide. The latter took Roosevelt to the Chimney Butte, or Maltese Cross, Ranch. It was about 7 miles south of Medora and operated by Joe's brother, Sylvane, and his partner, William J. Merrifield. Roosevelt and his guide then traveled to their hunting base, the ranch of Gregor Lang, on the Little Missouri River about 50 miles south of Medora.

During his brief stay, Roosevelt's association with the Ferris brothers, Lang, and Merrifield fired his enthusiasm for the prospects of the cattle industry on the northern Plains. By the time the hunt ended, he had decided to invest in ranching. Before returning to New York, he bought the Maltese Cross Ranch. In a contract he signed with Sylvane Ferris and Merrifield, Roosevelt agreed to stock the ranch with about 400 head of cattle. In return, Ferris and Merrifield were to operate it for 7 years, at the end of which time they would return to Roosevelt his original investment plus half the increase. The other half was to be theirs.

Returning to New York, in November Roosevelt won reelection to his last term in the legislature. By the next summer, however, grieving over the loss of his wife and mother, both of whom had died on the very same day the previous February, he returned to North Dakota seeking to regain his sense of purpose. He found that a ranching boom was in progress. Encouraged by the success of his ranch, he purchased 1,000 head of cattle and selected a site for a second on the Little Missouri River, the Elkhorn Ranch, about 35 miles north of Medora. The buildings, begun in the autumn of 1884, were completed in the early summer of 1885. The ranchhouse, one of the finest in the Badlands, became headquarters for Roosevelt's cattle operations, which reached a peak in 1885-86. At that time, he probably owned between 3,000 and 5,000 head.

During his periodic visits to the Badlands, when not participating in ranching chores, Roosevelt turned to writing. At the Maltese Cross Ranch, he completed one book, *Hunting Trips of a Ranchman* (1885); at the Elkhorn Ranch, he wrote most of his *Life of Thomas Hart Benton* (1886). He also helped organize and served as chairman and then president of the Little Missouri Stockmen's

Association and was a member of the Montana Stockgrowers Association.

The winter of 1886-87 brought disaster to the range cattle industry on the northern Plains. During the preceding summer, many southern Plains cattlemen, plagued by almost continuous drought and frequent brush fires and seeking new forage areas, drove their stock northward onto the already overstocked ranges of the western Dakotas, Wyoming, and Montana, which were also in poor condition. By the time winter broke, most cattle herds were in a weakened state. A brutal cycle of heavy snowfall, partial thawing, and subzero freezing ensued, crusting the ground with impenetrable ice. Thousands of animals froze, starved, or fell prey to predators. Newspapers estimated the total loss of stock as high as 75 percent. When Roosevelt returned to Medora in the spring of 1887, he found that more than half his herd had perished. From that time on, his family and political career occupied more of his time and he visited the Badlands less frequently.

Between 1890 and 1892, Roosevelt abandoned the Elkhorn Ranch and shifted his headquarters to the Maltese Cross Ranch. In the latter year, he formed a partnership, the Elkhorn Ranch Company, with some other Dakota ranchers and increased his stock, hoping to make up some of his losses. The company achieved limited success, but Roosevelt, whose burgeoning political life demanded more and more of his time, became disenchanted with the cattle industry. In 1898 he sold out to Sylvane Ferris. Roosevelt did not return to Medora until 1903, the year he made a Presidential tour of the West. At that time, practically the entire population of the Badlands turned out to greet him. His last visit, in 1911, was brief.

Despite his failure as a rancher, Roosevelt felt that his associations with the West immeasurably enriched his life. He once wrote, "I have always said I never would have been President if it had not been for my experience in North Dakota." Certainly, he always regarded his life on the range as an idyllic interlude and contended that "the romance of my life began" there. He admired the rough virtues and the rugged integrity of the men with whom he rode in the Dakotas. They inspired him to help organize the Rough Riders, which brought him fame during the Spanish-American War (1898) and furthered his political aspirations. He also idealized his frontier experiences in his multivolume *The Winning of the West* (1889-96).

Scene at Theodore Roosevelt National Memorial Park.

The park consists of about 110 square miles. It is divided into three units along the Little Missouri River: the South Unit, near Medora; the North Unit, near Watford City; and the Elkhorn Ranch site, west of and about midway between the other two units. To reach the latter site, accessible only by a rough dirt road, the Little Missouri River must be waded or forded. Local inquiry should be made before attempting to reach it. Neither the ranchhouse nor any other buildings remain at the site today, but a diorama at the Medora visitor center provides an accurate reproduction. The site has been excavated and nearly all the original ranch features have been located.

Motorists entering the South Unit at the Medora entrance should first stop at the visitor center, which features exhibits on the history and natural history of the park. To the north of the center is the Maltese Cross cabin, built by Sylvane Ferris and William Merrifield in 1883-84, the only surviving building from either of

Roosevelt's ranches. Removed in 1904 from its original location (now south of the park boundaries on privately owned land), it was exhibited in various cities and stood for many years on the State capitol grounds at Bismarck, N. Dak. There, the State and the Daughters of the American Revolution administered it as a historic site. In 1959 the National Park Service acquired it, moved it to Medora, and restored it to its original appearance.

The cabin is a three-room structure of hand-hewn pine logs. There are two doors, several glass-paned windows, mortar chinking, and a high-pitched shingled roof. The roof provides an extra half-story, accessible by a ladder and trapdoor in the kitchen and used for storage and as a sleeping loft for ranch hands. All the furnishings are representative of the 1880's and a few of them are Roosevelt items.

The park is open all year, but spring, summer, and autumn are the best seasons to visit. Camping and picnic facilities are in the North and South Units. The badlands landscape—tablelands, buttes, canyons, and rugged hills—is of considerable scenic beauty and geologic interest. Although the climate is semiarid, much interesting plant and wildlife may be seen. A major attraction is a herd of buffalo that has been introduced into the park.

Medora, still an active cowtown, contains a number of historical structures that help round out the picture of frontier life in the 1880's. The town of Little Missouri no longer exists.

Harding Home, Ohio △
Marion County, 380 Mount Vernon Avenue, Marion.

Except for the years he spent in the U.S. Senate, when he resided mainly in Washington, D.C., Warren G. Harding lived in this house throughout the three decades preceding his election to the Presidency in 1920. These years spanned his rise from a young, small-town newspaper editor through his senatorial service.

In 1890 Harding and Florence Kling DeWolfe designed the home and arranged for its construction, in anticipation of their marriage, which took place in the large front hallway of the completed structure in July 1891. Conducting the major portion of his 1920 Presidential campaign from the wide front porch, Senator Harding welcomed and spoke to thousands of people from it. To accommo-

Harding Home.

date the crowds, the lawn was covered with gravel. After his election triumph, he left Ohio for Florida on a lengthy vacation and leased his residence prior to returning to Washington for his inauguration.

President Harding died suddenly in August 1923, during his term in office. After a state funeral in Washington, his body was returned to Marion for interment. Mrs. Harding soon moved back to the city, but took up residence elsewhere and did not dislodge the tenants who were occupying her house. She survived her husband by only a little more than a year.

A 2½-story frame structure in the Queen Anne style, the residence has a gabled roof, green clapboard siding, and cream-colored trim. The large Colonial Revival porch, of which one end is rounded, dominates the front of the house; it was probably added to the structure some years after the original construction. The base of the balustraded porch is fieldstone, as are also the pedestals, which support paired Ionic columns. The roof is galleried on a pattern that duplicates the first-level arrangement on a smaller scale.

Mr. and Mrs. Harding on the porch of their Marion home in 1920, the year before he assumed the Presidency.

On the first floor are a large front hallway, parlor, library, and dining room. The second floor contains the master bedroom, whose bay window overlooks the roof of the porch and the front lawn; two other bedrooms; a maid's room, and a bathroom. Almost all of the interior woodwork is oak.

Mrs. Harding willed the house and its furnishings to the Harding Memorial Association, which later opened some of the rooms to the public. In 1964-65 all of them were restored to their historic appearance. They display numerous pieces of Harding furniture and possessions. At the rear of the lot is a small detached building.

This single-story clapboard structure, painted white, served as a press headquarters in the 1920 campaign. Today it houses Harding memorabilia and contains the offices of the memorial association.

The association also owns and administers the Harding Memorial, at the corner of Vernon Heights Boulevard and Delaware Avenue in Marion. An ornate circular monument built of white Georgian marble and completed in 1927, it contains the tombs of President and Mrs. Harding.

Lawnfield, Ohio   ⚠

Lake County, 1059 Mentor Avenue, Mentor.

James A. Garfield purchased the Lawnfield estate in 1876, during his service in the U.S. House of Representatives, as a country home for his young and active family, which included five boys and a girl. From the residence, he conducted his successful race for President in 1880. In March 1881 he left for Washington to assume his official duties. Only a few months later, however, an assassin mortally wounded him.

The farmhouse at Lawnfield, erected in 1832 by James Dickey, was originally a small, 1½-story frame structure. Between 1877 and 1879 Garfield and his wife enlarged it to 2½ stories, added a porch across the front, and refurnished the interior. An enthusiastic farmer, he spent many hours tilling the soil and conducting a variety of agricultural experiments.

This idyllic interlude ended in June 1880, when Garfield unexpectedly won the Republican nomination for the Presidency. At Lawnfield, he conducted much of his successful campaign from his "front porch." He entertained an endless procession of visitors in his home, and used one of the outbuildings as a campaign office. The Lake Shore and Michigan Southern Railroad, whose tracks ran across the estate, routed special excursions to Mentor and scheduled a stop at Garfield Lane, a country road leading to the house.

In March 1881 Garfield moved into the White House. He was never to see Lawnfield again, for on July 2 an assassin shot him at a Washington train station. Lingering on for more than 2 months, at first in Washington and then at a seaside retreat in New Jersey, he died on September 19 and was buried in Cleveland's Lakeview

Lawnfield.

Early view of Lawnfield.

Cemetery, where an impressive memorial to him was later constructed. Four years later, Mrs. Garfield, who continued to live in the farmhouse for some time, completed their plans by adding a library wing and several rooms to the rear. The structure has remained largely unchanged since that time.

In 1936 the Western Reserve Historical Society, which had acquired Lawnfield from Garfield heirs and restored the first two floors, opened it to the public. It is presently administered by the Lake County Historical Society, which maintains a museum on the third floor and a library on the first. Other rooms on the first floor include the entrance hall, main hall, the bedroom shared by Mr. and Mrs. Garfield, that of his mother, a reception hall, a parlor, a nurse's room, and a dining room. The second floor contains additional bedrooms, the President's study, the memorial library built by Mrs. Garfield, and several other rooms. Both of these floors are furnished with original Garfield items and mementos, as well as period pieces.

At the northeast corner of the farmhouse stands the small, one-story frame building used first as a library and in 1880 as the campaign office. Equipped with telegraph facilities, it was used by Garfield's secretary and from it the election returns were received. The building is being converted into a museum. Not far from the main house is a replica of Garfield's log-cabin birthplace. Also on the grounds, dating from the period of the President's occupancy, are a windmill-pumphouse, carriage house, and barn.

McKinley Tomb, Ohio   ⚐

Stark County, Westlawn Cemetery, just off I-77 along Seventh Street NW., Canton.

Except for the White House, no other McKinley residence is extant. This tomb, in the city he was closely identified with throughout his adult life, is the only structure that is significantly associated with him. Following his death by an assassin's hand in 1901 at Buffalo, his body was temporarily interred in Westlawn Cemetery, where this memorial mausoleum was to be erected. It was dedicated in 1907, the year his wife succumbed and was buried with him.

The tomb stands on a 75-foot-high, grass-covered hill overlooking the city of Canton. It is circular and domed, has a pink granite

McKinley Tomb.

ashlar exterior, rises 96 feet above the ground, and measures 79 feet in diameter. Designed by Harold Van Buren Magonigle and financed by public subscription, it cost $558,452.91.

The floor of the mausoleum is formed by different-hued marble laid in a cross pattern. At the center, two polished, dark-green, granite sarcophagi, resting atop a 10-foot-square polished dark-maroon granite base, contain the bodies of McKinley and his wife. Each axis of the cross pattern on the floor leads to a semicircularly arched recess or bay. Each arch has a keystone, on which an eagle is sculptured. Doric columns flank each bay and support an entablature and frieze that extend around the bottom of the dome and bear an inscription from McKinley's last speech. Light-gray marble faces the interior walls.

The exterior of the double-walled tomb, whose platform measures 178 feet in diameter, is little ornamented. Festoons of ivy decorate the frieze, and a civic crown with a laurel wreath of gilded bronze surmounts the dome. Entrance is through huge double bronze doors which are set in a semicircularly arched opening. Each door measures 12 by 24 feet.

Originally a reflecting pool stretched some 750 feet from the base of the hill to the 108 stone steps leading to the tomb. The pool and steps were intended to symbolize the blade of the President's sword in time of war. A depressed lawn replaced the pool during the 1930's, but the sword effect remains. A tree-lined drive passes around the pool site to a parking area at the foot of the tomb. Midway up the steps, on a 13-foot-high pedestal, is a 9½-foot-high bronze statue of McKinley delivering his last speech in Buffalo. The work was rendered by Charles H. Niehaus.

The William McKinley Memorial Association owned and maintained the tomb until 1943, then turned it and approximately 20 surrounding acres over to the State. The Stark County Historical Society acquired the memorial in 1973.

Spiegel Grove, Ohio   ⚠

Sandusky County, at the intersection of Hayes and Buckland Avenues, Fremont.

The residence on this estate, the home of Rutherford B. Hayes from 1873 until his death in 1893, is still occupied by Hayes descendants. Also on the grounds are a memorial library administered by the State and the present burial site of President and Mrs. Hayes.

Sardis Birchard, a prominent Fremont merchant and uncle-guardian of Hayes, acquired the estate about 1846 as the prospective site of a home for himself and his nephew, who was practicing law locally. Because the reflection of the trees and lush vegetation in pools of water after a rain reminded Birchard of German fairy tales he had heard in his youth, he named the estate Spiegel (German for "mirror") Grove.

In 1849 Hayes moved to Cincinnati to pursue a career in law and politics. As a result, Birchard changed his plans and during the period 1859-63 constructed a 2½-story brick residence with veranda on the estate as a summer retreat for his nephew. The latter moved into it permanently in 1873, when he returned to Fremont after completing his second term as Governor of Ohio the year before.

At that time, Hayes also took charge of his aging uncle's affairs and, to better serve his family of six children, enlarged the house. It then consisted of a formal entrance hall, a large parlor, kitchen facilities, bedrooms, and storage space. The one-story frame addition, on the west side, extended the veranda and provided an office-library, drawing room, a new kitchen, wood house, and privy.

The next year, upon Birchard's death, Hayes inherited the estate. The year before, he had been elected to a third term as Governor, and in 1877 became President of the United States. Three years later, before retiring from office, he erected a major brick addition on the north. This duplicated the gabled front of the original portion of the structure and more than doubled its size. Also completely remodeling the interior, Hayes extended the master bedroom on the first floor, enlarged certain other rooms by

Spiegel Grove.

Reception held at Spiegel Grove by President and Mrs. Hayes on September 14, 1877, while on a visit from Washington.

constructing a three-story projecting bay, and built a cupola on the fourth level.

In 1889, the year his wife died, Hayes tore down the 1873 frame addition and replaced it with a 2½-story wing that included the present formal dining room, a kitchen, and several upstairs chambers.

Hayes derived much pleasure from maintaining and landscaping the grounds. He was especially fond of trees, and in 1877, during a reunion at Spiegel Grove of members of his Civil War unit, the 23d Ohio Volunteer Infantry Regiment, he christened five oaks on the estate in honor of comrades in attendance. These are sometimes

Hayes (standing), in retirement at the age of 67, his wife, and Hon. William H. Smith, on the porch of Spiegel Grove, during the winter of 1888-89.

referred to as the "Reunion Oaks." He subsequently dedicated other trees to prominent military and political guests.

After Hayes' death in 1893, one of his sons, Col. Webb C. Hayes, lived at the estate for many years. In 1909-10, acting as spokesman for the Hayes family, he presented it to the State of Ohio with the stipulation that it be reserved indefinitely for family use and that the State be required to build a memorial library-museum on the grounds.

Constructed between 1916 and 1922, partially with funds donated by Webb C. Hayes, and enlarged in 1967, the Rutherford B. Hayes Library, a short distance north of the house, is a large structure of gray sandstone in the Classical architectural style. Books, correspondence, diaries, pictures and photographs, scrapbooks, and other possessions of the Hayes family form the nucleus of the voluminous collections, which also contain valuable materials dealing with local, State, and National history. The museum section of the library exhibits a variety of items, including personal souvenirs of President and Mrs. Hayes, letters written and signed by many of the Presidents, objects associated with Abraham Lincoln, and some American Indian artifacts.

The rambling residence, which now has some 20 rooms, epitomizes 19th-century Victorian architecture. Its broad veranda, now screened, stretches along the double-gabled facade. The central hall, featuring white-walnut paneling, runs through the center of the house to the large formal dining room. From the hallway a butternut stairwell with black walnut balusters rises from the first floor to the fourth-level cupola. Because of the various renovations, only two rooms—the red parlor to the south of the entrance hall on the first floor and Sardis Birchard's bedroom above it on the second—remain in their original state. The first-floor brown-and-gold drawing room and the formal dining room were modeled after rooms in the White House. The first floor also contains a modern kitchen and a family dining room; the upper levels, bedrooms and guestrooms that largely reflect the tastes of later generations of the Hayes family.

The six entrance ways to the estate consist of impressive iron gates that were once at the White House. A monument of Vermont granite marks the tomb of President and Mrs. Hayes, south of the residence. Their remains were moved there from Fremont's Oakwood Cemetery in 1915. The house and grounds, library, burial site, and 25 acres of land are administered jointly by the Hayes family, the Ohio Historical Society, and the Rutherford B. Hayes and Lucy Webb Hayes Foundation as the Rutherford B. Hayes State Memorial. Except for the residence, which is still occupied by Hayes descendants, it is open to the public.

Taft National Historic Site, Ohio ★

Hamilton County, 2038 Auburn Avenue, Cincinnati.

Preserved at this location is the house in which Taft was born and lived for most of the first 25 years of his life. Although it has been extensively altered over the years, the National Park Service recently acquired and stabilized it.

Built sometime after 1840 in Mount Auburn, then a country suburb of Cincinnati, the residence was acquired in 1851 by Alphonso Taft, a prominent lawyer. On September 15, 1857, his son William Howard was born there, probably in the first-floor nursery in the rear ell. The latter resided in the house until 1874, the year he entered Yale University. In 1876-77, while Alphonso was serving as Secretary of War and then Attorney General under President Grant, the family moved to Washington, D.C.

Upon graduating from Yale in 1878, William Howard returned home to study law at Cincinnati Law School. In 1882, the year his father received an appointment as U.S. Minister to Austria-Hungary and departed with most of the family for Europe, he helped his brothers rent out the house and moved to other quarters in Cincinnati.

The Tafts reoccupied the house in 1885, and William Howard lived with them until after his marriage the next year, when he acquired his own residence in the city. Subsequently, his political career necessitated his relocation to Washington, D.C. In 1889 his parents leased their residence and departed for an extended trip to California, where in 1891 Alphonso died. His widow returned to Cincinnati for the funeral, but then went to Massachusetts to live with her sister. In 1899 she sold her home.

When Alphonso acquired the residence, it was a square brick structure in the Greek Revival style and had two stories over a basement. He immediately renovated the entire structure, including the erection of a small captain's walk, or observatory, on top of the almost flat roof. He also constructed at the rear a three-story brick ell, the first story of which was on a level with the original basement. In 1878 fire destroyed much of the second floor and roof of the main house. During the rebuilding, major changes included raising the second story and installing larger windows in it, erection of a new roof and cornice, and the addition of a bay on the south side of the structure. At the same time, the Tafts also undertook substantial interior repairs and alterations.

Taft National Historic Site.

Through the years, a succession of owners substantially altered the interior and exterior. One of them, between 1899 and 1904, removed the front veranda and replaced it with a one-story porch extending across the entire width of the house; razed a two-story, wooden piazza that was located in the crook between the main residence and the ell and built in its place a one-story conservatory; and demolished a two-story stable and two other outbuildings. In the 1940's the structure was converted into apartments.

By 1961, the year the William Howard Taft Memorial Association leased the property to preserve it as a shrine to the Taft family, the house was in a serious state of disrepair. Seven years later, the association acquired full title to the structure, and the following year transferred it to the National Park Service, which is currently formulating long-range restoration plans. Portions of the first floor are already open to the public and contain exhibits. The second floor will be utilized for a library, meeting room, and offices.

Visitors to this site may also wish to visit the Taft Museum, in the downtown area at 316 Pike Street, which has some associations with President Taft but was designated a National Historic Landmark primarily for its architectural significance. The Cincinnati Institute of Fine Arts operates it.

Eisenhower National Historic Site.

Eisenhower National Historic Site, Pennsylvania ★

Adams County, adjacent to the southwest boundary of Gettysburg National Military Park, Gettysburg.

Near the edge of historic Gettysburg stands the farm that Dwight D. Eisenhower purchased after his retirement from the U.S. Army. During his Presidential years, he used it as a retreat; later, it became his main residence.

In 1948, while serving as president of Columbia University after more than three decades of military life, Eisenhower, confident he could finally settle down at a permanent address, began searching for a home. At the suggestion of a friend, he decided to scout the Gettysburg, Pa., area for a farm. The locale appealed to Eisenhower for several reasons. For one thing, he possessed a sentimental attachment to the town, which had been his temporary residence during his early married life, in 1918, when he commanded nearby Camp Colt. Reinforcing this attachment was his historical appreciation of the nearby site of a major Civil War battle. Also, he desired to live in a rural setting but within convenient commuting distance of New York City and Washington.

Late in 1950, southwest of and adjoining Gettysburg National Military Park, the Eisenhowers purchased the only home they ever held title to, a 189-acre farm. It had been owned by the Allen Reddings since 1921 but predated that time. They had made considerable improvements. These included installation of plumbing and central heating in the farmhouse, enlargement and modernization of the barn, and construction of several outbuildings. The purchase included all livestock and farm equipment.

Eisenhower had planned to occupy the farm by April 1, 1951, but the preceding December President Truman recalled him to active service to organize and command the North Atlantic Treaty Organization. In April Gen. Arthur S. Nevins and his wife, friends of the Eisenhowers, took possession for them and assumed the management. Upon his return to the United States in June 1952, Eisenhower entered politics. His subsequent campaign for and election in November to the Presidency led to an indefinite postponement of his occupation of his new home. Late that same year, General Nevins, who had been hospitalized for tuberculosis, placed it under the management of its senior hand, Ivan Feaster, who operated it until the former recovered in 1954.

In 1954-55 the Eisenhowers completely rebuilt the Redding farmhouse, an ample, two-story, red brick structure; only the foundations and Dutch oven were retained. Many of the materials, however, including timber, bricks, floor planks, roof shingles, accessories, and fixtures, were reused. In addition, all new landscaping was provided, the barn was repainted, and the chickenhouse that was attached to the south elevation of the barn was converted into a garage and apartment. An open house, held by the Eisenhowers for newsmen on August 9, 1955, marked the official beginning of their residence there, though they continued to live primarily in Washington, D.C.

Eisenhower's first prolonged stay at the farm occurred in November-December 1955, while recuperating from a heart attack he had suffered in September at Denver. To carry out official duties, he utilized facilities in the town of Gettysburg. The next year, he conducted part of his second Presidential campaign from the farm and town. Thereafter, he visited the former more regularly, often entertaining visiting dignitaries and heads of state there. Among his guests were Prime Minister Jawaharlal Nehru of India (1956), Field Marshal Bernard Montgomery of Great Britain (1957), Chancellor Konrad Adenauer of West Germany (1957), ex-British Prime Minister Sir Winston Churchill (1959), Premier Nikita Khrushchev of the Soviet Union (1959), and President Charles de Gaulle of France (1960). On January 20, 1961, Eisenhower retired

Mr. and Mrs. Eisenhower in their garden during his retirement.

from the Presidency. The following day, Gettysburg honored him
and his wife with a grand "welcome home" dinner at the Hotel
Gettysburg.

During retirement, Eisenhower devoted much more personal
attention to farm management than he had before. From 1961 until
1966, he bred Black Angus show cattle, but in the latter year
switched to feeders. The herd, which at a maximum numbered
about 250, was sold each year to packing companies in Philadel-

phia, Baltimore, or Lancaster. A dedicated conservationist, Eisenhower utilized his profits to improve his land and soil. Also, for expansion and preservation of the rural setting, friends acquired several tracts of adjacent land.

Except for the winters, which he spent in California, Eisenhower resided at the farm until his death at Washington's Walter Reed Hospital in March 1969; he was buried in the chapel near the Eisenhower Library and Museum, Abilene, Kans., which incorporates his boyhood home. Some 2 years earlier, he had donated the farmhouse and 230 acres of land to the U.S. Government for preservation as a historic site. The agreement insured him lifetime occupancy rights, but required his wife to vacate the premises within 6 months after his death. In 1969 the Government waived the latter requirement; Mrs. Eisenhower now possesses lifetime rights to the farmhouse and 14 acres.

The main focus of historical interest at the farm are the residence and adjacent structures. The former, 2½ stories high and painted white, consists of two sections. The northern part, in which the entrance way is centered, is of frame. It contains the living room; dining room; and at the eastern, or rear, facade, a glass-covered porch overlooking the lawn. In the brick south section are the kitchen; the "Old Dutch Room," which preserves the original Dutch oven and fireplace; a study; two bedrooms; two baths; and a laundry room. Six bedrooms, five baths, and a studio occupy the second floor; a studio, half-bath, and storage area, the attic. Directly to the south of and connected to the main house is a small, 1½-story stone addition that houses the library.

Northwest of the farmhouse is a two-room guest cottage that was originally a garage. To the southeast are an ivy-covered brick teahouse with fireplace and flagstone patio, behind which are two greenhouses. Rounding out the immediate grounds are the large stock barn, various utility structures, a skeet-shooting range, and a putting green.

Eisenhower National Historic Site comprises about 493 acres. Still the home of Mrs. Eisenhower, it may not be visited by the public.

Independence National Historical Park, Pennsylvania   ★

Philadelphia County, in downtown Philadelphia, visitor center at the corner of Third and Chestnut Streets.

In this park, at Congress Hall, during the period that Philadelphia served as the Nation's Capital (1790–1800), occurred the inaugurations of George Washington, for his second Presidential term, and John Adams. Other structures in the complex also have associations with the Presidents. The park, in the old portion of the city, was also the scene of many major aspects of the Nation's founding and initial growth and several momentous national events. These include meetings of the First and Second Continental Congresses; adoption and signing of the Declaration of Independence, which marked the creation of the United States; and the labors of the Constitutional Convention of 1787, which perpetuated it.

Restored Assembly Room, Independence Hall, one of the meeting places of the Second Continental Congress, where the Declaration of Independence and the Constitution were also debated, adopted, and signed. Future Presidents Washington, John Adams, Jefferson, Madison, and Monroe helped found the Nation in this room.

The nucleus of the park and its outstanding historical building is Independence Hall. [For a detailed history and description of the hall as well as a discussion of historical events associated with it, see *Founders and Frontiersmen, Signers of the Declaration,* and *Signers of the Constitution,* Volumes VII, XVIII, and XIX respectively in this series.] Constructed as the State House for the Province of Pennsylvania between 1732 and 1756, it served as the principal meetingplace of the legislature until 1799, though in 1775-77 and in 1778-83 the Second Continental Congress convened there, as did also the Constitutional Convention in 1787. Serving in those bodies were future Presidents Washington, John Adams, Jefferson, and Madison. The carefully restored, stately, and symmetrical hall, a 2½-story red brick structure, is the most beautiful 18th-century public building of Georgian style surviving in the United States.

The interior focus of interest is the Assembly Room, the east one on the first floor, where the Declaration of Independence and the Constitution were formulated and signed. It has been restored to its appearance at the time of the Continental Congress, though only a few original items remain in the room.

When the Federal Government moved from New York City to Philadelphia in 1790, the city council offered for the use of Congress a recently constructed building on Independence Square, at the southeast corner of Sixth and Chestnut Streets just west of Independence Hall. Built between 1787 and 1789 as the County Court House (subsequently known as Congress Hall), it is a two-story brick structure with a projecting south bay and a peaked roof, topped by a cupola.

Congress convened there in December 1790, the Senate meeting in a small chamber on the second floor and the House of Representatives in a larger one on the first. Some Members of Congress during this period—Madison, Monroe, Jackson, and William Henry Harrison—were later Presidents; and Vice Presidents John Adams and Jefferson presided over the Senate at the time. In March 1793 in the Senate Chamber, George Washington recited the oath of office for his second term as Chief Executive. In a similar ceremony 4 years later in the House Chamber, John Adams succeeded him.

After 1800, the year the Federal Government relocated to Washington, the city of Philadelphia utilized Congress Hall. Except for the enlargement of its south facade in 1793, it has changed little throughout the years. The National Park Service has restored and refurnished the interior of the hall to approximate the appearance while it was the meetingplace of Congress.

For short periods in 1793 and 1794, during yellow-fever epidemics in Philadelphia, President Washington resided at the Deshler-Morris House, 5442 Germantown Avenue, in Germantown, part of the park though 7 miles away.

The site of one of two no-longer extant adjoining homes (1785-90 and 1790-95) once owned by Robert Morris, on the southeast corner of High (present Market) and Sixth Streets, is related to the Presidency. In the first of these, Washington stayed with Morris during the Constitutional Convention. During the period when Philadelphia was the U.S. Capital, Morris also made the house available as a temporary Presidential mansion, and Washington and John Adams occupied it.

In 1797 the city of Philadelphia completed an official Presidential mansion outside the boundaries of the present park, but it was never utilized for that purpose and has long since disappeared.

In connection with the U.S. Bicentennial commemoration, the National Park Service has reconstructed the Jacob Graff, Jr., House and City Tavern. Jefferson, a roomer, wrote the Declaration of Independence in the 3½-story brick Graff House, 2 blocks from Independence Hall on the southwest corner of Seventh and Market Streets. The first floor contains displays; the parlor and bedroom that Jefferson lived in on the second floor have been restored and are furnished with period pieces. City Tavern, at the northwest corner of Walnut and Second Streets, where members of the Constitutional Convention and Continental Congress and Government officials, including some future Presidents, stayed while in Philadelphia, is furnished and operated as an 18th-century tavern.

The American Philosophical Society, founded in 1743 by Benjamin Franklin and the oldest learned society in the United States, maintains its headquarters in Philosophical Hall (1787). Its distinguished membership has included many Presidents.

Many other sites and buildings in 22-acre Independence National Historical Park, most of which are open to the public, are related to other themes of history than the Presidency. Properties that are owned by the city of Philadelphia but administered by the National Park Service consist of Independence Hall, Congress Hall, City Hall (1791), and Independence Square. In recent years,

Congress Hall.

House Chamber in restored Congress Hall.

to enhance the setting of the area, the Commonwealth of Pennsylvania has created Independence Mall in the three blocks across Chestnut Street directly north of Independence Hall; the National Park Service administers it. The Liberty Bell, a worldwide emblem of freedom, is displayed in a special pavilion on the mall.

Federally owned buildings include the First Bank of the United States; the Second Bank of the United States (Old Custom House), which features the park's extensive collection of historical portraits; Deshler-Morris House, operated by the Germantown Historical Society; Todd House; Bishop White House; New Hall (Marine Corps Museum); Pemberton House (Army-Navy Museum); and the Philadelphia (Merchants') Exchange. Among those privately owned properties whose owners have cooperative agreements with the National Park Service are Carpenters' Hall and Christ Church, both National Historic Landmarks, and Gloria Dei (Old Swede's Church) and Mikveh Israel Cemetery National Historic Sites. The American Philosophical Society holds title to Philosophical Hall, another Landmark and the only privately owned building on Independence Square, but also operates Library Hall, on Federal land.

In 1948, upon recommendation of the Philadelphia National Shrines Park Commission, Congress created Independence National Historical Park. This act specified the Federal Government's role in the commemoration of existing historic sites and buildings and in the acquisition and management of others. The entire undertaking is guided by an advisory commission of distinguished citizens. Many individuals and private and civic organizations have contributed to the preservation and beautification of the park.

Wheatland, Pennsylvania ⚠

Lancaster County, 1120 Marietta Avenue (Pa. 340), on the western outskirts of Lancaster.

James Buchanan lived at Wheatland for the last two decades of his life. During that period, in 1856, it was the scene of one of the early "front porch" campaigns for the U.S. Presidency.

In 1828 William Jenkins, a wealthy Lancaster banker, built "The Wheatlands" (later shortened to Wheatland), which he named for its vista of waving wheatfields. In 1845 William M. Meredith, a prominent Pennsylvania lawyer who was later to serve as U.S. Secretary of the Treasury, purchased it. Three years later, James Buchanan, who at that time held the office of Secretary of State, bought the estate. It then consisted of the house and a 22-acre tract. From there, in 1856 he conducted a "front porch" campaign for the Presidency. Wheatland became its symbol, and in many areas Buchanan supporters formed "Wheatland Clubs" to promote his election. Successful in his bid, he served one term (1857-61) in the White House and then returned to his estate to pass his remaining years. He died there in 1868 and was buried at the local Woodward Hill Cemetery. Subsequently, several owners held the residence before its acquisition in the 1930's by the Junior League of Lancaster, which later organized the James Buchanan Foundation for the Preservation of Wheatland, the present owner.

Wheatland.

A large brick structure, Wheatland combines Colonial and later architectural features, but possesses a basic Georgian-style symmetry. The 2½-story central section, with a central hall and matching rooms on either side, is flanked by three-story wings. The rooms total 17. The front of the main section is dominated by a Doric-columned porch; steps on three sides lead up to the entrance. Few changes have occurred over the years except for some interior improvements made by Buchanan. These included installation of a furnace and central heating, replacement of the open hearth in the kitchen by a cast-iron stove, and addition of such conveniences as a tin bathtub.

The rooms on the first two floors have been furnished with appropriate period pieces. Many of the items, especially those in the library, belonged to Buchanan. First-floor rooms include the "warming" kitchen, breakfast room, dining room, parlor, and library. From the central hall, a stairway ascends to the second floor, which contains bedrooms, dressing rooms, and a museum room exhibiting memorabilia of Buchanan. He died in a plainly furnished backroom on this floor. On the third level are five unrestored rooms that originally quartered servants.

Wheatland today consists of the well-preserved house and about 4½ acres. Hostesses costumed in period dress conduct tours. The grounds are attractively landscaped. Outbuildings include the old smokehouse-icehouse and a stable now used for other purposes by the Junior League of Lancaster. The original water spring, Buchanan's favorite retreat, may still be seen.

Mount Rushmore National Memorial, South Dakota   ★

Pennington County, about 25 miles southwest of Rapid City and 3 miles southwest of Keystone, just off U.S. 16 on Horse Thief Lake Road.

Carved into the granite face of Mount Rushmore, a sheer peak rising 6,000 feet above sea level in the Black Hills of South Dakota, are the colossal images of four Presidents: Washington, Jefferson, Lincoln, and Theodore Roosevelt. In paying tribute to them, this national memorial also commemorates the growth of the United States through the early part of the 20th century. An incredible engineering feat, the monument was constructed over the course of 14 years at a cost of nearly $1 million. Unique among world sculpture and practically immune to the ravages of time and nature, it also stands as an enduring tribute to the genius of sculptor Gutzon Borglum.

The idea of a mountain sculpture in the Black Hills originated with South Dakota historian Doane Robinson, who in 1923 enlisted the support of U.S. Senator Peter Norbeck for such a project. The next year, Robinson acquired the services of sculptor Borglum, who enthusiastically agreed to direct operations. He had been engaged in a similar endeavor at Stone Mountain, near Atlanta, Ga., where he had begun carving a huge Confederate memorial, but the undertaking had failed. Rejecting Robinson's conception of a monument to prominent western heroes, Borglum envisioned a national memorial on an immense scale. He initially considered carving into a mountainside the images of Presidents Washington and Lincoln complete from the waist up.

In 1925 Senator Norbeck succeeded in obtaining the passage of laws by the South Dakota legislature and by the U.S. Congress authorizing the project. The former body, apparently assuming that another peak near Mount Rushmore in the Black Hills was the likely site, also created an administrative unit, the Mount Harney Memorial Association. In August Borglum selected Mount Rushmore, an imposing peak of smooth-grained granite near the town of

Mount Rushmore National Memorial.

Keystone. In addition to a picturesque setting, the mount enjoyed the advantage of facing the sun for most of the day, an ideal lighting arrangement.

On October 1 Borglum dedicated Mount Rushmore before a crowd of about 1,000 people. He undoubtedly held the ceremony to stimulate public interest, for almost no construction funds had yet been raised. During the next 2 years, he consumed most of his time raising money in the East and in perfecting his design. Eventually choosing as his subjects the faces of Presidents Washington, Jefferson, Lincoln, and Theodore Roosevelt, he believed they would effectively represent not only the westward expansion of the Nation but also its entire history from the time of the American Revolution to his own generation. Meantime, the Mount Harney Memorial Association had managed to acquire some support from Rapid City businessmen, a few State organizations, and a couple of philanthrophists.

The funds collected were rapidly exhausted. By 1927 the project seemed to be on the verge of failure. The rededication of the mountain on August 10 of that year by President Coolidge, however, brought wide national press coverage and some new contributions. Nonetheless, after a few months of work, Borglum was forced to cease operations. Aware that more substantial financial support was needed, he appealed to the Federal Government for aid. In February 1929 Congress responded by creating the Mount Rushmore National Memorial Commission to replace the Mount Harney Memorial Association and by authorizing Federal appropriations up to $250,000, provided they were matched by private subscriptions. About a decade later, the Federal Government assumed complete financial responsibility for the project.

Creation of the memorial required the use of some unique engineering techniques that Borglum had earlier originated at Stone Mountain. After designing a group of figures to conform to the contour of the mountaintop, he made individual plaster models of each of them to serve as guides for his workmen. The models measured 5 feet from the top of the head to the bottom of the chin; 1 foot on a model equaled 12 feet on the mountainside. Sometimes, for measuring purposes, the models were suspended from the mountaintop by cables.

All the workers were local men trained by Borglum. Using ladders hewn out of pine trees to climb the mountain, they installed a tramway of cables and winches from its base, where they constructed shelters and storage shacks. An elaborate scaffolding system was devised to accommodate drilling and blasting. Drillers, using jackhammers to drill holes for dynamite, were lowered from the peak to the scaffolds in leather swings by hand-operated winches. Microphones and loudspeakers relayed messages for the lowering and raising of the swings. Surface rock had to be blasted away with dynamite to eliminate deep fissures and cracks until only solid granite remained. The actual carving involved a tedious cycle of measuring, blasting, drilling, wedging, and smoothing. A blacksmith shop at the base of the mountain serviced the drills, as many as 400 of which needed to be resharpened each day.

The Washington face was unveiled on July 4, 1930. Jefferson's image proved to be far more difficult. Originally to the north of Washington, in 1933, because of imperfections in the granite, the partially completed figure had to be blasted away and begun anew at a different location. Three years later, on August 29, 1936, President Franklin D. Roosevelt traveled to Mount Rushmore and dedicated it. The remaining figures, those of Lincoln and Theodore Roosevelt, were dedicated on September 17, 1937, and July 2, 1939. Each head in the group, carved to the scale of a man 465 feet tall, averaged about 60 feet from top to bottom. Each had a nose 20 feet long, a mouth 18 feet wide, and eyes 11 feet across.

But the memorial had not yet reached completion. Besides refinements in the images already carved, Borglum was planning to inscribe a brief history of the United States into the mountain alongside the four figures. Even more fantastic, he had already begun blasting a huge hall of records in the interior of the mountain. The hall was to be a gigantic room filled with busts of individuals representing all phases of U.S. history, bronze and glass cabinets containing historical records carved on aluminum sheets, artifacts of American civilization, and various works of art. Access to the hall was to be via an enormous flight of steps rising 400 feet from a huge granite disk at the base of the mountain.

Borglum's sudden death in March 1941 brought an end to such grandiose schemes. His son Lincoln, who had assisted him for many years, supervised the final work, completed in October. Construction had extended over a period of 14 years, though much of that time the laborers had been idle because of financial difficulties and weather conditions. The cost had almost reached $1 million. At the base of the mountain lay 450,000 tons of stone rubble, which has never been removed.

By 1941 the National Park Service had assumed full responsibility for the memorial. Since that time, it has greatly enhanced administrative and visitor accommodations. Uniformed rangers, informational signs, leaflets, and museum exhibits provide interpretive services. Each evening from June through September a dramatic lighting ceremony is held in the amphitheater.

Johnson (Andrew) National Historic Site, Tennessee ★

Greene County, visitor center at the corner of Depot and College Streets, 1 block east of Main Street, in downtown Greeneville.

Andrew Johnson National Historic Site dramatically illustrates Johnson's rise from very humble beginnings to the Presidency.

Early view of Andrew Johnson's tailor shop, which is now preserved inside a brick shelter.

Three structures, at separate but nearby locations, represent nearly 45 years of his life: the tailor shop he owned for many years and two of his residences. The cemetery in which he is buried is also in the national historic site.

In the fall of 1826 Johnson, a 17-year-old and almost illiterate tailor's apprentice, arrived in Greeneville, Tenn., from North Carolina with his impoverished family, consisting of his mother, brother, and stepfather. Unable to find employment there, Andrew moved on to Rutledge, about 40 miles to the west, and possibly other towns and villages in eastern Tennessee, working as a tailor.

The next spring, however, by which time conditions in Greeneville had improved, he returned.

Within a short time, Johnson married Eliza McCardle and settled down in a two-room frame-puncheon board house on Main Street, which he apparently rented. He used one room as a shop and resided in the other. In this crowded structure, his wife gave birth to two of their five children. She also taught him to write and helped improve his rudimentary knowledge of reading.

In 1831, his tailor business prospering, Johnson acquired a more substantial two-story brick dwelling at the northeast corner of Water and Main Cross (present College and Depot) Streets. About the same time, he purchased a lot across Water Street opposite the house. He may have moved there from another location, for use in his tailor business, a one-room frame structure or may have utilized one already standing on the site.

In 1830 Johnson, who for some time had been participating in civic affairs, became mayor. In 1835 he was elected to the Tennessee legislature. Subsequently, as his public duties increased, he spent less and less time in his tailor shop. After 1843, the year he won election to the U.S. House of Representatives, he left it in charge of a manager and five or six journeymen.

Johnson Home (1851-75).

In 1851, toward the end of his decade of service in the House and by which time his family had long since outgrown its residence, Johnson purchased a larger, two-story brick structure on South Main Street. It was to be his permanent home for the rest of his life, though official duties and other activities were to keep him away for long periods of time. While owning it, he held the offices of Governor of Tennessee, U.S. Senator, Vice President, and President. At the outbreak of the Civil War in 1861, his allegiance to the Union made him so unpopular in Tennessee that he and his family were forced to flee from Greeneville. During their exile, both Confederate and Union troops occupied his house; the former used it as a barracks and hospital.

Upon leaving the Presidency in 1869, Johnson and his family returned to their Greeneville home. His residence, damaged extensively during his absence, required considerable repair and refurnishing. About this time, closets and diagonal corner cupboards were added, Greek Revival mantels installed, fireplaces bricked up, and the second story and veranda added to the rear ell. In 1875 he returned to the U.S. Senate, the only ex-President ever to do so. Within a few months, however, while visiting the home of one of his daughters, near Elizabethton, Tenn., he suffered a stroke and died. Mrs. Johnson survived him only until the next year.

By the time he assumed the Presidency, Johnson had leased his tailor shop. It later became a residence but remained in the ownership of the family until 1921. The State, which then purchased it, enclosed the structure in a brick shelter and administered it as a historic shrine until the Federal Government acquired it in 1941. A small one-room frame building, the shop has a high ceiling and steep roof covered with shingles. The exterior walls have yellow poplar weatherboarding. The interior walls and floor are of pine, and a large fireplace occupies one end of the room. The shop is furnished with items Johnson used, including tailoring bench, heating stove, iron, pair of candle molds, and water pitcher.

Johnson's first Greeneville home (1827-31) has not survived. The 1831-51 residence, also known as the Kerbaugh House, passed through the hands of many owners after the Johnsons. The National Park Service gained possession from the Kerbaugh family in 1963, and began restoring it 5 years later. A two-story brick structure, probably constructed in the 1820's, it originally had

Memorial to President Johnson and burial plot where he and his wife are interred.

four rooms: living room and kitchen/dining room on the first floor and two bedrooms on the second. Additions apparently made by Johnson include an ell on a slightly lower level adjoining the east end of the house, a porch along the south end, and a portico at the Water (College) Street entrance. The ell provided space for a dining room over a basement which at certain times served as a kitchen, and was later filled in. At the time of the additions, the original kitchen/dining room in the main house probably became a bedroom.

The 1851-75 residence, built not long before Johnson purchased it, stayed in the possession of his heirs until 1942, the year the

Federal Government acquired it. It had undergone considerable alteration throughout the years, including an extensive remodeling in the Victorian style in 1884-85. The National Park Service has restored and refurnished it to its 1869-75 appearance. It now consists, as it did then, of a two-story, brick main house and a two-story, brick ell at the rear.

The brickwork is Flemish bond on the front and common bond on the sides. A double veranda extends along the rear of the main section and the northeast side and end of the ell; the exposed basement level gives the effect of three stories on this side. The front of the house sits flush on the street. The structure contains 10 rooms: kitchen and storeroom (also servants' quarters) in the basement; parlor, dining room, and two bedrooms on the first floor, one of which rooms was possibly the original kitchen; and four bedrooms on the second. The rooms of the main block on the first and second floors are divided into pairs by central halls. Each floor of the ell contains two rooms, one behind the other and separated by a chimney wall; these rooms open onto the porches.

About half a mile distant from the general area in which the homes and tailor shop are located is the 15-acre cemetery in which Eliza and Andrew Johnson are buried. It was carved out of a 23-acre tract he purchased in 1852. In 1875 his family interred him on Signal (later Monument) Hill in the center of the tract, and 3 years later marked the gravesite with an elaborately decorated 26-foot-high marble shaft. In 1901 Martha J. Patterson, one of Johnson's daughters, bequeathed the cemetery to the Federal Government. Between 1906 and 1948, the Department of War administered it as Andrew Johnson National Cemetery and then transferred it to the National Park Service; today it is part of the national historic site.

The park headquarters is at the tailor shop. In an attached annex a museum features Johnson exhibits, offices, and a visitor center.

Polk Home, Tennessee ⚏

Maury County, on U.S. 43, just west of its intersection with U.S. 31, Columbia.

Although James K. Polk lived in this house for only a few years during his early manhood and was away at college a large part of the time, it is the only extant structure closely associated with him.

Polk Home.

Now preserved as a memorial, it contains many items and furnishings commemorating him and his career.

Polk was a 21-year-old student at the University of North Carolina in 1816 when his father, Samuel, built this modest brick residence. The former probably spent his vacations and holidays with his family. After his graduation in 1818, he also lived at home for a time. In 1819 he moved to Nashville to study law, after which he began practicing back in Columbia, married, and apparently resided in a home of his own there until 1839, when he was elected Governor and moved to Nashville.

The next year, Polk acquired a mansion, Polk Place. Upon his death in 1849, he left instructions that it be presented to the State for preservation after the death of his wife. For some reason, when she succumbed in 1891, her husband's instructions were not followed. The mansion, the garden of which was Polk's original burial site, was later demolished; his remains, as well as those of his wife, now rest on the State capitol grounds.

The Columbia residence remained in the Polk family for many years. It then changed hands several times. In 1929 the State of Tennessee and the James K. Polk Memorial Association of Nashville acquired it. The following year, the association, which had earlier obtained many Polk mementos by bequest, opened it to the public. Subsequently, the association and the James K. Polk Memorial Auxiliary of Columbia restored the house and furnished it with Polk items and period pieces; obtained adjacent property, including a home that had been occupied by Polk's two sisters; reconstructed a detached kitchen-dining room building on its original foundations; and laid out a memorial garden. Today maintained by State appropriations and funds raised by the association and auxiliary, the site is administered by the latter organizations as a historic house museum and memorial to Polk.

A two-story, brick structure typical of the Federal style as constructed in Tennessee, the residence features a gable roof and a handsome doorway with fan-shaped transom. The bricks, woodwork, window frames, and sashes are all handmade. The first floor consists of a large side hall; front and rear parlors; and a rear porch, now enclosed as a museum. The second floor contains a hall and three rooms. The mantels in most of the rooms and the stone hearth in the front parlor have never been replaced. The downstairs floors are built of wide boards of white ash held together by wooden pegs; hand-pinned yellow poplar predominates upstairs.

The furnishings include an outstanding collection of historical portraits, prints, lithographs, engravings, and photographs; items originally used in the house; and objects employed by President and Mrs. Polk in the White House and at Polk Place. To the rear of the Polk Home, a brick-lined courtyard leads to the reconstructed kitchen building. It is also of brick and is furnished with appropriate period pieces.

Adjoining the Polk Home is the residence of Polk's sisters, which will eventually be restored for offices and museum space. Behind it, lies a memorial garden patterned after typical formal gardens of the Polk era. Carefully landscaped and surrounded by a brick wall, the garden features moss-covered brick walkways, a rose trellis made of slender Grecian columns, flower beds outlined by English boxwoods, Italian statues, Grecian urns, a sundial, a circular stone bench, and the iron fountain that once stood in the garden at Polk Place.

The Hermitage, Tennessee ⚐

Davidson County, on Old Hickory Boulevard, just off U.S. 70N, about 12 miles northeast of Nashville.

For more than four decades, during which time Andrew Jackson rose from a frontier militia commander to the Presidency, he made this estate, in the rolling middle Tennessee hills, his home. The residence preserved there today is the one he completed during his second term as President and appears almost exactly as it did at the time of his death.

Between 1791, the year Jackson married Rachel Donelson Robards, daughter of one of the founders of Nashville, and 1804 he lived on various tracts in the vicinity. In the latter year, however, he purchased 625 acres of land, the nucleus of a permanent estate, The Hermitage, and moved into a group of log structures already standing on the property. The Jacksons used a large two-story structure that had once served as a blockhouse as their principal living quarters and three smaller cabins for storage and guest accommodations.

Jackson settled down to the life of a planter. Although he derived his main income from cultivating cotton and corn, he held interests in various other enterprises, including part ownership of a tavern, a racetrack, and a boatyard. As he prospered and emerged as one of the prominent men in the region, he entertained various distinguished guests in his log home. Among them were Aaron Burr and President James Monroe.

In 1813 Jackson's career took a significant turn. During the Creek Indian uprising of that year in Alabama, he commanded the Tennessee militia and attained the rank of major general. His success at the Battle of Horseshoe Bend (1814) earned him a major

The Hermitage.

general's commission in the U.S. Army. His victory over the British in January 1815 at the Battle of New Orleans, the final action in the War of 1812, made him a national hero.

Jackson returned to The Hermitage, where he remained until 1817, when he left once more, this time to conduct a 2-year campaign against the Seminole Indians and Spanish forces in Florida. When the Spaniards ceded Florida to the United States in 1821, Jackson was appointed as provisional Governor of Florida

The Hermitage, Jackson's dome-shaped tomb, and the Andrew J. Donelson residence, Tulip Grove.

Territory. After a short tour of duty, however, he resigned and again trekked back to The Hermitage. In 1823-25 he served in the U.S. Senate.

Meantime, in 1818–19 Jackson had erected a brick house near the log structure he had lived in for 15 years. The new residence was a square building two stories high. On each floor were four rooms, each with fireplace, divided into pairs by large central halls. At his estate, Jackson, who continued to prosper in private and public life, entertained many nationally prominent figures, including La-fayette in 1824. That same year, he ran for President but lost.

In January 1829, when Jackson departed for his Presidential inauguration in Washington, he left behind the grave of his beloved wife, Rachel, who had died only a few weeks earlier. Two years later, his grief was somewhat assuaged by the marriage of his adopted son, Andrew Jackson, Jr., to Sarah York, a favorite of the President. Learning that the couple intended to move into The Hermitage, he ordered that it be remodeled. Alterations included the addition of a one-story wing at each side and front and rear porches. The front one extended across the first story of the house except at the entrance, where it rose to two stories and was topped by a pediment. Other improvements included construction of a stone memorial over Mrs. Jackson's grave and the erection of a detached kitchen and smokehouse. The entire house was also freshly papered and painted.

In 1834 fire gutted the interior. During the rebuilding, completed in the following year, Jackson made several changes. He raised the ceilings of all the rooms, enlarged and rearranged the windows, converted both the porches to two-story galleries with Corinthian columns, and bricked in a covered entrance in the east wing to create a side hall. The front elevation of the house was painted white to hide smoke damage. In 1837, at the end of his second term in the White House, Jackson retired to The Hermitage. He lived out the rest of his days there as an elder statesman, entertaining the great and near-great. In 1845 he died and was laid to rest in the garden beside his wife.

Mantel of rough-cut hickory in the dining room at The Hermitage.

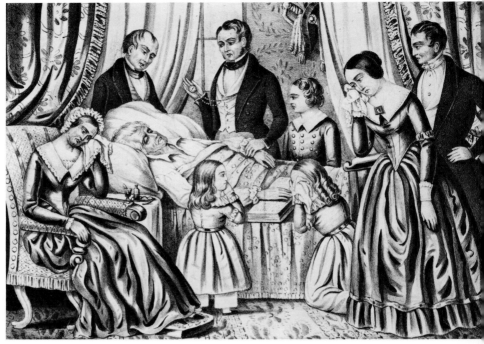

Fanciful version of Jackson's death.

At that time, The Hermitage consisted of about 1,200 acres. Andrew Jackson, Jr., who inherited it, was a poor manager and soon lost all but 500 acres. In 1856, hopelessly in debt, he sold the remainder of the property, including the residence, to the State. It subsequently considered donating the estate to the Federal Government as the site for a military academy, but never did so.

Andrew, Jr., who moved to Mississippi in 1858, returned to The Hermitage 2 years later at the request of Gov. Isham G. Harris to serve as custodian. In 1865 he died. His widow, Sarah, and son, Andrew III, lived in the house until the former's death in 1887. Two years later, the Ladies' Hermitage Association, which was conceived by Mrs. Andrew Jackson III and incorporated that year, applied to the State for permission to administer the mansion as a Jackson shrine. Subsequently, the State conveyed to the association the house, tomb, outbuildings, and 25 acres.

Except for the tree-lined, guitar-shaped driveway, which dates from 1837, The Hermitage today appears as it did after the 1835 reconstruction. From the broad front portico with flagstone floor, double doors lead to the central hall, which is dominated by a circular staircase. The walls of the hall are covered with scenic French wallpaper. To the left of the hall are double parlors connected by folding doors. Each of these chambers has a marble mantelpiece. From the front parlor, a doorway enters into the dining room and pantry in the west wing. To the right of the central hall are a cross hall and two bedrooms. The hall leads to the east wing, which contains an entry hall; a library-office; and the steward's, or overseer's, room. Four bedrooms and a central hall are upstairs.

The Ladies' Hermitage Association has furnished the house with Jackson possessions and has acquired about 600 acres of adjacent land. A few historic outbuildings are extant on the property, including what is believed to be the original log Hermitage, other log cabins, and a stone springhouse. A museum structure and a log cabin used by the association are of recent origin. The tomb of President and Mrs. Jackson is in the garden.

Directly across the highway from The Hermitage is Tulip Grove, also operated by the Ladies' Hermitage Association and open to the public. This fine brick residence, completed in 1836, was the home of Andrew Jackson Donelson, Rachel Jackson's nephew and secretary to her husband. Donelson's wife, Emily, acted as the White House hostess during most of the Jackson administration. Adjacent to Tulip Grove stands "Rachel's Church," a small structure erected in 1823 with Jackson's financial assistance.

Johnson (Lyndon B.) National Historic Site, Texas ★

Blanco and Gillespie Counties, headquarters in the Federal Office Building, Johnson City.

Throughout his life, President Johnson was closely identified with the Texas hill country. This park contains three residences and several other structures that commemorate him. Spanning the years from his birth to his death, they illustrate his ascendancy from modest origins to the office of President.

The first child of Rebekah Baines and Sam Ealy Johnson, Jr.,

The ranchhouse as it appeared in 1963, the year Lyndon B. Johnson assumed the Presidency. It looks essentially the same today except that the antenna has been removed and the shrubbery is larger.

Lyndon was born on August 27, 1908, at a farm on the banks of the Pedernales River near Stonewall in Gillespie County, Tex. Two more children, Rebekah Luruth and Josefa Hermine, also first saw the light of life in this home, a two-bedroom structure that was the smaller of two on their grandparents' farm.

In 1913 the Johnsons moved to Johnson City, about 13 miles to the east in Blanco County. They purchased a handsome, one-story frame building facing Ninth Street. There, two more children, Sam Houston and Lucia Huffman, were born. During his years in Johnson City, Sam Ealy pursued careers in real estate, newspaper work, and politics. Meantime, Lyndon had continued with his elementary education.

In 1920 Sam rented out his home and returned to the Gillespie County farm, which he had acquired from the other heirs of his parents. By this time, he was more active in politics than any other field. Because of his long absences while he was serving in the legislature, Lyndon often found himself in charge of the farm. In 1921, however, because of the lack of high schools in the Stonewall vicinity, he moved in with relatives at Johnson City and began his freshman year there. The next year, his family sold the farm and moved back to their Johnson City home.

Upon graduation from high school in 1924, temporarily uninterested in further learning, Lyndon traveled to California, where he held various minor positions before returning home the next year. In 1927, after a couple more years of drifting from job to job, he entered Southwest Texas State Teachers College in San Marcos. After receiving an elementary teacher's certificate, however, he dropped out the next year to become principal and teach grade school at Cotulla, but reentered the following year and received his Bachelor of Science degree in August 1930. A few months later, he accepted a high-school teaching position at Houston.

That same year, Sam Johnson decided to move once again, this time to San Marcos; 4 years later, he again went back to Johnson City. After his death in 1937, his widow rented out the Ninth Street home and moved to Austin. She remained there until she passed away in 1958.

Meantime, in 1934 Lyndon had married Claudia Alta ("Lady Bird") Taylor of Marshall, Tex., and his political career had flourished. He spent much of his time in Washington, D.C., but returned to Texas as often as his official duties allowed. In 1951 he purchased the LBJ Ranch, about a mile west of the site of his birthplace. It had been owned by an aunt and uncle for four decades. Johnson's permanent home until his death early in 1973, it served as the "Texas White House" during his Presidency (1963-69).

Johnson Birthplace.

The birthplace home, which had been constructed by Lyndon's grandfather about 1889, passed through the hands of various owners after Sam Johnson sold it in 1922 and was torn down in the 1930's. In 1964 Johnson family interests repurchased the site, deeded it to the Johnson City Foundation, and commissioned Austin architect J. Roy White to begin a reconstruction. He based it on a thorough archeological investigation, information supplied by family members and others who remembered the house, and contemporary photographs. Some of the materials utilized in the reconstruction came from an existing building nearby and may once have formed a part of the birthplace. The Johnson City Foundation, which opened the structure to the public in 1966, donated it to the Federal Government 4 years later, the year after Congress authorized the establishment of Lyndon B. Johnson National Historic Site.

The reconstruction is a typical Texas farmhouse of the late 19th century. An open central hallway, or "dogtrot," runs between two

Lyndon and Lady Bird Johnson at the entrance to their ranch while he was serving as Senate Majority Leader.

large rooms on the east and west sides. In the outer wall of each room is a stone fireplace with wooden mantel. A wooden porch, the western end of which is enclosed to provide a "shed room," extends across the entire front of the structure. An ell to the rear of the western room contains a dining room, old kitchen, and a modern kitchen that did not exist in the original house. To the east of the dining room is a back porch, a shed room, and a modern bath. The house is furnished with Johnson family items or period pieces.

The boyhood home in Johnson City, erected by W. C. Russell in 1901, was originally a small framehouse, L-shaped and one story high. It contained a front parlor, east bedroom, hall, dining room, and kitchen. In 1907 Russell added a west wing to provide two additional bedrooms. Two L-shaped porches flanked the front, a screened porch was situated to the rear of the eastern bedroom and hall, and an open porch and a bath were behind the west wing. Except for minor improvements made by the Johnsons in 1934, the basic floor plan remained essentially unaltered until 1964.

In the latter year, the Johnson family remodeled the structure for use as a community center. Major changes included the removal of interior partitions in the eastern section of the house to provide a large room for group meetings, conversion of the west wing into a caretaker's apartment and bath, and modernization of the kitchen. Also, the rear screened porch was glassed in and the house was carefully refurnished with original or other Johnson family items. In 1965 the Johnson City Foundation acquired the structure and opened it to the public. Five years later, the foundation deeded it to the National Park Service. The house, grounds, and outbuildings have been restored to their appearance as of 1925.

After Johnson decided not to seek another full term in March 1968, he briefed all the Presidential candidates. Here, in August, on the porch outside his office at the ranch, he counsels Republican candidate Richard M. Nixon.

Late in 1972, not long before his death, Lyndon B. Johnson donated part of the LBJ Ranch, including the house and more than 200 acres of land, to the National Park Service. His widow occupies the two-story, frame ranchhouse, but visitors may tour the property and view the exteriors of the buildings. One interesting structure is an airplane hangar that Johnson often used for press briefings.

Other donations by the Johnsons have enabled the National Park Service to acquire a 36-acre tract and log house near Johnson City that the President's grandfather used as a headquarters for his cattle operations and the one-room Junction School in the vicinity of the birthplace that Johnson attended for a short time when he was only 4 years of age. The log house and adjoining rock buildings have been restored and an interpretive facility built.

In addition to the properties under the jurisdiction of the National Park Service, three other pertinent sites are in the area. Johnson's grave is in a family cemetery adjacent to the birthplace. Lyndon B. Johnson State Park, across the Pedernales River from the LBJ Ranch, interprets the region and its influences on his life through exhibits and programs. The Lyndon B. Johnson Library, on the campus of the University of Texas at Austin and operated by the General Services Administration, serves as a center of scholarly research and a historical museum.

Coolidge Homestead, Vermont ⚠

Windsor County, just north of Calvin Coolidge Memorial Highway (Vt. 100A), in the village of Plymouth (Plymouth Notch).

This modest frame and clapboard farmhouse, nestled in the remote and picturesque hill country of Vermont, was the boyhood home of Calvin Coolidge. Although he spent most of his adult life outside the State, he often returned to the old homestead to visit his family and never lost his fondness for it. During the early hours of August 3, 1923, he took the Presidential oath of office there.

In 1876, when Coolidge was 4 years old, his father, "Colonel" John Coolidge, purchased the homestead, a simple, 1½-story farmhouse connected to a barn by a shed. He repaired the house, bought some new furniture, and added the front piazza and bay windows in the sitting room, but subsequently made few other changes. Calvin lived in the house until 1887, the year he entered

Coolidge Homestead.

Black River Academy, in nearby Ludlow. In 1895, upon graduating from Amherst College, he took up the practice of law and settled in Northampton, Mass.

Through the years, while pursuing a successful political career, Coolidge returned to Plymouth to call on his family as often as duty would allow. On one of these occasions, during the night of August 2, 1923, when he was serving as Vice President of the United States, he was awakened with news of President Harding's sudden death in San Francisco. In a dramatic ceremony, held about 2:47 a.m. in the sitting room of the homestead, Coolidge's father, a notary public and justice of the peace, swore him into office as President. Witnessing the ceremony were Mrs. Coolidge; U.S. Representative Porter H. Dale, who happened to be staying nearby; L. L. Lane of the Railway Mail Association; and Coolidge's chauffeur and stenographer. Later, Coolidge repeated the oath in his apartment at the Willard Hotel in Washington, where he was staying pending Mrs. Harding's departure from the White House.

When his father died a few years later, Coolidge inherited his boyhood home, but continued to spend most of his time in

Northampton, where he died in January 1933. The homestead remained in the possession of the Coolidge family until 1956, when Coolidge's only surviving son, John, donated it and all the furnishings to the State. The next year, following the death of Mrs. Calvin Coolidge, it formally accepted the gift, dedicated the building as a historic shrine, and opened it to the public. It appears almost exactly today as it did on the night of the inauguration. Because Coolidge's father had refused to install modern conveniences such as electricity, gas, and telephones and because no alterations occurred after his death, the house is exceptionally well preserved.

The State still owns and administers the boyhood home, the first floor of which is open to the public. The main house is connected to the barn by a series of rooms, including the buttery, woodshed,

Upon President Harding's sudden death, Calvin Coolidge took the oath of office from his father at his boyhood home in Vermont during the early hours of August 3, 1923. Watching (left to right) are Vermont Senator and former Representative Porter H. Dale, L. L. Lane of the Railway Mail Association, and Mrs. Calvin Coolidge.

Calvin Coolidge in his Vermont fields.

toolroom, laundry room, and shed bedroom. The latter features the bed in which Coolidge was born at a nearby residence and a quilt he made in his youth.

The most elaborate room in the main house, a formal parlor that was used only on special occasions, contains the black walnut, horsehair-covered furniture that "Colonel" Coolidge purchased at the time he bought the house, as well as the original rug, lace curtains, and cast-iron stove. The sitting room, known as the "Oath of Office Room" because it was the scene of Coolidge's inauguration, displays the table, Bible, and kerosene lamp used in that ceremony. Because the upper floor is inaccessible to the public, the State has refurnished a first-floor bedroom with items from the upstairs bedroom that President and Mrs. Coolidge occupied when visiting. The kitchen, which overlooks the front porch, contains, among other original items, a cast-iron wood stove and a table set for four. Adjacent to the kitchen is the pantry.

Elsewhere in Plymouth, several other historic structures associated with Coolidge are extant, some of which are open to the public. Directly across the street from the homestead is Union Church, a typical New England church attended by Coolidge throughout his life when he was in town. Adjacent to it stands a structure that incorporates Coolidge's birthplace, a 1½-story house at the rear, and a large, two-story ell, a later addition at the front, in which Coolidge, Sr., operated a general store. During the Presidential campaign of 1924, Coolidge maintained an office on the second floor of the store, probably because his father would not permit telephones to be installed in the homestead. The State acquired the entire structure in 1967 and has partially restored it.

Another State-owned structure is the Wilder House, a two-story building just east of the homestead that was once the home of Coolidge's aunt and uncle and the birthplace of his mother. It serves as a restaurant and hospitality center. Across the street and to the east of the Wilder House stands the Farmer's Museum, originally the Wilder barn but now a State-owned and operated museum of 19th-century farm and household items. Not far to the west of the homestead is the Cheese Factory, established about 1890 by "Colonel" Coolidge and reactivated by Calvin's son John in the early 1960's. Near it is an old schoolhouse, presently operated as a gift shop.

Plymouth Notch Cemetery, about a mile southwest of the homestead on the south side of Vt. 100A contains the graves of President and Mrs. Coolidge, their youngest son, Calvin, Jr., who died in 1924 at the age of 16, and several Coolidge ancestors.

Berkeley, Virginia ⚠

Charles City County, on the south side of Va. 5, about 8 miles west of Charles City.

In historical interest this fine mansion has few rivals among the James River plantations. It was the birthplace and lifelong home of Benjamin Harrison V (1726-91), signer of the Declaration of Independence and three-term Governor of Virginia, as well as the birthplace and boyhood residence of his son, William Henry (1773-

Berkeley.

1841), ninth President of the United States and grandfather of Benjamin (1833-1901), the 23d President.

Benjamin Harrison IV, the signer's father, built the structure in 1726. In 1773 it was the birthplace of William Henry. During his youth, in 1781 British troops under Benedict Arnold plundered the plantation, but did not seriously harm the mansion. When Benjamin V died in 1791, William Henry's oldest brother, Benjamin VI, inherited Berkeley. Sometime in the 1790's, one of the Harrisons, probably Benjamin VI, made some architectural alterations and redecorated the interior in the Adam style.

As a young man, following attendance at Hampden-Sydney College and a fling at medical education, William Henry emigrated to the Northwest Territory to seek his fortune and never again lived permanently at the plantation. He did, however, visit his family there, and in 1841 paid a last visit after his election to the Presidency. At that time, he apparently wrote his inaugural address in the room in which he had been born; he died only a month later in the White House and was interred in a private cemetery, present Harrison Tomb State Memorial, in North Bend, Ohio.

By the time of the Civil War, the plantation was known as Harrison's Landing. In 1862 it served as a supply base and camp for the Union Army of the Potomac following its retreat from Malvern Hill, Va., which ended the Peninsula Campaign. Gen. George B. McClellan utilized the mansion as his headquarters. While quartered nearby, Gen. Daniel Butterfield composed the famous bugle call "Taps."

By 1915 the early Georgian mansion was in poor condition. Subsequent owners have restored it to its 18th-century appearance. This included removal of a 19th-century porch on all four sides, replacement of the window sash and exterior door framings, and reconstruction of the center stairs. The exterior has been altered somewhat over the years, but retains much of the original structure and character.

The house is 2½ stories high and has a dormered, gable roof with two tall interior ridge chimneys and distinctive pedimented gable ends, including modillioned cornices. The brick walls are laid in Flemish bond. Gauged brick is employed in the flat window arches, the belt course, and door pediments. The broad-piered central doors on the north and south elevations, with pediments in gauged brick, are reconstructions. Two detached, two-story, brick dependencies, set slightly south of the house on the river side, were built in the 1840's to replace similar structures that had been erected sometime before 1800.

The center hall plan has been slightly modified. The hall bisects the four rooms on the first floor into pairs. A small stairs in the northwestern corner was probably inserted about 1800. Most of the interior finish reflects the Adam alterations of the 1790's. The upper floors are used as a private residence, but the basement and first floor may be visited. The unmarked grave of signer of the Declaration Benjamin Harrison is in the family cemetery, a quarter of a mile southeast of the plantation.

Monroe Tomb.

Monroe Tomb, Virginia ⚐

Hollywood Cemetery, 412 South Cherry Street, Richmond.

This tomb, a small-scale architectural masterpiece, contains the
remains of President James Monroe. Upon his death in New York
City on July 4, 1831, his body was interred in that city's Marble
(Second Street) Cemetery. In 1858, the 100th anniversary of his
birth, municipal officials and representatives of the State of
Virginia decided that the remains should be returned to his home
State for reburial. The Virginia legislature appropriated funds for
this purpose. On July 5 the body, accompanied by the 7th Regiment
of the New York National Guard, arrived in Richmond on the

The exhumed body of President Monroe, who had died in 1831, lies in state in New York City's City Hall in 1858, before being returned to his home state, Virginia, for reburial.

steamboat *Jamestown.* That same day, an impressive burial ceremony, highlighted by a speech delivered by Gov. Henry A. Wise of Virginia, was held at the gravesite, on a high bluff overlooking the James River, in Richmond's Hollywood Cemetery.

The tomb is an ornate Gothic Revival structure. Designed by Alsatian architect Albert Lybrock, it was erected in 1859. The innovative and imaginative use of cast iron, obtained from the Philadelphia firm of Wood and Perot, provided the opportunity for a delicacy and intricacy of design that was not possible on the same scale in stone.

The tomb is in the form of a rectangular "cage" surrounding Monroe's simple granite sarcophagus. Each facade is decorated with a lancet arch in the style of a cathedral window. At the top of each of these arches is a rose window tracery; below each tracery are three round arches. On the two longer sides of the rectangle, two subordinate lancet arches flank the main ones. At each of the four corners, a colonette supports a small tabernacle that rises above the top of the facades. The "cage" sits on a solid but elaborately decorated base and is surmounted by an ogive canopy featuring delicate tracery. A low stone wall encircles the tomb.

Hollywood Cemetery, on a rolling ridge overlooking the James River, also contains the graves of President John Tyler, near that of Monroe; Jefferson Davis; Gen. J. E. B. Stuart; and thousands of other Confederate soldiers.

Monticello.

Monticello, Virginia ⚠

Albemarle County, just off Va. 53, about 2 miles southeast of Charlottesville.

"Monticello," Italian for "Little Mountain," is an enduring tribute to the genius and versatility of Thomas Jefferson, who personally designed and supervised erection of the splendid mansion. He resided in it for many years of his long life, his spirit lives on in its architectural perfection and the ingenious devices with which he equipped it, and he is buried nearby. Sitting amid pleasant gardens and lawns on a hilltop, the residence overlooks Charlottesville; the

University of Virginia, which Jefferson founded and some of whose buildings he designed; and the green rolling hills of the surrounding countryside. Until his death, at the age of 83 on July 4, 1826, the prominent men of his age made pilgrimages to Monticello. To this day it is visited by the humble, as well as the great—all who admire Jefferson's character and accomplishments.

In 1757 Jefferson's father bequeathed the property, consisting of some 1,053 acres, to him. Eleven years later, while in his early twenties, he began leveling the hilltop, which at the time was considered to be a highly unconventional site for a home, and constructing a road-path system to link all parts of the plantation. In 1770 fire destroyed his modest, nearby residence and birthplace, Shadwell, and he moved to Monticello, where he had already begun building a mansion. The first part of it completed was the small south pavilion (1769-70), which he occupied as a bachelor's quarters until January 1772, when he brought his bride, Martha Wayles Skelton, to share it with him. It is still known as "Honeymoon Cottage."

The first Monticello, vastly different from the present one, was begun in 1770 and basically completed by 1779. Constructed of red brick, and trimmed with white cut stone, it consisted of a central two-story unit, which had a pedimented gable roof, at the sides of which were 1½-story wings whose gabled roofs were perpendicular to the central unit. The chief architectural accent was the main two-story portico, Doric below and Ionic above. Small polygonal bays projected from the ends of the wings. Just after the War for Independence, Jefferson made numerous alterations and major changes.

The present two-wing structure, built in stages between 1793 and 1809, incorporates the original rooms of the house on the west, or garden-rear, side. The design, modeled on the Hôtel de Salm in Paris, reflects Jefferson's shift in architectural preference from Georgian to Roman Revival, elements of both of which are represented. He was almost entirely responsible for starting the Roman Revival movement in the United States.

The mansion consists of 2½ stories over a basement and contains 35 rooms. The dominating exterior features are the Doric-columned east and west porticoes, which feature fanlighted pediments; the central dome just beind the west portico; the balustrade crowning the second floor; the Chinese Chippendale railing on the top level;

could the dead feel any interest in Monu-
-ments or other remembrances of them, when, as
Anacreon says: Ολιγη δε κεισομεσθα
                    Κονις, οστεων λυθεν]ων
the following would be to my Manes the most
gratifying.
On the grave
       a plain die or cube of 3.f without any
mouldings, surmounted by an Obelisk
of 6.f. height, each of a single stone:
on the faces of the Obelisk the following
inscription, & not a word more
       Here was buried
       Thomas Jefferson
author of the Declaration of American Independance
       of the Statute of Virginia for religious freedom
       & Father of the University of Virginia.'
because by these, as testimonials that I have lived, I wish most to
be remembered. ~~the stone~~ to be of the coarse stone of which
my columns are made, that no one might be tempted
hereafter to destroy it for the value of the materials.
my bust by Ciracchi, with the pedestal and truncated
column on which it stands, might be given to the University
if they would place it in the Dome room of the Rotunda.
on the Die, of the Obelisk might be engraved
       Born apr. 2. 1743. O.S.
       died ——   ,

Jefferson's directions for the monument at his tomb.

the set-back upper half story; and four interior chimneys. Behind the east portico the half-windows of the low second story are set near the floor immediately above the lintels of the first-floor windows.

The rooms on the first floor are grouped around the large, two-story entrance hall, which is partly surrounded by a balcony connecting the second-story rooms. Chambers of special interest on the lower level include Jefferson's bedroom, in which he died; library; glassed-in piazza; dining room; and the semioctagonal parlor, behind the entrance hall and opening on the west portico. Two steep and narrow staircases, concealed in alcoves off the lateral halls, provide access to the upper levels, including the dome room.

The house is furnished largely with Jefferson belongings, including a replica of the small portable desk on which he probably wrote the Declaration of Independence. The exhibits in the entrance hall are of special interest. Some of the clever devices in the residence are a 7-day calendar-clock and a dumbwaiter. The drawing room contains one of the first parquet floors in the United States. The upper levels are not shown to the public.

Before Jefferson built Monticello, every plantation had a group of small outbuildings such as the laundry, smokehouse, dairy, stable, weaving house, schoolhouse, and kitchen. Jefferson sought to render these as inconspicuous as possible and increase the efficiency of the facilities they provided by constructing two series of rooms for these purposes dug into the sides of the hill beneath two long L-shaped terraces extending from the house. Below the south terrace, beyond the angle of the ell, are the kitchen, the cook's room, servants' rooms, room for smoking meat, and the dairy. At the end of this terrace, on the aboveground level, stands "Honeymoon Cottage."

Under the far side of the north terrace are the stables, carriage house, icehouse, and laundry. Jefferson used the small building terminating this terrace, adjacent to which is the paddock, as an office. An underground passageway—containing storage rooms for wine, beer, cider, and rum—connects the basement of the main house with the series of service rooms along the outer sides of the ells. Jefferson is buried in the family graveyard, which is adjacent to the road leading from the house. Still visible are remains of his "roundabouts," or paths, which were built at various levels on the hillside and were part of the road network.

Upon Jefferson's death in 1826, his daughter Martha inherited Monticello, but was soon forced to sell it, to the first of a series of private owners. In 1923 the newly organized Thomas Jefferson Memorial Foundation purchased the estate, the following year opened it to the public, and has retained ownership to the present day.

Montpelier, Virginia   △

Orange County, on Va. 20, about 4 miles west of Orange.

Montpelier, or Montpellier, was James Madison's residence for nearly all his life. Born at his grandmother's home in King George County in 1751, he soon traveled with his mother to his father's farm, a tract in Orange County that had been in the family since 1723 and that became the nucleus of Montpelier. There, he first lived in a modest wooden house, constructed by his grandfather, Ambrose Madison, about two decades earlier and probably located a half mile south of the present mansion. The early, or central, portion of the present Georgian residence was constructed by his father, also named James, about 1760. When the latter died in 1801, he bequeathed the house and part of the estate to his oldest son, James.

Madison's frequent absences were mainly for education or public service. Upon completion of his second term as President, he and his wife, Dolley, retired to Montpelier. They held court for a succession of visitors, including the Marquis de Lafayette, James Monroe, Thomas Jefferson, and Daniel Webster. After Madison died at Montpelier in 1836, his wife returned to Washington, D.C., where she resided until she succumbed 13 years later. They are both buried at Montpelier.

The mansion was originally a brick rectangular structure, two stories in height over an elevated basement. It consisted of two large rooms and a central hall on each floor. During his first term as President, in 1809-11, Madison retained architects William Thornton and Benjamin H. Latrobe to remodel the house. The former enlarged the main building, and the latter added step-down, one-story wings. The exterior brick walls were also stuccoed. Apparently the huge Doric portico was added at a later date. In 1907 the wings were enlarged to 2½ stories.

Montpelier.

Madison, who was interested in horticulture and agriculture, planned the gardens and landscaping of the estate, which had grown to more than 1,000 acres, many of which were under cultivation. Tobacco and corn were the principal crops. During his absences, Madison left an overseer in charge.

The mansion and the beautifully landscaped grounds have been carefully maintained. Three-bay wings flank the seven-bay central section of the hip-roofed mansion. Four huge Doric columns support the two-story portico, which has a triangular pediment containing a semicircular window. The double-door front entrance is framed by sidelights and a fanlight. A pair of chimneys stand at either end of the main building, and a chimney at the end of each wing. A dentiled cornice adorns the roofline and the pediment.

Privately owned, the estate, except for the Madison family cemetery, is not accessible to the public.

Mount Vernon.

Mount Vernon, Virginia △

Fairfax County, at the southern terminus of the George Washington Memorial Parkway, about 7 miles south of Alexandria.

Overlooking the Potomac River in a setting of serene elegance and beauty is George Washington's plantation estate, Mount Vernon. Its sweeping lawns, beautiful gardens, magnificent mansion, and carefully planned outbuildings superbly represent a Virginia plantation home. Many shrines commemorate Washington as President, military leader, and statesman, but Mount Vernon best reveals the plantation farmer and country gentleman.

Mount Vernon was Washington's home for several years during his childhood and all his adult life—though he was absent for long periods while serving the Nation. At the estate, he entertained many U.S. and world dignitaries. He also hosted the Mount Vernon Conference (1785), after its initial sessions at nearby Alexandria. This meeting led to the Annapolis Convention (1786), the immediate forerunner of the Constitutional Convention (1787).

The history of the estate dates back to the late 17th century. In 1674 John Washington, the great-grandfather of George, and Nicholas Spencer obtained a 5,000-acre grant along the Potomac, and 16 years later their heirs divided it. In 1726 Mildred Washington (Mrs. Roger Gregory), who had inherited the Washington half, which was then known as Hunting Creek Plantation, sold it to her brother Augustine, George's father.

Augustine probably constructed the first portion of the present mansion over the foundations of a smaller, earlier dwelling that may have been erected by his father, Lawrence Washington, or his grandfather. From about 1735 until 1738, Augustine and his family, including young George, resided there after living at Wakefield, and in the latter year moved to the "Strother estate" (Ferry Farm), along the Rappahannock River opposite Fredericksburg. In 1740 Augustine deeded Mount Vernon to his eldest son, Lawrence, George's half-brother, who settled there at the time of his marriage 3 years later, and renamed the plantation Mount Vernon after Admiral Vernon, under whom he had served in the Caribbean. George spent part of his youth at the estate with Lawrence, who may have modified or rebuilt the house.

In 1754, or 2 years after Lawrence's death, George leased the property, then over 2,600 acres, from Lawrence's widow who had a lifetime right to it; upon her death in 1761, George inherited it. In 1757-58, in preparation for his marriage the following year to Martha Custis, George thoroughly rebuilt the 1½-story Georgian structure, which then contained four rooms bisected by a central hall on each floor. He enlarged the residence to 2½ stories and remodeled it to a more impressive Palladian form. Because of his long absences on military duty in the French and Indian War until late in 1759, the bulk of the construction was supervised by William Fairfax, a neighbor.

For the next 15 years after his marriage in 1759, Washington lived as a prosperous planter, and made no further changes of consequence in his residence. In 1773 he decided to enlarge it, but he had hardly begun to do so when, in 1774-75, he went to Philadelphia to serve in the First and Second Continental Congresses. In the latter year, he was appointed as commander in chief of the Continental Army.

While Washington was away during the War for Independence, a distant kinsman, Lund Washington, carried out his plans for the

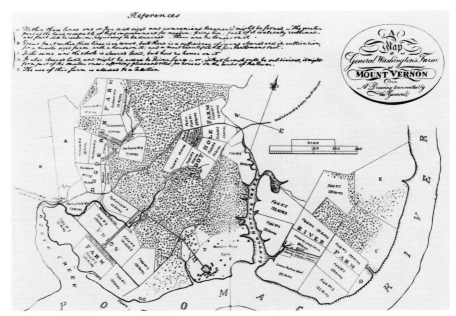

Washington's sketch of his Mount Vernon estate.

estate. Lund enlarged the relatively modest main house from five to
nine bays; constructed the piazza; added the detached, flanking
wings, which connected to the central mansion by means of
curving light arcades; built outbuildings; landscaped the grounds;
and extended the gardens.

George found the mansion almost completed in 1781, when he
stopped off on his way to and from Yorktown. After resigning his
commission 2 years later, he returned to Mount Vernon; and in
1787 concluded the remodeling, when he placed the large octagonal
cupola on the center of the roof.

That summer, Washington again traveled to Philadelphia, where
he served as president of the Constitutional Convention. Two years
later, elected as U.S. President, he departed once more and for the
following 8 years was able to return only about twice a year. In
1797 he did so a final time, to retire; he died at Mount Vernon 2
years later. His wife lived there until she passed away in 1802. His
nephew, Bushrod Washington, inherited the property, which
remained in the family until 1858.

The mansion is an excellent example of Georgian architecture. Most striking is the high-columned, two-story piazza, which extends the full length of the structure and overlooks the Potomac. A triangular pediment tops the west elevation. Both the latter and the river facade have a central entrance and two side entrances. Two large interior chimneys mark the earlier ends of the dormered, hip-roofed mansion. A dentiled cornice adorns the roofline and the pediment. The exterior wood siding is beveled, and its paint contains sand to give the appearance of stone. Windows of both facades are shuttered.

On the first floor are the musicroom, west parlor, banquet hall, a bedchamber, dining room, and library. The second floor contains the blue bedroom, Lafayette's bedroom, the yellow bedroom, Nelly Custis' bedroom, and George Washington's bedroom. The third floor includes three bedrooms and two storerooms. The kitchen is outside but adjacent to the house.

A courtyard and bowling green, flanked by flower and kitchen gardens, extend from the west, or land, front of the house. To the north of the flower garden is a greenhouse. Various outbuildings, including smokehouse, workshops, and stables, have been restored in detail, as have the gardens and lawn. One modern building, built in 1928 in the same style as the other outbuildings, serves as a museum. The tombs of George and Martha Washington lie to the south of the mansion.

At its peak, during Washington's lifetime, the plantation contained more than 8,000 acres and was partitioned into five farms. After his death, four of them were divided and subdivided. By 1858 the estate had dwindled to 200 acres.

In 1858 the Mount Vernon Ladies' Association of the Union, concerned about the condition of the property, acquired title from Washington's great-grandnephew, John A. Washington, Jr. He had been unable, while operating the farm, to handle the numerous visitors or properly care for the house and grounds. By that time, none of the original furnishings remained. The association restored the buildings and grounds; eventually gained title to an additional 300 acres; and procured period pieces, many of them originals.

Oak Hill, Virginia ⚠

Loudoun County, on U.S. 15, about 1 mile north of its junction with U.S. 50 at Gilberts Corner and about 8 miles south of Leesburg.

James Monroe began building this palatial mansion at the height of his career, during his first term as President (1817-21), drafted the Monroe Doctrine in it, and retired there at the end of his public service.

In 1808 Monroe inherited the property on which the mansion stands from an uncle, but lack of funds prevented him from beginning construction of a home for at least a decade. Thomas Jefferson designed the mansion, and James Hoban, architect of the White House and Capitol, provided architectural assistance. Constructed of brick kilned nearby, the structure was completed in 1823. Monroe furnished it with pieces from his Ash Lawn estate, near Charlottesville, Va., which he later sold.

Spending much time at Oak Hill, Monroe made horseback trips to and from the Capital. On the grounds, among numerous locust and poplar trees, he planted an oak for each State in the Union, and thereby gave the estate its name. In 1825 he left the White House and retired at Oak Hill, where he entertained such notables as John Quincy Adams and the Marquis de Lafayette. Financial difficulties eventually forced him to dispose of all his property, including Oak Hill. In 1830, the year his wife died, he moved to New York City to live with his daughter. On July 4, 1831, he died there.

The mansion originally consisted of a two-story central portion with small, one-room wings. In 1923 the owner enlarged the wings to two full stories. The south portico, two stories high and supported by seven Doric pillars, is the most striking feature of the residence. The basement contains the kitchen, servants' dining room, and various storage and service rooms. On the first floor are an entrance hall, two drawing rooms, dining room, sitting room, library, master's room, guestroom, and pantry. Bedrooms, servants' quarters, and four sun decks occupy the second floor. The attic is used for storage. A number of outbuildings remain, including a smokehouse, springhouse, law office, and "Monroe's Cottage." The latter is a small frame structure that served as his residence before he built the present mansion. Privately owned Oak Hill is not open to the public.

Oak Hill.

Poplar Forest.

Poplar Forest, Virginia ⚠

Bedford County, on the east side of County Route 661, about 6½ miles west of Lynchburg.

In 1806-19 Thomas Jefferson designed and built this architecturally notable octagonal house on his 4,000-acre Bedford County plantation as a summer home and retreat. He occupied it intermittently until his death in 1826.

The plantation came into Jefferson's possession through Martha Wayles Skelton, whom he married in 1772. For many years, whenever he visited it to superintend its management, he resided in a two-room cottage, the only dwelling. In June 1781, just after abdicating the governorship and narrowly escaping capture with a group of legislators during a British raid on Charlottesville, he temporarily moved his family to the cottage. Before the month was out, a horse threw and injured him. During his recuperation, he wrote *Notes on the State of Virginia*, a study of social and political life in 18th-century Virginia. In 1806-19, during which time he retired from public office, he erected Poplar Forest. When visitors became too numerous at Monticello or the fancy struck, he took up residence at his retreat for a month or two, usually twice a year. As time went on, he refined the structure.

In 1845 a fire destroyed the roof and interior, leaving only the four chimneys, the brick walls, and possibly the portico columns. That same year, the present unadorned roof, octagonal and hipped like its predecessor, and dormers were added. Prior to the fire, a skylight and balustraded deck at the edge of the roof, with a Tuscan cornice below, extended around the building. The one-story brick residence is set over a high basement. Because of the sloping ground on the rear side, the structure is two stories high there. One- and two-story tetrastyle Tuscan porticoes are attached to the front and rear of the house respectively. The front one is pedimented; the unpedimented rear one is built over a one-story arcade.

The original interior plan is unchanged. Four elongated octagonal rooms are grouped symmetrically around the present dining room, a square central chamber that was once lighted from above by a skylight, not replaced in 1845. No aboveground traces remain of a flat-roofed office wing, referred to by Jefferson, but a kitchen and smokehouse still stand.

Poplar Forest, in good condition, is a private residence and is closed to public visitation.

Sherwood Forest, Virginia ⚠

Charles City County, on Va. 5, about 4 miles east of Charles City.

John Tyler, who was born in Charles City County and retained life-long ties to Tidewater Virginia, acquired this residence during his Presidency and made it his retirement home.

In 1842, about 2 months after the death of his first wife in the White House, Tyler purchased Creek Plantation, a 1,200-acre estate only about 3 miles from his birthplace, Greenway. Considering himself something of a political "outlaw," he whimsically renamed his new home "Sherwood Forest," after the legendary Robin Hood's hideout.

At the time Tyler bought the property, the main house, built about 1780 and then known as the "Grove" for its setting in a grove of oaks, was a 2½-story, clapboarded structure with two 1½-story wings. About the time of his second marriage, in 1844, he renovated the structure. He added a covered colonnade to connect a 1½-story detached kitchen-laundry to the east wing, and duplicated this pattern on the west end of the house to provide space for an office

Sherwood Forest.

and ballroom. The completed building, only one room deep, spanned 300 feet and was one of the longest private residences in the country. Tyler used the present rear of the mansion as the front; that side faces the James River and he found it convenient to use the road that then passed between his house and the river.

Tyler's expanded home served the requirements of his ever-growing family; he and his second wife, Julia, had seven children during the years they lived in it. He retired there after leaving the Presidency in 1845, though he maintained a summer cottage near the ocean at Old Point Comfort (present Hampton), Va., and usually spent some time each year with his wife's mother on Staten Island, N.Y. Living quietly for many years, he devoted himself to raising his family and tending to agricultural pursuits.

In February 1861 Tyler journeyed to Washington, where he chaired the unsuccessful Peace Convention. Later in the year, he participated in the Virginia secession convention, and won a seat in the Confederate Congress. He died the next January in Richmond. Soon after his demise, his wife and their younger children crossed Union lines and joined her mother in New York. Before long, Union troops ravaged Tyler's estate, cut down the grove of trees, and destroyed many of his possessions. By 1864 the house stood deserted, but members of the family returned after the end of the war.

Although the estate has been divided, largely among Tyler descendants, the house is still owned by one of them and is a private residence. It has changed relatively little through the years, and contains a number of original furnishings and mementos of President Tyler's life. The mansion, which is painted white, is surrounded by a large yard, in which traces of the old formal garden can be seen. At the east end of the house stands an 18th-century wine house; at the west end, a dairy; and two other dependencies near the house are extant. Some buildings also survive on other portions of the original estate, which remains mainly in agricultural use. The present owner of Sherwood Forest plans to restore and repair it, and may eventually open a portion of it to the public.

Tuckahoe, Virginia   ⚠

Goochland County, on the south side of Va. 650, about 13 miles west of Richmond.

Tuckahoe, situated along the James River, was the boyhood home of Thomas Jefferson for 7 years and the place where he obtained his elementary education. The mansion, outbuildings, and surrounding gardens and lands constitute an outstanding example of a southern colonial plantation.

The land on which Tuckahoe stands was patented in 1695 by William Randolph. His son Thomas inherited the plantation and built the north wing of the mansion about 1712. Sometime between 1730 and 1745, William Randolph II enlarged the residence to its present proportions. When Randolph died in 1745, Peter Jefferson moved his family, including 2-year-old Thomas, from Shadwell to

Tuckahoe.

Tuckahoe to fulfill a promise Peter had made to Randolph, his wife's cousin, to act as guardian of his son, Thomas Mann Randolph. In 1752 the Jeffersons returned to Shadwell.

Tuckahoe is an outstanding and rare example of an H-shaped structure of early Georgian style in the Colonies. It is a large, two-story, frame structure lined with brick nogging and exterior weatherboarded walls, except for the two solid brick ends of the south wing. Two long gabled wings are connected by a broad central block. Tall slender chimneys accentuate the narrow gable ends and the marked verticality of the structure, which is further enhanced by the high brick foundations. The chimneys in the frame ends of the north wing project, but those in the south brick ends are flush with the walls. The second-floor level is marked by a wooden belt course and the roofline by a modillioned cornice.

The central doorways on the north and south sides have low porches with square posts supporting gable roofs. The south porch is approached by a long flight of stone steps, splayed but lacking a balustrade; the north porch is near ground level. The doors in the center block, on the east and west elevations, are sheltered by pedimented hoods. All four paneled exterior doors, one in each wing and two in the central block, are original, as are also the weatherboarding and sash.

On the first floor of each of the wings are two rooms, divided by a center cross hall. The north wing contains two parlors; the south, a dining room and "children's" room. The central connecting block contains one large room, or salon. The second floor repeats the plan of the first floor except that, of the original five bedrooms, the one in the central block has been modernized and subdivided into several rooms.

The interior decoration and trim, of the finest workmanship, is remarkably unaltered and in fine condition. All the walls are covered with fine wood paneling. The original wide floorboards remain throughout the structure. The hall stairways, especially the north one, with elaborately turned and spiraled balusters, are outstanding examples of the early Georgian style. Mantels throughout the house date from the 19th century, but the marble fireplace facing in the west bedroom of the north wing is original.

East of the mansion is a small, one-room, brick, one-story schoolhouse, possibly the one Jefferson attended, as well as fine boxwood gardens. A short distance west of the main house is a plantation street, containing a complex of buildings of uncertain date, all in excellent condition and little altered. They include the plantation office, kitchen, storehouse, slave quarters, smokehouse, and barn.

Since Tuckahoe passed out of the possession of the Randolph family in 1830, a succession of individuals have owned it. It is still a private residence, not accessible to the public.

Washington Birthplace National Monument, Virginia ★

Westmoreland County, just east of Va. 3, about 38 miles east of Fredericksburg.

The memorial mansion at this site along the Potomac symbolizes Wakefield, where George Washington was born on February 22, 1732, and spent the first 3 years of his life. His family then moved farther up the river to the Little Hunting Creek plantation that later came to be known as Mount Vernon.

In 1717 or 1718 Augustine, George's father, bought land fronting on Popes Creek, a mile southeast of his home on Bridges Creek. On this tract, some three-quarters of a mile above the point where the creek empties into the Potomac, probably in the 1722-26 period he built the residence that became known as Wakefield. He and his family soon moved in. His first wife, Jane Butler, died in late 1729. Two years later, he brought his new wife, Mary Ball, to reside there.

George Washington, who was born the next year, as their first child, never owned Wakefield. Upon the death of his father in 1743, it passed to George's older half-brother, Augustine, Jr. At that time, George, aged 11, may have returned for awhile to attend a nearby school. Because he was close to his half-brother, in subsequent years he visited often.

When Augustine, Jr., died in 1762, his son William Augustine was only 5 years old. The latter inherited the plantation in 1774, when his mother passed away. Although he was only 17, that same year he married and assumed responsibility for the estate. After fire accidentally destroyed the home in 1779 or 1780, he moved to another location. The house was never rebuilt.

For many years, the site of Wakefield lay neglected and forgotten. The first person to place a marker there was George Washington Parke Custis, grandson of Martha and erstwhile ward of George

Memorial house at Washington Birthplace National Monument.

Washington. In June 1816 he held a memorial ceremony at the probable house site and placed a freestone slab marker; eventually it disappeared.

In 1856 William Lewis Washington, a family heir, offered to donate a small plot of land at the site of the house and the nearby family burial ground to the State. Two years later, Virginia accepted the donation, planning to mark and preserve the sites, but the political turmoil generated by the approach of the Civil War was likely the reason this was not done.

In 1882 the State donated the property to the Federal Government, which the next year acquired additional acreage. In 1895-96 the Government placed a granite shaft at the site. In 1923 the Wakefield National Memorial Association organized to reconstitute and preserve the plantation as a national shrine. Several years later, Congress authorized the creation of a house at Wakefield as nearly as possible like the one built by Augustine Washington. By 1931-32 the association, aided by John D. Rockefeller, Jr., had transferred to the Government enough land to bring the holdings to about 394 acres.

Extensive research failed to yield reliable information about the appearance of the birthplace home. Consequently, the memorial house is only a general representation of a Virginia plantation residence of the 18th century. Its design is based on tradition and surviving homes of the period. Archeological excavations by the National Park Service and others, however, have revealed foundation remnants near the site of the present house that might well be those of the original structure.

The memorial house was built in 1931-32, at which time workers moved the granite shaft to its present location, near the entrance to the national monument. The Federal Government paid part of the construction and landscaping costs.

The typically Georgian residence, of brick made from clay obtained in an adjoining field, is 1½ stories high. It has pairs of buttressed chimneys at each end and a gabled roof. Four rooms are downstairs and four upstairs. Central hallways divide the chambers on each floor. A tilt-top table in the dining room is the only piece of furniture that may have been in the original residence. The rest of the furnishings, however, date from the first half of the 18th century.

About 50 feet from the house is a typical Colonial frame kitchen, built on the traditional site. One of its two rooms is furnished to represent a plantation kitchen during the period of Washington's youth; the other displays artifacts recovered on the grounds.

Plantings near the house may be derived from those that grew on the place when Washington lived there as a boy. The nearby garden features only those flowers, vines, herbs, and berries common to Virginia gardens of his time. South of the garden a grove of eastern red cedar trees covers Burnt House Point, which juts out into Popes Creek.

About a mile northwest of the memorial mansion, on the banks of Bridges Creek, are the family burial plot and the site of the home that John Washington, George's great-grandfather, purchased in 1664. The burial plot, surrounded by a brick wall, includes the graves of George Washington's father, grandfather, great-grandfather, and half-brother, Augustine, Jr. George was buried at Mount Vernon.

An additional feature of the national monument is a "living farm." It recreates a typical agricultural setting of Washington's day. The livestock, poultry, and crops are the same types and varieties raised then and are nurtured by colonial methods.

Wilson Birthplace, Virginia   ⚠
24 N. Coalter Street, Staunton.

In 1846 the First Presbyterian Church of Staunton built this residence, the birthplace of President Wilson, for use as a manse. Nine years later, the Rev. Joseph R. Wilson, who had come to Virginia in the early 1850's to teach at Hampden-Sydney College, accepted an appointment with the Staunton Church and moved in. He also served as chaplain of nearby Augusta Female Seminary (later Mary Baldwin College). On December 28, 1856, his wife Jessie gave birth to their first son and third child, Woodrow.

About a year later, however, Reverend Wilson took a pulpit in Augusta, Ga., and relocated there with his family. In December 1912, after his election to the Presidency, Woodrow returned to Staunton and spent a night in his birthplace; he had visited the town frequently as a youth. Pastors succeeding the Reverend Wilson used the manse until 1929, when the church deeded it to Mary Baldwin College. The college retained title until about 1938,

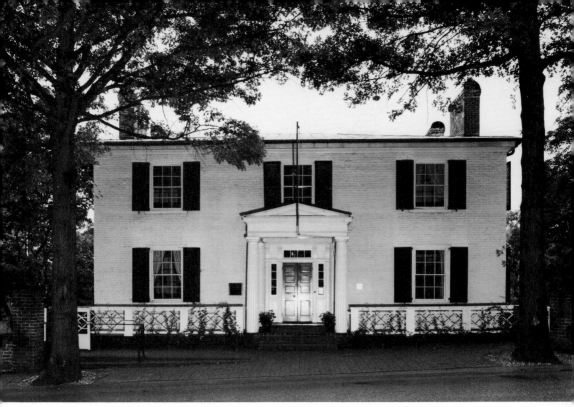

Wilson Birthplace.

and then transferred the property to the Woodrow Wilson Birthplace Foundation, Inc., which now owns and administers it.

The rectangular brick structure, painted white, represents the Greek Revival style. It sits on the slope of a steep hill. Because the ground floor is below street level on the street side, the house presents two stories on that side and three at the rear. The rooms number 12; four, divided by a wide central hall, are on each level. Architectural features of interest include the one-story, pedimented portico that covers the central entrance on the street side and a wider and more impressive rear three-story portico with huge Doric columns and double balcony overlooking a terraced Victorian garden.

The garden, created in 1933 by the Garden Club of Virginia, features brick walkways and bow-knot flower beds bordered in century-old boxwood. One of the walkways leads to a garage, in which is displayed a Pierce Arrow automobile that Wilson used while in the White House and during his last years. Beyond the garden in the distance stands the church where Wilson's father preached and where in 1857 Wilson was baptized. Today it serves as the chapel for Mary Baldwin College.

The house contains many Wilson family possessions. Among those on display are the family Bible, in which Reverend Wilson recorded Woodrow's birth; the bookcase the youth bought with his first earned money and used while a student at the University of Virginia; personal letters; items of furniture that belonged to his parents, among which is the cradle he occupied as an infant; furniture owned by Wilson himself, including the canopied four-poster bed he slept in while he was president of Princeton University; and musical instruments belonging to him and members of his family. Mrs. Edith Wilson, the President's widow, and associates and friends assisted in furnishing the structure.

Suggested Reading

AIKMAN, LONNELLE. *The Living White House*. Washington: White House Historical Association with the cooperation of the National Geographic Society, 1975.

AMERICAN HERITAGE. *The American Heritage History of the Presidency* (1 vol.) and *The American Heritage Pictorial History of the Presidents of the United States* (2 vols.). New York: 1968.

BINKLEY, WILFRED E. *The Powers of the President: Problems of American Democracy*. New York: Russell, 1973.

DURANT, JOHN and ALICE. *Pictorial History of American Presidents*. New York: Castle Books, 1975.

FREIDEL, FRANK. *Our Country's Presidents*. Washington: National Geographic Society, 1975.

———. *The Presidents of the United States of America*. Washington: White House Historical Association with the cooperation of the National Geographic Society, 1975.

HYMAN, SIDNEY. *The American President*. New York: Greenwood, 1974.

JENSEN, AMY L. *The White House and Its Thirty-Five Families*. New York: McGraw-Hill, 1970.

KANE, JOSEPH N. *Facts About the Presidents: A Compilation of Biographical and Historical Data*. New York: H. W. Wilson, 1974.

KLAPTHOR, MARGARET B. *The First Ladies*. Washington: White House Historical Association with the cooperation of the National Geographic Society, 1975.

KOENIG, LOUIS W. *The Chief Executive*. New York: Harcourt, Brace, Jovanovich, 1975.

LORANT, STEFAN. *The Glorious Burden: The American Presidency*. New York: Harper and Row, 1968.

MUGRIDGE, DONALD H. *The Presidents of the United States, 1789-1962: A Selected List of References*. Washington: Library of Congress, 1963.

ROSSITER, CLINTON L. *The American Presidency.* New York: Harcourt, Brace, and World, 1960.

WHITE HOUSE HISTORICAL ASSOCIATION. *The White House: An Historic Guide.* Washington: White House Historical Association with the cooperation of the National Geographic Society, 1975.

WHITNEY, DAVID C. *The Graphic Story of the American Presidents.* Garden City, N.Y.: Doubleday, 1975.

WHITNEY, DAVID C. and RICHARD P. KLUGA. *American Presidents: Biographies of the Chief Executives from Washington through Ford.* Garden City, N.Y.: Doubleday, 1975.

Criteria for Selection of Historic Sites of National Significance

A. National significance is ascribed to buildings, sites, objects, or districts which possess exceptional value or quality in illustrating or interpreting the historical (history and archeology) heritage of our Nation, such as:

1. Structures or sites at which events occurred that have made a significant contribution to, and are identified prominently with, or which outstandingly represent, the broad cultural, political, economic, military, or social history of the Nation, and from which an understanding and appreciation of the larger patterns of our American heritage may be gained.

2. Structures or sites associated importantly with the lives of persons nationally significant in the history of the United States.

3. Structures or sites associated significantly with an important event that outstandingly represents some great idea or ideal of the American people.

4. Structures that embody the distinguishing characteristics of an architectural type specimen, exceptionally valuable for a study of a period, style, or method of construction; or a notable structure representing the work of a master builder, designer, or architect.

5. Objects that figured prominently in nationally significant events; or that were prominently associated with nationally significant persons; or that outstandingly represent some great idea or ideal of the American people; or that embody distinguishing characteristics of a type specimen, exceptionally valuable for a study of a period, style, or method of construction; or that are notable as representations of the work of master workers or designers.

6. Archeological sites that have produced information of a major scientific importance by revealing new cultures, or by shedding light upon periods of occupation over large areas of the United States. Such sites are those which have produced, or which may reasonably be expected to produce, data affecting theories, concepts, and ideas to a major degree.

7. When preserved or restored as integral parts of the environment, historic buildings not sufficiently significant individually by reason of historical association or architectural merit to warrant recognition may

591

collectively compose a "historic district" that is of historical significance to the Nation in commemorating or illustrating a way of life in its developing culture.

B. To possess national significance, a historic or prehistoric structure, district, site, or object must possess integrity. For a historic or prehistoric *site*, integrity requires original location and intangible elements of feeling and association. The site of a structure no longer standing may possess national significance if the person or event associated with the structure was of transcendent importance in the Nation's history and the association consequential.

For a historic or prehistoric *structure*, integrity is a composite quality derived from original workmanship, original location, and intangible elements of feeling and association. A structure no longer on the original site may possess national significance if the person or event associated with it was of transcendent importance in the Nation's history and the association consequential.

For a historic *district*, integrity is a composite quality derived from original workmanship, original location, and intangible elements of feeling and association inherent in an ensemble of historic buildings having visual architectural unity.

For a historic *object*, integrity requires basic original workmanship.

C. Structures or sites which are primarily of significance in the field of religion or to religious bodies but are not of national importance in other fields of the history of the United States, such as political, military, or architectural history, will not be eligible for consideration.

D. Birthplaces, graves, burials, and cemeteries, as a general rule, are not eligible for consideration and recognition except in cases of historical figures of transcendent importance. Historic sites associated with the actual careers and contributions of outstanding historical personages usually are more important than their birthplaces and burial places.

E. Structures, sites, and objects achieving historical importance within the past 50 years will not as a general rule be considered unless associated with persons or events of transcendent significance.

Acknowledgments

Advisory Board on National Parks, Historic Sites, Buildings, and Monuments

Hon. E. Y. Berry, *Rapid City, S. Dak.*
Hon. Alan Bible, *Reno, Nev.*
Laurence W. Lane, Jr., *Menlo Park, Calif.*
A. Starker Leopold, *University of California, Berkeley.*
Mrs. Rogers C. B. Morton, *Easton, Md.*
Linden C. Pettys, *Ludington, Mich.*
Mrs. Paul T. Rennell, *Greenwich, Conn.*
Steven L. Rose, *La Canada, Calif.*
Douglas W. Schwartz, *School of American Research.*
William G. Shade, *Lehigh University.*
Edgar A. Toppin, *Virginia State College, Petersburg.*

Consulting Committee for the National Survey of Historic Sites and Buildings

James Biddle, *National Trust for Historic Preservation.*
Walter L. Creese, *University of Illinois.*
Richard H. Howland, *Smithsonian Institution.*
John W. Huston, *U.S. Naval Academy.*
Herbert E. Kahler, *Alexandria, Va.*
Charles E. Lee, *South Carolina Department of Archives and History.*
Henry A. Millon, *American Academy in Rome.*
Frederick D. Nichols, *University of Virginia.*
Dorothy B. Porter, *Washington, D.C.*
Patrick G. Porter, *Harvard University.*

National Park Service

Leigh M. Ablondi, *Clerk-typist, Historic Sites Survey.*
Elmer S. Atkins, *Assistant Director, White House Liaison, National Capital Parks.*
Doris D. Barber, *Graphics Clerk, Branch of Reference Services, Harpers Ferry Center.*

Edwin C. Bearss, *Supervisory Historian, Historic Preservation-East, Denver Service Center.*

Frederick R. Bell, *Picture Librarian, Office of Public Affairs.*

Jack E. Boucher, *Supervisor of Photography and Pictorial Records, Office of Archeology and Historic Preservation.*

S. Sydney Bradford, *Historian, Historic Sites Survey.*

Patrick M. Burkhart, *Architect, Historic American Buildings Survey.*

John A. Burns, *Architect, Historic American Buildings Survey.*

Mary O. Callander, *Secretary, Historic Sites Survey.*

Mark S. Carroll, *Chief, Professional Publications Division.*

James E. Dillon, *Architectural Historian, Historic Sites Survey.*

Virginia S. Fairman, *Secretary, Historic Preservation-East, Denver Service Center.*

Robert S. Gamble, *Historian, Historic Sites Survey.*

Richard E. Greenwood, *Historian, Historic Sites Survey.*

David K. Hansen, *Curator, Fort Vancouver National Historic Site, Wash.*

Sarah S. Hawkins, *Printing Specialist, Division of Organization and Methods.*

F. Ross Holland, *Associate Regional Director, Professional Services, North Atlantic Regional Office.*

Patrick A. Hurley, *Design-Production Specialist, Professional Publications Division.*

Robert R. Jacobsen, *Superintendent, Shenandoah National Park, Va.*

Henry A. Judd, *Chief Historical Architect, Park Historic Preservation.*

Benjamin Levy, *Senior Historian, Historic Sites Survey.*

Stephen M. Lissandrello, *Historian, Historic Sites Survey.*

John F. Luzader, *Manager, Historic Preservation Team, Denver Service Center.*

John D. McDermott, *Assistant Executive Secretary, Advisory Council on Historic Preservation.*

Barry Macintosh, *Historian, Park Historic Preservation.*

Michele Mangan, *Research Assistant, Historic Sites Survey.*

Joseph S. Mendinghall, *Historian, Historic Sites Survey.*

J. Frank Mentzer, *Assistant to the Director, Southwest Regional Office, Santa Fe.*

A. Russell Mortensen, *Assistant Director (retired), Archeology and Historic Preservation.*

W. Brown Morton III, *Architectural Historian, Historic Sites Survey.*

J. Leonard Norwood, *Associate Director, Administration.*

Harry W. Pfanz, *Chief Historian.*

Carolyn Pitts, *Architectural Historian, Historic Sites Survey.*

Franklin C. Pridemore, *Superintendent, Catoctin Mountain Park, Md.*

Polly Matherly Rettig, *Historian, Historic Sites Survey.*

Karen P. Ross, *Professional Assistant, Historic Sites Survey.*

Christine L. St. Lawrence, *Writer-Editor, Historic American Buildings Survey.*

William J. Savannah, *Printing Officer, Division of Organization and Methods.*

Blanche H. Schroer, *Historian, Historic Sites Survey.*

Horace J. Sheely, Jr., *Chief, Historic Sites Survey.*

James W. Sheire, *Historian, Historic Sites Survey.*

Marcella M. Sherfy, *Historian, Park Historic Preservation.*

Charles W. Snell, *Historian, Historic Preservation-East, Denver Service Center.*

Robert M. Utley, *Assistant Director, Park Historic Preservation.*

Lee A. Wallace, Jr., *Historian, Branch of Reference Services, Harpers Ferry Center.*

Marilyn D. Williams, *Clerk-typist, Historic Sites Survey.*

Marilyn Wondrous, *Graphics Researcher, Branch of Reference Services, Harpers Ferry Center.*

Other Individuals

Jacqueline W. Allder, *Office of Presidential Libraries, National Archives.*

Lavinia P. Banner, *Visual Information Specialist, United States Information Agency.*

Leroy Bellamy, *Reference Librarian, Prints and Photographs Division, Library of Congress.*

Leonard Bikowski, *Chief, Circulation Section, Office of Library and Information Services, U.S. Department of the Interior.*

Lee H. Burke, *Historian, Bureau of Public Affairs, U.S. State Department.*

Elizabeth C. Churchwell, *Chief Photo Librarian, United States Information Agency.*

Herbert R. Collins, *Associate Curator, Division of Political History, Smithsonian Institution.*

Sam V. Daniel III, *Reference Librarian, Prints and Photographs Division, Library of Congress.*

Hazel Dawson, *Interlibrary Loan Assistant, Office of Library and Information Services, U.S. Department of the Interior.*

John H. Elder, *Business Manager, Parks and History Association.*

William R. Emerson, *Director, Franklin D. Roosevelt Presidential Library, N.Y.*

Richard L. Holzhausen, *Audiovisual Archivist, Eisenhower Presidential Library, Kans.*

Sibley Jennings, *Architect, Commission of Fine Arts.*

Jerry L. Kearns, *Head, Reference Section, Prints and Photographs Division, Library of Congress.*

Charles J. Kelly, *Library Assistant, Prints and Photographs Division, Library of Congress.*

Jack E. Kightlinger, *Photographer, White House.*

William H. Leary, *Archivist, Audiovisual Archives Division, National Archives.*

Mary C. Long, *Art and Reference Division, Office of the Architect of the Capitol, Washington, D.C.*

John J. McDonough, *Manuscript Librarian, Manuscript Division, Library of Congress.*

Rosemary McEachern, *File Clerk, Photo Library, United States Information Agency.*

Ray Mackland, *Chief, Pictures Branch, United States Information Agency.*

Andrea M. Mattei, *Intern, Office of Educational Programs, National Archives.*

Charles S. Marshall, *Executive Secretary, Eastern National Park and Monument Association.*

Franz Mayr, *Manager, Commonwealth Club, Richmond.*

Moses J. Newson, *Executive Editor, Afro-American Newspapers.*

Ruth F. Nicholson, *Manuscript Librarian, Manuscript Division, Library of Congress.*

Mark S. Samuelson, *Archives Technician, Office of Educational Programs, National Archives.*

Richard W. Schoepf, *Reference Librarian, Office of Library and Information Services, U.S. Department of the Interior.*

Lenore A. Stein, *Chief, Photo Library, United States Information Agency.*

Hillory A. Tolson, *Executive Director, White House Historical Association.*

J. Patrick Wildenberg, *Audiovisual Archivist, Hoover Presidential Library, Iowa.*

Don W. Wilson, *Assistant Director, Eisenhower Presidential Library, Kans.*

Francis L. Wolfe, *Photographic Archivist, Lyndon B. Johnson Presidential Library, Tex.*

Elizabeth D. Woodbury, *Reference Librarian, Office of Library and Information Services, U.S. Department of the Interior.*

Art and Picture Credits

The National Park Service gratefully acknowledges the assistance of agencies and individuals furnishing illustrations and granting permission to reproduce them. Except where otherwise indicated, all oil paintings are on canvas. Where available, names of photographers and dates of photographs are indicated.

Page

Page

40   Library of Congress.

42   Oil (undated) by Gilbert Stuart. Pennsylvania Academy of the Fine Arts.

43   United Press International, Inc.

45   Lithograph (1881) by W. T. Mathews. Library of Congress.

48   Wide World Photos, Inc.

49   National Park Service (Cecil W. Stoughton, 1963).

51   Engraving, in John R. Young, *Around the World with General Grant* (1879). Library of Congress.

52   United Press International, Inc.

54   *Eisenhower,* Wide World Photos, Inc.; *Truman,* National Archives; *Harding,* United Press International, Inc.; *Carter,* The White House (detail).

55   United Press International, Inc.

56   Oil (ca. 1797) by Gilbert Stuart. All color portraits in this volume are from the official White House Collection; identifications courtesy Betty C. Monkman, Registrar, Office of the Curator of the White House. White House Historical Association.

58   Oil (1824) by John Trumbull. Architect of the Capitol.

59   Library of Congress.

61   Oil (1796) by Edward Savage. National Gallery of Art (Andrew W. Mellon Collection).

63   Oil (1878) by Edgar Parker.

64   Oil (1819) by John Trumbull, after an earlier painting (1786-95). Architect of the Capitol.

65   Oil (1815) by Gilbert Stuart. National Gallery of Art (gift of Mrs. Robert Homans).

67   Library of Congress.

70   Oil on panel-mounted canvas (1800) by Rembrandt Peale.

73   Oil mural (1870-73) by Constantino Brumidi, in the Senate Reception Room, U.S. Capitol. Architect of the Capitol.

74   *Aurora General Advertiser* (Philadelphia) (Mar. 6, 1801). Library of Congress.

76   Library of Congress.

78   Oil (1816) by John Vanderlyn.

81   Oil (ca. 1856) by Junius Brutus Stearns. Virginia Museum of Fine Arts.

82   Engraving (detail) (1814) by Alexander Anderson, after a drawing (1814) by John W. Jarvis, in the *New York Evening Post* (Apr. 25, 1814). Library of Congress.

83   Engraving, published by G. Thompson. Library of Congress.

84   Oil (1819) attributed to Samuel F. B. Morse.

87   Smithsonian Institution (Ralph E. Becker Collection).

88   National Archives.

89   Oil (undated) by Clyde O. Deland. Philadelphia Board of Public Education.

91   Oil (1864) by George P. A. Healy.

92   Oil (1796) by John Singleton Copley. Boston Museum of Fine Arts (gift of Mrs. Charles Francis Adams).

Page

93 Oil (1914) by Sir Amédée Forestier. National Collection of Fine Arts, Smithsonian Institution.

95 Lithograph (1848) by Nathaniel Currier. Library of Congress.

96 Oil (1819) by John W. Jarvis.

99 Engraving (probably 1858) by Thomas Phillibrowne, after a painting (undated) by Alonzo Chappel. Library of Congress.

100 Lithograph (1832). Library of Congress.

101 Lithograph (1836), published by H. R. Robinson. Library of Congress.

104 Oil (1858) by George P. A. Healy.

106 Engraving. Library of Congress.

107 Engraving (1841), in the *Weekly Herald* (New York City) (Mar. 6, 1841). Library of Congress.

108 Lithograph (1848) by Nathaniel Currier, published by Peter Smith. Library of Congress.

110 Oil (1879) by Eliphalet F. Andrews, after James H. Beard (1840).

112 Engraving (1800) by Charles B. J. Fevret de Saint Mémin. Library of Congress.

114 Lithograph (1840) by Gimber, published by Ferdinand C. Unger. Library of Congress.

115 Engraving (undated) by W. Ridgway, after a drawing (ca. 1860) by [John C.?] Chapin. Library of Congress.

116 Oil (1859) by George P. A. Healy, probably after his 1842 version.

119 Engraving. Library of Congress.

120 Lithograph. Library of Congress.

121 Chicago Historical Society.

123 Oil (1858) by George P. A. Healy.

124 Library of Congress.

126 National Archives.

127 Engraving, in the *Illustrated London News* (ca. 1845). Library of Congress.

128 Oil (undated) by an unknown mid-19th-century artist.

130 Engraving (undated) by William Wellstood, after a painting (undated) by Alonzo Chappel. Library of Congress.

132 Lithograph, published by H. R. Robinson. Smithsonian Institution (Ralph E. Becker Collection).

133 Song sheet (1848), published by Horton & Co. Library of Congress.

137 Oil (1857) by George P. A. Healy.

139 *Daily American Organ* (Washington, D.C.) (Feb. 26, 1856). Library of Congress.

140 Lithograph (1856) by Nathaniel Currier. Library of Congress.

141 Engraving, in *Harper's Weekly* (June 27, 1857). Library of Congress.

143 Oil (1858) by George P. A. Healy.

145 Lithograph (1852) by Nathaniel Currier, after a daguerreotype by Cutting. Library of Congress.

146 Lithograph (1852) by Thomas Bonar. Library of Congress.

Page

147   Engraving, in *Gleason's Pictorial* (1854). Library of Congress.

148   Oil (ca. 1902) by William M. Chase.

151   Engraving by John Sartain. Library of Congress.

152   Engraving, in *Frank Leslie's Illustrated Newspaper* (1857). Library of Congress.

154   Library of Congress (Mathew B. Brady, ca. 1859).

157   Oil (1868) by George P. A. Healy.

159   Library of Congress.

161   Library of Congress (Mathew B. Brady).

163   National Archives.

165   Oil (1880) by Eliphalet F. Andrews.

167   Library of Congress.

168   Lithograph (1866) by A. Hageboeck, published by I. A. Wetherby. Library of Congress.

169   Library of Congress.

170   Oil (1875) by Henry Ulke.

173   Missouri Historical Society.

174   Library of Congress (Mathew B. Brady, 1864).

177   Library of Congress (1885).

179   Oil (1884) by Daniel Huntington.

181   Photograph (1879 or 1880) by G. W. Pach of a lithograph by an unknown artist, after a photograph by Mathew B. Brady. Library of Congress.

182   Top, engraving, in *Frank Leslie's Illustrated Newspaper* (1878), Library of Congress; bottom, engraving probably by T. De Holstrup, after a drawing by W. M. Rouzee, in *Harper's Weekly* (Jan. 22, 1881). Library of Congress.

185   Oil (1881) by Calvin Curtis.

186   Library of Congress (Mathew B. Brady or assistant).

188   Lithograph (1880) by Currier & Ives. Library of Congress.

189   Engraving, after a drawing by William A. Rogers, in *Harper's Weekly* (July 23, 1881). Library of Congress.

190   Oil (1885) by Daniel Huntington.

193   Engraving, after a drawing by Frederick Dielman, in *Harper's Weekly* (Feb. 28, 1885). Library of Congress.

194   Engraving, in *Frank Leslie's Illustrated Newspaper* (Oct. 28, 1882). Library of Congress.

195   Engraving, in *Harper's Weekly* (1884). Library of Congress.

196   Oil (1891) by Eastman Johnson.

199   Copyrighted by the Waring Hat Manufacturing Co. Library of Congress.

200   Drawing by G. Y. Coffin. Library of Congress.

202   Library of Congress.

205   Oil (1895) by Eastman Johnson.

207   Library of Congress.

208   Copyrighted by the Waring Hat Manufacturing Co. Library of Congress.

210   Engraving by Charles Graham, in *Harper's Weekly* (Nov. 18, 1888). Library of Congress.

Page

212 Oil (1902) by Harriet A. Murphy.

214 Smithsonian Institution (Ralph E. Becker Collection).

215 Library of Congress.

217 Smithsonian Institution (Ralph E. Becker Collection).

218 Oil (1903) by John Singer Sargent.

221 Cartoon (ca. 1905) by Louis Dalrymple, in *Judge* magazine (Jan. 7, 1905). Harvard College Library (Theodore Roosevelt Collection).

223 Library of Congress (ca. 1903).

224 Brown Bros.

227 Oil (1911) by Anders L. Zorn.

229 Copyrighted (1908) by Kurz & Allison. Library of Congress.

230 Library of Congress.

231 Cartoon by Clifford K. Berryman, in the *Washington Star* (1912). Library of Congress.

232 Oil (1936) by F. Graham Cootes.

235 Library of Congress.

236 Library of Congress (Pach Bros., 1912).

238 Library of Congress.

241 Oil (1922-23) by E. Hodgson Smart.

243 Cartoon by Clifford K. Berryman, in the *Washington Star* (1920). Library of Congress.

244 Library of Congress.

245 Library of Congress.

246 Oil (1932) by Charles S. Hopkinson.

248 Library of Congress.

249 Smithsonian Institution (Ralph E. Becker Collection).

251 Library of Congress (Underwood & Underwood).

252 Oil (1956) by Elmer W. Greene.

255 United Press International, Inc.

257 Cartoon by Clifford K. Berryman, in the *Washington Star* (1930). Library of Congress.

258 National Archives.

260 Oil (1947) by Frank O. Salisbury, after his life portrait (1935).

263 Wide World Photos, Inc.

266 National Park Service.

268 Harris & Ewing.

270 Oil (1947) by Martha G. Kempton.

273 Harris & Ewing.

275 United Press International, Inc.

277 National Archives.

279 Oil (1967) by J. Anthony Wills.

280 Eisenhower Presidential Library.

Page

282   United States Army.

284   United Press International, Inc.

287   Oil (1970) by Aaron Shikler.

289   United Press International, Inc.

290   National Park Service (Special Collection).

291   National Park Service (Special Collection).

295   Oil (1968) by Elizabeth Shoumatoff.

297   Lyndon B. Johnson Presidential Library.

298   National Park Service (Special Collection).

300   National Park Service (Special Collection).

302   Photograph (1968) by Robert S. Oakes.

305   National Park Service (Special Collection).

306   National Park Service (Special Collection).

309   Wide World Photos, Inc.

311   Photograph (1974) by David Hume Kennerly.

313   National Park Service.

314   National Park Service (Special Collection).

317   National Park Service (Special Collection).

319   Photograph (1977) by Karl Schumacher.

320   National Park Service (Special Collection) (1946).

322   Black Star (Eugene Anthony, 1976).

323   National Park Service (Special Collection) (1977).

329   Top, Library of Congress (Beach and Bodurtha, 1876); bottom, National Park Service (Fred Bell, 1976).

331   Top, Eisenhower Presidential Library; bottom, National Park Service.

338   National Park Service (John D. McDermott, 1969).

339   National Park Service (Stoughton, 1968).

340   Franklin D. Roosevelt Presidential Library.

342   National Park Service (Boucher, 1976).

345   National Park Service (Boucher, 1976).

347   Library of Congress.

349   National Park Service (Boucher, 1976).

352   National Park Service (Boucher, 1976).

353   Engraving, after a drawing by Edwin F. Faber, in *Harper's Weekly* (May 6, 1865). Library of Congress.

354   National Park Service (Boucher, 1976).

356   National Park Service (Boucher, 1976).

358   National Park Service (Boucher, 1976).

361   National Park Service (Boucher, 1976).

362   Library of Congress.

364   National Park Service (Boucher, 1976).

365   National Park Service (Boucher, 1976).

366   National Park Service.

Page

369   National Park Service (Boucher, 1976).

371   National Park Service (Boucher, 1971).

374   National Park Service (Boucher, 1971).

376   National Park Service (Boucher, 1976).

377   Library of Congress (Mathew B. Brady).

378   National Archives (Alexander Gardner, 1865).

379   Library of Congress.

380   United Press International, Inc.

382   National Park Service (Boucher, 1976).

384   National Park Service (Jack Rottier, 1967).

386   National Park Service (Boucher, 1976).

388   National Park Service (Stoughton).

389   Engraving apparently by C. Upham, probably in *Frank Leslie's Illustrated Newspaper* (date unknown). Library of Congress.

390   Engraving, after a sketch by Miss Georgie A. Davis, in *Frank Leslie's Illustrated Newspaper* (Apr. 3, 1880). Library of Congress.

391   Engraving probably by T. De Holstrup, in *Harper's Weekly* (June 12, 1886). Library of Congress.

392   National Park Service (Special Collection).

396   Library of Congress.

397   United States Army.

398   National Park Service (Stoughton).

399   White House Historical Association (James P. Blair, National Geographic Society, 1966).

401   National Park Service (Boucher, 1976).

402   Library of Congress.

403   Engraving, after a sketch by James E. Taylor, in *Frank Leslie's Illustrated Newspaper* (June 6, 1868). Library of Congress.

405   Library of Congress (Frances Benjamin Johnson).

407   Library of Congress.

408   Harris & Ewing.

409   Library of Congress (Architect of the Capitol Collection).

412   National Park Service (Wilbur Dutton).

414   National Park Service (Boucher, 1964).

415   Library of Congress.

417   National Park Service (Hruska-Kray, 1976).

419   National Park Service (Richard Frear, 1972).

420   Library of Congress (J. A. Whipple, 1860).

421   Illinois State Historical Library.

423   National Park Service (Frear, 1972).

425   National Park Service (Dave Beatty Studios, 1976).

427   Engraving, after a sketch by Thomas Hogan, in *Frank Leslie's Illustrated Newspaper* (May 27, 1865). Library of Congress.

429   National Park Service (Boucher, 1975).

Page

432   Top, President Benjamin Harrison Memorial Home; bottom, National Park Service.

435   National Park Service (Boucher, 1962).

438   National Park Service (Charles C. Keely, Jr.).

439   National Park Service (W. S. Keller, 1966).

440   Hoover Presidential Library.

442   National Park Service (Allan Rinehart).

443   National Park Service (Boucher, 1959).

444   Library of Congress (J. F. Wieners, 1906).

446   National Park Service (Lin Caulfield, 1976).

448   Oil (undated) by Dwight D. Eisenhower. David H. Marx, Shrewsbury, N.J.

450   Wide World Photos, Inc. (Paul Vathis, 1961).

452   National Park Service (Steve Rosenthal, 1976).

454   National Park Service (Rosenthal, 1976).

455   National Park Service (Frear, 1972).

456   Watercolor (1798) by E. Malcolm. Adams National Historic Site.

458   Top, National Park Service (Stoughton, 1972); bottom, National Park Service (Stoughton, 1972).

460   National Park Service (Frear, 1974).

461   National Park Service (Stoughton, 1969).

463   National Park Service (Rosenthal, 1976).

465   National Park Service.

467   National Park Service (Robert S. Gamble, 1971).

469   Photo Researchers, Inc. (Bradley Smith, 1952).

471   Truman Presidential Library.

472   National Park Service (Edwin W. Small, 1972).

473   National Park Service (Steven Zane, 1976).

474   Library of Congress.

476   National Park Service (Zane, 1976).

477   Engraving, after a sketch by J. W. Alexander, in *Harper's Weekly* (Oct. 1, 1881). Library of Congress.

478   National Park Service (Boucher, 1976).

480   Lithograph, after a contemporary print by Cornelius Tiebout. Library of Congress.

483   National Park Service (Hare Photographs, Inc., 1976).

484   Globe Photos, Inc.

485   Library of Congress (Carvalho, ca. 1885).

486   Museum of the City of New York (James Binder, 1897).

488   National Park Service (Zane, 1976).

490   United Press International, Inc.

491   United Press International, Inc.

493   National Park Service (Zane, 1976).

496   National Park Service (Frear, 1971).

498   National Park Service (Boucher, 1964).

Page

500   Library of Congress (Pach Bros.).

501   Library of Congress.

503   National Park Service (Frear, 1973).

505   National Park Service (Glenn S. Cook and Son, 1976).

506   National Park Service.

509   National Park Service (Boucher, 1958).

511   National Park Service (S. Sydney Bradford, 1965).

512   Harding Memorial Association.

514   Top, National Park Service (Robert R. Riggin, 1976); bottom, wash drawing by C. Corwine, Library of Congress.

516   National Park Service (George R. Adams, 1974).

518   Rutherford B. Hayes Library.

519   Rutherford B. Hayes State Memorial (1877).

520   Library of Congress.

523   National Park Service (Frear, 1972).

524   National Park Service (James Aycock, 1967).

526   Wide World Photos, Inc.

528   National Park Service (Boucher, 1974).

531   National Park Service (Boucher, 1974).

532   National Park Service (Boucher, 1974).

534   National Park Service (Mel Horst Photography, 1976).

536   National Park Service (Boucher, 1959).

539   Library of Congress.

540   National Park Service (Moody Studio).

542   National Park Service (Benjamin H. Davis, 1956).

544   National Park Service (Boucher, 1976).

547   National Park Service (Boucher, 1971).

548   Lithograph (1856) by Endicott & Co., apparently after a drawing by architect Francis W. Strickland. Library of Congress.

549   National Park Service (Boucher, 1971).

550   Lithograph (1845) by J. Baittie or Baillie. Library of Congress.

552   Lyndon B. Johnson Presidential Library.

554   National Park Service (Fred Mang, Jr.).

555   Bill Shrout (1958).

556   Lyndon B. Johnson Presidential Library (Michael Geissinger, 1968).

558   National Park Service (Ralph M. Brouchoud, 1976).

559   Lithograph, in the *Boston Sunday Post* (Mar. 1, 1925). Library of Congress.

560   Library of Congress.

562   National Park Service (Boucher, 1976).

564   National Park Service (Edward F. Heite, 1969).

565   Engraving, in *Frank Leslie's Illustrated Newspaper* (July 17, 1858). Library of Congress.

566   National Park Service.

Page

☆ U.S. GOVERNMENT PRINTING OFFICE : 1977   O—239-651

No mention of Yalta Conference.
Instead of referring to Ford's Theater as a unit
of the national park System, wouldn't it be
better to say that it is in National Park Service
care? (See top of page 383)

As the Nation's principal conservation agency, the Department of the Interior has responsibility for most of our nationally owned public lands and natural resources. This includes fostering the wisest use of our land and water resources, protecting our fish and wildlife, preserving the environmental and cultural values of our national parks and historical places, and providing for the enjoyment of life through outdoor recreation. The Department assesses our energy and mineral resources and works to assure that their development is in the best interests of all our people. The Department also has a major responsibility for American Indian reservation communities and for people who live in Island Territories under U.S. administration.